A SCHOOL COUNSELLOR CASEBOOK

A SCHOOL COUNSELLOR CASEBOOK

VIKRAM PATEL, MRCPsych, FMedSci
Professor of International Mental Health &
Wellcome Trust Senior Research Fellow in Clinical Science
London School of Hygiene and Tropical Medicine, UK
Sangath Centre, Goa, India
Public Health Foundation of India

LISA ARONSON, MSW, JD, PhD
Clinical Child Psychologist and Clinical Social Worker
Faculty, Graduate Center for Child Development and Psychotherapy
Los Angeles, California, USA

GAURI DIVAN, MRCPCH
Paediatrician
Sangath Centre, Goa, India

BYWORD BOOKS™

First published October 2013
Reprinted January 2018, July 2023

ISBN 978-81-8193-115-3 (print version)
ISBN 978-81-8193-118-4 (e-book version)

Cover design: Netra Shyam
Illustrations: Shreya Kharbanda
Typesetting: Jacob Thomas

Published by
Byword Books Private Limited
GF-15, Virat Bhavan
Mukherjee Nagar Commercial Complex
Delhi 110009, India; Phone: 011-47038040
email: bywordbooks@gmail.com
website: www.bywordbooks.in

Printed at Replika Press Private Limited, Kundli, Haryana, India

For Our Parents

BHARATI and HARSHAD PATEL
JAN and GERALD ARONSON
SMITA and ANIL DIVAN

CONTENTS

PART B: CASE STUDIES

PART A: LIST OF BOXES AND FIGURES

CHAPTER 1

CHAPTER 2

CHAPTER 3

CHAPTER 4

PART B: LIST OF PANELS

Preface

'So when you are listening to somebody, completely, attentively, then you are listening not only to the words, but also to the feeling of what is being conveyed, to the whole of it, not part of it.'

—J. Krishnamurti

Our motivation

It is estimated that a quarter of India's population, about 300 million people, is of school-going age. No doubt many of these young people are not, in fact, in school, but a substantial proportion is and this number is growing. These young people are our future and the way they negotiate their school years determines not only their own future well-being but also the overall development of their communities. Although the school years tend to be the healthiest period of life, they are also the time when mental health problems often begin or become more apparent. This is due, in part, to the challenges posed by the expectations in the spheres of education and socialization, as well as the physical and developmental changes that occur during these critical years. By far, the majority of youth negotiate these challenges well, drawing upon a range of resources to do so: innate reserves of resilience, healthy coping strategies, and supportive school and home environments. However, every now and then, a young person falters and stumbles. Gentle support and guidance, informed by knowledge and skills, can make all the difference for the troubled youngster. Providing this informed support and guidance is the role of the school counsellor. We believe that every school must have at least one counsellor, and possibly more, depending on the size of the school and its cultural diversity. This casebook is intended to provide the counsellor with a solid foundation for counselling practice in schools.

Counselling youth who have mental health problems and participating in their recovery are among the most gratifying jobs: after all, what other job allows one to help a child cope with a personal difficulty and assist him in taking steps towards building the foundation for a healthy and successful life? In addition, the establishment of a mutually rewarding working relationship with the school staff and the wider school community to promote a youth's mental health has a positive impact on the morale and environment of the entire school and simultaneously creates an empathetic school environment which acknowledges and includes all children, irrespective of their individual differences.

Our sources

The inspiration for this casebook is the work of Sangath, a non-governmental organization based in Goa, with which we have been associated (www.sangath.com). Sangath has pioneered a low-cost model to provide mental health care to schoolchildren, integrated with other interventions for the promotion of health, and has developed training programmes and resource materials for lay school counsellors. Its work in these areas, which includes an evaluation of the lay school counsellor programme, has been published.* This casebook is based primarily on case material from the Sangath counsellors' work in primary and secondary schools in Goa and the work of nurse-counsellors trained by Sangath mental health experts in several other states of India (Maharashtra, Bihar, Madhya Pradesh, Orissa and Rajasthan).

In addition, the authors bring to this book their rich experience working with youth with mental health problems in various clinical settings. The diversity of the professional backgrounds of the three authors has made it possible to present the subject of the mental health of youth from various perspectives, including psychiatry, paediatrics, child psychology and clinical social work. Vikram Patel is a psychiatrist with the Centre for Global Mental Health at the London School of Hygiene and Tropical

* Rajaraman D, *et al.* The acceptability, feasibility and impact of a lay health counsellor-delivered health-promoting schools programme in India: A case study evaluation. *BMC Health Services Research* 2012;12:127.

Medicine. He co-founded Sangath in 1996 and has led its adolescent and youth health programme. His particular interest and expertise lies in sharing the task of carrying out psychosocial interventions with less specialized and less expensive human resources as a strategy to bridge the severe shortage of mental health professionals in India. Lisa Aronson, a clinical child psychologist and clinical social worker, enhanced her skills to train non-specialists to provide mental health care to youth in under-resourced settings while a Fulbright–Nehru Scholar affiliated with Sangath. She is an experienced child/youth/and family psychotherapist, clinical supervisor and educator. She served as the Director of Child Evaluation at the UCLA Trauma Psychiatry Service and Director of the Center for the Study of Mind and Human Interaction at the University of Virginia and is on the faculty of the Graduate Center for Child Development and Psychotherapy. Gauri Divan is a developmental paediatrician who helped a number of schools in Goa establish circle time for the promotion of mental health, and then expanded these into life skills programmes to address the needs of children. Her experiences with children with disabilities and their families motivates her to work for their inclusion in mainstream educational settings. Individual chapters were initially drafted by experienced psychologists and other mental health professionals within Sangath. These included, apart from the authors, Gracy Andrew, Pacienca Cardozo, Achira Chatterjee and Prachi Khandeparkar. In addition, Neerja Chowdhary and Saumya Singh contributed to several sections of this book. We have also been inspired by the established literature on youth development and on counselling and mental health interventions for youth. A list of the main resources we have consulted can be found in the Appendix.

Who is the casebook for?

School counsellors constitute a relatively new professional group in India yet to be defined by the regulations that apply to other mental health professionals. This may have a downside in terms of the standardization of knowledge, skills and competencies but, at the same time, is potentially liberating as it permits a wider range of persons to become counsellors than would be possible in India if strict rules were applied.

The lack of specialized mental health professionals is a major barrier to the improvement of access to mental health care in India (and many other countries) and it is very unlikely that specialized professionals will be available for every school in India (and other countries) in the foreseeable future. Because of this, counsellors coming from a wide range of backgrounds can provide counselling in schools; for example, they may have completed a higher degree in clinical or counselling psychology or may be lay counsellors drawn from the local community (a model championed by Sangath) who have had more limited or no formal training in counselling. The role of a school counsellor requires a varied set of skills, including skills for working with the individual youth; with the youth's family; with teachers and the school staff; and at times, with other health professionals. School counsellors must also have the skills to work in both the school and community settings. As a result, this casebook needed to address these diverse backgrounds and roles, and finding the right balance between a description that would be too basic for some and too complicated for others posed a challenge for us. Our hope is that we have reached out to the majority. In considering the diagnostic and counselling approaches that we recommend for school counsellors, we have chosen those which a graduate in any field is most likely to have the capability to use, given some basic understanding or training in psychology. We also hope that this casebook will be a resource for more experienced mental health practitioners and for mental health professionals who supervise the work of school counsellors. We would expect the school counsellor to use this book as one of many resources to build and maintain her competency, as well as an aide for the critically important process of ongoing supervision of her counselling by her peers or seniors. While this edition of the casebook has been written primarily for school counsellors in India and is based on case material derived from our experiences in school settings in India, we believe that it may be applicable to other settings (such as community centres) and other countries as well because of its developmental and evidence-based approach to youth mental health. In any event, we would be delighted if this casebook were adapted for use in other settings and could serve as a basis to support training programmes.

ORGANIZATION AND STYLE OF THE CASEBOOK

The casebook is divided into two parts. Part A gives the reader a fundamental grounding in school counselling. This part covers: normal child and adolescent development; the mental health problems that young people may experience; the counselling relationship; assessment and case management processes; counselling skills; counselling strategies and supportive interventions; counselling settings and formats; counsellor ethics; and suggestions for the counsellor on the maintenance and strengthening of counselling skills, professional development and personal well-being. Part B comprises 20 case studies, each of which presents a youth with a mental health problem that the counsellor may encounter in the school setting. Each case study is divided into two sections. The first section contains the case study of a specific youth, including the assessment for this youth; the case formulation; and the counselling strategies and supportive interventions recommended to address the youth's problem. The second section of each case study provides an overview of the general approach to the mental health problem covered in the specific case study. The 20 case studies represent mental health problems that occur among children across the developmental spectrum, from young children attending primary school to adolescents in higher secondary schools. They are based on actual cases of young people seen by our colleagues or who have been seen in Sangath's school programmes. The case study material has been altered to the extent necessary to protect the individual's confidentiality. The case studies are arranged according to the age group, beginning with younger children in primary school, followed by older children in primary school and finally, adolescents in secondary school. The casebook ends with an Appendix of resources such as sample counselling record forms and recommended reading materials.

We have attempted to keep the language of the book as simple as possible, while at the same time, not diluting the concepts or technically important words and terms. Our approach to the categorization and description of mental health problems and the description of selected counselling strategies and supportive interventions reflect this delicate balance. We generally use the term 'youth' to describe anyone of school-going age and the term 'child' when referring to the relationship between a parent/family member and the student, and at times, for a younger child. Each chapter consistently uses either 'she' or 'he' for the young person. The exception is when we are talking about a disorder which is more commonly found in a particular sex (e.g. in Chapter 2 we have described attention deficit hyperactivity disorder with reference to a male). Reflecting the predominance of women counsellors in the Indian context we have used the female pronoun 'she' for the counsellor in Part A; in Part B, we have occasionally used the male pronoun to represent a male counsellor.

To assist the reader, we have extensively cross-referenced between chapters of the casebook and within the chapters. It is advisable that the reader become familiar with Part A before consulting Part B.

Our thanks

Finally, we wish to acknowledge the important contributions of others in making this casebook possible. We thank the many school counsellors who have contributed their case study materials and the knowledge gained from their counselling experiences with youth, which are at the heart of the casebook. We are grateful to our colleagues in Sangath for contributing to sections of chapters. We thank the funders which have supported Sangath's school-related programmes, notably, the John and Catherine MacArthur Foundation, the United Nations Family Planning Association and the Dempo Mining Corporation. One of the authors (Vikram Patel) has received support from the Wellcome Trust for nearly 20 years, which has been instrumental in helping him to lay the foundation for Sangath's school programmes. Lisa Aronson is grateful to the United States–India Educational Foundation for extending its support to allow her to spend time in India on a Fulbright–Nehru Scholar grant. Gauri Divan is grateful to her parents and teachers who instilled in her the importance of an education which is beyond books. We thank the teachers, members of the school management and students with whom Sangath has established a richly rewarding partnership over the years. We are extremely grateful to Theresa Betancourt and Mark Jordans, our two reviewers, who went through earlier drafts of this casebook with a fine-toothed comb and have provided invaluable inputs. We are grateful to Shreya Kharbanda for the wonderful illustrations and the publishers for their patience and guidance. As always, we are indebted to the young people and families with whom we work and whose resilience inspires us on a daily basis. Finally, we thank you for consulting and reading this book and, in particular, for the feedback we anticipate both on how useful you found it, as well as how it could be improved for future editions.

VIKRAM PATEL, LISA ARONSON, GAURI DIVAN

September 2013 (e-mail: casebook@sangath.net)

Abbreviations

ADHD	attention deficit hyperactivity disorder
ASD	autism spectrum disorder
BA	behavioural activation
CD	conduct disorder
ID	intellectual disability
IEP	individualized education programme
IQ	intelligence quotient
MSE	Mental Status Examination
OCD	obsessive–compulsive disorder
ODD	oppositional defiant disorder
PTSD	post-traumatic stress disorder
SDQ	Strengths and Difficulties Questionnaire
SJPU	Special Juvenile Police Unit
SLD	specific learning disabilities
WHO	World Health Organization

Part A

BASICS OF COUNSELLING

BASICS OF COUNSELLING

CHAPTERS

CHAPTER 1

CHILD AND ADOLESCENT DEVELOPMENT

When a child makes the transition from a home or pre-school environment to primary school, he is increasingly ready to explore the world independently while continuing to depend upon his caregivers for many physical and emotional needs. As the young person passes through middle childhood and the exciting and challenging adolescent phase, his social and cognitive skills grow and he becomes increasingly self-sufficient. In this casebook, the development of a young person is divided broadly into two phases: the primary school period and the middle and high school period. Each age group is characterized by specific issues in the sphere of mental health and development. To distinguish between the two broad groups, this casebook employs the terms 'child' or 'children' to refer to 6–10-year-olds and 'adolescent(s)' to refer to 11–18-year-olds. However, the counsellor should keep in mind that these are not rigid boundaries and the issues affecting older children are often similar to those affecting younger adolescents. In this casebook, the terms 'young person' or 'youth' refer both to children and adolescents.

The course of an individual's development varies from person to person, although there are broadly defined 'milestones' within each domain of development (Box 1.1) that the individual should optimally reach by a particular age. Each milestone achieved is the building block for the development of future skills. For example, a child in primary school can copy a letter because he was able to hold a crayon and scribble in early childhood. It is important to understand the unique developmental path of each young person, while at the same time, keeping in mind the expected milestones. There is a wide but normal variation in the rate at which children acquire skills (e.g. one child may begin walking a few months before another). Also, an individual child may show variations in different areas of development. This means that although the individual

acquires skills in a developmental sequence (e.g. sitting before crawling), he may develop some skills more rapidly and others more slowly (e.g. a 6-year-old may be able to cycle and somersault, but find it difficult to hold a pencil).

Many factors influence the path of a young person's development. Protective factors promote development, while risk factors slow down and occasionally even reverse it (*see* Chapter 2). Similarly, how a young person develops and the way in which he approaches the world and handles challenges, are influenced by the 'traits' he inherits from his parents and by his 'temperament' (Box 1.2).

An understanding of normal child and adolescent development and developmental theories provides the counsellor with a foundation so that she can judge whether and to what extent a young person has departed from the expected developmental path. This foundation helps the counsellor to assess and address the young person's mental health needs.

Developmental milestones and goals

This section describes the developmental stages that a young person passes through from the time he enters school, at around 6 years of age, to when he completes school, at around 18 years of age. This chapter describes the main physical changes, cognitive (thinking) achievements,

BOX 1.1: DOMAINS OF DEVELOPMENT

- **Motor development:** This refers to the functioning of both large muscle groups (e.g. walking, running, riding a cycle) and small muscle groups (e.g. the manipulation of small object with the hands in order to eat, draw and play).
- **Language development:** This refers to the development of receptive (i.e. understanding what is spoken) and expressive language skills (i.e. communicating either through words or actions).
- **Cognitive development:** This refers to the ability to solve problems through intuition (i.e. common sense), perception and reasoning. It includes the ability not only to learn and understand, but also to retain information and apply it as needed.
- **Social/emotional development:** This refers to the ability to form and maintain relationships and respond to others.

BOX 1.2: TEMPERAMENTS AND TRAITS

Alexander Thomas and Stella Chess (1977) studied infant and child behaviour and concluded that there are three main groups of *temperaments*. Although not all children can be placed neatly in any one of these groups, at least two-thirds of children fit into one of these patterns. Forty per cent fit the 'easy' pattern, 10% fall into the 'difficult' pattern and 15% are 'slow to warm up'. The remainder have features of more than one pattern. Each temperament category has its specific strengths and weaknesses, and no one temperament is superior to another.

- **The easy child:** This child has regular eating, sleeping and elimination cycles (bowel movements), and a positive response to new situations. He manages frustration with little fuss.

(*continued*)

BOX 1.2: TEMPERAMENTS AND TRAITS (*continued*)

Such children adapt quickly to change (e.g. eating new food or attending a new school). Their mood is calm most of the time.

- **The difficult child:** Such children have irregular eating, sleeping and elimination cycles. They display a negative response to new situations (e.g. they cry frequently or throw tantrums when frustrated). They are slow to adapt to change and need more time to get used to new foods, new people or new situations.
- **The slow-to-warm-up child:** These children have mildly negative responses when exposed to new situations, but they slowly adapt with repeated exposure. They have fairly regular eating, sleeping and elimination cycles.

Traits are characteristics that shape the way a particular person looks at events, responds to the world and feels emotionally. Certain traits, while influenced by the environment, may have a genetic underpinning. Such traits include conscientiousness (e.g. being organized and taking good care of toys and books), openness (e.g. being ready for adventure and excited about taking risks), agreeableness (e.g. being friendly and compassionate), neuroticism (e.g. having an anxious disposition) and extroversion (e.g. displaying confidence and a love of being the centre of attention). Thomas and Chess also stressed the 'goodness of fit', which refers to whether and how the temperament of a child, the temperament of the parents and cultural factors mesh or do not align; this 'goodness of fit' has an effect on whether the child's temperament is accepted or creates challenges for the parent. To take an example, some children prefer to sleep in the parental bed, but bed-sharing is not acceptable in all cultures and may result in a 'problem' for the parent.

emotional changes and the evolution of social relationships associated with each developmental stage. The section on adolescence also includes a description of sexual maturation.

When entering school

The 6-year-old entering school has grown significantly in the previous year, is physically more confident and is ready to explore new challenges. The primary developmental task in early childhood is for the child to achieve a sense of stability within himself and be able to turn his attention to the external world with the help of his growing physical and cognitive skills.

Physically: The child is able to run, jump and hop with increasing confidence. However, some 6-year-olds continue to be unsure of their physical skills. Simultaneously, the child's fine motor skills have become stronger, enabling him to hold a pencil, colour within lines and use scissors.

Cognitively: The ability to concentrate over a length of time varies from child to child. Some children are able to complete schoolwork with ease, while others find this more challenging. This variation in the ability to concentrate is often linked to how long the child is able to sit in one place for a prolonged period of time, as required in a classroom setting. Some children can read by this age and understand the concept of time. The language skills of children of this age are evolving rapidly and the child can typically express himself clearly. It is not unusual for the 6-year-old to confuse and reverse certain letters and numbers. Children of this age usually enjoy puzzles and creative toys. They have a wonderful fantasy world, which may occasionally be scary, including

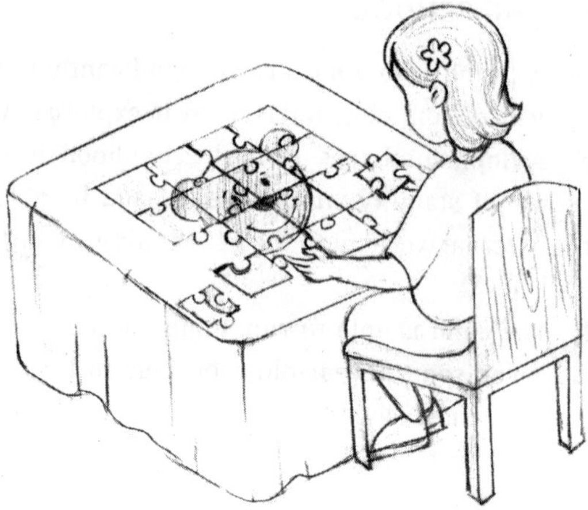

monsters and ghosts. They make use of toys and other materials to play out these fantasies. The child begins to develop a sense of humour and enjoys telling jokes (which may include slang words that he borrows from the adult world).

Emotionally: The 6-year-old can be boastful, and generally understands the world from his own point of view. This means that he can occasionally be rigid, unadaptable and prone to tantrums. Though he is seemingly independent and brave, he remains anxious to please, often requiring reassurance and praise from adults. His ability to tell right from wrong is evolving and he needs adult guidance to make these distinctions. He has the capacity to feel guilt and remorse when he does something wrong, and is beginning to understand others' emotions.

Socially: The 6-year-old chooses his own friends. He can play cooperatively with others and is learning to share toys. Simple rule-based games can be introduced, although he is most likely to prefer role-playing games (e.g. teacher–student or cops and robbers).

Middle childhood (6–10 years of age)

The primary developmental task in middle childhood is to acquire skills which will help the child move beyond the realm of the family and home and begin to cope with increasingly complex issues related to his social environment. This is often the time when developmental delays and behavioural problems start to become apparent as the child's ability to cope with the new challenges may not yet be sufficient for the social and educational demands he encounters.

Physically: The rate of growth slows down during this period. There is a refinement in fine motor development, enabling the child to hold a pencil and write with increasing skill. Near the end of this period, some children begin to enter 'puberty' (Box 1.3), indicated by rapid physical growth and the development of secondary sexual characteristics. Girls tend to enter puberty earlier than boys. The process of pubertal growth occurs between 9 and 19 years of age. The average age for a growth spurt among girls is 11–13 years and among boys, 13–15 years. The changes which occur during puberty are elaborated upon in the section on adolescence.

BOX 1.3: PUBERTY

Puberty is the period of development when the body matures sexually and the sexual organs become functional. It occurs when the reproductive hormones become active in adolescents. In addition to the obvious physical changes that can be seen externally, internal physical, psychological and emotional changes also occur. The precise age of the onset of puberty varies from individual to individual and is often influenced by genetics, nutrition and other environmental factors.

Cognitively: The child now communicates confidently and is increasingly interested in the world around him. He is able to address and tackle problems in a logical manner, but without the flexibility of abstract thinking. The child is now also able to understand similarities and differences, and to organize objects or items into groups (e.g. fruits, animals and the family).

Emotionally: Children in this age group are able to identify and express their emotional needs using more specific vocabulary. Caregivers need to be firm but gentle about their behavioural expectations because the child is sensitive to criticism. As he tries hard to achieve new tasks with his emerging skills, the child often encounters failure;

encouraging him and bolstering his confidence helps him to develop into a self-assured young person. This is also an important time to help the child develop resilience and the flexibility to deal with setbacks, face disappointments and manage emotions. Some children often experience a strong desire for independence. Schools and counsellors can encourage the healthy expression of independence by allowing such children to learn from their mistakes, as long as there is no danger involved. These experiments with independence can help the child understand the world around him in a safe manner.

Socially: The young person's world is expanding beyond the family. Though the child remains affectionate towards his family members, his emerging drive for independence is reflected in his desire to spend time with friends. This is also the age when the young person develops a sociocultural identity. For example, 'What kind of work do your parents do?' and 'What kind of house do you have?' are common questions asked at this age. This is the ideal age for children to understand and appreciate diversity, and to develop a positive sense of self. It is also at this stage that value education should be introduced into school curricula. Some children may display undesirable reactions to differences and diversity, and this period is critical for monitoring early signs of bullying behaviour. A school can help a child recognize and avoid bullying if it engenders the values of compassion and caring for others (*see* Chapter 6). At this stage, peer groups become increasingly important and most children choose

groups of the same sex to spend time with. Being accepted as part of a group is often a key aspect of a child's sense of self in this period. Group affiliations influence the way a young person uses language (especially slang), how he chooses to dress, his social attitudes, as well as his values. Friendships become increasingly complex, evolving from the pre-school 'playmate' relationships to friendships based on trust. Gender roles (*see* Box 1.5) become established at this stage. For example, in many Indian households, girls take on more responsibilities, especially with regard to their younger siblings, while boys are often exempt from household chores.

ADOLESCENCE (11–18 YEARS OF AGE)

The term 'adolescence' derives from the Latin 'adolescere' ('to grow into maturity'). It is an exciting time in a young person's life: his body is changing, his emotions are intense and he is ready to explore the world. For some young people, it can also be a time of increased stress and responsibility. The primary developmental tasks in adolescence are the formation of a personal identity and achieving independence. Adolescents try to take on new roles, expand their social worlds, experiment with new ways of thinking and behaving, and explore ideas and values which are different from those of their families and diverge from societal expectations.

Physically: The age at which a young adolescent enters puberty varies. As mentioned earlier, the onset of puberty is, on average, two to three years earlier among girls than boys. Among boys, the onset of puberty is heralded by the growth of the testes and scrotum, together with the appearance of pubic, facial and underarm hair; an increase in the size of the penis; deepening of the voice; and a growth in muscle bulk and stature. Among adolescent girls, the first sign of puberty is the development of the breasts. This is followed by the appearance of pubic hair and the physical growth of the body (especially the hips). Next, menstruation begins and generalized growth of hair takes place (e.g. underarm hair). Along with these changes, both sexes experience an increase in perspiration, as well as acne. Adolescent girls begin to menstruate every month in preparation for the function of reproduction. Though boys of all ages

get erections, they are more frequent and are associated with sexual feelings during adolescence. These erections can be quite embarrassing for the adolescent boy. Night emissions or 'wet dreams' (when a small amount of semen is ejaculated during sleep) may also occur, and this can be somewhat upsetting if the boy is unaware that it is a perfectly normal experience. Since adolescents have many questions concerning how their bodies are changing, it is important to introduce the subject of reproductive and sexual health in school curricula. As the adolescent begins to experience the changes in his body, his concerns now centre around personal attractiveness. Due to differences in the onset, the experience and the process of puberty, some adolescents require reassurance that they are 'normal'. Cultural and traditional approaches to pubertal milestones may affect the adolescent's participation in activities (e.g. adolescent girls may not be allowed to participate in social activities when they are menstruating). Adolescents often do not get enough sleep because of changes in their sleep cycle. This can cause academic problems with daytime tiredness. It is important that the adolescent continues to get adequate nutrition, sleep and exercise. It is useful to channellize their energy into sport. Physical maturity is reached by 18 years of age among women and 21 among men, and most young adults become comfortable with their bodies by this time.

Cognitively: During the earlier years of adolescence, the youth is more interested in his present than his future. Problem-solving, which has been primarily 'concrete' (i.e. understanding what is visible and obvious), becomes more flexible and abstract. These abstract thinking abilities include understanding cause and effect, as well as comprehending and contemplating what could happen in the imagined future ('foresight'). Due to this increased comprehension and appreciation of a future, adolescence is the ideal time to provide education on the consequences of high-risk behaviours, such as smoking, and to provide information on career choices. By the time the adolescent enters young adulthood, his well-established skills for abstract thinking are mobilized in the direction of making career plans and setting personal goals. At times of stress, however, the young person may revert to concrete thinking. An adolescent is intensely curious and has varied, though often not sustained, interests. One can build upon the young adolescent's desire to be an active learner by providing many different learning avenues, such as lectures, projects, practical demonstrations and debates. A mixture of individual and group-based activities encourages different learning styles and optimizes learning.

Emotionally: The adolescent is prone to mood swings, characterized by confidence and happiness on the one hand, and unexplained irritation, bad moods and self-doubt on the other. This occurs especially during early adolescence. There is a growing need for an independent identity and the acceptance of this identity by other people. This, coupled with embarrassment and awkwardness about one's changing body, often results in great sensitivity to personal criticism. Occasional doubts related to issues such as, 'Do I look good?' and, 'Do my friends really like me?' are common. The adolescent is beginning to construct a personal value system and to evaluate the world around him. Adolescents experience a need for privacy, which can give rise to feelings such as 'nobody understands me' and feelings of loneliness. Establishing a personal identity includes being increasingly independent with respect to one's physical needs, not always requiring a parent's approval for one's actions, being able to seek help from people outside the family and beginning to feel comfortable about being different and distinct from others. In later adolescence, the youth begins to openly challenge family authority and conflicts may emerge about his increasing independence. Families, schools and communities should encourage healthy independent decision-making and provide positive decision-making opportunities for adolescents (e.g. allowing them to decide how they would like to spend their time off, either with friends or with the family).

Socially: Adolescents develop intense relationships. Early adolescence is characterized by strong peer allegiances and the adolescent experiences sexual urges while exploring special friendships. While the need to belong to a group remains important, one-on-one romantic relationships begin to develop. Peer pressure may influence the adolescent's experiments with 'high-risk behaviours' (Box 1.4). As the adolescent loosens his ties to his family, his relationships with others in the community become stronger. Peer influence increasingly shapes the attitudes and values of the young adolescent; and this can cause him to challenge authority, especially within the family. The adolescent uses various methods to expand his horizons (e.g. using the Internet to access networks and groups beyond traditional boundaries). The adolescent begins to make independent decisions regarding his degree of religious belief and participation in religious events. Idealism is one of the hallmarks of late adolescence and the individual often envisions a positive future for himself, his community and his country. As they approach young adulthood, adolescents become increasingly clear

BOX 1.4: RISK BEHAVIOURS

Risk behaviours are behaviours that can have a negative impact on the development and health of a person. These behaviours (e.g. fighting and smoking) can have an immediate impact, such as an injury, or long-term negative consequences on health, such as cancer. These behaviours may also prevent the young person from enjoying experiences and relationships that are typical of their age group. For example, a teenager who becomes pregnant may have to discontinue her education. Importantly, risk behaviours can endanger the life of the young person, as in the case of an accident due to driving while drinking. Also, they can interfere with the development of skills required for the next stage of development. For example, drug dependence may cause a youth to drop out of school, which is likely to affect his ability to pursue an adult vocation later. The three broad groups of risk behaviour are: substance use (alcohol, drugs, smoking and chewing tobacco); early and unprotected sexual activity; and delinquency and antisocial behaviour.

about their personal identity within the larger group, understanding how they fit in and how they can contribute. At this stage, cultural and social norms and expectations often determine how interdependent or independent the adolescent is relative to the family and the community. Some family structures support independence, while more traditional households value collective decision-making. This may be particularly pertinent when it comes to the choice of an occupation and a life partner. The dramatic expansion of the social worlds that the adolescent inhabits, coupled with the emergence of a distinct personal identity, may bring an adolescent into conflict with others (e.g. his family).

Sexually: Adolescence is a period of sexual awakening and physical maturation (Box 1.5). In early adolescence, the youth develops intense same-sex relationships and interactions with the opposite sex often occur only in a group setting. At this stage, same-sex attractions do not necessarily indicate a homosexual orientation; rather, they are most likely a phase that the adolescent is passing through. As the adolescent grows, the cultural milieu determines how young people dress, behave and socialize with the opposite sex. In later adolescence, the youth often develops relationships with the opposite sex and interactions frequently occur in private rather than group settings. This is the age of sexual experimentation, and the counsellor should encourage and empower the parents to act as their children's primary sex educators.

The counsellor should also strengthen the school's programmes to help the youth make healthy decisions with respect to all aspects of their personal health. A person with a sexual orientation which is different from that of the majority is usually aware of their sexual preference by early adolescence. As they progress through adolescence, they often develop a strong sense of being 'different' from others. Owing to cultural pressures, these individuals may suppress their sexual orientation,

BOX 1.5: TERMS DESCRIBING ASPECTS OF ADOLESCENT SEXUAL DEVELOPMENT

- **Sex** refers to the biological and physiological characteristics that differentiate men and women.
- **Gender roles** refer to socially constructed roles, behaviours, activities and attributes that are considered appropriate for men and women (e.g. women do the housework and men work outside the house).
- **Gender identity** refers to how the individual views herself and is usually in accordance with one's biological sex. In a small percentage of the population, the gender identity of the individual may not be aligned with their biological sex. In these cases, the individual truly feels that they should be the opposite gender. Such persons are sometimes referred to as 'transsexual' or 'transgender'.
- **Sexual orientation** refers to whether a person is attracted sexually to persons of the opposite biological sex (heterosexual), of the same biological sex (homosexual) or to both sexes (bisexual). The colloquial expression to describe homosexual males is 'gay', while the equivalent for homosexual females is 'lesbian'. Heterosexual people are sometimes referred to as 'straight'. Studies suggest that up to five out of every 100 persons are homosexual (the percentage is higher among males than females), and that the remainder are heterosexual.

which sometimes leads to mental health problems. On the other hand, if they are open about their sexuality, they may face a greater risk of being bullied and victimized by their peers and rejected by their families. The acceptance of differences in sexual orientation is certainly influenced by one's social and cultural environment, but counsellors need to understand that individuals with sexual orientations which are different from that of the majority require support, and that such support must be non-judgemental. Above all, it is important to accept that a homosexual orientation is not a disorder or a mental health problem, but it may bring on mental health problems due to feelings of guilt and discrimination.

THEORIES OF CHILD AND ADOLESCENT DEVELOPMENT

A number of theories explain the progression of the individual from childhood through young adulthood. These also help explain how adult personalities are formed during this transition. This section summarizes the key features of some major developmental theories and aims to provide the counsellor with a basic foundation in child and adolescent development. This casebook does not advocate a particular theory but, rather, recommends a pragmatic approach which borrows elements from different theories with an eye to their usefulness in different contexts.

SIGMUND FREUD

Sigmund Freud (1856–1939) was a Viennese physician who developed a theory on how the mind works and a therapeutic approach to mental suffering, called 'psychoanalysis'. His theory was based on his observations that a person's personality is the result of a compromise between his sexual and aggressive instincts and the demands of his family and society. Freud described sequential phases of psychosexual development: the oral phase (birth to 1 year), the anal phase (1–3 years), the phallic–oedipal phase (3–6 years), the latency phase (6 years to puberty) and the genital phases (puberty to death). Each phase is dominated by a primary sexual zone and the pleasure received from that zone. Thus, during the oral phase, children focus on the pleasures of sucking and biting. In the anal phase, the child's pleasure shifts to the anus as they begin toilet training and attempting to control their bowels. In the phallic–oedipal phase, the child's pleasure zone moves to the genitals. During the phallic–oedipal phase, children turn their interest and affection towards the parent of the opposite sex, resent the parent of the same sex and ultimately, identify with the parent of the same sex. During latency, sexual urges and interests are temporarily suppressed. Finally, once the child reaches adolescence, he enters (and remains in) the genital phase, in which adult sexual interests and activities predominate. Freud's 'metapsychology' identified a number of 'structures of the mind': the 'id' as the home of unconscious instinctual and selfish urges; the 'ego' as the home of reality testing and judgement; and the 'superego', or 'conscience', as the home of values and rules. Many psychologists and child development researchers have attempted to empirically test Freud's theories. Their observations have confirmed some aspects of his theory and modified or rejected others. Freud's theory remains important and influential today because it linked early childhood experiences to the development of the adult personality, and the psychological and biological pathways of development.

Anna Freud

Anna Freud (1895–1982) followed the path of her influential father, contributing to the field of psychoanalysis and founding the field of child psychoanalysis. In addition to developing therapeutic approaches for children and methods to support their psychological well-being, she expanded on Sigmund Freud's understanding of defence mechanisms. She explained more thoroughly how the individual uses defence mechanisms to protect himself from psychological pain caused by internally or externally overwhelming experiences. The defence mechanisms described by Sigmund Freud and Anna Freud continue to influence clinical practice today (Box 1.6).

Erik Erikson

Erik Erikson (1902–1994) used Sigmund Freud's work as a starting point

BOX 1.6: DEFENCE MECHANISMS

- **Repression:** This is the involuntary exclusion of negative thoughts and memories from one's consciousness. For example, a young adult does not recall being bullied as a child.
- **Suppression:** The conscious exclusion of painful thoughts is known as suppression. For example, the child says, 'I don't want to think about that.'
- **Denial:** The failure to recognize a painful reality is termed denial. For example, although a child's parents are divorced, he states that his father 'has gone away for work'.
- **Reaction formation:** This is when the individual unconsciously transforms an impulse into its opposite. For example, a jealous sister becomes overprotective of her new sibling.
- **Regression:** When the young person falls back to a previous developmental stage due to stress, he is said to have regressed. For example, a 6-year-old resumes bedwetting when a sibling is born.
- **Identification with the aggressor:** This takes place when an individual overcomes his fear of someone who is aggressive towards him by unconsciously adopting the traits of the aggressive individual in order to feel powerful instead of fearful. For example, on seeing his father physically attack his mother and fearing that the father could turn his aggression on him, a youth himself becomes aggressive.

for his psychosocial theory of human development from birth through childhood and, ultimately, into old age. Unlike Freud's psychosexual emphasis, Erikson's focus was on how a person's identity develops within the context of society and how he learns to live within a larger community. The theory describes the situations that would be ideal at each stage of development for the individual to become a well-adjusted person, as well as the challenges that the individual may face if the environment is not favourable. For example, during the first psychosocial stage of 'trust versus mistrust' (birth to 1 year), if the infant's basic needs (food, clean nappies and love from caregivers) are consistently provided for, he learns that he can trust people in his environment and he will believe that the world is good. If, on the other hand, he is neglected, he will doubt his caregivers' constancy and trustworthiness. In Erikson's scheme, learning to trust others is the first essential step in learning how to have loving and supportive relationships with others and in developing a positive self-image in later life (Box 1.7). Erikson views the individual's experiences with his relationships and his life experiences as central to his developmental process over the course of his lifetime.

Lawrence Kohlberg

Lawrence Kohlberg (1927–1987), in his theory of moral development, put forward the idea that as the young person develops, he learns to differentiate right from wrong and his moral reasoning becomes increasingly sophisticated. Kohlberg described three stages of moral development, each of which builds upon the abilities gained in the previous stage/s. Kohlberg concluded that moral development is a lifelong task and many people fail to reach the more advanced stages of moral understanding even in adulthood. In the first stage, the 'pre-conventional stage', understanding is dictated by consequences and the child's decision-making is based on the avoidance of trouble. In the second stage, the 'conventional stage', the adolescent follows social and cultural norms because he believes that this will promote good personal relationships and a healthy community. In the final stage, the 'post-conventional stage', morality is based on a highly nuanced personal code, such that people make their moral judgements on the basis of a set of personal values or beliefs. For example, there may be an unwritten rule in a hostel that physically harassing new students is acceptable; however, an individual who has evolved to this last stage may question this approach, viewing it as being violative of the rights of the individual. Kohlberg believed that these stages result from the evolution of the person and are not dependent on his environment. Kohlberg's theory adds to our understanding of how an individual's moral reasoning develops as he matures.

BOX 1.7: ERIK ERIKSON'S PSYCHOSOCIAL STAGES OF DEVELOPMENT*

Stage	Basic conflict	Important events	Outcome
Infancy (birth to 18 months)	Trust versus mistrust	Feeding	Children develop a sense of trust and confidence when caregivers are reliable and provide them with care and affection. Without this, they will mistrust the world.
Early childhood (2–3 years)	Autonomy versus shame and doubt	Toilet training	The development of a sense of personal control over his physical abilities provides the child with a sense of independence and self-sufficiency. The failure to achieve this results in feelings of shame and doubt about his abilities.
Pre-school (3–5 years)	Initiative versus guilt	Exploration	Children need to feel that they can stimulate change in their environment. Success leads to a sense of purpose; failure leads to a feeling of guilt.
School age (6–11 years)	Industry versus inferiority	School	Children develop skills to meet social and academic demands within the school system. Success leads to a sense of competence; failure leads to a feeling of inferiority.
Adolescence (12–18 years)	Identity versus role confusion	Social relationships	Adolescents develop a sense of personal identity that allows them to remain true to their beliefs. Failure at this stage results in confusion about their role in society.
Young adulthood (19–40 years)	Intimacy versus isolation	Romantic relationships	Young adults develop intimate, loving relationships with other people. Failure to achieve this leads to loneliness and isolation.

*Adapted from Lerner R, Easterbrooks M, Mistry J. *Developmental Psychology*. New Jersey, USA: John Wiley; 2003.

Jean Piaget

Jean Piaget (1896–1980) put forward the theory of cognitive development, describing how a child's thinking capacities develop through his interactions with the world around him. Infants and young children understand the world in a different way than do adults. As he explores and plays, the child learns how to think in ways that increasingly fit with reality. Piaget describes four stages, the first of which is the 'sensorimotor stage' (0–2 years). Children of this age are beginning to learn through their interactions with the environment, using their five senses and developing motor skills. During the 'preoperational stage' (2–7 years), children start to use mental symbols to understand and interact with the world. They begin to acquire language skills and engage in pretend play. In the 'concrete operational stage' (7–12 years), children gain the ability to think logically, which enables them to solve problems and organize information. During the 'formal operational stage' (12 years onwards), adolescents solve problems using abstract and symbolic thought. Piaget's contribution to the understanding of cognitive processes is his theory that the way children view and understand the world develops as they are exposed to and interact with it, through distinct stages of cognitive development.

Urie Bronfenbrenner

Urie Bronfenbrenner (1917–2005) developed the ecological systems theory to explain how the child's environment affects his growth and development. He identified four environments that make up the human world: the microsystem, the mesosystem, the exosystem and the macrosystem. The microsystem is the small, immediate environment the young person lives in. It includes his interaction with his family/caregiver, school and friends. The influences of the family/caregivers and school in the early years continue to shape the youth as he grows up. For example, in a traditional household, the family may be of the view that a son should be brought up in such a way as to discourage him from performing household chores, and this, in turn, influences his later attitudes towards the roles of men and women. The mesosystem refers to how the different parts of a child's microsystem can work together to benefit the child. For example, if a child's caregivers play an active role in matters related to his school (e.g. going to parent–teacher meetings) and the teachers are actively interested in the child's progress, this synergy will benefit the child. The exosystem includes the people, places and events that the young person may not routinely interact with, but which may have a significant impact on him. For example, if one of the youth's parents has long working hours, he may have to spend a significant amount of time by himself at home and may start watching too much television as a result. The macrosystem is the farthest from the young person's immediate environment. It is made up of the people, places and events which potentially have a great influence over the young person (e.g. the relative freedoms permitted by the government, cultural values, the economy, wars). Bronfenbrenner's theory gives us insights into how diverse the environmental influences on a child's mental health are, and how they operate at different levels and interact with each other.

NANCY EISENBERG

In 1987, Nancy Eisenberg developed the theory of prosocial reasoning. Prosocial behaviours are those which benefit others. These behaviours are more likely to be present among the youth who are capable of 'empathy' (the ability to understand another person's point of view, as

well as the ability to feel what the other person may be feeling). For example, although a child is hungry, he may share his food with another child who has left his tiffin at home because he understands that the other child is also hungry and feels what it must feel like to be that child. The child's emotional reaction to the other child turns into empathic concern for that child once he not only understands that child's unhappiness, but actually feels what it must be like to be so hungry. Eisenberg describes this ability to 'put oneself in another's shoes' as most often being related to the youth's age and life experience, i.e. his level of maturity. Eisenberg describes that the young child initially uses self-centred and needs-oriented reasoning; then, as he develops, he uses approval-oriented reasoning, followed by empathic reasoning; and is finally guided by internal moral principles.

TRADITIONAL INDIAN THEORIES OF CHILD DEVELOPMENT

Ayurvedic literature describes the child's development, commencing with conception. Psychological development occurs from the third month of pregnancy, when the mind of the foetus is stimulated and functions as a single unit along with the mother's mind. The mother's desires during conception and pregnancy are thought to reflect the child's future character. The core concepts in Ayurveda are that the basic personality of the individual is laid down *in utero* and that the child cannot be treated as an independent unit, but is instead, part of a dyad with the mother, especially through its infancy. Ayurveda also recognizes certain unique stages of development of the child, referred to as 'samskaras'. These are related to the child's level of dependency. Each level is associated with prescribed rituals, which help the child make the transition into adult society and roles. Some examples of these rituals are the naming ceremony at the age of 1 month, the tonsure ceremony at 3 years of age, and a specific ceremony to induct the child into reading and writing between 5 and 7 years of age. This traditional Indian system recognizes the various 'ages and stages' that a child evolves through and marks these ceremonially, in a manner which is generally accepting and nurturing. The counsellor may come into contact with families which raise their children in accordance with this traditional perspective.

In conclusion, the diverse theories of child development help the counsellor understand the phases that the young person passes through from different theoretical perspectives. In order to understand the young person's development and mental health, it is useful for the counsellor to appreciate that the phases through which the young person passes are overlapping and sequential, that his experiences during the earlier phases influence the later phases, and that diverse temperamental and environmental factors influence development.

CHAPTER 2

DISTRESS, DISORDERS AND DISABILITIES

Most individuals make the journey from childhood through adolescence into young adulthood without any significant health problems. During this journey, individuals adapt to many challenges. However, this ability to adapt to, manage and make the best use of environmental and personal challenges and opportunities varies from person to person. It depends on the nature of the challenges, the individual's make-up, the developmental level reached and the characteristics of her home and community life. In some instances, the young person may develop a mental health problem during this journey.

Mental health problems during childhood and adolescence can be broadly classified into three categories: mental health *distress*, mental health *disorders* and developmental *disabilities*. In general, the distress states tend to be strongly associated with environmental factors and do not last long, while disorders and disabilities tend to have a greater association with 'biological' factors and tend to be longer-lasting (even over the course of a lifetime, in the case of developmental disabilities). These mental health problems interfere to varying degrees with the youth's capacity to manage her emotions and her environment and to participate in activities typical of her developmental stage. This chapter guides the counsellor on how to understand what is troubling the youth and how to determine the best way to help her. It is divided into the following sections:

- **Child and adolescent mental health problems:** This section summarizes the main types of distress, disorders and disabilities which a counsellor may encounter in school-going youth.
- **Life course approach to mental health problems:** This section describes the problems observed most often among different age groups.

- **Burden of child and adolescent mental health problems:** This section summarizes what we know about how common mental health problems are and their impact on the lives of youth.
- **Risk and protective factors affecting mental health:** This section summarizes what we know about the factors which can lead to mental health problems, as well as those which can protect youth from developing problems.

CHILD AND ADOLESCENT MENTAL HEALTH PROBLEMS

Although childhood and adolescence proceed well for most individuals, as many as one in 10 youth develop a mental health disorder or disability and many more are troubled by mental health distress. This section includes descriptions of mental health distress and the mental health disorders and developmental disabilities that the counsellor may encounter among youth in the school setting. For each condition, the information is organized as follows:

Common presentation and possible variations: A description of the features typical of the problem, as well as any specific age- or situation-related variations which may occur. Other conditions which commonly 'coexist' with the primary problem are also mentioned here.

Consequences: The important consequences of suffering from the specific mental health problem are described.

Counselling strategies and supportive interventions: The key counselling strategies and supportive interventions most suitable for addressing the problem are listed here and described in greater detail in Chapter 6.

The categories of mental health problems described in this chapter are:

- Mental health distress
- Mental health disorders

  ⇒ Emotional disorders

  —Depression

  —Anxiety disorders

—Trauma-related emotional disorders or post-traumatic stress disorder
- ⇒ Behavioural disorders
  - —Disruptive behaviour disorders (oppositional defiant disorder and conduct disorder)
  - —Attention deficit hyperactivity disorder
- ⇒ Substance use disorder
- ⇒ Serious mental disorders
  - —Schizophrenia
  - —Bipolar disorder
  - —Obsessive–compulsive disorder

- Developmental disabilities
  - ⇒ Intellectual disability (mental retardation)
  - ⇒ Autism spectrum disorder
  - ⇒ Specific learning disabilities (scholastic disabilities)
  - ⇒ Locomotor and sensory disabilities

Mental health distress

A young person's emotional stability can be shaken by unexpected challenges, changes in the circumstances of her life or an increase in stressors, particularly when she does not have the necessary coping capacities to manage the stressful circumstances or lacks the support system required to weather the challenges. As a result, she may be overwhelmed by feelings that she cannot manage and experience mental health distress. Common examples of challenges that may temporarily affect a young person's adjustment include: a change in the family structure (e.g. the parents divorcing or remarrying, the birth of a sibling); a loss (e.g. the death of a parent, moving to another home or school); greater academic expectations (e.g. change in the medium of instruction from the local language to English); an uncertain future (e.g. a lack of vocational opportunities as graduation approaches); parental disapproval (e.g. parents disagreeing with the youth on her romantic involvements); physical health difficulties (e.g. anticipating or having undergone a medical procedure); and sudden unexpected events (e.g. a sudden death in the family, witnessing or being a victim of an accident or natural disaster) which can take the youth by surprise.

Mental health distress reactions are generally closely related in time to a stressful event(s); of a relatively short duration and a mild intensity; and improved circumstances, strengthened coping skills and family/ counsellor support can often reduce the youth's distress. On the other hand, if the intensity of the youth's reaction endures despite the passage of time following a stressful event(s) and the support provided, it may indicate that she is suffering from a mental health disorder, which will require more extensive counselling or a referral.

Common presentation: Increased emotional distress may temporarily interfere with the youth's mood and adjustment as she absorbs and adjusts to altered circumstances. The level of distress experienced and the ability to manage it varies from one person to another. If the youth does not have adequate skills or support, she may experience unusually strong reactions. The feelings of distress can include fear, nervousness, guilt and shame, a loss of control, vulnerability, self-doubt, confusion, loneliness, sadness and anger. These feelings are manifested in a number of ways, either through symptoms of anxiety and/or depression or through impulsive behaviours. Anxiety and/or depression may be manifested as moodiness, withdrawal, changes in core biological functions (e.g. sleeping and/or eating more or less), physical symptoms of anxiety (*see* Anxiety disorders), regression to earlier ways of managing feelings (e.g. seeking comfort by sleeping in the parents' bedroom) and regression to earlier stages of development (e.g. wetting the bed at night despite being toilet trained). Sometimes, young people respond to increased stress with 'acting out' behaviours, e.g. throwing tantrums or having outbursts. These

actions may provide some relief from inner tension, especially in the case of those who tend to express their feelings through actions rather than words ('acting out'). Some youth experiencing stress may overreact to minor events that may not have caused noticeable problems for them in the past. For example, a youth may yell or push a friend who has taken her pencil and paper without asking, rather than responding in her usual way, which would have been to simply ignore what happened.

Consequences: There may be a temporary decline in the academic performance of a youth experiencing mental health distress. Social withdrawal (e.g. reduced contact with friends, refusal to go to school) can also occur. 'Acting out' may result in conflict with peers, family members and the school staff, further aggravating the adverse circumstances which led to the distress.

Counselling strategies and supportive interventions: A range of counselling strategies can be used to help a youth suffering from mental health distress, crisis counselling and youth psychoeducation being the foremost among them. In addition, depending on the specific circumstances, the following strategies can be helpful: anger management counselling, social skills counselling, relaxation exercise and problem-solving counselling. Simultaneous family psychoeducation is necessary if it is the youth's environment that is the source of stress. Supportive interventions in the home and the community and supportive interventions in the school are very important to reduce additional stress, e.g. by modifying academic expectations. If the event the youth is reacting to has also had an impact on the parents or caregivers (e.g. a death in the family), they, too, will benefit from crisis counselling and supportive interventions in the home and the community.

Mental health disorders

Mental health disorders are characterized by a cluster or pattern of distressing emotions, thoughts or behaviours, which typically occur together with a frequency, severity and pervasiveness that seriously affect and impair normal functioning and prevent the individual from achieving age-appropriate developmental goals. In order to diagnose health problems the World Health Organization (WHO) has designed the

International Statistical Classification of Diseases and Related Health Problems. Currently, the version in use is the 10th Revision (ICD-10) (WHO, 1996).[#] This comprehensive classification of physical and mental health problems contains more than 10,000 different diagnostic codes and covers more than 100 mental health conditions. The system makes it possible for health practitioners and researchers to diagnose and record information on individuals in any part of the world, helping to increase the global understanding of the frequency and causes of these problems, and to ensure appropriate treatment. For the purposes of this casebook, WHO's *Multi-axial Classification of Child and Adolescent Psychiatric Disorders: The ICD-10 classification of mental and behavioural disorders of children and adolescents*[†] has been adapted so that descriptions of mental health disorders and disabilities of youth are practically applicable for counsellors working with youth in the school setting.

This casebook organizes the many types of mental health disorders into three broad groups, each group sharing related features. The first group, the emotional disorders, comprises disorders which primarily affect the feelings or emotional states of the person. This group includes depression, anxiety disorders and disorders following a traumatic experience. The second group, the behavioural disorders, comprises disorders characterized by behavioural disturbance. This group includes hyperactivity disorder, substance use disorder and conduct disorder. The third group comprises the serious mental disorders, which are characterized by unusual thoughts and sensory experiences. This group includes the psychoses (schizophrenia and bipolar disorder) and obsessive–compulsive disorder. Note that these are pragmatic groupings and there are overlaps between groups and specific differences between disorders within the same group. This casebook does not include some disorders, such as eating disorders, because they are rare or require specialist care.

[#] http://www.who.int/classifications/icd/en/

[†] WHO. *Multi-axial Classification of Child and Adolescent Psychiatric Disorders: The ICD-10 classification of mental and behavioural disorders of children and adolescents*. Cambridge: Cambridge University Press; 1996.

Emotional disorders

Depression

Feeling unhappy is common during childhood and adolescence, and indeed, at some point or another in everyone's life. For example, a young person may feel sad when her best friend moves to a different neighbourhood or school. This sadness is usually specific and in response to a particular event or experience. Some may become more acutely distressed if the event is unexpected or severe, their sadness taking the form of mental health distress (*described earlier*). Most youth recover naturally from these bouts of sadness after a period of adjustment. For a young person to be described as suffering from 'depression', however, she must exhibit a group of specific symptoms of an intensity that impairs daily functioning for a prolonged duration. Depression is more common among adolescents than children, among girls than boys and among youth who have a family history of depression.

Common presentation: Depression is characterized by a change in the person's mood (how they feel), which, in turn, affects how they behave. Although the name of the disorder may suggest that for a young person to be diagnosed with this disorder he must complain primarily of feeling sad, in fact, many youth complain of physical discomforts or other types of emotional distress. Young people with this disorder may have unexplained episodes of crying, experience an overwhelming sense of hopelessness and helplessness or unusual levels of irritability and anger, and complain of being tired or of aches and pains, or of losing interest in what they used to find enjoyable. In many cases, there are difficulties with relationships; lowering of self-esteem and feelings of guilt; a loss of appetite and loss of weight or increased appetite and weight gain; or sleep problems (either reduced or increased). Among younger children, depression may not take the form of 'feeling sad', but may manifest as fatigue or multiple physical complaints which seem to be unfounded. These may be accompanied by grouchiness or irritability, or by a change in sleep patterns (Box 2.1). One should make a diagnosis of depression only if these symptoms have persisted for at least two weeks, have been present for most of the day during that period, cause considerable personal distress and affect the individual's social functioning. Many

BOX 2.1: COMMON SYMPTOMS OF DEPRESSION IN A YOUNG PERSON (*see* Case Study 18)

- Sadness
- Tearfulness
- Loss of interest in activities that were previously pleasurable
- Irritability
- Feelings of worthlessness or excessive guilt
- Changes in appetite: eating less or more
- Poor concentration and fatigue
- Unintended changes in weight
- Sleep problems (either reduced or excessive sleep)
- Social withdrawal
- Suicidal thoughts

youth with depression also show features of other emotional disorders, notably anxiety disorders.

Consequences: Depression impairs the youth's concentration, thus affecting her academic performance. Young people who are depressed may become isolated, which, in turn, can interfere with their recovery. They may misuse substances, such as cannabis and alcohol, in order to feel better, but this only makes their problems worse. Although most young people with depression will recover with or without treatment, many are at risk of suffering a 'relapse' (recurrence of the disorder) later in life. The most serious consequence of depression is self-harm, which can be either impulsive or planned, and might lead to the death of the young person.

Counselling strategies and supportive interventions: When depression is mild or moderate, i.e. when the symptoms are not getting in the way of the youth's daily life to any significant extent, the counsellor can make use of options such as youth psychoeducation, cognitive restructuring, problem-solving counselling, behavioural activation and, where appropriate, family psychoeducation. If these strategies do not help, or if the depressive symptoms are very severe and are affecting the young person's social functioning in a number of settings (e.g.

home, school, with peers), the counsellor must assess the person for the possible risk of suicide and take appropriate action (*see* Chapter 4). The youth's recovery can be facilitated by supportive interventions in the school, such as advising teachers to decrease the academic pressure until the youth's depression eases.

Anxiety disorders

Anxiety is characterized by feelings of tension, fear and/or nervousness when faced with a situation which is or feels unfamiliar, stressful or dangerous to the individual (e.g. on seeing a snake or before an examination). These feelings are valuable signals which help the individual recognize that they are in or about to enter a dangerous or stressful situation. These feelings help them anticipate and prepare for, or avoid, such situations. Everyone experiences anxiety many times in the course of their lives. However, the anxiety may be considered a disorder when the feelings of anxiety do not match the situation, e.g. they occur even though the situation does not call for them, or they are objectively out of proportion to the circumstance; when they interfere with normal functioning; or when they persist after the stressful situation has passed. Anxiety disorders have been observed more frequently among girls than boys.

Common presentation: The changes which accompany mild anxiety include a quietening down of motor activity, an increased level of concentration and a heightened awareness of the surroundings. More sustained or severe anxiety is associated with distressing symptoms, such as light-headedness, faintness or dizziness, headaches, disturbed sleep or feeling aroused or awake, chest pain and/or feeling one's heart beat fast and loud, shortness of breath, dry mouth, diarrhoea, increasing urgency to pass urine, restlessness, flushing of the face, sweating, and numbness and tingling of the hands and feet. Sometimes, the anxiety occurs in an acute (sudden), extremely intense and relatively short-lasting (a few minutes) form, resembling an 'attack'; this is called a 'panic attack' (*see* Case Study 8).

Specific types of anxiety disorders, some associated with specific triggers, which may occur among children and adolescents include the following:

Separation anxiety disorder: It is normal for pre-school children to feel anxious when separated from a parent or caregiver. However, when separation from a specific caregiver creates severe symptoms of anxiety and causes extreme worry (i.e. the worry that terrible harm might befall the caregiver during the separation), the child is considered to be suffering from separation anxiety disorder. This disorder is manifested in various ways. At home, for example, the child may refuse to sleep alone or stay with a babysitter when her parents are out. With regard to school, the young person may throw temper tantrums on the way to school, leave the classroom midway through a lesson, call home repeatedly from school or downright refuse to go to school. Severe separation anxiety disorder can result in physical symptoms, such as stomach aches and/or vomiting, and/or nightmares, and/or acting out behaviours.

Phobic anxiety disorder: From time to time, children experience a number of fears, such as a fear of the dark, ghosts or animals (Box 2.2). However, when any of these normal fears becomes so intense that it affects the child's daily functioning or is unreasonable, it is termed a phobia and she is suffering from a phobic anxiety disorder. Children with this disorder harbour unreasonable fears about relatively non-threatening situations, and their daily lives and social interactions are greatly restricted as a result. For example, many children have a fear of dogs, whether or not they have had a bad experience with a dog; if the child refuses to go to a park or visit a friend's home because of the

BOX 2.2: 'NORMAL' FEARS AND AGE OF PRESENTATION IN CHILDREN AND ADOLESCENTS

Stage	Age	Common fears
Infants/ toddlers	Infancy to 3 years	Loud noises, strangers, separation from parents, large objects, baths, toilet training
Pre-school children	3–6 years	Imaginary figures and possibilities (e.g. ghosts, monsters, supernatural beings, the dark, noises, sleeping alone, thunder, floods)
School-age children/ adolescents	7–16 years	More realistic fears (e.g. physical injury, health, school performance, death, thunderstorms, earthquakes, floods, burglary, new situations)

fear that she might come across dogs, it may be considered a phobia. Individuals with a phobia cannot be convinced to approach the feared object or situation and do not respond to reassurance. Panic attacks may be a prominent feature of phobic anxiety disorder. This disorder sometimes persists into adolescence and adulthood. The individual may, for example, be unable to travel in a bus or go to the market because she is afraid of being in a closed or crowded space.

Social anxiety disorder of childhood: This is the persistence of 'stranger anxiety' beyond the age of 3 years (stranger anxiety is normal up to the age of 3 years). A child with this disorder usually has a good relationship with his family members and individuals familiar to him, but avoids interactions with less familiar or unfamiliar persons, such as school peers. Social anxiety disorder causes the child to actively avoid social interactions in specific settings, and may persist into adolescence and adulthood.

Consequences: Anxiety disorders can severely limit the youth's ability to participate in school and social events. This can give rise to the perception that the child is different from her peers and she may become socially isolated. Social isolation can also occur because the child begins to avoid specific situations which provoke anxiety. Avoidance of such situations usually makes the anxiety disorder worse. Adolescents may misuse drugs and alcohol in order to control their symptoms of anxiety. Anxiety can interfere with the young person's ability to concentrate on her studies and examinations, adversely affecting her academic performance. For example, 'going blank' just before or during an examination is a consequence of severe anxiety.

Counselling strategies and supportive interventions: Youth psychoeducation is essential. Relaxation exercises, problem-solving counselling and social skills counselling are useful interventions, depending on the trigger for the anxiety. Family psychoeducation should also be given, especially when a youth avoids school, which can aggravate the disorder further. In family psychoeducation, the counsellor would guide the family to reintroduce their child to school in a step-wise manner. The counsellor can advise the parents to actively discourage avoidance of everyday activities even though they may be the cause of the anxiety. Supportive interventions in the school, such as the counsellor helping the teachers understand that the youth's inability to study is linked to her anxiety rather than defiance, can create a more supportive school atmosphere for the youth.

Trauma-related emotional disorders or post-traumatic stress disorder

'Trauma' refers to an exposure to an exceptionally threatening or calamitous single acute event (e.g. a natural or man-made disaster, a terrible car accident, an episode of domestic violence), or to repeated overwhelming events (e.g. child abuse, parental violence). In the instance of a single acute event, it is natural for the exposed individual to feel overwhelmed and frightened for a period of time. The youth may present to the counsellor in a distressed state (*described earlier*, Mental health distress). With the passage of time and with support, the youth will gradually recover. Some individuals, however, continue to experience distressing emotions and disturbing memories of the trauma. These individuals are considered to be suffering from post-traumatic stress disorder (PTSD). Repeated traumatic events (i.e. ongoing trauma) are not only associated with a greater risk of persistent emotional difficulties, but can also lead to other emotional disorders (*see above*, Emotional disorders).

Common presentation: A young person suffering from PTSD presents with three clusters of symptoms. The first cluster of symptoms involves *re-experiencing the trauma*, which may include distressing recollections of the event (children may often re-enact the event, repeating the event in some detail in their play), vivid sensations of reliving the traumatizing experience ('flashbacks') and/or nightmares. The second cluster consists of *symptoms of hyperarousal*, including feeling jumpy and checking for threats. In addition, interrupted sleep, hyper-vigilance and physical symptoms of arousal, such as a fast heartbeat and breathing rate, are symptoms of hyperarousal. The third cluster consists of *symptoms of active avoidance*. In other words, the young person actively avoids any mention, thoughts of and/or contact with situations, settings and people associated with or reminiscent of the traumatizing event. These symptoms often affect the youth's concentration (*see* Case Study 3).

Consequences: Symptoms of PTSD may affect the youth's school performance and cause her to withdraw from her usual activities and friends. For example, hyperarousal makes it difficult for the youth to concentrate. Many young people with PTSD also experience features of depression and some adolescents may abuse drugs or alcohol to try to alleviate the distress. Youth exposed to ongoing trauma may present with oppositional defiant disorder (ODD) in childhood or conduct disorder (CD) in adolescence.

Counselling strategies and supportive interventions: Crisis counselling in the period immediately following the traumatizing event can help the youth (and, where relevant, the family) better manage their feelings, such as ongoing fear, guilt and anger, as well as the symptoms of PTSD. The youth psychoeducation component of crisis counselling helps the youth understand the reasons for their distress and the link between their distress and the traumatic incident. Problem-solving counselling can enable the youth to identify ways of managing practical problems affecting her mental health and/or delaying her recovery. Supportive interventions in the school can help the teachers understand that the youth's behaviour in school is related to the traumatizing event she has been through, e.g. that the youth is unable to concentrate because she is preoccupied with memories of the event. The family psychoeducation component of crisis counselling can help the caregiver manage the youth's distress and support her at home. When the event that the youth is reacting to has also had an impact on the family members, as in the case of a natural disaster, they too will benefit from counselling.

Behavioural disorders

All children and adolescents occasionally behave in an impulsive and defiant manner and 'act out' under different circumstances. However, when these behaviours are persistent, disruptive and beyond the norm for their age, they could be symptomatic of a disorder.

Disruptive behaviour disorders

When the youth behaves in a socially unacceptable manner repeatedly and the behaviours are disruptive, the youth could have an oppositional defiant disorder (ODD) or a conduct disorder (CD). These behaviour disorders are more frequently encountered among boys.

Common presentation: When a youth is continuously defiant, tends to provoke others, refuses to admit mistakes, is spiteful and vindictive in his words and actions, and when such behaviours begin before the age of 10 years, he can be considered to be suffering from ODD. Unlike the youth who may be simply mischievous or argumentative, the youth with ODD is disruptive and uncooperative to an extent that is beyond what would be considered normal for his age. Such children usually deliberately ignore requests, break rules to annoy others, tend to become angry and resentful, and are quick to blame others for their problems. CD affects children who are older. These children are repeatedly aggressive towards people or animals, and are excessively prone to fighting with or bullying others. They may be destructive towards property, e.g. setting fires and indulging in vandalism; may repeatedly indulge in lying, stealing and truancy from school; or be persistently disobedient and violate rules. These antisocial behaviours are often impulsive, and threaten the safety and violate the rights of other people. The antisocial behaviours displayed by a young person with CD can range from less severe forms, such as chronic lying, to more severe forms, such as burglary or physically harming others (*see* Case Study 16).

Consequences: A significant number of children with ODD progress to increasingly disruptive behaviours that characterize CD in adolescence. Youth with disruptive behaviour disorders do not inspire sympathy from adults or their peers and hence, become increasingly isolated. Their schooling is often interrupted, and characterized by poor academic performance and failure. They may indulge in high-risk and antisocial behaviours, including precocious sexual activity, substance abuse and crime, which can have adverse social consequences and affect their health. Many youth with disruptive behaviour disorders can also experience emotional disorders, especially depression.

Counselling strategies and supportive interventions: Both ODD and CD are challenging and difficult disorders to manage. However, it is worthwhile to try the strategies of anger management, social skills counselling and problem-solving counselling in such cases. Simultaneous family psychoeducation, targeting maladaptive parenting behaviours (which may be aggravating the youth's disruptive behaviours), may help. Supportive interventions in the home and the community, such as encouraging the youth to get involved in a boys' club in the community, and supportive interventions in the school, such as advising the teachers on the management of the youth's disruptive behaviours, may assist the youth's recovery.

Attention Deficit Hyperactivity Disorder

In their pre-school years, many children go through periods in which their levels of activity are high and impulse control is poor; these are considered developmentally appropriate behaviours at this age. However, when these behaviours persist into the school years and are unusually intense, attention deficit hyperactivity disorder (ADHD) should be suspected. ADHD, also referred to as hyperkinetic disorder in the ICD-10 (*described earlier*), is more common among boys than girls.

Common presentation: This disorder has three distinct components: attention deficit, hyperactivity and impulsivity. Attention deficit is a difficulty with concentrating on a given task and paying attention to details. It can be manifested as a difficulty in paying attention in class; distractibility; not listening to instructions; forgetting school items; difficulty completing tasks, especially those that take more than several minutes; and disrupting other students' work. Hyperactivity includes a motor restlessness, with the child always being 'on the go', an inability to sit quietly for more than a few minutes and fidgeting while sitting down.

Impulsivity makes it difficult for the child to control his impulses, and can be manifested as the child answering impulsively before a question has been completed. Further, as a result of impulsivity, the child has problems waiting in line or taking turns; he may interrupt conversations or activities; he might talk at inappropriate times; and he may have trouble controlling his behaviour, for example, he might fly off the handle with little provocation. Importantly, in order for these behaviours to qualify as ADHD, they need to occur across a number of settings (school, home and during playtime), to have commenced before the age of 7, to have been present for more than six months and to be severe enough to affect the youth's daily functioning in various settings (*see* Case Study 5). Girls with this disorder often display less hyperactivity and greater inattentiveness than boys, and may appear to be 'daydreamers'. Specific learning disabilities (*see below*), CD and anxiety disorders may coexist with ADHD.

Consequences: In addition to scholastic underachievement due to inattention, the youth's impulsivity and distractibility often cause social isolation. Poor academic performance may lead the youth to drop out of school and increase the risk of his subsequently developing high-risk behaviours, such as substance abuse. Often, the symptoms of hyperactivity settle with time, though the difficulties with attention may persist into adulthood.

Counselling strategies and supportive interventions: Youth psychoeducation and family psychoeducation are useful counselling strategies for youth with ADHD. Family psychoeducation can help parents manage their child's disruptive behaviours at home. Social skills counselling and problem-solving counselling may also be helpful for the youth. Supportive interventions in the school are useful. The counsellor can offer suggestions for the management of the youth in the classroom, e.g. a seating adjustment which ensures that the student has more personal space in the classroom or specific methods of instruction which take into account the attention problem of the student. Coexisting mental health problems, such as specific learning disabilities (SLD), should be addressed. Since ADHD is one of the few mental health disorders of children that can be effectively treated with medicines, referral to a physician is recommended if the counselling strategies and supportive interventions do not have favourable results or the symptoms are very severe.

Substance use disorder

A number of drugs are available for use and misuse (Box 2.3). Some of these, such as 'recreational drugs', are accepted socially in certain circumstances, while others (e.g. heroin) are neither socially nor legally acceptable. Young people have easier access to socially accepted substances, notably, tobacco and alcohol, than to other substances. However, the use of these substances is illegal for school-going children in India and they are dangerous both for physical and mental health. A youth using any substance is engaging in risky behaviour and could benefit from counselling. Tobacco and alcohol are the most frequently used recreational drugs due to their easy availability. Glue and paint

BOX 2.3: SUBSTANCES ASSOCIATED WITH ABUSE

- Tobacco
  - ⇒ Smoked, e.g. cigarettes, beedies
  - ⇒ Chewed, e.g. gutkha
- Alcohol
  - ⇒ Beer
  - ⇒ Wine
  - ⇒ Spirits, e.g. rum, whisky
  - ⇒ Locally brewed alcohol, e.g. feni in Goa
  - ⇒ Illegally brewed alcohol
- Cannabis products, e.g. charas, ganja, bhang
- Opiates, e.g. heroin
- Cocaine
- 'Party drugs', also known as 'herbal highs' or 'pep pills'
- Prescription medicines, e.g. sleeping pills or 'stimulants' (used legally to treat ADHD; illegal if not prescribed)
- Glue and paint thinners (sniffing and inhalation of fumes, respectively)

thinner, which are very dangerous, are often sniffed and inhaled by youth 'living rough', e.g. on the streets, or by those living in extreme poverty. Cannabis is another commonly used illegal drug (typically smoked). A youth may abuse one or more drugs simultaneously. The choice of the substance and the tendency to use a particular substance are strongly influenced by the youth's cultural context, notably the youth's socioeconomic background, the nature of his family life (e.g. whether a family member uses the substance) and the larger social environment. For example, the use of bhang (a liquid preparation which contains cannabis and is drunk) is acceptable during certain festivals. Opiates are used in some regions of India (e.g. in Punjab and the Northeast), where they may be used in injectable forms which are extremely dangerous. The use of 'party drugs' may be observed among adolescents frequenting nightclubs or dance parties. Substance use has rarely been observed among younger children, and is more typical of the older adolescent (especially boys), who may use substances to belong to a group or to create a specific kind of identity for himself.

Common presentation: The *recreational* use of some drugs (such as tobacco) may not produce any obvious adverse health or social effects. Nevertheless, these drugs have important consequences for the person's future health. Other drugs (alcohol, cannabis, heroin, prescription drugs), even when used recreationally, can lead to acute intoxication, which is manifested as a state of altered consciousness, including sleepiness, distractibility, poor concentration, slurred speech and poor motor coordination. Sometimes, the recreational use of a substance becomes a habit, leading to harmful use and dependence. *Harmful use* refers to the frequent use of a substance, resulting in harm to the person's physical or mental health, e.g. accidents due to the consumption of alcohol, chronic cough due to smoking, emotional problems due to the use of any substance and disruptive behaviours due to the use of heroin. *Dependence* refers to the development of a psychological or physical need for the substance, which makes it difficult for the individual to control how much he uses and when he uses it. Dependence can be said to exist when the individual experiences withdrawal symptoms upon not using the substance (e.g. experiencing anxiety when he has not had a drink), and needs more of the substance to experience its effects, i.e. he has developed a 'tolerance'. Often, a youth with harmful or dependent use of a substance engages in disruptive behaviours, such as stealing, to support the habit.

Consequences: The use of substances, in particular, harmful use or dependence, has grave consequences, such as academic under-achievement, including school failure. Social isolation, police and legal action prompted by criminal and disruptive behaviours, injuries and accidents, and deteriorating physical and mental health are among the other serious consequences. Heavy use of cannabis can trigger psychosis in vulnerable individuals.

Counselling strategies and supportive interventions: As a young person seldom approaches a counsellor primarily for help for substance use, the counsellor should always be alert for signs suggesting substance use and explore this possibility during the assessment (*see* Chapter 4). This is particularly relevant in the case of older adolescents whose academic performance has deteriorated recently or who have developed any other mental health problem. Youth psychoeducation specific to the youth's drug of choice may be a helpful counselling strategy. Family psychoeducation and supportive interventions in the school (e.g. the counsellor requesting the teacher to help the student engage in school activities with peers who are not using substances) can also be considered, while ensuring that the person's confidentiality is not breached (*see* Chapter 7). Support groups have been successful in weaning youth away from the substance, especially in the case of alcohol dependence (e.g. Alcoholics Anonymous). Although abstinence, i.e. the complete cessation of the use of the substance, should ideally be the goal, the more practical approach of 'harm reduction' should also be considered for the youth when it is not realistic for him to stop the use of the drug immediately. Harm reduction entails gradually lowering the amount of alcohol consumed and could, for example, mean that the youth agrees not to drive while drinking as a first step towards the ultimate goal of abstinence. Motivational interviewing is a specific specialized counselling strategy used to treat substance abuse and other disorders (this specialized strategy is not described in this casebook). In addition to these individually focused interventions, all schools must put health promotion programmes in place, with the aim of preventing high-risk behaviours (*see* Chapter 6), including substance use.

Serious mental disorders

Serious mental disorders profoundly disrupt several or all aspects of an individual's mental health, notably cognition (thinking) and social relationships, and severely limit an individual's capacity to function. These disorders are often associated with persistent or relapsing symptoms over an extended period of the person's life. There is a strong genetic component involved and a family history of mental disorder is often present. These conditions are very rarely found among school-aged youth. Early recognition of the disorder and referral to mental health professionals are very important to support the youth's mental health.

Schizophrenia

This is one of the most disabling of all mental disorders. Its onset is usually during late adolescence and young adulthood. This disorder affects how an individual thinks and perceives the world. Schizophrenia is more common among males than females. A stressful life event or the use of cannabis can precipitate the onset of schizophrenia in a vulnerable individual. Schizophrenia typically has a gradual and subtle onset, but occasionally, the presentation is acute, with severe features.

Common presentation: The earliest symptoms are confusion; assigning unusual and sinister meanings to everyday occurrences; and fears related to one's misperceptions and misconceptions. The youth may become increasingly isolated and withdrawn, and display unusual behaviours. This is followed by a slow decline in self-care. Disordered thought is often reflected in the way the person expresses himself (becoming incomprehensible and using nonsensical words or phrases), and in bizarre beliefs ('delusions'), often of a persecutory nature, e.g. believing that people intend to harm him. Also, the person assigns special significance to unremarkable objects, events or people. Schizophrenia is also characterized by abnormal visual and auditory sensory experiences ('hallucinations'). The other features associated with the disorder include changes in mood and/or motor activity, so that the individual may exhibit periods of agitation and restlessness at one time and extreme slowing down at other times (*see* Case Study 17).

Consequences: Schizophrenia is a severe disorder which profoundly affects the social functioning of the individual. If untreated, the majority of persons with the disorder experience a decline in functioning, and experience increasing isolation, academic failure and family problems. There is a significant risk of suicide among individuals with schizophrenia.

Bipolar disorder

Individuals with this condition, sometimes also referred to as 'manic–depressive disorder', present with episodes of 'high' and 'low' moods and energy levels. All people go through mood shifts, but in bipolar disorder, these shifts are extreme in intensity, last for weeks or months and profoundly influence the functioning of the individual. This disorder is rarely seen among school-aged youth. While the onset of a manic episode is typically acute, the depressive phases are often difficult to recognize in the early stages.

Common presentation: The low moods are similar to those described under depression earlier in this chapter. In the manic mood, the person feels elated or 'euphoric' (very happy), out of proportion with the circumstances. Typically, this 'positive' feeling is accompanied by irritability and a short temper. Simultaneously, the person becomes restless and excessively energetic, sleeps very little, cannot concentrate and has a low attention span, experiences a 'flight' of thoughts which are often connected to each other only very loosely and speaks excessively and rapidly. Often the individual may behave in ways which are 'out-of-sync' with her normal character, e.g. wearing revealing clothes, spending unusual amounts of money and talking in a disinhibited way. Typically, the person has very grand ideas about herself and makes unrealistic plans.

Consequences: When a young person is going through an episode of mania, the youth's unrealistically inflated opinion of herself and her overbearing behaviour and grand plans may cause peers to avoid her and cause difficulties with her family members and the community. The consequences of the depressive phase are similar to those of depression. Bipolar disorder is strongly associated with the risk of suicide.

Obsessive–compulsive disorder

The manifestations of obsessive–compulsive disorder (OCD) can vary in severity; however, often, by the time the youth comes to the notice of the counsellor, the young person's OCD symptoms are severe. However, unlike the other serious mental disorders, OCD is often a 'hidden' condition because the youth is often embarrassed about the problem and it is rare for her to actively seek help for it. Nor is her disorder easily noticed by others.

Common presentation: The main feature of this disorder is the presence of unwanted repetitive and intrusive thoughts ('obsessions'), which may be accompanied by unnecessary and repetitive behaviours (rituals or 'compulsions'). Most commonly, the obsessional thoughts are in the form of intrusive words or phrases, which are deeply upsetting to the affected person. The thoughts may be related to the fear of contamination (i.e. becoming dirty) or be sexual or 'blasphemous' in nature, i.e. against one's religious beliefs. Another variety of obsession is 'rumination', in which the person has repeated worries about irrational themes, as opposed to worries about 'normal' issues. The person engages in rituals linked to the obsession to relieve her anxiety, e.g. repetitive washing, cleaning, checking and touching. The individual feels that by performing these rituals, she may prevent some unlikely event from occurring (e.g. a future accident). The young person may try to resist these thoughts and rituals because they know that they are peculiar, but they may be hard to overcome and the youth may ultimately resist them less and less.

Consequences: When the obsessions and compulsions become chronic and severe, they can affect the youth's daily activities and impair her general functioning at home, with friends and at school. For example, her bathing rituals may take so long that she ends up being late for school. Because the obsessional thoughts are so intrusive, they can also make it hard for the individual to concentrate on her studies, leading to academic failure.

COUNSELLING STRATEGIES AND SUPPORTIVE INTERVENTIONS FOR SERIOUS MENTAL DISORDERS

Schizophrenia, bipolar disorder and OCD are all serious mental disorders which need thorough diagnostic assessment and, often, treatment with medication or structured psychological treatments. The primary role of the counsellor is to detect the disorder as early as possible, and then provide guidance to the youth and her family on seeking appropriate help from a mental health professional. The counsellor should help arrange the referral and follow up on the outcome with the mental health professional. Continuing care by the counsellor in the school setting includes the provision of family psychoeducation regarding the nature of the illness and the importance of adherence to medication, and how to manage their child's distressing symptoms. This is helpful to the family whose child is suffering from a serious mental disorder. The youth may be able to benefit from youth psychoeducation, problem-solving counselling and social skills counselling depending upon the severity of her disorder and following a period of stabilization. Supportive interventions in the school guide teachers on how to help the youth with her social relationships. For example, a 'buddy' can be designated for the youth. Supportive interventions in the home and the community, such as obtaining support from members of the youth's extended family to help the family care for her, can benefit the youth and her family.

DEVELOPMENTAL DISABILITIES

Developmental disabilities are present at birth or develop in early childhood. They limit an individual's ability to learn and function independently. They are relatively 'permanent', lasting through the length of the person's life, though their impact can be modified by interventions. They can be of varying severity. When the disability is severe, the individual may require help in self-care and remain dependent on others for assistance. Developmental disabilities may affect a single area of development, such as intellectual development, or several areas, such as motor and intellectual development.

The counsellor should note any variations in the course of development. These can be of several types, as described below:

- *Developmental delay:* The child achieves developmental milestones more slowly than other children her age, but nonetheless progresses in keeping with the anticipated sequence. Some children may ultimately achieve age-appropriate milestones, while others 'lag' behind in the final achievement of milestones (*see* Case Study 4). The children who lag behind may reach a plateau with skills that are appropriate for an age lower than their chronological age.
- *Deviance:* The child has differing rates of development in different domains, and development does not follow the expected sequence. For example, normally, 'receptive language' skills (understanding what is said) are ahead of 'expressive language' skills (using language to communicate), i.e. the young child understands more than she can say. In certain disorders, this process is reversed and children may use language that sounds like adult language without really understanding the words they are using (*see* Case Study 1).
- *Regression:* This is the loss of previously acquired milestones. For example, a child who has been acquiring language skills at a normal pace until 2 years of age becomes unable to use the words she had learned and begins to communicate through gestures rather than words (such as pointing at an object she wants rather than naming it).

The diagnosis of a developmental disability has profound implications for the child and her family, and the process of diagnosis is a complex and technical one. Many children with such disabilities are diagnosed even before they enter school. However, several factors may result in a delay in the diagnosis until the child has begun attending school. Notable among these are a lack of awareness (*see* Case Study 1) and a lack of access to appropriately skilled health practitioners or facilities. Diagnosis may also be delayed when the disability is relatively mild (*see* Case Study 14). Other disabilities, such as specific learning disabilities, become evident only when the child is faced with specific academic challenges (*see* Case Studies 4 and 12). In such situations, as with serious mental disorders, the primary role of the counsellor is to be alert to the possibility of a developmental disability, refer the family to an appropriately trained professional, such as a child development professional (*see* Chapter 4), and then support the child and family in adjusting to the disability (*see* Chapter 6). It is also important not to forget that, like all other children, those with developmental disabilities are also at risk for mental health distress and disorders. Diagnosing and treating the mental health problems of children with developmental disabilities can be a challenging task. Counsellors working in specialized school settings for children with developmental disabilities require specific diagnostic and treatment skills. These skills are not described in this casebook as it is intended primarily for mainstream school counsellors.

Intellectual disability (mental retardation)

Intellectual disability is a condition in which there is a significant delay in learning that affects many areas of a youth's life, including her thinking and problem-solving skills, her ability to reason, use language and look after herself. Intelligence is measured by standardized tests which generate an 'intelligence quotient' (IQ). This is the level of intellectual ability a person has as compared to others from a similar background. An IQ of 85–115 is considered average or 'normal'. Box 2.4 describes the types of intellectual disability on the basis of IQ scores. In a small percentage of individuals, one can identify a precipitant that has led to an intellectual disability (Box 2.5); in most individuals, however, no cause can be found.

Common presentation: A youth with intellectual disability learns more slowly than others of the same age and has difficulties learning the range of skills that are necessary to live independently. These skills include communication, self-care, social skills and personal safety skills. Their thinking skills are below their chronological age, e.g. in areas such as reasoning, retaining and organizing information, and paying attention. They may also have trouble seeing how things or events are related to each other or in understanding abstract concepts. For example, they may find it difficult to understand that bananas, apples and mangoes all belong to the same overall category of fruit. Children who are 'slow learners' have an IQ of above 70 (usually between 70 and 84). However, their potential for scholastic learning is limited and they are often slow in achieving all their developmental milestones (*see* Case Study 4). The features associated with the different degrees of severity of intellectual disability are given in Box 2.4.

Consequences: Individuals with an intellectual disability find

BOX 2.4: THE SEVERITY OF INTELLECTUAL DISABILITY (ID)

	IQ range	Level of functioning
Borderline intellectual functioning (also termed 'slow learner')	70–84	These individuals are rarely considered to need assistance and manage their self-care properly. They may, however, struggle with academics and need additional support through the school system.
Mild ID	50–69 (intellectual ability of a 9–12-year-old)	These individuals require sustained support in an educational setting, but can be well integrated in mainstream schools. They can manage self-care independently. Academically, they can attain the level of up to Standard V or VI (and occasionally higher) but will require an individualized education programme (IEP). They may need support in building social relationships.
Moderate ID	35–49 (intellectual ability of a 6–9-year-old)	These individuals can learn simple functional and life skills with special educational inputs. Rarely are they able to manage a mainstream academic curriculum, but they can be involved extensively in the non-academic activities of school, such as sports and music.
Severe ID	20–34 (intellectual ability of a 3–6-year-old)	These individuals find basic self-care, language skills and intellectual tasks difficult to master and need constant supervision. They often require a special educational setting. However, if the environment of the mainstream school can be adapted significantly, they can spend the better part of their time in a resource room.
Profound ID	Below 20 (intellectual ability of less than a 3-year-old)	These individuals are dependent on others for all their personal needs and are rarely part of the formal education system.

BOX 2.5: COMMON CAUSES OF INTELLECTUAL DISABILITY

- Effects on the developing brain during pregnancy; for example, the mother taking certain medicines, drinking alcohol or having had an infection (such as rubella)
- Prematurity or very low birth weight
- Difficulties during the birth process that affect the brain; for example, an injury or the baby not getting enough oxygen
- Genetic causes; for example, Down Syndrome
- Childhood problems that affect the brain; for example, infections (such as meningitis), head injuries and exposure to toxins (such as lead)

it difficult to cope with mainstream curricula, especially when the academic demands increase in the later school years. This often leads to academic failure or the child drops out or transfers to a 'special school' (where children with disability are taught functional life skills, with less focus on academics). Children with intellectual disability often become socially isolated and have few friends. They may be bullied, suffer an erosion of their self-esteem and may develop emotional and behavioural disorders. They may also experience difficulties in coming to terms with their emerging sexuality during adolescence, which compounds their isolation and sense of low self-esteem. Take, for example, an adolescent girl who is a slow learner and has attended classes which have explained the menstrual cycle; she may not be able to put the information to use when she starts menstruating and, as a result, will need instruction repeatedly with the task of maintaining hygiene being taught as smaller steps. Parents are often devastated by the diagnosis of intellectual disability because they feel dismayed that their child will not be academically successful and is likely to remain dependent on them throughout their life.

Counselling strategies and supportive interventions: One of the primary goals of the counsellor is to work collaboratively with the child, parents and teachers to identify and work with the child's strengths, with the goal of ensuring that the child is included in the mainstream school if this meets her needs (Box 2.6). Family psychoeducation helps the family understand the strengths and challenges associated with their child's level of functioning. Supportive interventions in the school make the teachers and school aware of the specific educational structures and support that the child with the intellectual disability requires. The kind of structure recommended depends on the degree of disability, as well as the level of support provided by the school management and educational authorities. Examples of educational support for slow learners include concessions, such as extra time for assignments, multiple-choice questions rather than essays and assistance from readers/writers and adapted curricula (Box 2.7). As for young people with more severe forms of intellectual disability, the amount of academic learning they can absorb may be limited, so their curriculum should be modified so that it centres on developing self-help, social and vocational skills.

Autism spectrum disorder

Autism spectrum disorder (ASD) is a developmental disability characterized by difficulties in social communication and social interaction (how people respond to and communicate with each other), as well as the presence of restricted, repetitive patterns of interest, behaviours and activities. Much like intellectual disability, autism is a 'spectrum disorder', which can affect individuals to varying degrees. Usually, the presence of autism becomes apparent within the first two years of life, after a period of seemingly normal development. It is much more common among boys.

Common presentation: The features characteristic of this condition are: a significant impairment in the child's way of responding to and establishing relationships with others; differences from other children in the way language is used while communicating (ranging from late language development, loss of language after an early period of normal speech development to an unusual way of using language, i.e. too literally or precisely); a lack of imaginative or creative play; and restricted, repetitive patterns of behaviour, interests and activities. The child with autism often shows an obsessive desire for sameness, and their repetitive behaviours, some of them unusual, such as whirling around and rocking. The young person may have highly specific areas of interest. Many

BOX 2.6: THE EDUCATION OF YOUTH WITH DEVELOPMENTAL DISABILITIES

The majority of young persons with developmental disabilities in India are excluded from school environments. However, the Right of Children to Free and Compulsory Education (RTE) Act, 2009; as well as the Rights of Persons with Disabilities Bill, 2012, which is under review by Parliament, give all children with disability the right to receive inclusive, free and appropriate educational support until the age of 18 years. Currently, there are two models of educational services for youth who have developmental disabilities:

Mainstream schools
These encourage an inclusive environment for learning by linking resource rooms to regular classes. In such schools, a youth with a developmental disability is placed in a resource room within the mainstream school to remediate her specific learning problems and her mainstream curriculum is modified (Box 2.7), so as to allow her to spend most of the schoolday in the regular classroom. Special educators in resource rooms may also teach functional skills, such as those related to socialization and the activities of daily living, to youth with greater learning impairments. Ideally, each youth in a resource room should have a detailed individual educational programme (IEP) that specifies her specific learning needs and sets goals based on her unique strengths and difficulties.

Special schools
These impart education exclusively to youth with developmental disabilities. The special school may serve the educational needs of youth who have the same disability, e.g. a school for those with hearing impairments, or may serve youth with a range of disabilities. As with mainstream schools with resource rooms, special schools utilize IEPs.

BOX 2.7: MODIFYING THE CURRICULUM

Though the counsellor is not expected to modify the curriculum, it is useful for her to understand the approaches that a teacher or special educator may utilize to support youth with developmental disabilities. The purpose of modifying the curriculum is to include children of varying abilities in the same classroom, so that each student learns at her optimum pace in the mainstream environment. The curriculum can be modified using one or all of the following techniques:

- Changing the way instructions are given to the youth, e.g. written instead of verbal
- Changing where these instructions are given, e.g. in a quiet corner of the classroom
- Utilizing a different assessment method, e.g. multiple choice instead of a subjective answers
- Allowing the youth more time to learn and complete tasks
- Simplifying the content, e.g. multiplying single digit numbers instead of three digit numbers
- Providing assistance during instruction, e.g. through a teaching aide or a 'buddy'
- Decreasing the amount of information the youth has to learn, e.g. details of only one country instead of two
- Considering alternatives to how a youth participates in group activities, e.g. allowing the youth to paint a project chart instead of contributing content
- Changing the learning goals for the youth, e.g. learning the name of a country's leader rather than both the name and the political party
- Creating an alternative curriculum to match the child's needs, e.g. creating an individualized educational plan (IEP).

individuals with autism may have sensory hypo- or hypersensitivities; i.e. being either less responsive or exquisitely responsive to stimuli in any of their senses (e.g. touch, smell, sight, taste, hearing or balance). Almost a third of all children with autism will have an associated intellectual disability and epilepsy (Box 2.8) and significant behavioural difficulties. They appear to be in a 'world of their own'. Individuals on the milder end of the spectrum, sometimes referred to as Asperger syndrome, do not have delayed language development or intellectual disability. However, those with Asperger syndrome do manifest the core features of ASD, including impairment in social functioning and difficulties in communication and social interaction; being more at ease

BOX 2.8: EPILEPSY

Epilepsy is a brain disorder characterized by seizures or convulsions. It is caused by uncontrolled electrical activity in the brain. The most common type of seizures are called generalized tonic–clonic seizures, which result in thrashing movements of the arms and legs, upward rolling of the eyeballs, a loss of consciousness and possibly, the loss of bladder control. A rarer type of seizure, though common among children, is the 'absence' seizure. During this type of seizure, the child seems to blank out

(*continued*)

BOX 2.8: EPILEPSY (*continued*)

for a moment or a few moments and is unresponsive, but does not fall down or lose consciousness. It is important to recognize and treat epilepsy; if untreated, it can be life-threatening and cause permanent damage to the brain. Any child suspected to have epilepsy or a seizure must be referred immediately to a medical specialist for further assessment and treatment (*see* Chapter 4). In most young persons, epilepsy can be easily treated with medicines. The school activities of a child with epilepsy need not be restricted, with the possible exception of some sport activities, such as swimming. Epilepsy may coexist with intellectual disability or autism spectrum disorder or may occur by itself.

It is important for the school staff to know how to manage a seizure if there is a youth with epilepsy in the school. The following are among the steps that can be taken to assist a youth having a seizure:

- Stay calm and call for help.
- Stay with the young person until the seizure stops and he regains consciousness.
- To prevent injury, remove anything that can be dangerous from the area surrounding the youth.
- If possible, move the youth to a safe place, but do not force him to move. If he wears glasses, remove them so that they do not break.
- If possible, gently roll the youth's head and upper body to the right so that any fluids can drain out of his mouth. (It may be necessary to wait until he has stopped shaking.)
- If there is anything around the youth's neck, loosen it to make breathing easier. Also, loosen buttons or belts that are tight.
- Do not put anything into the youth's mouth. If he has food in his mouth, do not attempt to take it out since this may actually push it in further.

BOX 2.9: KEY FEATURES OF AUTISM/ASPERGER SYNDROME

- Difficulty in social communication, which may include a lack of desire to interact with peers, a lack of appreciation of social cues, and socially and emotionally inappropriate behaviours
- A narrow area of interest which tends to occupy the young person to the exclusion of other interests
- A rigid desire and need for routines
- Speech and language problems, including delayed language development and/or pedantic, formal use of language, with odd and peculiar vocal characteristics
- Problems with non-verbal communication, reflected in a limited use of gestures, limited or inappropriate facial expressions or a peculiar stiff gaze
- Motor clumsiness, causing poor performance in school sports

with adults than peers; not understanding social cues; interrupting others; obsessively talking about their own areas of interest; and not understanding the rules of to-and-fro conversations. Sometimes, an individual with Asperger syndrome has an unusual, pedantic way of talking and his gestures, too, are unusual. This makes him stand out and he appears different from the members of his peer group (Box 2.9; *see* Case Studies 1 and 14).

Consequences: ASD can lead to significant impairments in academic achievement. Youth at the severe end of the spectrum will be unable to complete mainstream schooling due to associated intellectual disability. As for those in the milder segment of the spectrum, their communication problems and unusual interests and behaviours make it difficult for them to fit into their peer group. They may become victims of bullying, suffer anxiety or depression and as a result, drop out of mainstream education. Youth with milder symptoms may have coexisting specific learning disabilities (SLD) which may hinder them from achieving their academic potential (*described below*).

Counselling strategies and supportive interventions: Family psychoeducation is important for the parents of all children on the autism spectrum once they have received a diagnosis. It includes explaining the diagnosis and the need for further professional input from a mental health or child development professional, as well as providing tips on how to manage the child's difficult behaviours at home. If a local support group for the parents of such children exists, the counsellor should suggest that the family participate in its activities. Youth with milder ASD can benefit from social skills counselling. This can include instruction on how to participate in a conversation, respond to teasing and become part of a group. It can also give them practice in understanding social interactions. The counsellor can use supportive interventions in the school, e.g. suggesting that the teachers obtain inputs from special educators to help with the modification of the curriculum. If necessary, she can suggest that the young person be placed in a resource room for part of the day. Almost all individuals at the severe end of the autism spectrum will need individual educational programmes and speech and behaviour therapies.

Specific learning disabilities (scholastic disabilities)

Youth with specific learning disabilities (SLD) can have difficulties in reading, writing or mathematics, memorizing and/or other areas of academic functioning. As the term suggests, not surprisingly, these disabilities are first detected in school settings. Usually, the child has normal intelligence, but does not perform in keeping with academic expectations. A young person should not be labelled as having an SLD unless a proper attempt at instruction has been made and she has been assessed with appropriate educational tests (*see* Chapter 4).

Common presentation: A problem with reading and spelling is commonly termed dyslexia, the most common form of SLD. Those with dyslexia have trouble recognizing shapes and their connection to letters, as well as their relationship to sounds. This makes it challenging for the child to read. In addition, since children with dyslexia find it difficult to connect speech sounds to different letters, while reading they substitute, distort or add sounds which are not present (e.g. reading 'lice' as 'like'). Children with dyslexia may have problems reading accurately or have a slow rate of reading, which is characterized by frequent pauses. They may also have difficulty comprehending what they are reading. Dysgraphia

is a difficulty with written expression. The youth with dysgraphia may write slowly and untidily, have trouble organizing paragraphs and have problems with composing written texts. Dyscalculia refers to difficulty in learning mathematical concepts or retaining mathematical information. This may affect the person's ability to understand the steps in a problem, and also includes misaligning numbers or putting decimals in the wrong place, confusion with mathematical signs and/or difficulty memorizing and recalling tables and formulae. Dyspraxia affects the planning and organization of motor movements. Those with dyspraxia may experience difficulties at school and home, including problems with self-care, outdoor sports, handwriting, concentration and producing speech sounds (*see* Case Study 12).

Consequences: The youth with a specific learning disability usually falls behind her peers as academic pressures increase. Since those with SLD usually have a normal level of intelligence and seem to either be making careless mistakes or submitting work of poor quality, they may be labelled as 'lazy'. Youth with SLD may find themselves in a vicious cycle: they perform poorly scholastically, leading to a lowering of self-esteem, leading to misbehaviour and poor concentration, leading to punishment, leading to a loss of interest in studies and a further decline in scholastic performance.

Counselling strategies and supportive interventions: The counsellor can initiate a referral to a professional trained to evaluate learning disorders, and who can identify the nature of the learning disorder and provide suggestions on modifications of the teaching methods and curricula (*see* Chapter 4). Though the special educator would take the lead in managing the educational modifications and supportive strategies that would suit the child with the SLD, it would benefit the youth if the teacher, special educator and counsellor functioned as a team. Many examination boards in India make concessions for young people with SLD. Modification of curriculum (Box 2.7) and remedial assistance should be introduced as soon as possible to prevent the young person from falling behind their peers academically. Youth and family psychoeducation help the youth and family understand how learning disorders can trigger emotional and behavioural difficulties. Problem-solving counselling can help the youth address issues which negatively affect his feelings.

Locomotor and sensory disabilities

These disabilities include the developmental disabilities of cerebral palsy (and other motor impairments), and hearing and visual impairment. Youth who have severe locomotor and sensory disabilities are typically educated in specialized school settings. The condition of youth with locomotor and visual impairments is commonly identified early in childhood. It is important for the counsellor to keep in mind the possibility of visual and hearing impairments (*see* Case Study 6) which have their onset in the school years. An example is short-sightedness, which can affect the child's academic performance and cause behavioural difficulties, and which can be easily reversed (e.g. with glasses). Younger children who have behavioural difficulties which have no apparent reason should be referred for a hearing test (*see* Chapter 4) to make sure that their difficulties do not stem from a hearing impairment so that the proper solution (e.g. a hearing aid) can be identified. Youth who have sensory impairments and are using compensatory devices, such as a hearing aid, can be taught in a mainstream setting with educational modifications that enable them to participate in all activities (*see* Case Study 6).

LIFE COURSE APPROACH TO MENTAL HEALTH PROBLEMS

The most common ages of the onset and presentation of mental health problems are described below, on the basis of the life course perspective. However, it must be noted that mental health problems can occur at any time during the youth's life course, depending on the youth's reactions to unexpected challenges, changes in life circumstances or an increase in stressors.

- **Pre-school age group:** Developmental disabilities, especially locomotor, sensory and severe intellectual disabilities, are identified during these early years, when the parents notice that their child is not making as much progress in various domains as are other children in the same age group. However, some disabilities may be 'hidden' from view for various reasons. For example, the diagnosis of autism is relatively infrequent in most parts of India and the young person's unusual behaviours may be attributed to personal eccentricity. The disorder may be noticed by the family only when the child faces specific challenges upon entering school.
- **Primary school age group:** The most common mental health problems among children of this age group are mental health distress and anxiety disorders, such as persistent phobias and separation anxiety. This is usually the period when developmental disorders not already detected in the pre-school years become apparent. As scholastic expectations increase, ADHD and SLD become evident.
- **Adolescence:** The major mental health problems affecting this age group are mental health distress, depression and conduct disorder. Substance use disorders and serious mental disorders, though rare, also have their onset in the later years of adolescence. Disorders and disabilities which have begun earlier, such as intellectual disability, continue to affect the adolescent and produce specific challenges related to this developmental phase. For example, in relation to sexuality, the adolescent girl with intellectual disability will need to be taught skills to help her manage her menstrual period.

Another important concept to be kept in mind is that of co-morbidity, i.e. the presence of more than one mental health problem at the same time (the term 'coexistence' is used to describe this throughout the casebook). The following are common examples of coexistence that the counsellor may come across:

- The coexistence of any behaviour disorder or disability with mental health distress and/or an emotional disorder, e.g. ADHD with anxiety symptoms and depression;
- The coexistence of any disruptive behaviour disorder with substance use disorder, e.g. conduct disorder with smoking;
- The coexistence of different types of disabilities, e.g. autism with intellectual disability;
- The coexistence of behaviour disorders with disabilities, e.g. ADHD with a SLD;
- Physical illness can also coexist with mental health problems. Typical examples are the coexistence of problems which affect one's appearance (such as obesity and skin diseases) with emotional disorders, and that of epilepsy with developmental disorders.

BURDEN OF CHILD AND ADOLESCENT MENTAL HEALTH PROBLEMS

It is estimated that up to 10% of children worldwide suffer from a mental health condition. By far, the most common conditions are mental health distress states and emotional disorders, followed by behaviour disorders. Considering that about 300 million people in India are in the school-going age range of 6–18 years, then at least 30 million youth have at least one or another type of mental health condition. Within this larger group of mental health conditions, the categories of developmental disabilities and serious mental disorders together affect at least 3 in every 100 young people. Thus, at least 10 million school-aged youth in India suffer from serious mental health problems.

Both on the societal and personal levels, mental health problems have a profound impact on the life of the young person, their families and the community. The following are some of the major effects:

- **Mortality:** The school-going period is generally one of the healthiest periods of life, when the risk of dying is the smallest. However, death does occur, though rarely, during this period, most often due to suicide and high-risk behaviours. Suicide is a leading cause of death during adolescence and young adulthood. Mental health distress and emotional disorders are the major causes of suicide in this age group. Youth with mental health problems are relatively more likely to engage in high-risk behaviours, many of which have a direct bearing on mortality, e.g. drinking resulting in accidents.
- **Suffering:** The symptoms of mental health problems cause immense suffering. In addition, they prevent a child or youth from achieving her potential for growth and development.
- **Social isolation and exclusion:** Mental health problems, particularly the serious mental disorders and disabilities, are associated with social isolation and a reduction in participation in everyday activities.
- **Academic underachievement and dropping out:** Many mental health problems lead to academic underachievement, and are a major reason for school failure and dropping out. This affects the youth's prospects of finding employment and her productivity over the course of her life.
- **Family distress:** Having a child or adolescent with a mental health problem increases the stress on all caregivers. Due to this burden, the caregivers themselves can develop mental health problems, e.g. a mother whose child has developmental disabilities can develop depression. Siblings can also suffer. For example, the parents may neglect them because their attention is focused on caring for the child with mental health difficulties. Among the other areas of concern for the family are the costs of treatment, the loss of income due to the need to take days off work to attend to their child's special needs and the concern for long-term care.
- **Stigma:** Discriminatory or hurtful practices by community members towards the youth concerned and her family (e.g. name-calling and social exclusion) cause social isolation and further suffering for the youth and her family.

Risk and Protective Factors Affecting Mental Health

Risk and protective factors are influences which respectively increase or reduce the chances of developing a mental health problem. The related concept of 'strengths and difficulties' refers to the individual's attributes, such as temperament and genetic make-up. Strengths and difficulties may contribute to resiliency or enhance vulnerability, respectively. Resilience is a protective characteristic which enables the individual to contend with adversity without suffering a major impact. Generally, resilience refers to positive mental health and developmental outcomes despite exposure to significant adversity. Vulnerability, on the other hand, refers to the possibility that the individual, if exposed to various risk factors, will suffer a negative mental health outcome. A resilient youth has the ability to cope with and adapt to the stressors and negative changes she is exposed to in her internal or external environment, such as a death in the family or failure in an examination.

The common risk and protective factors are listed in Box 2.10. Knowing the risk and protective factors for a particular youth helps the counsellor understand why the youth has developed a mental health problem. Furthermore, an understanding of these factors helps the counsellor determine the optimal course for promoting the youth's improvement and recovery. Risk and protective factors can operate at the individual, family, neighbourhood, community and societal levels (*see* Chapter 1). The most powerful risk and protective factors affecting mental health are summarized below:

- **Experiences in early life:** The mother's health during pregnancy, the period of childbirth and the early neonatal period are periods that are critical for healthy development. Problems during these periods, e.g. infections and prolonged childbirth, can influence the course of development and mental health throughout life. On the other hand, secure mother–child bonding which, for example, might occur through exclusive breastfeeding for four to six months after birth, promotes the child's physical health and development, and builds the child's resilience.

BOX 2.10: RISK AND PROTECTIVE FACTORS FOR CHILD AND ADOLESCENT MENTAL HEALTH

Protective factors	Risk factors
Individual characteristics	
Easygoing and adaptable temperament, positive self-esteem, good social skills	Difficult temperament or slow to warm up; inflexible approach to change
Normal intellectual functioning	Developmental disorders
Good school performance	Poor school performance
Good stable peer relationships	A lack of a positive peer group
Responsible attitude towards sexual activity	Early initiation of sexual activity
Secure upbringing	Abuse or neglect
Normal delivery and a healthy neonatal life	Difficulties during delivery and ill health during the early period of life
Parent and family characteristics	
Good maternal health during pregnancy	Poor maternal health during pregnancy
Secure mother and infant bonding	Insecure attachment; institutional upbringing; maternal mental illness
High level of maternal education	Low level of maternal education
Stable traditional family structure	Non-traditional family structure
Authoritative and firm parenting, with consistent discipline	Parenting style too lax or too harsh
Supportive extended family network	Isolated family
Positive parental expectations and good role-modelling	Parental illness; substance abuse; family violence; death in family
Stable employment	Unemployment
Social/environmental characteristics	
Comfortable socioeconomic conditions	Poverty

(*continued*)

BOX 2.10: RISK AND PROTECTIVE FACTORS FOR CHILD AND ADOLESCENT MENTAL HEALTH (*continued*)

Protective factors	Risk factors
Social/environmental characteristics	
Adequate housing, healthcare and leisure activities	Inadequate housing, healthcare and leisure activities
Adequate school environment	Poor school environment
Positive peer groups	Negative peer groups
Stable community	Transient community, such as migrant camps
Safe neighbourhood, with a high level of trust	Unsafe neighbourhood, with a low level of trust

- **The child's temperament:** Temperament (*see* Chapter 1) is influenced both by genetic factors (traits inherited from the parents) and environmental factors during early life, e.g. bonding with the mother. A child with an easygoing and optimistic outlook, for example, is likely to be able to take on challenges in her environment with much greater ease than one who is short-tempered or pessimistic.
- **The family characteristics:** The family and community environments play an important role in shaping the individual's development. Parenting approaches are profoundly influential. Overcritical, punitive and inconsistent parenting is associated with mental health problems, while authoritative and firm parenting is protective. The socioeconomic status of the family and the quality of intra-familial relationships are also important. Direct experience of abuse and violence is a major determinant of mental health problems.
- **The community in which the family lives:** Living in a secure neighbourhood, in which the level of trust is high, can promote mental health. Going to a school which promotes healthy policies, such as anti-bullying policies and inclusive education for children with disabilities, and which has strong networks with the community is also beneficial for the youth's mental health.
- **Exposure to adverse events:** Children and youth who are exposed to

adverse conditions, such as extreme poverty, violence and abuse, may be more vulnerable to mental health problems.

A youth whose protective factors clearly outweigh the risk factors is at a lower risk for mental health problems and is more likely to recover quickly if she develops one. On the other hand, a youth whose risk factors clearly outweigh the protective factors is at a high risk for mental health distress and disorders, and is likely to need support to recover. Building on the protective factors and minimizing the impact of the risk factors are of key importance in promoting the improvement and recovery of a vulnerable youth. During the assessment process, the counsellor must gather sufficient information on the youth's personality, family and environment (*see* Chapter 4), so that she can plan and provide the counselling strategies and supportive interventions that will have the highest degree of success.

CHAPTER 3

The counselling relationship

The quality of the counselling relationship is critical to the success of counselling. The elements of how to promote and sustain this relationship are described in the following sections:

- Introducing the counsellor's role to the teachers and school staff
- Introducing the counsellor's role to the students
- The importance of 'engagement'
- Making a counselling plan
- Sustaining the counselling relationship
- Structuring each session
- Working with the youth's family members
- Managing changes in the counselling relationship

This chapter emphasizes that the success of the counselling relationship, in addition to the strategies employed, is rooted in the approach and attitude of the counsellor towards the youth. Ideally, the approach should consist of always maintaining a caring, enquiring, respectful and non-judgemental attitude; working with the youth in a flexible and collaborative manner to make the most of the counselling; assuring the youth of predictable and continual contact; and communicating with important people in the young person's life so that he may receive more support to help him recover.

Introducing the counsellor's role to the teachers and school staff

When the counsellor first begins working in a school, it is important for her to inform the teachers, school management and students about the availability and purpose of counselling. The counsellor should aim to

quickly become a member of the school team, and a valuable and trusted resource for the teachers and principal. Because the principal, teachers and counsellor have the mutual goal of promoting the well-being of the youth, it is expected that they will work together on the youth's behalf. However, this does not 'happen naturally'. In order for the school staff to refer a student for counselling and for the counselling process to proceed well, the counsellor needs to clearly explain her *role*, make every effort to *build a rapport* with the principal and teachers, and *provide regular feedback* to her school colleagues on her work as a counsellor at the school (and, when appropriate, on the progress of a particular young person's condition, within the boundaries of confidentiality) (*see* Chapter 7).

Explaining the Counsellor's Role to the School Staff

It is critically important for the counsellor to clarify to the school staff what her role is with respect to youth. It is equally important to inform the school staff what her role does not include. The counsellor needs to clarify that her role includes:

- Assessment of a young person's emotional or behavioural problem;

- Provision of counselling to help the young person address his problems;
- Referral of the youth to other professionals, as needed;
- Partnering with teachers and/or family members to assist the young person with his problem.

The counsellor may need to clarify that her role does not include:

- Disciplining a young person
- Being a substitute teacher.

BUILDING RAPPORT WITH THE TEACHERS AND SCHOOL STAFF

In order to successfully build rapport with the teachers and school staff, the counsellor must demonstrate respect for the school staff and principal. After explaining the role she expects to play, the counsellor should listen and respond to the concerns or questions of the teachers and school staff, keeping in mind that they know their students very well. As a member of the school staff, who shares with them the goal of ensuring that all students and the overall school community should function optimally, the counsellor should tell the school staff that she looks forward to learning about their students from them, and also, about their efforts to help the students. Despite these efforts, the counsellor may still find it difficult to gain full acceptance at the school. If there is a supervisor working with the counsellor (*see* Chapter 8), he may step in to support the counsellor's work. He may, for example, discuss with the school staff the difficulties encountered by the counsellor in the school and the remedies that might be available, such as a meeting between the supervisor and the counsellor and school team members so that all parties can air concerns.

ADDRESSING SCHOOL STAFF CONCERNS

The common concerns of the teachers and school staff about the counsellor's role include:

- That the counselling sessions will reduce the time that the youth spends on his studies;

- That the counsellor is 'pampering', instead of firmly disciplining, the young person (teachers might feel this particularly with regard to a youth with disruptive behaviour problems);
- That the counsellor may learn negative things from the student about the teachers and/or their classroom management techniques.

The counsellor can respond to these concerns as follows:

- **Taking time away from studies:** Typically, a counselling session lasts from 30 minutes to one hour, depending on the specific problem of the youth. The counsellor should ask the teacher when it would be best to hold the counselling session to ensure that it does not interfere with the youth's studies (e.g. during breaks in the school day).
- **Pampering the youth:** The counsellor should explain that her goal and the school's goal is ultimately the same: increasing the likelihood of the youth achieving academic success. She can explain to the teachers that since the young person has not responded to the school's efforts, the counsellor will assist him by using additional strategies and supportive interventions. The counsellor can describe some of these strategies and supportive interventions (*see* Chapter 6). She should assure the members of the school staff that she will keep them up to date on the youth's progress, while protecting the youth's confidentiality (*see* Chapter 7). She should also tell them that she will seek their feedback on the youth's progress in the classroom.
- **Learning negative things about the school or teacher:** The members of the school staff are unlikely to express this concern to the counsellor, though it might be worrying them greatly. For this reason, it is important to let the teachers know in various ways that they are valued. For example, the counsellor can acknowledge that managing large classes is very stressful and praise the teachers for their positive classroom practices. It is also important for the counsellor to be supportive to the teacher. For example, she can make an effort to find out about the circumstances which are hard to manage, either in the context of a particular class or a particular young person, and offer to think together with the teacher about the classroom approaches that can be utilized to address these difficulties (*see* Chapter 6). The counsellor should always be empathetic towards both the teachers and the youth.

Sometimes, a teacher or another member of the school staff seeks help from the counsellor for his own problems. This is a sensitive issue and the counsellor should always offer the teacher the opportunity to talk with her about his problems. If appropriate, she should suggest that the teacher seek help from a mental health professional (on the basis of the referral resources the counsellor has collated, *see* Chapter 4).

Providing regular feedback

In order to nurture the relationship between the counsellor and school staff, the counsellor should provide regular feedback to the staff about her activities at the school. Ideally, staff meetings should be organized for this purpose. The counsellor can give information on her monthly/term activities during such meetings. She should use a general approach while providing information, e.g. she can enumerate her school-based projects, discuss her plans for further activities and present statistics on individual counselling sessions, *avoiding discussion of a specific youth.* The counsellor should also invite suggestions from the staff and try to incorporate them into her school-based activities when this is feasible.

It is essential that the counsellor maintains strict confidentiality regarding the youth she is assessing and counselling (*see* Chapter 7). It is also good practice to have small sessions with senior members of the staff and the principal to discuss and try to find solutions to sensitive issues, such as specific incidents of bullying.

Introducing the counsellor's role to the students

After introducing herself to the school staff, the counsellor may request an opportunity to introduce herself and the counselling service to the students (Box 3.1). The counsellor should present herself, with a brief introduction, either to each class or to the entire school at a school assembly. In general, the former is preferable because the setting is smaller and more intimate, and gives the students a better opportunity to ask questions and seek clarifications.

BOX 3.1: INFORMING STUDENTS ABOUT THE COUNSELLOR'S ROLE

Introducing counselling to a class

'Hello. My name is Miss X. I am new to you and to your school. I am a counsellor. Have any of you heard about counsellors and counselling? [Some youth may offer ideas which could be useful to guide the discussion. Continuing…] *Sometimes a young person might have some problems. These include things like having trouble with schoolwork, having worries and feeling tired or upset. A counsellor can help you by discussing these concerns with you and suggesting ways to cope with them. There are also some situations that are difficult to solve alone, and as your counsellor I can try to help you with these situations. All our counselling meetings will be private and as your counsellor I will not talk to anyone about what has been discussed at our meetings without discussing it with you first.'*

(continued)

BOX 3.1: INFORMING STUDENTS ABOUT THE COUNSELLOR'S ROLE (*continued*)

Understanding the counsellor's role

'When you face problems in your daily life, your parents, teachers and close friends may provide you with caring and helpful guidance. This is very important and is often enough for you to deal with a problem. However, sometimes this support may not be enough to help you. At other times, it may be difficult to ask your parents, teachers or close friends certain questions or talk to them about certain issues and feelings. And sometimes, the issues may be related to your relationship with a friend or your home. As a counsellor, I have special training to help young people with their feelings, worries and concerns. I will use this knowledge to try to help you enjoy every day, do well in your studies and be happy with your friendships and your school life.'

Informing the students about how to make contact

'There are a number of ways you can contact me. You can put your name on a note in the "Speak out box", you can tell your class teacher that you would like to speak with me or you can come directly to my office.'

A 'Speak out box' is a box with an opening into which a student can insert a note describing a problem. The student may include his name and class in the note. The counsellor can suggest to the principal that the school provide such a box. If a Speak out box is made available, the counsellor should check the box regularly and respond to the notes in a timely fashion. It is important that only the counsellor have access to this box to ensure that students feel comfortable sharing sensitive issues.

The main goals of the introduction are to:

- Explain that the counsellor's role is to help youth experiencing difficulties;
- Clarify how the counsellor's role differs from that of a teacher or parent;
- Emphasize the confidential nature of the counselling relationship;
- Emphasize that counselling services are available in a growing number of schools (to legitimize the presence of counselling services in the school);
- Inform the students how to make contact with the counsellor.

THE IMPORTANCE OF 'ENGAGEMENT'

'Engagement' forms the foundation for a successful counselling relationship. Engagement refers to the relationship formed between the counsellor and young person and the agreement made between them to work together to successfully address the problem facing the youth. There are a number of ways in which the counsellor can evaluate whether the youth has engaged in the counselling relationship successfully. The engagement can be said to be successful if the youth is attending the counselling appointments; if the youth is willing to share his feelings, thoughts and problems; and if the youth is completing any home practice tasks that have been agreed upon.

The likelihood that the youth will accept and adhere to the counselling plan is optimized if the youth feels that the counsellor understands his needs and perspective. This is most likely if the counsellor communicates this understanding clearly to the youth. In addition, the source of the referral and the youth's understanding of the counselling process greatly influence how he engages with the counsellor. The youth may have initiated his own referral ('self-referral') and may be very open about his difficulties; on the other hand, he may have been 'forced' to see the counsellor by a teacher and may be angry, hostile and mistrusting. The counsellor needs to modulate how she initiates the counselling process, depending on the source of the referral, as well as the youth's understanding and expectations of counselling.

The first meeting between the counsellor and the young person is of the utmost importance in promoting successful engagement (Box 3.2).

BOX 3.2: THE FIRST SESSION

Introduction to counselling

'Hello. It is good to meet you. My name is Miss X. As you may already know, my job is to help students with any problems and worries that they may have.' The counsellor then waits for any questions or comments and notices the youth's body language to see whether he is comfortable with the introduction.

Addressing confidentiality

'Your teacher has suggested that I see you, but what we talk about is between you and me. It is private. There may be particular issues that I may need to discuss with others, but I will do so only after discussing this with you and obtaining your permission.'

Addressing meeting others in the young person's life

'If you and I decide that it would help you if I had a discussion with your family, teacher or principal, I will.'

Explaining how counselling works

'We will think, talk and work together to understand why you are having these problems; then we will work out ways in which you can overcome them. We will meet regularly over a period of time at a time which will not interfere with your studies.'

The counselling space

The counsellor should pay attention to the comfort and confidentiality of the room used for counselling. Ideally, the room should be well-lit, well-ventilated and quiet, with a door that can be closed to ensure privacy. It should be large enough to comfortably accommodate at least two chairs, which can face each other. Preferably, it should be able to accommodate up to four chairs, in case there are family meetings. To increase privacy, a sign saying 'do not disturb' can be put up on the door when the counselling room is in use.

At this meeting, the counsellor's first task is to create an environment of emotional safety. To accomplish this, the counsellor should:

- Ensure privacy, e.g. the office door must be closed and there should be no one else in the room;
- Introduce herself and her role clearly;
- Assure the youth about the confidential nature of the counselling;
- Give the youth sufficient time to tell his story;
- Show respect for and concern about the youth throughout the meeting;
- Use open-ended questions (*see* Chapter 5), since this form of enquiry is more likely to encourage the young person to speak about himself and his concerns and interests;
- Make empathic statements which indicate that the counsellor understands the young person, e.g. paraphrasing the youth's own words in a warm, accepting and non-judgemental manner to show that she understands the feelings and thoughts behind these words (*see* Chapter 5);
- Express her sincere praise for the young person's efforts to cope with his difficulties and for his decision to seek counselling.

Making a Counselling Plan

It is important to help the young person understand the uniqueness of the counselling relationship from the first meeting itself. The relationship between the counsellor and the youth is 'therapeutic', an 'alliance' or 'partnership' and a 'working' interaction. The relationship is therapeutic because the counsellor is trained to help the youth understand and overcome his difficulties. It is an alliance because the counsellor is working with the youth and the youth is working with the counsellor to discover the reasons for the youth's problems and to address them. The relationship is a working alliance because both the young person and counsellor are actively working together on the youth's problems with the goal of finding a solution.

After the counsellor introduces herself to the young person, she should encourage the young person to tell his story and speak about his understanding of why he has sought counselling (or been referred by someone else, if that is the case). If the youth hesitates, the counsellor should explain her own understanding of the reasons. This explanation should be a straightforward one, stated in a calm, matter-of-fact and simple way. Following this, in the first session, and possibly over a number of sessions, the counsellor must assess the nature of the youth's problem (*see* Chapter 4). Once the counsellor has done so, she should develop a counselling plan for the youth and explain to him how the plan will address his problem areas and concerns.

The counselling plan, which is based on the assessment and case formulation (*see* Chapter 4), must cover the following points:

- The mutually agreed upon counselling goals;
- The frequency of the counselling sessions, e.g. weekly or more or less frequently, as needed;
- The location of each session;
- The likely duration of each session (generally ranging from 30 minutes to one hour);
- The likely duration of the entire counselling process;
- The counselling strategies and supportive interventions that the counsellor suggests to help the youth (*see* Chapter 6);
- How the youth or the counsellor will notify each other if a change of appointment is necessary;
- The reasons for consulting significant others who interact with the youth, e.g. his teachers (*see* Chapter 4);
- The reasons for referring the youth to other specialists, if such referral is required (*see* Chapter 4).

Sustaining the Counselling Relationship

The same counsellor should see the youth over the entire course of the counselling. Of course, there may be unusual circumstances that make this impossible. Regular, planned meetings with the same counsellor are very important to the youth's progress for the following reasons:

- To create a sense of purpose, hopefulness and continuity.

- To help the young person better manage distressing emotions between sessions.
- To help the young person feel that he has value.

Another critically important aspect of sustaining the counselling relationship is ensuring successful engagement between the youth and the counsellor. In order to nurture and sustain the relationship, the counsellor needs to maintain a caring, enquiring and non-judgemental attitude from session to session and between sessions, e.g. if she should meet the young person in the school hallway or neighbourhood. It could be a challenge for the counsellor to maintain this attitude if the young person behaves in a difficult manner with her, e.g. skipping sessions without informing the counsellor ahead of time and arriving late for sessions. The counsellor can draw attention to the young person's difficult behaviours during one of their discussions. However, the counsellor should remain calm, remembering that her objective is to understand the meaning of the young person's behaviour. She should convey her understanding to the youth, without criticism, to increase the youth's self-awareness. Throughout the course of counselling, the counsellor should consistently be interested in the youth and his progress, and value and care about him. Above all, it is imperative that the counsellor must never become hostile towards or angry with the young person, irrespective of the provocation. Equally importantly, she must not do anything that breaks any agreement that she has made with the young person, e.g. about not sharing a particular fact with a particular teacher.

STRUCTURING EACH SESSION

In general, each session should have three parts, as follows:

- The counsellor should begin with brief welcoming remarks, which include praising the youth for his efforts to come to the sessions and work together on his difficulties. Next, the counsellor should set out the plan for the session (sometimes referred to as 'setting the agenda'). In the initial sessions, she may take the lead in guiding the course of the session. Later on, this responsibility may be shifted to the young person, though in younger children or youth who are less verbal, the counsellor may need to guide the course of most of the sessions. The shift may be accomplished by asking the youth, 'What would you like to talk about today?'

- The second part of the session consists of the following:
  - — A review should be made of the primary problem(s). The counsellor should then ask the youth whether there has been any change in his problem(s) and if so, what these changes are. She should enquire whether the youth feels better or worse and if he can provide an explanation for his progress or lack of progress.
  - — The counsellor and youth should discuss any new problems/difficulties which have arisen since the last session.
  - — If the counselling strategy includes home practice assignments, the counsellor should enquire if he has completed them; if so, these should be reviewed. If the youth has had any difficulty doing or completing them, the counsellor should find out why. She should determine whether the home practice can be done together with her during the session, or whether it needs to be set aside or left out of the counselling altogether if it is hindering the counselling process. It is important to remember that the fact that the home practice has not been done should not be an obstacle to proceeding with the session.
  - — The counsellor should implement the specific counselling strategies (*see* Chapter 6) that have been selected to help the youth with his problem(s).
- Closing the session includes the following:
  - — Praising the youth for having participated cooperatively with the counsellor to achieve their goals;
  - — Briefly summarizing what was achieved during the session;
  - — Summarizing any home practice assigned during the session;
  - — Agreeing upon the time, place and date of the next appointment.

There will be some exceptions to the structure of the counselling session that has been described above. For example, changes may be necessary if the young person has dropped in for an unplanned session at the end of the day, when time is short, or if the youth is in extreme

BOX 3.3: MANAGING EMERGENCY MEETINGS

There may be instances when a youth comes to the counsellor, or is referred to the counsellor, at the end of the day. In such instances, the counsellor should take time to assess if the youth is facing an emergency that cannot wait for a scheduled appointment the following day.

If the youth is facing an emergency, e.g. fearing family violence or sexual abuse, the counsellor should spend some time with him and consult the school principal to make plans for the youth's immediate safety (*see* Chapter 7).

distress. If the youth has dropped in for an unplanned session and if it is not an emergency situation (Box 3.3), the counsellor should briefly address the issue that is troubling him and set a time for following up on the issue the next day.

Working with the Youth's Family Members

At the beginning of the counselling relationship, the counsellor told the young person that the counselling relationship is private and that she will not discuss the content of their meetings with anyone else. However, she mentioned an exception to this: ***'There may be particular issues that I may need to discuss with others, but I will do so only after discussing this with you and obtaining your permission.'*** Under exceptional circumstances, concerns about a youth's safety may take precedence over the need to maintain confidentiality. In these situations, the counsellor must help the youth understand that it is necessary to provide information that he has shared during counselling to people who can protect him from danger.

Meeting the members of the youth's family or others may be necessary for an adequate assessment or for his protection in situations such as the following:

- In younger children, to get a comprehensive history from an adult caregiver;
- When a youth displays disruptive behaviours in school and the counsellor would like to get an idea of his functioning at home to determine whether these behaviours occur across various settings;
- When the counsellor suspects a developmental disability and a detailed developmental history would contribute essential information to the diagnostic process (*see* Chapter 4);
- When a problem at home is contributing to the youth's difficulties, e.g. if a parent mistreats the child or a parent is ill;
- When the counsellor is concerned about the youth's health and/or safety, e.g. if the adolescent is abusing substances or is at risk of suicide;
- When an adolescent has been or is facing any form of physical or sexual violence in any setting (*see* Chapter 7);
- When a referral to another professional is needed (*see* Chapter 4).

Meeting certain family members may, in some instances, pose a threat to the youth's emotional well-being. For example, if a youth living in an abusive family has shared information about the abuse with the counsellor, the risk of violence against him might increase. Because of this, the young person must be consulted while planning a meeting with the family members concerned. Since he knows his family the best, he will often be in a good position to judge, together with the counsellor, whether the counsellor should meet his family members and, if so, with whom, how and where. Additionally, the young person should understand that the meeting is intended for his benefit, and that only relevant information will be shared and all else will be kept confidential.

The following is an example of an explanation that can be given to the young person about meeting his parent:

'It seems to me that your main problems stem from your experiences with your father, who gets extremely angry with you, to the point of beating you. This is affecting your concentration and studies, which makes your father even angrier. Perhaps we could try to explain to your father how his anger is affecting your studies. What do you think? [Wait for the young person's responses and respond to them.] ***What would be the best way to approach your father?*** [Wait for the young person's responses and respond to them.] ***Do you think involving your mother in a discussion may be of help?'***

MANAGING CHANGES IN THE COUNSELLING RELATIONSHIP

At times, there are planned and unplanned changes in the counselling relationship. Examples of *planned changes* include a planned closure of counselling (*see* Chapter 4), a planned change in the date or time of a counselling session and changes related to the end of the school term. Examples of *unplanned changes* include the absence of the counsellor for a session due to illness, a premature end to the counselling relationship because the counsellor has left her job or the youth discontinues without warning. When changes in the counselling can be foreseen, the counsellor should make sure she prepares the young person. Without preparation, the youth may be taken by surprise at a minimum or overwhelmed by feelings of being abandoned at a maximum. If the counsellor has caused the unforeseen event, she should explain this in a subsequent meeting with the youth, keeping in mind that being on the receiving end of unexpected events can be emotionally painful for the youth.

The following is an example of how the counsellor can prepare the young person for an anticipated change:

'The school term is coming to a close next month. We have been steadily working together on your worries for some months. We have one month to think together about your plans for and concerns about the summer break ahead. This will be our last bit of work together. I will not be returning to this school next year, so we will also have to say goodbye. [Wait for the youth's responses and respond to them.] ***This may give rise to feelings that we will have a chance to discuss. Let us mark the calendar so that we can keep track of how many more meetings we will have, and when it might be the right time to discuss your thoughts and concerns about the summer and the next academic year.'***

The following is an example of how the counsellor can tackle the issue of an unplanned change after it has occurred:

'Last week, I could not come to school and was unable to contact you. I am sorry. Sometimes, young people worry that their counsellor has forgotten about them, or even that she is angry with them when an appointment has been missed. I wonder how you felt. [Wait for the youth's reaction and respond. Then, proceed.] ***In the future, I will always try to get in touch with you if I am unable to keep to an appointment. But at times, this may not be possible because something urgent might come up and I might be unable to get in touch. I hope you understand and do not take it personally.'***

In general, unless there is an unforeseen emergency, the counsellor should never discontinue the counselling without notifying the young person in advance and discussing the situation with him. In addition, in the event that she has to discontinue counselling, she should make arrangements for the youth's continuing care, as necessary; e.g. making a referral for further counselling. The counsellor should consult a supervisor if she is considering changes in the counselling relationship (*see* Chapter 8).

CHAPTER 4

CASE MANAGEMENT

Case management refers to the entire process of assisting the youth with a mental health problem, beginning from when the counsellor first meets the youth and assesses her problem until her condition has improved. Each of the case studies in Part B of this casebook follow the case management process described in this chapter. This chapter consists of the following sections:

- Assessing the problem
- Case formulation, planning treatment and monitoring progress
- Making a referral
- Closure of the counselling

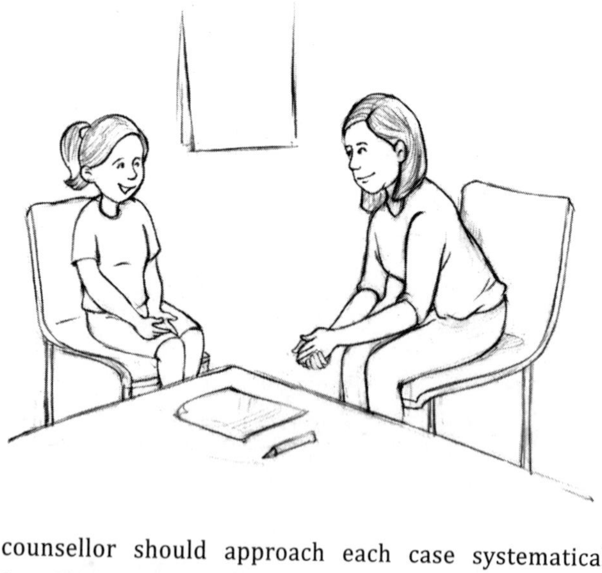

The counsellor should approach each case systematically. The Generic Case Management Diagram on page 87 details the step by step counselling process from assessment through closure.

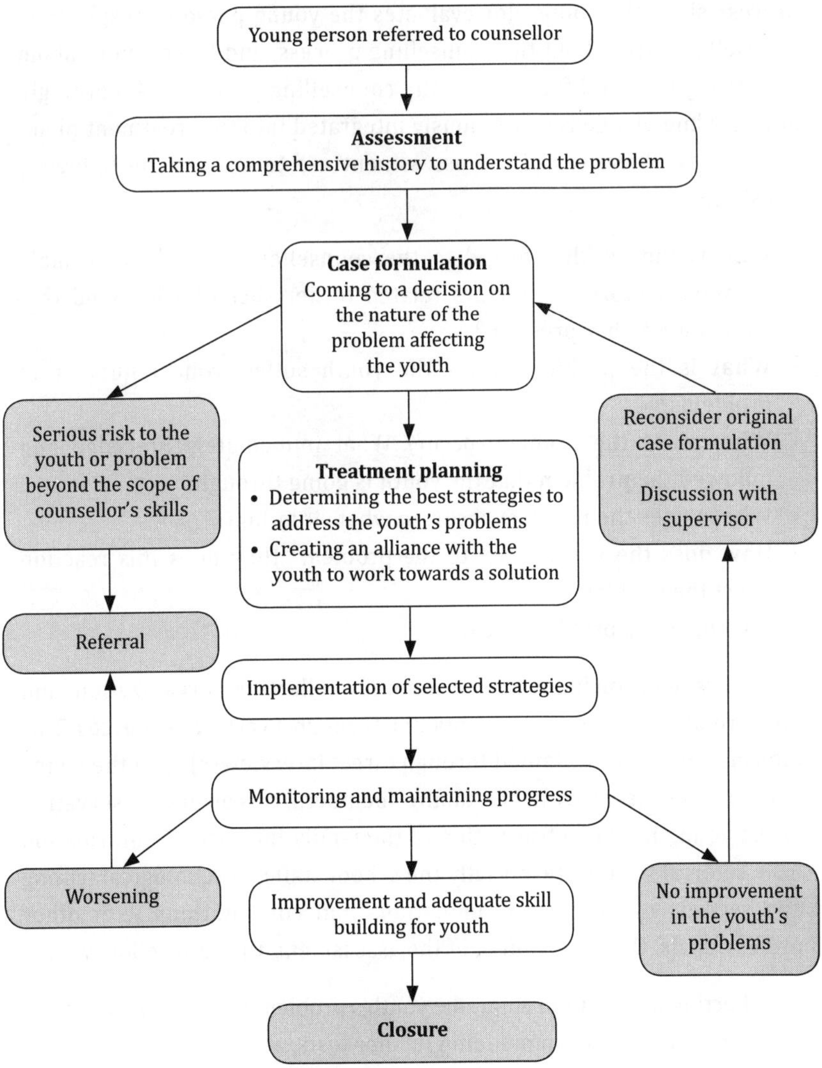

Generic Case Management Diagram

Assessing the Problem

The goal of the assessment is to understand the youth's overall functioning and life circumstances in order to develop a counselling plan tailored specifically for the individual youth. Assessment is a continuous process since the counsellor evaluates the young person's response to counselling throughout the counselling process, and learns more about her strengths and difficulties as the counselling proceeds. Accordingly, any new knowledge is continuously integrated into the treatment plan.

The key objectives of the assessment are to answer the following questions:

- **Who** is the youth referred to the counsellor? What are the main personal factors and factors related to her social background that contribute to her problem?
- **What** is the problem? Does the youth suffer from a number of problems?
- **When** does the problem occur? What immediately preceded and followed the problem that the youth is going through?
- **Where** does the problem occur; in what situation(s)?
- **How** does the youth react to the problem? How does this reaction affect the problem?
- **Why** does the problem occur?

Assessment includes the systematic collection, organization and interpretation of information obtained through a variety of sources. This information can be obtained through direct interview(s) with the young person, interviews with her family members/caregivers, observation of the young person, observation of the family interaction, information from referral sources (especially the school staff), psychological testing and records of previous examinations and consultations with other professionals. Over the course of the assessment, the counsellor will be:

- Collecting information about the youth's problem from various sources;
- Carrying out or recommending further tests, as needed;
- Reviewing this information to make sense of the youth's problem.

Each of these steps is described below.

Collecting information

The critical components of the information to be gathered during the assessment include the following:

- Demographic information
- The reason for referral
- The youth's presenting problem
- The developmental history of the youth, including any specific health issues (mental or physical)
- The psychosocial history of the youth, which includes:
  —her family history
  —her academic history
  —her social history
- Substance use history, when appropriate
- Mental status examination (MSE)
- Assessment of risk of suicide, when necessary
- Information from psychological tests and tools

Information from varied sources gives one a richer and more accurate understanding of the problems and circumstances of the young person. As a general rule, the counsellor should try to obtain as much information from the young person as possible. Collaterals, such as parents, teachers and family physicians, can be important informants, but the counsellor should always bear in mind the need to maintain the confidentiality of the youth when speaking to others involved in her care (*see* Chapter 7).

A home visit can provide additional information on the youth. Visiting the home can be useful when:

- The counsellor is not certain that the youth will convey the counsellor's request that the family contact her for a meeting (e.g. a youth with a developmental disability or one who is at risk of self-harm);
- The youth has a disruptive behaviour problem and the counsellor wants to assess whether it occurs in various settings (e.g. hyperactive behaviour needs to be present at school, home and other places to be diagnosed as such);
- The counsellor thinks that the youth might live in a vulnerable setting and wants to clarify the extent of adversity in the home setting (e.g. the level of poverty);
- The counsellor thinks that a meeting with the parents would be important to her understanding of the youth's circumstances, but the

parent has not attended a counselling session at the school despite several requests.

Demographic information

This includes the youth's age (and birth date), contact address, place of residence, sex and preferred language, as well as her parents' occupations (*see* Appendix). This information provides the counsellor with information about the youth's socioeconomic and cultural context.

Reason for referral

The first step in the assessment is to understand the reason for which the youth is seeking help or others are seeking help for her. It is important to note whether the young person has come on her own or has been referred by her parents or others, since this may influence the counsellor's interaction with her. For example, if the young person has not come on her own, she may be hostile or reluctant to engage with the counsellor. If the youth has not sought help on her own, the counsellor should find out the reason for referral directly from the source of referral, (e.g. the school staff or family). In this context, it often helps to meet the person who has made the referral, either separately or together with the young person.

The presenting problem

The counsellor should be aware that if the young person has not sought help on her own, she may not divulge information on her problem and may even deny that she has a problem at all. Successful engagement with the young person and developing a rapport are critically important steps in the early stages of counselling (*see* Chapter 3). It is useful to begin the assessment by asking the youth a general question about whether she has experienced any difficulties recently, rather than focusing on the reason for the referral. The presenting problem can then be explored by asking questions related to the reason for referral. These include:

- What is the reason you have come to see me?
- When did this problem start?

- How often do you feel this way?
- Has this problem changed over time? Why?
- What do you think are the likely causes of the problem?
- What have you done to improve the situation?
- What makes the problem worse/better?
- How do you think I can help you?

Developmental history

Since the young person is not always in a position to give a reliable and detailed developmental history, the counsellor will need to interview a parent, in particular, the mother or significant caregiver. This is true especially if facts related to pregnancy or early childhood are relevant for the counsellor's understanding of the youth's problems. A knowledge of the young person's developmental history, from pregnancy up to her present age, can help the counsellor understand if her current problems are related to significant events in her early history and/or difficulties or delays in the overall context of her development (*see* Chapters 1 and 2). A detailed history of developmental milestones and delays need not be obtained initially, unless there is a suspicion of a developmental problem, notably, academic difficulties or significant social delays.

The counsellor should obtain information on the following issues for each specific phase of development:

Pregnancy and birth: Complications during the pregnancy, such as high blood pressure, or around the time of birth, such as the baby not crying within a few minutes of being born, may be associated with developmental delays and intellectual disabilities.

Some questions that help the counsellor understand what happened during this period include:

- How was your pregnancy?
- Where did you deliver? Were there any problems around this time?
- How were your first few months with your baby?

Infancy and pre-school years: It is during these early years of a child's life that obvious developmental disabilities, such as locomotor problems and significant language delays, may be recognized.

Some questions to gain information about key milestones include:

- Was your child copying sounds by 6 months?
- Did your child sit by 9 months?
- Did your child say 'mama'/'papa' by 1 year?
- Did your child walk independently and say single words by 18 months?
- Could she make simple two-word sentences, follow instructions and kick a ball by 2 years?
- Was she playing make-believe games and having a simple conversation by 3 years?
- Could she tell simple stories and play happily with others by 4 years?
- Could she dress and undress by 5 years?

If the parent describes delays, the counsellor should ask for their understanding of the reasons and any actions they have taken. The counsellor should keep in mind that there may be a need for referral (*see* Making a referral) to understand the reasons for any delays.

Middle childhood: During this period, the child is in primary school. Difficulties with learning or social communication may become prominent at this stage. Mental health problems, particularly anxiety and behaviour disorders, may also emerge during this phase of development. Certain events which were particularly stressful for the child and/or her caregiver may have occurred and may have had an influence on the child's emotional development. While the parents or teachers are the key sources of information on this phase of the child's life, the child can also provide useful information.

Some questions that help the counsellor understand what happened during this period of life include:

- Can you describe your child's interactions with family members?
- Was your child cooperative or defiant? Did she throw frequent temper tantrums?
- Did she get into trouble with the teachers?
- Have any changes in her life circumstances, such as a divorce, the death of a parent, birth of a sibling and any crisis, occurred during this period?

Adolescence: This is the period when the youth is in secondary school. The risk of developing mental health problems is higher during this phase than during any other period of life (*see* Chapter 2). Key adults, such as parents and teachers, and the young person herself can provide reliable information. The areas of enquiry should include whether there have been any changes in the youth's family relationships, whether there have been particular stressors and, if so, whether they are persisting.

Since sexual feelings and interest in sexuality come to the fore during this period, it is important to understand the youth's attitudes and experiences in this area. Talking about sexuality can be challenging since the youth may feel uncomfortable sharing her interest or concerns with an adult. The young person may want to talk about the subject, but is unlikely to, unless specifically asked. It is best for the counsellor to introduce the topic by telling the youth that it is routine to ask questions about sexuality when developing an understanding of adolescents. She can go on to ask whether it is all right for her to proceed, and then ask questions.

Some useful questions are:

- Do you have any 'special' person in your life, that is, someone you are in love with?
- Are you currently involved in a sexual relationship? Would you like to tell me about it?
- If you are involved in a sexual relationship, are there any sexual health concerns that you might want to discuss? (Specific areas of enquiry may include pregnancies, birth control, the attitude of the family, abortions and infections.)
- Have you ever been sexually harmed or harassed in any way? If yes, when? By whom? Have you been able to do something to stop it?

Psychosocial history

This includes the child's early environment, her temperament over time and the youth's family, academic and social history.

The child's early environment: Infancy and the pre-school years are important for building a sense of security in the child. Because of this, the counsellor should enquire about any disruptions in the early environment. Some examples of disruption are birth of a sibling, a severe medical condition and separation from the primary caregivers. In addition, this is the earliest period to identify the beginning of problems. Some useful questions to understand the child's early environment are:

- What has your child's relationship with you been like since her birth; has it changed over time?
- Have there been any upsets in the family since the child's birth, for example a loss, a move?
- What were your child's early years like? Did she develop like other children around her?
- Have there been any major events in the child's life that were distressing or upsetting for her?

If the parent needs clarifications in order to answer this, the counsellor can offer examples of major events, such as losing a close relative or being in hospital. If there was a major event in the child's life, the counsellor should seek further details, e.g. when it occurred and how the child reacted to it.

The child's temperament over time: Understanding the youth's temperament over time (Chapter 1) can also help the counsellor understand the current mental health problems. For example, it would help to know whether the child was a worrier if the current problem is an anxiety disorder, or whether the child was uncomfortable with strangers if the current problem is related to a lack of friends.

A useful question is:

- How would you describe your child's temperament? Have you seen any changes over time in her temperament?

Family history: It is important to understand the family history and the interactions within the family since the family plays a key role in the life of a young person. Challenging behaviours are sometimes produced by disturbed family relationships, adversity that the family is going through or the inability of parents to effectively manage their child's behaviour. A child's mental health may also be affected by gender-based expectations. For example, in some families, a young girl feels unfairly treated as compared to her brother. When the family history is obtained in a family session, the counsellor has the opportunity to observe the nature of the interactions among the family members, e.g. the degree of warmth between them, and this adds to her understanding of the youth's family context. Since a family's structure is sometimes complicated, as in the case of an extended family, it is useful to obtain a detailed description of everyone who lives in the home and influences the youth and her environment.

Some questions that can help the counsellor gain a clear understanding of the family structure and the youth's perception of her home life include:

- Who lives with you at home? Can you help me by drawing a picture of all the people in the home and how they are related to each other?
- Who makes decisions at home?
- How do your parents/family members get along with each other?
- What aspects of your life do you look after for yourself (e.g. getting to school on your own, filling your own tiffin)?

During the adolescent period, many young people are prone to strong feelings which often affect their relationships, particularly their family relationships. Some useful questions that can help the counsellor learn about intra-family relationships from the adolescent are:

- How are your relationships at home? Are you happy with your relationships with your family members or do you feel angry or irritable with your family members? If you feel angry or irritable, what causes this?
- Do you feel that you are being treated fairly at home?

Academic history: This covers issues related to coping with studies and the results of examinations. Academic performance can be an important window into the young person's overall functioning. If she is on target academically, it often means that she is functioning well in general. If her academic performance is not in keeping with the expected level for her grade or if she is having difficulty coping with academic expectations, it may reflect emotional and intellectual problems and can also lead to mental health problems.

Asking the youth the following questions may be useful:

- How do you like school these days? And your teachers?
- How do you think you are doing with your studies? Do you have

difficulty with any particular subject? How does this make you feel?
- Are you satisfied with your performance? If not, why? How do your parents feel about your performance?
- For adolescents: What are your plans for the future? What are your plans for further education?

It is also important to obtain information from the youth's teachers to clarify what her academic difficulties are. This should be done only with the youth's permission. The subject books and school report card are also useful sources of information. The academic history can be a relatively 'neutral' subject to explore, compared to, for example, the youth's relationship with her family, and may offer an avenue for building a rapport with her and engaging her.

Social history: This covers how the youth functions with her peers and the environmental factors which affect her functioning in a social setting.

In order to gain an understanding of the young person's social relationships and environment, the counsellor could enquire about possible factors in the home or neighbourhood which make her vulnerable, such as gangs of older youth. On the other hand, there might be aspects of the youth's immediate environment which nurture positive skills, such as local sport clubs.

Some questions to ask include:

- What social support is available for you?
- Who are your role models/mentors?
- Are there situations in your neighbourhood which make you feel unsafe?
- Which relationships do you find supportive?

Peer relationships play an increasingly important role as the young person develops her world beyond the family. The number and nature of these relationships are important indicators of whether the youth's psychosocial development is proceeding well.

Asking the youth the following questions provides the counsellor information on her peer relationships as well as other relationships:

- Can you name some of your good friends?
- What do you enjoy doing with your friends?

Bullying and social isolation are important risks in the school age years. They often have an impact on the social participation and academic performance of a youth (*see* Case Study 9).

Some questions which may allow a counsellor to explore the often hidden issue of bullying are:

- Have you ever been hurt physically or emotionally by classmates?
- What did you do when this happened? Who did you tell?
- What are your feelings about these incidents now?

Substance use history

This is also a sensitive area which the youth may find difficult to discuss and the counsellor should not attempt to enquire about it until a rapport has been established. Enquiring about a substance use history is necessary for any adolescent above 14 years of age; however, for younger youth, it need not be obtained unless the counsellor has reason to believe that the youth is engaged in substance use.

Some useful questions include:

- Have you ever tried tobacco? Alcohol? Any other drugs?
- If so, when did you first use this? Are you currently using it? How often?
- Do you think that this is a problem for you? Why? What have you done to try to stop it?

The medical history

It is important to learn about the young person's overall health since it is related both to her physical and emotional functioning. The counsellor should ask if the young person has had any major illnesses in the past or if she has any at present, and about any treatment that she has received or is receiving. If the need arises, medical records can be consulted for clarifications, but these can be obtained only with the permission of the young person, or of the parent if the youth is unable to provide permission due, for example, to a severe intellectual disability.

The Mental Status Examination

The Mental Status Examination (MSE) helps establish an overall picture of the young person's current mental health and is particularly useful in assessing the type of mental health problem (*see* Chapter 2). The MSE is carried out by observing the young person's behaviour during a meeting with her, and by asking her specific questions about her thoughts and feelings. The MSE covers the following areas:

Attitude to the interview: The counsellor observes the youth's approach to the interview and to the counsellor. Is she friendly and open? Is she secretive, i.e. possibly hiding something or holding back some information? Is she evasive, i.e. avoids answering questions or does not answer them directly?

General appearance: The counsellor observes the youth's dress, style of walking and posture. Unkempt hair and dirty clothes, for example, might indicate that the youth is suffering from a disruptive behaviour disorder or serious mental disorder, or that her social circumstances are difficult.

Behaviour: The counsellor observes whether the youth is distracted, attentive, focused, fidgety, aggressive or restless, and whether she makes direct, occasional or no eye contact. To take a few examples, restlessness, inattentiveness and fidgeting could indicate attention deficit hyperactivity disorder or the presence of anxiety; being withdrawn may be a sign of depression or mental health distress; and poor or no eye contact may be a sign of mental health distress or autism spectrum disorder (*see* Chapter 2).

Speech: The counsellor observes the youth's speech, i.e. how it sounds, its pace and clarity (e.g. whether her speech is clear and understandable, too much, too little, too loud, too low, too fast or too slow), as well as what she says. Young people with autism spectrum disorder or specific learning disabilities often have difficulties with speech. For example, speaking very little or in a peculiar monotonous, didactic way may indicate autism spectrum disorder. Slurred speech may be a sign of substance use. Stammering (*see* Case Study 8) is an obvious speech impairment, which can be associated with mental health problems. Occasionally a speech problem may also indicate a hearing problem.

Affect: This is the emotion that can be observed in the person's facial expression, e.g. whether the young person appears to be sad, happy or anxious. The counsellor takes note of the quality, range and intensity of the 'affect' (the observable emotion in the person's facial expression), as well as any changes in it. Does her affect change unpredictably? Does her affect match what she says she feels? For example, does she say she is sad but is smiling and laughing? When her affect does not match the situation she describes, it is considered 'incongruent' (not matching, inappropriate) and may indicate a serious mental disorder.

Mood: The counsellor should encourage the youth to describe her mood. The counsellor may ask, ***'Now, I would like to ask you some questions about how you have been feeling these days.'*** The counsellor should pay close attention to words which indicate how the young person is feeling. For example, does she describe feeling discouraged, depressed, low, brimming with energy, extremely happy, out of control, angry or irritable? The counsellor should enquire specifically about whether the young person feels low, has lost interest in pleasurable activities, feels irritable, and feels worried or anxious. If there is evidence that the youth feels low, the counsellor must explore the possibility of the presence of suicidal thoughts (*see* Suicide risk assessment).

Thought process: This refers to the content, quantity and 'form' (logical sense) of thought, as well as the rate of thought flow. One can draw conclusions about the person's thought processes by observing her speech or asking her to describe her thoughts. In some youth with mental health problems, thoughts rush through their head, while in others, the thoughts move very slowly; others present a pattern of disorganized thought. Any of these could indicate intellectual disability or a serious mental disorder. During the interview, the counsellor should carefully observe the young person's thought processes from the following perspectives:

- *Form:* Do the young person's thoughts make logical sense, are they relevant to the situation described, are they organized and do they flow logically in response to the questions? If not, the youth may have a 'thought disorder'.
- *Content:* Does the young person say that she is preoccupied with a particular distressing thought (an 'obsession')? Is she worrying a lot about something in particular? Does her description of her thoughts convey that she has some beliefs that are not true ('delusions')? The counsellor may need to specifically explore the content of these beliefs

if she thinks that they are unusual, e.g. if the young person expresses the suspicion that others are trying to harm her. If the counsellor detects the presence of unusual thoughts, she should ask whether the young person has experienced any unusual sensory experiences, e.g. does she see things or hear voices (visual or auditory 'hallucinations')? Although such experiences are uncommon, it is important to be alert for them, as they are a feature of a serious mental disorder and are often accompanied by a thought disorder.

Cognitive ability: This refers to the young person's attention, memory, orientation and intelligence. Like the other aspects of the MSE, these abilities can be assessed through observations during the interview and by asking specific questions. Impairments in cognitive ability are generally very rare and, if observed, usually indicate a developmental disability or certain disorders such as attention deficit hyperactivity disorder. The aspects of cognitive ability are as follows:

- *Attention:* This is the ability to focus attention on the task at hand. The ability to focus on the interview indicates a good level of attention. The counsellor can also assess attention by asking the youth to repeat sequences of numbers in forward then backward order.
- *Memory:* Memory consists of recent, remote and immediate recall. These can be assessed by asking what the youth did in the morning, last year and earlier in the week, to assess recent and remote memory. Immediate memory can be assessed by asking the youth to repeat three unrelated words, e.g. cat, piano and skirt. The counsellor then asks the youth to recall these words after 5 minutes.
- *Orientation:* The awareness of time and place is referred to as orientation, which can be assessed by asking the youth about the date/day and where she lives.
- *Intelligence:* This refers to the ability to reason and think abstractly. It can be assessed, in part, through information about the young person's developmental history, e.g. checking whether there has been a consistent delay in achieving cognitive milestones. In assessing intelligence, the counsellor must also observe whether the young person's behaviours and skills are appropriate for her age. A youth who is coping well academically probably has age-appropriate

intelligence. However, intelligence tests are usually required for a definitive assessment when the counsellor is uncertain (*see* Box 4.7).

Insight and judgement: Insight refers to the youth's awareness and understanding of her problem. It can be assessed by observing if she seems affected by or concerned about her problem, and by specifically asking her whether she thinks she has a problem, what kind of problem it is, what has caused it and how she thinks it can be addressed. Judgement, which is related to insight, is the ability to make and act upon sound and responsible decisions and plans, and behave appropriately in social situations. Insight and judgement are very helpful for a successful counselling experience and, if limited, may be a focus of counselling.

Suicide Risk Assessment

Suicidal behaviour: Suicidal behaviours are behaviours intended to harm oneself. Sometimes a distinction is made between harming oneself with the goal of dying (suicide) and harming oneself without the intention of dying. It is often difficult to make this distinction in practice. In any case, people who deliberately harm themselves without the specific goal of killing themselves are at a greater risk for attempting to kill themselves in the future. For this reason, both these situations (self-harm with or without the intention to die) are considered 'suicidal behaviours'.

Suicidal thoughts and behaviours vary in degree and intensity. At the 'mildest' end are fleeting thoughts of ending one's life. These thoughts are usually transient, and occur relatively more frequently in adolescence. At the next level are suicidal thoughts which are more persistent and distressing, and which signal the possibility of a mental health problem. At the more extreme end of the spectrum, the young person makes detailed plans to end her life, e.g. she works out the exact method she plans to use to harm herself. This serious stage precedes the suicide attempt. In youth, suicidal attempts are often impulsive and triggered by acute suicidal thoughts.

Suicide is one of the leading causes of death among people between the ages of 15 and 29, in India. Many suicides can be prevented through an adequate assessment and timely intervention.

What influences the risk of suicidal behaviour? The risk of suicide is determined by the balance between the risk and protective factors (Box 4.1), as well as the frequency and type of suicidal thoughts. Three levels of risk and the associated actions that the counsellor can take are described below.

- *High risk:* The risk for suicide can be considered high if there are persistent suicidal ideas, with definite plans; severe mental health problems; or multiple immediate risk factors and limited protective factors. In this situation, the counsellor should discuss the youth's level of risk with a supervisor and urgently make a referral (*see* Chapter 4).
- *Moderate risk:* The risk is moderate if there are persistent suicidal ideas, with no concrete plans; moderate-to-severe mental health problems; or one or more immediate risk factors and limited protective factors. In this situation, the counsellor should discuss the youth's level of risk with a supervisor and consider a referral.
- *Low/no risk:* There is a low risk or no risk if suicidal ideas cross the person's mind occasionally or not at all, or if she makes only brief and infrequent mention of suicidal ideas, e.g. 'I'd be better off dead.' The same goes for those with mild mental health problems, and those with no immediate risk factors and adequate protective factors. In these situations, the counsellor should monitor the youth's risk.

Assessing the risk of suicide: A counsellor needs to always keep the risk of suicide in mind when working with young people who have a mental health problem since suicidal acts can be sudden and impulsive.

The following signs indicate the need for a suicide risk assessment:

- Symptoms of depression;
- When a young person loses interest in and withdraws from her usual social interactions with her friends or family members;
- When a young person is no longer motivated to study;
- When a young person with depression drops out of counselling;
- When a young person makes attempts to gain access to means of committing suicide, e.g. buying large amounts of medicines (this is an indicator of a high risk of suicide and requires immediate intervention).

BOX 4.1: FACTORS CONTRIBUTING TO RISK OF SUICIDE AMONG YOUNG PERSONS

Risk factors

Social and demographic factors

- The risk of suicide is low below the age of 15, but then rises quickly, peaking in young adulthood (the early twenties).
- Being female
- Low socioeconomic status
- Social isolation and lack of support
- Academic stress, e.g. failure in examinations
- Difficulties with relationships, e.g. break-up of a romantic relationship
- Having experienced violence or abuse
- Having a family member or close friend who has committed suicide

Mental health factors

- Having a current mental health disorder, particularly depression
- Having a chronic medical disorder, especially conditions associated with disability or conditions affecting one's appearance
- Feelings of hopelessness
- Having attempted suicide in the past
- The use of alcohol and/or drugs

Protective factors

- Strong, secure ties with family or friends
- Doing well in studies
- Religious and cultural beliefs which hold that suicide is morally wrong
- Involvement in school or community activities
- Optimistic temperament, positive coping styles and problem-solving abilities
- Plans for the future

The first question that needs to be addressed is whether the youth has ideas of self-harm (Box 4.2). It is a myth that asking a young person about suicidal ideas introduces suicidal wishes or ideas into her mind; on the contrary, this is the only way to identify suicidal ideas and to provide the help necessary for preventing a suicidal act. It is also important to keep in mind that the youth may feel guilty or embarrassed about

BOX 4.2: QUESTIONS TO ASSESS SUICIDAL THOUGHTS AND BEHAVIOURS

Enquiring about the presence of suicidal thoughts

- In the past few weeks, have you felt it would be better if you did not wake up in the morning?
- I can see that you are going through a very difficult period. In your situation, some people feel that carrying on with life is not worth it. Have you ever felt this way?
- Have you felt that the problems in your life are so difficult that you would be better off if you were not alive?

Enquiring about the severity of suicidal thoughts or behaviours

- Have you been having thoughts of harming yourself?
- How frequently do you have these thoughts?
- How have you been trying to deal with these thoughts? Are you able to distract yourself from these thoughts?
- Have you been feeling that nothing can help you? (feelings of helplessness)
- Have you been feeling that you are a burden on others/you are a loser? (feelings of worthlessness)
- Have you been feeling as if there is no way out of your current problems? (feelings of hopelessness)
- What effect are these thoughts having on you?
- Have you made any plans to harm yourself? Can you tell me something about these plans?
- Have you told anybody else about your plans? What have you told them?
- Have you ever tried to harm yourself in the past?

sharing suicidal ideas with the counsellor, which makes it especially important to ask about the presence of any such thoughts in a gentle and non-judgemental manner. Obviously, it is easier to assess the risk if the counsellor has a good rapport with the young person.

The counsellor should be aware that the risk of suicide may change over time. A change in the circumstances or mental health of the youth should prompt the counsellor to reassess the risk. If a young person admits to suicidal thoughts, a more thorough assessment of the risk of suicide should be carried out. This would include assessing the presence of the various risk and protective factors, as well as the specificity of the person's suicidal ideas and plans (Box 4.2). When in doubt about whether or not the risk of suicide is high, it is always better to overestimate the risk and to consider an urgent referral to a mental health professional for further assessment.

Finally, the counsellor should always remember that most people have mixed feelings about committing suicide. A person usually goes back and forth between wishing to die and wishing to live. In reality, most young people who express suicidal thoughts do not really want to die, but rather, are temporarily unhappy with their lives. If they are given support and their wish to live is bolstered, the risk of suicide most often decreases.

Information from psychological tests and tools

While interviews and observations are the most useful sources of information about the young person, a range of psychological tests and tools (self-report or counsellor-administered questionnaires) are also available for the assessment and diagnosis of mental health problems. Of the range of tests available, the one which may be used by school counsellors is the 'Strengths and Difficulties Questionnaire' (SDQ) (Box 4.3). The SDQ has been translated and used in India, and is available at no cost. A full description of other psychological tests and tools is beyond the scope of this book, as most tests should be administered only after appropriate training. Some tools screen for a particular condition, some confirm the diagnosis and some throw light on the young person's functioning. While standardized tools can be useful for assessment and

BOX 4.3: THE STRENGTHS AND DIFFICULTIES QUESTIONNAIRE (SDQ)

The SDQ was developed by Robert Goodman and has become one of the most widely used rating questionnaires for assessing the mental health of young people in the world. It is most often used as a screening tool for youth between the ages of 3 and 16 years. It has 25 questions which provide scores on four scales: emotional symptoms, behavioural symptoms (conduct and hyperactivity), peer relationships and social behaviour. Each of these scales includes questions addressing both the positive and negative aspects of the specific area. The answers reflect the frequency of the behaviour being enquired about. The results are interpreted in terms of a range of scores from 'normal' through 'borderline' to 'abnormal'. 'Abnormal' scores in any of the four scales suggest that the person has a mental health problem related to that scale. For example, depression is suspected if the scores in the emotional scale are abnormal, and conduct disorder is suspected if those in the behaviour scale are abnormal. Separate questionnaires and follow-up questionnaires are available for parents and teachers, as is a self-assessment questionnaire for older youth. Although these questionnaires are designed as self-report questionnaires, the counsellor may find it helpful to discuss or go through the questionnaire with the youth and parent.

The counsellor can use the SDQ in the following ways:

- It can be used to strengthen the initial assessment of a young person's problem.
- It can be used before and after the application of specific counselling strategies to help evaluate the impact of the counselling on the youth's mental health.

The SDQ, as well as further instructions on its use, can be downloaded from *www.sdqinfo.com*.

the planning of treatment, the counsellor's clinical impression, combined with appropriate specialist inputs, where necessary, is always the most valuable 'tool' for developing the treatment plan.

Case formulation, planning treatment and monitoring progress

Case formulation is the conceptualization of the youth's mental health problems which informs the counselling plan. Planning treatment is the process of using the case formulation to design a counselling plan which identifies selected strategies and supportive interventions to achieve specific outcomes. This plan should be agreed upon by the youth and, when appropriate, her caregivers and teachers. Monitoring of progress is the process of evaluating the benefits of the counselling and making appropriate changes, when necessary, to the treatment plan and, sometimes, to the case formulation itself as the counsellor gains additional information. These three steps are in 'dynamic' interaction, i.e. they inform each other throughout the counselling process.

Case formulation

On the basis of the information gathered during the assessment phase, the counsellor arrives at an understanding of the youth's current functioning, whether she may be suffering from a mental health problem and, if so, the nature of that problem (*see* Chapter 2).

Arriving at a decision on whether the youth is suffering from mental health distress, a disorder or a disability, and ascertaining its specific nature, is key to the case formulation. This casebook describes three broad categories of mental health problems (mental health distress, mental health disorders and mental health disabilities) and the conditions within each category to guide the counsellor's decision-making (*see* Chapter 2). Should a counsellor wish to consult a more detailed system for the diagnosis of disorders and disabilities, she may consult the *WHO's Multi-axial Classification of Child and Adolescent Psychiatric Disorders: The ICD-10 classification of mental and behavioural*

BOX 4.4: THE SIX AXES OF CHILD AND ADOLESCENT DISORDERS

- **Axis I** refers to mental health disorders, e.g. depression. The severity of the problem is also described, e.g. severe depression.
- **Axis II** refers to specific disorders of development, e.g. the developmental disability of autism.
- **Axis III** refers to the level of intellectual capability and, as with Axis I, the degree of the intellectual disability is also described.
- **Axis IV** refers to coexisting medical conditions, such as epilepsy.
- **Axis V** refers to associated abnormal psychosocial situations, such as exposure to violence or abuse.
- **Axis VI** pertains to a global assessment of psychosocial disability and reflects the young person's functioning at the time of the assessment. Four distinct areas of functioning may be considered: personal care, occupational functioning (including academic life), family functioning and social functioning.

disorders of children and adolescents, which utilizes six 'axes' to describe mental health problems (Box 4.4).

The goal of the case formulation is to summarize the assessment and to guide the development of the counselling plan. In addition, the case formulation provides a baseline which the counsellor can use to reassess the young person's condition and modify the counselling plan (and, sometimes, the diagnosis itself) as she gains more information during the counselling process. The case formulation is a one-to-two-paragraph summary of the findings. It covers the following:

- Important personal information, including the name, age, sex and family/living arrangement;
- The reason for referral and the young person's history with respect to the presenting problem;
- The youth's current level of functioning;
- Events closely related to the onset of the youth's problem;
- Past history of a mental health problem and/or significant medical problem;

BOX 4.5: CASE FORMULATION OF ABHIJIT, A YOUTH WITH ANXIETY

Abhijit, a 14-year-old boy studying in Standard VIII, was brought by his mother after he failed his last class examination. Abhijit lives with his mother and brother; his father died about a year ago from a heart attack. His primary problem is severe anxiety, especially before and during examinations. The problem seems to have started just before his final examinations last year. He used to rank among the top students in his class before his father's death. Abhijit was very close to his father. His mother is very supportive, and he has good relationships with his brother and friends in school. His psychosocial and developmental histories revealed nothing else that was out of the ordinary. During the assessment, Abhijit was friendly, well-groomed and attentive; his speech was clear and understandable. He reported that he has extremely distressing, worrying thoughts and fearful feelings about his future, and that these affect his ability to concentrate on his studies. He suffered from regular headaches. He denied experiencing any suicidal thoughts. The most likely diagnosis of Abhijit's condition is an anxiety disorder, precipitated by his father's death.

- Key aspects of the Mental Status Examination;
- The most likely diagnosis;
- The youth's strengths and difficulties, based on her psychosocial and developmental histories.

Box 4.5 gives an example of a case formulation. Each case study in Part B of this casebook contains a case formulation and can be consulted as additional examples.

PLANNING TREATMENT

The case formulation should be discussed with the young person in simple language and in a way that does not cause her worry, emphasizing that the counsellor can help her feel and do better. Whether or not a specific diagnostic label should be used depends on a number of factors, including the nature of the problem, whether the youth's mental health problem can be better described with the help of such a label, and the certainty of the diagnosis. In general, when speaking to a young person, it is not necessarily advisable to use diagnostic labels for mental health distress and emotional and behaviour disorders. In these situations, it is generally more appropriate to summarize the symptoms and give an explanation for them. For example, instead of telling the youth, ***'You have depression'***, the counsellor could say, ***'It seems that you are very overwhelmed at the moment and feel that everything around you is bleak. Through our counselling sessions, we can...'*** On the other hand, it may be important to communicate the diagnostic term to the youth and/or her family for the more severe and enduring mental health disorders and disabilities, such as autism, specific learning disabilities or schizophrenia. In these instances, understanding the diagnosis could help the family and youth understand the challenges facing them and the need for specialized services. Such diagnoses, however, should only be made and communicated by a specialist with appropriate expertise.

After the case formulation has been discussed with the youth, it is important that the youth has an opportunity to give feedback to the counsellor on what has been communicated to her. The counsellor may encourage this by asking questions such as, ***'Do my impressions match the way you feel?'*** or ***'What do you feel about my understanding of your difficulties?'*** This process helps to confirm the extent to which the counsellor's understanding of the problem matches the young person's view of it and to identify discrepancies which need further exploration. In addition, the discussion can help build a rapport with the young person, since it indicates that the counsellor has listened to the youth attentively and made an effort to understand her concerns.

Once the youth has had sufficient opportunity to ask questions and clarify her doubts, the counsellor should explore the hopes or expectations she nurtures with respect to the counselling and begin to develop counselling goals. For example, the counsellor could ask, ***'What change do you hope for in your current situation?'*** The overall aims of

BOX 4.6: AN APPROACH TO GOAL-SETTING IN THE PLANNING OF COUNSELLING

Qualities of the goal			Examples
S	Specific	Needs to be clear and should define the behaviour that the youth wants to change	'I will not get into fights with Suraj.'
M	Measurable	Needs to be quantified and verifiable on follow-up	'I will not hit Suraj during the next week.'
A	Adequate	Needs to match the severity of the problem	'I will walk away when I am angry with Suraj.'
R	Realistic	Needs to be achievable and attainable, i.e. within the young person's reach	'I will tell Suraj why I am angry with him and then walk away.'
T	Time-limited	Needs to be achieved within a specific time-frame	'I will achieve this within the next two weeks.'

this discussion are to build a working relationship with the youth, to involve her in choosing the counselling goals and to develop a treatment plan to pursue these goals (Box 4.6).

On the basis of this discussion, the counsellor can go on to propose a treatment plan. While proposing the plan, the counsellor should:

- Explain how the problem can be effectively addressed through counselling;
- Agree with the youth on the counselling goals (Box 4.6);
- Describe the counselling strategies and supportive interventions that she is recommending to help with the youth's recovery (*see* Chapter 6);
- Explain that counselling consists of 'collaboration', i.e. it is a mutual working relationship, between the counsellor and the youth (*see paragraph below*);
- Discuss with the youth the likely number of sessions and over what period of time the counselling will take place;

- Review how the treatment plan will address the young person's expectations.

While describing the collaborative nature of counselling, the counsellor should try to make the youth appreciate that the two of them will work together to help the youth with her problems. It should be emphasized that 'working together' requires both of them make a commitment to the counselling plan. The counsellor can minimize the possibility of the youth dropping out of or otherwise resisting counselling if, during her discussion with the youth, she actively explores the barriers that might hinder the counselling. The counsellor can, for example, gently ask, ***'Do you see any reasons why it might be hard to work on your problems during counselling?'*** With the help of the youth, she can identify some possible barriers. These may be practical, e.g. the worry that the time spent on counselling will take away from her class work; psychological, e.g. the youth holding a very different view of her problem than the counsellor; or social, e.g. there being a stigma attached to seeing a counsellor. By identifying and talking over each barrier, the counsellor may increase the likelihood of the young person engaging in counselling. However, in certain situations the young person might not want to participate in counselling even after discussing the possible barriers. If this should happen, the counsellor should always leave the door open for the young person and offer a review appointment to continue the discussion. The counsellor should remember that in all sessions, including those devoted to assessment and treatment planning, she must demonstrate an interest in and respect for the youth and instil the hope that counselling will help to reduce the youth's problems and make her feel and fare better.

Monitoring progress

The goal of monitoring progress is to evaluate the youth's mental health over the course of the counselling and the extent to which the outcomes of the planned intervention are being achieved. Accordingly, appropriate counselling modifications may be made, if necessary. Goal-setting using SMART (*see* Box 4.6) can help to evaluate specific changes in behaviour.

A critically important component of monitoring progress is keeping adequate records, both of each session as well as of other information that the counsellor obtains on the young person between sessions, e.g. a report from a teacher.

Examples of counselling record forms, which cover assessment, case formulation, planning of treatment and monitoring of progress, can be found in the Appendix.

The goals of monitoring progress are:

- Assessing and noting changes in the youth's functioning, particularly whether there are any changes in the symptoms or problem she presented with and whether any new symptoms or problems have emerged;
- Observing and noting which counselling strategies are helping the young person improve and which are not;
- Implementing additional interventions, if needed (e.g. referrals, meetings with teachers or others);
- Supporting the youth when there are setbacks to her progress and working with her to help her understand the reasons for any setback.
- Determining if and when the young person has made enough progress to bring the counselling to an end.

The counselling goals formulated after the assessment can be modified as the counselling proceeds based on a number of factors, such as the severity of the youth's problems, the improvement or lack of improvement in her condition, changes in the young person's coping capacities, the level of social support available to her, her expectations of the counselling and her motivation.

In addition to monitoring the youth's progress, the counsellor must promote the young person's ability to maintain and build on the skills she learns throughout the counselling process. This will help the youth to practise and generalize her new skills and prepare for closure (*see* Closure of counselling). The following are useful in this context:

- Helping the youth consolidate what she has learnt, e.g. suggesting that she summarize the main skills and strategies she has learnt for dealing with problem situations;

- Building the young person's skills by encouraging her to apply the lessons learnt during counselling to real-life situations, e.g. applying her ability to engage in conversations during role-play with the counsellor to initiating conversations with her peers;
- Identifying potential future difficulties and helping her develop useful strategies to address these, e.g. accessing support and resources from her friends and/or family;
- Emphasizing that coping with her problems and maintaining her progress require continuing practice and improvement of the skills learnt during the counselling.

Making a referral

It is critically important for the counsellor to be able to recognize when the young person needs to be referred to another professional for further assessment and/or management of her problem (Box 4.7). A 'referral' is a recommendation to the young person (and her family, where appropriate) that she consult another professional in addition to, or instead of, the counsellor. The need for a referral may arise at any point during the course of the case, from the time of assessment to the closure of the counselling.

When to refer

As a general rule, if the counsellor is feeling out of her depth while trying to understand and/or address the young person's problem, referral to another professional is advisable. Some examples of situations in which a referral may be required are discussed below.

When there is a serious risk of self-harm: Earlier in the chapter, the assessment of the risk of suicide was discussed. The counsellor should attempt to manage mild risk; however, youth at serious risk should be discussed with a supervisor and referred to an appropriate health professional (*see* Where to refer). When the level of risk worsens or the risk persists, e.g. if a mild risk becomes more serious or continues, the counsellor should also consider referral.

When there is a possibility of physical and/or sexual abuse,

neglect or extremely adverse circumstances: If the counsellor suspects that the youth is facing overwhelming circumstances, including abuse, neglect and/or extreme poverty, she should discuss the situation with her supervisor and consider referral to the appropriate social services (*see* Chapter 7).

When there is a serious degree of disruptive or impulsive behaviour: A referral is necessary if a disruptive behaviour problem (such as aggressive behaviour towards peers) or a problem of impulsive or distractible behaviour is causing serious problems in the school setting and the young person is not responding to counselling. The counsellor should remember that medication might be useful to tackle some of these problems, notably those associated with attention deficit hyperactivity disorder, and a referral to an appropriate specialist may be necessary to evaluate whether medication (and which medication) should be prescribed.

When the young person has a medical problem: Any physical health problem should be referred to the family doctor, paediatrician or the primary health centre. Common examples of the health problems that the counsellor may encounter are difficulty seeing or hearing, persistent aches and pains unrelated to emotional distress, and skin problems, such as acne, which often trouble adolescents. Reproductive and sexual health is an important and delicate health issue during adolescence. Some girls may suffer from heavy vaginal discharge and/or menstrual problems. Some counsellors have the training and skills to address a few of these concerns, but it is usually a good idea to refer the young woman to a gynaecologist. If a young woman is involved in a sexual relationship and has exposed herself to the risk of pregnancy, a referral is essential to confirm whether she is pregnant and to make a plan for antenatal care. In the case of both males and females who are sexually active, the counsellor needs to bear in mind the possibility of sexually transmitted infections. These youth may complain of urinary or genital problems, such as pain while passing urine, and will require a medical referral.

When the young person may have a serious mental disorder or disability: Features suggestive of a serious mental disorder or disability (*see* Chapter 2) require a referral to a mental health professional for further assessment, diagnosis and treatment. Some prominent features of a serious mental disorder or disability are hallucinations, bizarre beliefs or delusions, odd behaviour(s) such as talking to oneself or repeated hand-washing, severe social withdrawal or isolation, severe anxiety leading to refusal to attend school, drug abuse and/or serious academic difficulties.

When the counselling has not produced the desired changes or the problem worsens: As described earlier, a core component of case management is monitoring the progress of the youth's condition. If there is no improvement despite the best efforts of the counsellor, or if the problem(s) worsens, the young person should be referred to a mental health professional.

Other situations which may require a referral:

- When a young person is confused about the choice of career or vocation, a referral to a career guidance or vocational counsellor may be useful.
- When a young person is unable to cope with her studies due to a learning disability (*see* Chapter 2), the counsellor should refer her for a psychoeducational assessment (Box 4.7) to possibly qualify her for access to additional resources, e.g. for participation in a resource room in the school.
- If the counselling relationship becomes untenable, e.g. because the youth has developed an unhealthy affection for the counsellor. In such cases, the counsellor could refer the youth to another counsellor, after consulting with her supervisor.
- A referral can be useful if the young person does not believe in the treatment offered. For example, she may feel that talking about her problems to a counsellor does not help. In such cases, a counsellor could suggest that the young person meet her supervisor with a view to clarifying the need for counselling.

It is good practice to obtain the youth's consent before approaching her parents or caregivers to discuss the referral. However, in some situations, the counsellor may need to approach the parents without obtaining the youth's consent (*see* Chapter 7).

BOX 4.7: ASSESSMENTS CONDUCTED BY SPECIALISTS

Developmental assessment: This is performed by a paediatrician or child development professional. A paediatrician should routinely perform developmental monitoring to determine whether a child or youth is maintaining and achieving her age-appropriate developmental milestones. When the paediatrician notices problems or delays, a thorough developmental assessment is needed. This comprehensive evaluation assesses the youth's physical, intellectual, language, emotional and social development. In addition, it includes an examination for neurological problems, and either screening or diagnostic questionnaires for mental health disorders and developmental disabilities.

Psychoeducational testing: Such testing is usually performed by a clinical or educational psychologist. It evaluates the youth's current intellectual and educational abilities. The assessment includes gaining an understanding of the individual's background, as well as her developmental and psychosocial histories (*see* Assessing the problem). The assessor utilizes a variety of tests. A final report is made on the basis of the scores achieved on specific tests, as well as their interpretation. The tests may include evaluations of intellectual functioning (IQ tests), social and adaptive achievements (such as self-help skills) and scholastic difficulties. The final report is of particular use to the special educator, counsellor and teachers as it relates to the youth's intellectual and educational strengths and difficulties.

Hearing and visual assessments: These are recommended in order to rule out sensory impairments or disabilities. Mild hearing and visual impairment can have an impact on a child's performance at school and result in behavioural problems in the classroom. For example, the child can become inattentive and easily distracted due to an inability to see the blackboard or hear the lesson. Both assessments are conducted by specialists

(continued)

BOX 4.7: ASSESSMENTS CONDUCTED BY SPECIALISTS (*continued*)

(audiologists for hearing and ophthalmologists for vision), although many schools conduct an annual health screening to identify these impairments.

Special educational needs assessment: Such assessments are conducted by a special educator, who is a teacher specifically trained to work with individuals with developmental disabilities. Incorporating information from the student's developmental and psychoeducational reports, the special educator works directly with the student to determine her specific learning capabilities and styles. With the help of the knowledge that she has gained, she advises the teachers on how to modify the curriculum to suit the individual's needs and how to design an individualized education programme (IEP) (*see* Chapter 2). She may work as part of a team with the mainstream classroom teacher and specialized therapists to implement the student's IEP. Some special educators work in a specialized school setting (*see* Chapter 2).

Aptitude testing: These assessments are usually performed and interpreted by psychologists. They determine the individual's strengths, weakness, learning styles and areas of interest, and then match these with vocation and career choices.

Therapists: Therapists are specialists in rehabilitation who work across a range of disabilities. Speech and language therapists help individuals with communication disorders, such as a language delay or autism. Physiotherapists work with individuals with a physical disability in order to help them achieve or regain a range of functional movements and reduce the impact of impairments which result from the disability. Occupational therapists evaluate the individual's needs in the school and home settings, and help those with a disability to achieve independence in their 'functional skills' (activities of daily living).

Where to refer

Every counsellor must prepare and keep at hand a list of the names and contact numbers of the following professionals, centres, services, organizations and authorities in the neighbourhood of the school:

- Paediatricians
- Psychiatrists
- Educational and clinical psychologists
- Disability professionals and centres, e.g. speech therapists
- Family doctors and primary health care clinics
- Ophthalmologists
- Ear, nose and throat doctors
- Gynaecologists
- Dermatologists (skin specialists)
- Child or family guidance centres
- Vocational/career guidance counsellors
- Social workers
- Special Juvenile Police Unit (SJPU) or equivalent protective authority
- Childline 1098 (a helpline for children) (*see* Chapter 7)
- Child rights organizations

It is a good idea for the counsellor to contact each of these referral resources to introduce herself and inform them about the services she provides in the school, as well as the possibility that she may occasionally refer a youth. In addition, the counsellor should request that, should she make a referral, the referral resource provide her with a report on the young person's condition and the recommended treatment. The counsellor should aim to build a collaborative relationship with the professional to whom she refers the family/child. In situations where the counsellor is unable to locate local referral resources, the next best option is to refer the youth to the nearest professional available, even though this may involve a longer journey for the family. In such instances, the counsellor should try to facilitate the process of the youth obtaining appropriate leave from the school so that the family can complete the referral.

How to refer

Once the counsellor has decided that a referral is needed, she must convey this to the young person. The suggestion, as well as the reasons for it, should be discussed with the young person and, where appropriate (*see below*, final paragraph of this section), with the family. The counsellor might suggest a referral to the youth in the following way:

'After talking to you during the last session/s and understanding more about your problem, I think it would be helpful for you to meet Dr X (name of health professional), who could add to our understanding of your problems because of her specialized training. I will need to speak to your parents and ask them to take you to Dr X. If Dr X decides that there is a better way to help you overcome your difficulties than coming to me for counselling, she will make recommendations to you and your family. I am always available here in the school to clarify what Dr X has told you and your family, and will be here for you if you need my help.'

When a referral is necessary, it is usually best to talk to the parents or caregivers separately from the youth to explain the reason the referral has been recommended (and to provide the contact information for the referral) since parents often feel more comfortable asking questions about the purpose of the referral in the child's absence. The counsellor needs to be aware that many parents and young people are very anxious about a referral, especially because it may mean facing an outcome that is stigmatizing, e.g. the diagnosis of an intellectual disability. For this reason, the counsellor must be extremely sensitive while explaining why the referral has been suggested. As a general rule, she should emphasize that the referral has been suggested to benefit the youth and to ensure that she receives appropriate care for her problem. The counsellor should not state the specific mental health problem she suspects, but should broadly describe some of its features (e.g. that the youth seems to be having great difficulty with social relationships, instead of telling the parents that she suspects that the youth may have autism).

It is good practice for the counsellor to write a referral note summarizing the case formulation and the specific reason for referral. Where possible, the counsellor should also telephone the referral resource to arrange an appointment for the youth.

In some cases, it may be necessary to make a referral without informing the family. Some examples of when this may need to be done are if the older adolescent has explicitly requested, with good reason, not to share the information she has disclosed with the parent/family; if a family member is sexually or physically harming the youth (*see* Chapter 7); and if an adolescent requires a sexual/reproductive health referral. The counsellor may suggest accompanying the youth to the referral agency in these rare circumstances.

Following-up after making the referral

Once the counsellor has made a referral, it is important for her to follow-up with the family, the youth and/or the referral source to confirm the outcome of the referral. The counsellor should make sure she learns about the recommendations both from the youth/family and from the referral including what diagnosis was made, whether the young person has been prescribed medicines and how the counsellor might be of help in the youth's continuing care.

Closure of counselling

When to close

The decision to close the counselling is made by the counsellor in consultation with the young person and, where appropriate, in consultation with the parent/caregiver. Closure should be well planned and approached with sensitivity. When the youth has received counselling over a long period of time, the original reasons for the counselling may have become less significant and possibly replaced by more recent issues. It is important for the counsellor to review the original issues and goals with the young person, determine the extent to which they have been addressed, discuss with the youth if recent issues require further counselling and explore the extent to which the counselling process has provided learning experiences to cope with her challenges.

In summary, the counsellor should prepare for closure of the counselling if:

- The young person reports a consistent improvement in her mental health problem, e.g. feeling less sad;
- The counsellor observes clear signs of progress, e.g. an improvement in social functioning;
- Significant others report progress, e.g. the teacher reports that the youth's academic performance has improved;
- The counsellor observes that the youth is able to adapt the counselling strategies she has learnt and utilize them across various situations.

The process of closure always begins with a discussion with the youth. The following are two examples of how the counsellor might introduce the discussion:

'We have met for eight sessions and you have been making good progress. I suggest we review our counselling plan and discuss what we wish to achieve in the remaining sessions. What are your thoughts about this?'

'After two more sessions, we will be closing our counselling work together, as we have discussed. I suggest we spend some time today discussing what you have learnt over the course of the counselling and how you can use your skills to deal with difficulties in the future. What are your thoughts about this?'

The young person may well have mixed feelings about bringing the counselling process to an end. On the one hand, she may feel more competent than earlier and relieved that the counselling is over; on the other, she may still have doubts about her ability to deal with real-life situations without the counsellor's help. Sometimes, the young person develops a strong attachment to the counsellor or has begun to depend on her to help her handle problems. Occasionally, the young person has additional concerns which she has not felt comfortable discussing but which she would benefit from discussing. The counsellor should facilitate an open discussion of the youth's feelings about closure, how she might cope with these feelings and if she needs an opportunity to discuss any additional concerns she may have (*see below*, Formats for closure). The counsellor can also share her own thoughts about the counselling relationship and the youth's progress. For example, she can say, ***'I am happy with the progress that you have made and we have worked well together'; 'It has been rewarding working together with you'; 'I admire***

the courage with which you are facing the situations in your life'; or, ***'If there are additional concerns that you have, we can make a plan to extend the counselling.'***

Types of Closure

Sometimes closure is premature and unplanned, e.g. if the young person suddenly changes school or abruptly decides to discontinue counselling. If the young person moves or there is a change of school, the counsellor could make a referral to the counsellor in the new school. Before doing this, she must seek the permission of the youth and, if appropriate, involve the family in obtaining this permission. However, if the premature closure is due to dissatisfaction with the counsellor or the progress of counselling, the counsellor should reflect on the reasons for this and take appropriate steps, where possible (Box 4.8).

When the closure is planned, a number of formats may be used for the closure, as described below.

- **Fixed closure:** When the treatment is being planned, the counsellor and the young person agree on a contract specifying the number of sessions and time-frame, e.g. weekly sessions over two months, and the focus of the counselling. The advantage of this format is that the clearly defined time-frame might motivate the youth to utilize the sessions. The disadvantage is that it might be difficult to adjust the counselling plan if new problems emerge or become evident during the counselling, or if the desired goals are not achieved within the preplanned time-frame.
- **Open closure:** In this format, the counselling concludes when the counsellor and the young person agree that sufficient progress has been made in attaining the youth's significant goals. According to this format, the number of sessions is not specified in advance. While this approach has the advantage of flexibility, some young people may feel that it does not allow them to clearly anticipate the length of counselling.

In practice, combinations of fixed and open closure can be used. For example, a fixed closure plan can be decided upon at the outset, but then

BOX 4.8: 'DROPPING OUT' OF COUNSELLING

Dropping out, or premature discontinuation of counselling, is unfortunately not an uncommon occurrence. The following are some warning signs of the possibility of a young person dropping out:

- There is a lack of agreement between the counsellor and youth about the nature of the problem.
- The youth has expressed frequent doubts about the usefulness of the counselling.
- The youth has displayed uncooperative or hostile attitudes during the counselling process.
- The youth denies that there is any problem at all.
- The youth misses appointments without informing the counsellor in advance.
- The youth does not respond to the counsellor's requests suggesting a new appointment.
- The youth does not get in touch with the counsellor for a period of time.

A young person could drop out of counselling for a number of reasons. The common ones are as follows:

- The youth has been referred to the counsellor against her wishes.
- The youth feels better due to relief of symptoms.
- The counselling has not resulted in the degree of improvement that was expected by the parent/young person.
- There is a mismatch between the counselling offered and what the youth expects or needs.
- There is peer pressure on the youth to not 'listen' to the counsellor.
- The youth fears being stigmatized by friends for visiting a counsellor.
- The youth does not want to listen to an 'adult', who she feels is 'telling' her how she should lead her life.

(continued)

BOX 4.8: 'DROPPING OUT' OF COUNSELLING (*continued*)

- The youth feels hopeless due to the number of problems she is facing or due to a mental health problem.
- The youth's family is putting pressure on her to discontinue.
- The counsellor does not adequately explain to the youth the nature of the problem she is suffering from and/or the counselling plan.

The counsellor should always reflect on the possible reasons a youth has discontinued counselling. She should use it as an opportunity to examine her own skills realistically and to discuss the development of skills with a supervisor, if required. It is important for the counsellor to develop the skill of self-evaluation, rather than engaging in self-criticism (*see* Chapter 8). The counsellor should also remember that people do drop out of counselling and this can be due to factors beyond her control. She can prepare herself for the possibility of a youth dropping out and take remedial action, where feasible, by being alert to the warning signs (*see above*).

It is important for the counsellor to remember that she should never become angry with the youth for dropping out of counselling, and she should always keep her door open should the youth wish to renew contact.

modified if unexpected issues arise during counselling. Some counsellors may choose to close the counselling gradually, e.g. from weekly meetings to fortnightly or monthly meetings. Others may prefer to continue at a regular pace and close the counselling when the youth and counsellor feel that the time is right. It can also be helpful, depending on the youth's problems, if the counsellor invites her for a meeting a few months after the closure (a 'booster session') to assess how she is faring, as well as to support and motivate her to work through any difficulties which she is currently facing by applying the skills she learnt during counselling. Informal reviews can offer opportunities for continuing contact outside

the formal counselling process to support the young person, make a quick assessment of her progress or gradually transform the relationship between the youth and counsellor from a formal professional relationship to a less formal one. Short meetings at the playground or technologies like e-mail can be used for this purpose. However, the counsellor should keep in mind that the boundaries between the counsellor and young person must always be respected, even after the formal counselling is over (*see* Chapter 7).

When closing the counselling, the counsellor must say goodbye in a realistic and friendly way, and in a manner which is appropriate to the counselling relationship. For example, she might say:

'We have been working together on your problems for four months and I think you have made great progress. As we discussed before, this is our last session and I want to thank you for having been punctual for our appointments and making the effort to help yourself. I hope you will continue to enjoy good health, but also remember that you can drop in to see me any time you would like to.'

If the closure is not well planned and well executed, the influence that the counselling has had on the young person and the motivation to maintain her skills may be weakened. As a result, she may leave feeling dissatisfied, rejected or inadequate.

How to close

A purpose of the closing evaluation with the youth is to review with the youth what she has learnt during the counselling and the resources which she needs to optimize her functioning. The areas which should be addressed include:

- The problem areas that troubled the youth when she came for counselling and how these have been addressed;
- The goals of counselling and the extent to which they have been achieved;
- The effective coping skills she has learnt over the course of counselling;
- The supportive resources the youth can continue to access.

The following are some of the key considerations the counsellor needs to bear in mind when preparing for closure:

- What is the youth's opinion about closure? Does she see it as a positive step? Does she feel that it is the right time for closure?
- How will closure affect the young person? Is there any indication that she may react negatively?
- Does the young person have support from her parents/teachers/ friends to deal with difficult situations?
- Is there evidence that she can use the skills she has learnt during counselling in coping with new difficulties?

Additional purposes of the closing evaluation for the youth are to strengthen the youth's confidence by identifying the new abilities she has learnt to deal with her problems, and to discuss with her how she is now in a better position to cope with the problems she encounters in herself and the environment. As for the counsellor, the closing evaluation is an opportunity for the counsellor to reflect on what went according to plan and what did not, and how to improve her own counselling skills, if indicated (*see* Chapter 8 and the Generic Case Management Diagram on page 87).

CHAPTER 5

Counselling skills

This chapter covers the eight core counselling skills that an effective counsellor makes use of throughout the process of case management (*see* Chapter 4). Each of these skills is described and then illustrated in the final section of the chapter (*see* A session transcript to illustrate core counselling skills). The eight core counselling skills are as follows:

- Attending behaviour
- Interviewing skills
- Observation skills
- Reflective listening
- Giving information
- Working with resistance
- Supporting self-efficacy
- Interviewing and counselling approaches for the youth who is less verbal

Attending behaviour

The counsellor's body language should indicate that she is listening to the young person and interested in helping him with his concerns and problems, i.e. she is giving the youth her undivided attention. An example of very poor attending behaviour is when a counsellor constantly checks her watch or answers calls on her mobile phone during the session. Attending behaviour facilitates the youth's engagement in the counselling process.

Attending behaviours include the following:

A welcoming stance: The counsellor should acknowledge the effort that the youth has made to attend the counselling session. For example, she should warmly welcome and guide the youth into the counselling room, introduce herself and make positive remarks about the fact that the youth has come to see her.

Good eye contact: The counsellor should maintain adequate eye contact with the young person, without making him uncomfortable. She should do so even if the young person has his eyes averted. However, determining the degree of eye contact that would be the most suitable with a particular youth is an art in itself. It is important to keep in mind factors relating to culture, gender and age. For example, in a very traditional setting, a male counsellor may need to modify the amount of eye contact he makes with adolescent female students.

Positioning: This is a very important part of building rapport in the counselling setting. Asking the youth to sit across a desk and staring into his face can result in discomfort for both the counsellor and the youth. However, placing a chair in such a way that the counsellor and youth are on the two ends of an 'L' allows both persons to feel that they can look away easily, if need be, without actively turning their heads. A low table can be placed near the two chairs, especially to provide the youth with an opportunity to express himself through drawing. For younger age groups, smaller chairs should be available both for the counsellor and child.

Attentive body language: The counsellor should use appropriate and encouraging gestures or facial expressions in response to what the youth is saying. The way the counsellor sits should convey that she is

listening attentively. For example, she could lean forward towards the youth (while keeping a professional distance).

Verbal and non-verbal behaviours ('encouragers'): The verbal and non-verbal behaviours of the counsellor should imply interest and encourage the youth to keep talking. For example, the counsellor could nod her head or make encouraging sounds such as 'uh-huh' in response to what the youth is saying.

Tone of voice: The counsellor's tone should be gentle and clear. She should modulate her tone to indicate empathy for the youth.

INTERVIEWING SKILLS

Interviewing skills are of critical importance in helping the counsellor obtain relevant information and in helping the youth clarify his problem. The following three types of questions can be used when interviewing a youth:

Closed questions: These invite a specific answer (typically 'yes' or 'no') and are typically aimed at seeking specific information. Some examples are, 'Are you comfortable?' and, 'How old are you?'

Open-ended questions: These encourage the youth to talk and provide him with the opportunity to speak openly. An example is, 'Could you tell me something about...?' The first word of an open-ended question often elicits certain types of responses. Questions starting with 'what' bring out facts; those starting with 'how' elicit information on feelings; and those starting with 'why' shed light on reasons. Often when a counsellor asks open-ended questions, the youth ends up speaking more than the counsellor, a sign that the session is going well. Open-ended questions can be used both to gently steer the session in a particular direction and to encourage the youth to elaborate on something which the counsellor believes is important to explore.

Probing questions: These can be used if the youth's answers are very brief, and the counsellor would like to encourage him to express himself and provide more information. An example is, 'Can you tell me a little bit more about that?'

Some general rules which the counsellor should follow in interviewing youth are:

- Use open-ended questions as far as possible in order to encourage the youth to talk and to avoid the pitfall of the counsellor doing most of the talking.
- Ask questions in a neutral, non-judgemental way that does not hint at the kind of answer you expect.
- Display good attending behaviours while asking questions.
- Ask one question at a time and guide the conversation with further questions based on the answer.
- Use words and concepts that are appropriate to the person's age.
- Avoid long sentences.

Important examples of questioning styles which should be avoided are as follows:

- *Bombardment/grilling:* 'Where were you yesterday? Weren't you supposed to be here for this session after lunch—I didn't know you had a class at that time?' Too many probing questions put the youth on the defensive.
- *A series of questions:* 'Tell me about your family. What does your father do? Your mother? Do you have a good relationship with them?' A question that is long or has too many parts can confuse the youth and make it difficult for him to think clearly or provide an appropriate answer.
- *Questions that make a statement:* 'Don't you think it would be helpful if you studied more?' Such questions make the counsellor's view obvious and can put the youth off.
- *Confrontational 'why' questions:* 'Why did you lie to me in the last session?' Such questions, if not put sensitively, can cause discomfort.

Observation Skills

Observing the youth and noting behaviours help the counsellor understand how the youth is feeling. Observing is a skill and, like all skills, needs to be practised and developed.

Observation should focus on the following three areas:

The youth's non-verbal behaviour: This consists of eye contact and body language. The counsellor may note, for example, that the youth breaks eye contact or shifts his gaze during periods of emotional distress. If the youth leans forward (body language), it may indicate that he is interested in what the counsellor is saying or what he himself is expressing, while if he folds his arms and looks away, it may indicate the opposite. Facial clues, such as furrowing of the brow, tightening of the lips and blushing, may indicate emotional reactions to what is being discussed. Large body movements, such as shifting his body in the chair, may indicate shifts in the youth's reactions or thoughts, or a reaction to a change in topic. For example, a young person who had been communicating well may suddenly seem tense, e.g. his body posture becoming rigid, when a sensitive topic is introduced.

The youth's verbal behaviour: If the youth changes the subject or refuses to answer a question, it may indicate that the topic is emotionally difficult for him. The counsellor should observe the quality of the youth's speech (its tone and volume) because it usually indicates something about what he is feeling. For example, a person who speaks loudly and rapidly may be angry.

Discrepancies: A discrepancy may be a statement that contains opposite ideas, such as, 'My father is perfect, but he doesn't respect me,' or a difference between what is said and what is done, e.g. the youth may say he is very concerned about his studies but skips classes. Another type of discrepancy is a difference between the youth's statement and the behaviour that accompanies it. For example, he might say, 'I really don't have any problem making friends' in a quiet tone and with an averted gaze. Discrepancies may indicate emotionally difficult issues and should prompt the counsellor to probe gently with an appropriate question. In order to encourage the youth to express more, she can highlight the discrepancy with a remark such as, 'I am sure that your father is perfect in many ways, except sometimes you feel that he does not respect you. Can you tell me why you feel this way?'

REFLECTIVE LISTENING

Reflective listening helps the youth feel that the counsellor has 'empathy', i.e. an accurate understanding and appreciation, for his experience. When the youth is convinced that the counsellor empathizes with him, he will feel that the counsellor is 'in his shoes'. Empathy is communicated through reflective listening. This entails responding to the youth using his own words, as well as the meanings and/or feelings these convey, in the form of a statement. These statements should be made in a warm, accepting and non-judgemental manner. They should be characterized by humility since the counsellor can never be certain that her understanding of the situation is entirely correct. While conveying her understanding of the meanings or feelings underlying the youth's words, the counsellor should avoid interpretations of the youth's hidden motives or make suggestions of the possible causes for his behaviours. For example, in the case of a student who is not attending class because a teacher has mocked him publicly for his performance in a test, the counsellor should point to the fact that the student is angry but should wait for the youth to specify why he is angry. The counsellor might ask, 'From what you have told me, it seems you are missing your classes because you are angry. Is that right?' Empathic statements by the counsellor are recognized and felt to be true by the youth. Interpretations, in contrast, may be perceived as coming from outside the youth's perspective and he either cannot immediately recognize them as true or false, or feels they are intrusive or unsettling. An example of an interpretation in the situation described above is, 'It seems that you are angry because the teacher made you feel belittled.' Drawing such a conclusion may offend or not suit the youth.

The techniques the counsellor can use for reflective listening include the following:

Clarifying: A counsellor using this technique refines and reflects what the youth has said to check on the accuracy of what she has heard. Clarifying can prompt the young person to talk in greater detail about issues that concern him and guides the counselling process towards a discussion of these issues. This technique also focuses overly talkative young people on the core issues that need to be addressed. An example of clarifying is: 'So let me try and understand what you just said; you are worried that you will not be chosen for the cricket team and that this will disappoint your parents.'

Paraphrasing: This is an extension of clarifying, in that the aim is to go beyond simply checking the accuracy of what has been said to providing a statement which indicates that the counsellor has understood the significance of the young person's words. Paraphrasing involves the use of a combination of new words along with words that the youth has used. This technique can be very useful for exploring the youth's feelings and laying the foundation for further action. Phrases which may be useful while employing this technique include: 'You appear to be saying...'; 'You appear to be unhappy about...'; 'It seems that you became angry when...'; and, 'It looks like you felt happy about....'

Reflecting: This technique entails reflecting back to the youth the feelings he may have expressed verbally and non-verbally during the counselling session. Reflecting allows the counsellor to clarify whether she has misinterpreted something. For example if a youth looks angry during a session, the counsellor may reflect, 'It appears that you are angry with me'; the youth may then clarify that he is angry with his class teacher and not with the counsellor, or confirm that he is angry with her.

Summarizing: This brings together the thoughts, feelings or concerns that the youth has expressed, and often includes the counsellor's understanding of how these fit together. Summarizing can help the counsellor ensure that she is understanding the youth's situation accurately, helps the youth see the connections between the things he has been telling the counsellor and prepares the way for the counsellor to shift focus or move on to the next part of the counselling process. Summaries are especially useful when moving from one subject to another, or when the counsellor wants to make complex issues or statements clearer for the youth. It is important not to give an opinion during the process of summarizing, as young people are more willing to work together with the counsellor if they feel confident that their own agenda has been taken seriously and understood. An example of a summary is: 'I am trying to put together what you have said—that you have been having a difficult time in school since you moved to the area; that though you like cricket, it has been hard to get into the team; and that the curriculum in maths is proving a bit challenging. Would this be correct?'

Giving information

There are times when direct information may need to be provided to the youth. Some examples of when information needs to be provided are:

- If the youth asks a question which requires a factual answer, e.g. concerns about reproductive health;
- If the counsellor has the impression that the youth's problems are partly due to lack of awareness or knowledge, e.g. not understanding the dangers of tobacco use;
- If the youth has destructive or false beliefs, e.g. that he is responsible for his parents' marital problems.

The information given should be clear and appropriate to the person's age. It should not be coloured by value judgements. Some examples are, 'I would like to give you some information on keeping yourself safe and healthy,' and, 'Let me give you a few facts about how smoking affects our bodies.' Providing relevant information may help the youth think over his actions more effectively. Further, it may increase his coping capacity and help him prepare for situations that he creates or finds himself in. Providing information does not mean convincing, advising or imposing. Rather, information should be provided objectively, while at the same time respecting the youth's perspective. Providing information can improve the counselling relationship and build trust, since the youth can see that the counsellor clearly cares enough about him to help him understand his situation and problems better. Providing information may also satisfy the youth who is expecting a more directive counselling approach, although ideally information should be offered in a collaborative manner (as indicated in the examples above, where the counsellor is asking the youth if she would like to hear the information).

WORKING WITH RESISTANCE

One of the core counselling skills pertains to enhancing the youth's commitment to make the most of the counselling. Young people often have both positive and negative feelings about counselling. This is also referred to as 'ambivalence'. 'Resistance' is the term used to describe how a youth's negative feelings about counselling interfere with the counselling relationship. Rather than challenging or confronting a young person who displays resistance, the counsellor should seek to understand why he is uncomfortable about counselling and try to gain his cooperation.

The techniques for working with resistance include the following:

Double-sided reflection (working with mixed feelings about counselling): When the youth has expressed or acknowledged that he has both positive and negative feelings about the counselling process, the counsellor reflects this back to the youth (*see* Reflective listening). Generally, the counsellor starts by reflecting the youth's wish to remain the same and then contrasts this with the youth's wish to change. For example, the counsellor might say, 'On the one hand, I hear from you that it is fine with you that you are failing your exams and, on the other, I hear that you want to attend college.' Mixed feelings about an issue can also appear as a discrepancy in the youth's statements. For example, the youth may claim that he does not need to see the counsellor while admitting that he is concerned about the serious deterioration in his academic performance in the past year. The counsellor can make a remark on the discrepancy between the youth's statements in order to enhance his motivation to go through with the counselling process. For example, she can say, 'I hear from you that you do not have any hopes for the counselling, while you also say that you are concerned about your academic decline.'

Amplified reflection (exaggerating the negative feeling towards counselling): When the youth has expressed or acknowledged that he has only a negative attitude towards counselling, the counsellor exaggerates or intensifies what the young person has said. This often leads the youth to correct the distortion, which then may lead him to a more positive attitude towards counselling. For example, the youth may start out by insisting, 'I am not a "mental case" who needs counselling'; to which the counsellor might reply, 'You seem to think that only mentally ill people need counselling; is that true?'; to which the youth may reply, 'Well, not always.'

Reframing (providing a different perspective on counselling): The counsellor presents what the young person has already said from a different perspective. For example, if the youth says, 'Counselling is for idiots,' the counsellor responds, 'Actually, counselling is for smart people who, like yourself, can increase their ability to solve problems.' Reframing is an extension of paraphrasing (*see* Reflective listening).

Emphasizing personal choice and control (allowing the counselling process and outcome to be within the youth's control): The counsellor assures the youth in a sympathetic tone that any decision to enage with counselling is ultimately his and that the counsellor has no wish to take that choice away.

Shifting focus (distracting from difficult issues): The counsellor temporarily shifts attention away from an area of potential or actual disagreement to one where common ground can be found, e.g. the counsellor could suggest, 'Let's talk about how things are with your classmates instead.'

SUPPORTING SELF-EFFICACY

Self-efficacy refers to a youth's beliefs about how likely his efforts are to result in success. The nature of these beliefs is a key determinant of whether a youth can be engaged in counselling since a person who does not believe that he can succeed is unlikely to try very hard to continue with a task (in this case, the counselling process). Young people with mental health problems often anticipate that they will fail in everything they do and believe that their prospects of feeling better are dim. To try to alter the youth's negative view of his ability to solve problems, the counsellor should actively look for opportunities to point out and support his strengths. The counsellor can discuss the details of how the youth had successfully managed a specific problem in the past, as well as the details of how he is currently facing a problem. Similarly, in order to encourage the youth to believe that counselling can make him feel better, if the youth expresses any belief in his 'ability' to come for counselling, work with the counsellor and/or make changes, the counsellor should highlight these statements and ask him to elaborate. If, despite the counsellor's efforts, the youth remains pessimistic about being able to sustain a commitment to counselling, the counsellor should reframe (*see* Working with resistance) the youth's doubts and use a counselling strategy that promotes positive self-evaluation such as cognitive restructuring (*see* Chapter 6).

Two additional techniques that build self-efficacy are 'affirmation' and 'positive asset search'.

Affirmation: The counsellor expresses her sincere appreciation of the youth's efforts to cope with the challenges in his life and to participate in the counselling process. To convey this, the counsellor can make helpful statements such as the following:

- 'Well done for trying so hard.'
- 'It sounds like you have had a difficult week, but despite this you still managed to achieve some of the goals we had set.'
- 'I am pleased to see that you are not giving up!'

Positive asset search: The counsellor recognizes the youth's positive assets or strengths and reflects them back to him. For example, if the youth is good at drawing but has been faring poorly in his academic subjects, the counsellor might say, 'You have such a strong ability to notice details around you and to capture them in your drawings.'

COUNSELLING APPROACHES FOR THE YOUTH WHO IS LESS VERBAL

The counselling strategies (*see* Chapter 6) often rely upon the youth's ability to express himself verbally about his concerns and to be an active collaborator or partner in the counselling process. When working with an individual who is less verbal, younger or reluctant, or who has a developmental disability, the counsellor needs to be creative and flexible. She must encourage communication in a variety of ways that are enjoyable, interesting and non-threatening. The following are some techniques that can enhance the counselling relationship and the counsellor's communication with and understanding of such individuals. Of course, these techniques are also useful for verbal individuals.

Drawing: When the youth is unable or unwilling to describe his problem or identify his feeling(s), the counsellor can encourage him to draw a picture of anything he wishes, supplying him with paper and colour pencils. If he does not have time to complete the picture during the session, he can take it up again during the next session if he wants. As he draws, and also once the drawing is completed, the counsellor can ask him about the drawing. Through this discussion, the counsellor learns about the youth's interests and concerns. The counsellor can then describe what she sees in the drawing, with a view to encouraging

the youth to contribute. For example, she can say to the youth, 'I see a picture of a house with many people around it. I wonder who these people are? Can you tell me?' The counsellor should not try to 'interpret' (*see* Reflective listening) the drawing in case her understanding of the drawing is wrong; the drawing should instead be seen as an opportunity for the youth to express himself.

Using toys or other materials for play and self-expression: Depending on his age, preferences and abilities, the young person will have an interest in particular play materials. These might include dolls, figures or other objects that can be used to represent people; pictures of facial expressions through which the person identifies feelings; and blocks or simple building materials that may be used to represent the youth's home, playground or town. As with drawing, the counsellor should provide an opportunity to use play materials in order to encourage self-expression, rather than with the aim of 'interpreting' the meaning of the play. The counsellor can offer to participate, asking, for example, 'Can I join in your play?' However, she must not interfere in the youth's self-expression. If the youth is playing with figures, the counsellor can encourage (not pressure) him to express himself by asking him what the puppets are doing or thinking about, or by pretending the dolls can speak and encouraging the youth to have his doll speak.

Developing a vocabulary for feelings: This might take the form of

creating, together with the youth, a 'personal dictionary' of the words that match his feelings. The dictionary can also be an illustrated one. For example, in the case of a youth who appears sad, the counsellor can encourage the youth to write the word 'sad' together with his definition of the word and to draw a picture of a sad face next to it. As the counselling proceeds, the youth can add to the dictionary.

Making up a story about a young person with a similar problem: The counsellor can make up a simple story about a young person with a problem similar to the youth's and describe how it made that young person feel and behave. Although the facts and problems described in the story are very similar to those the youth faces, taking this 'step away' from a direct discussion of his situation serves as a layer of protection for him, setting the stage for a more comfortable talk. For example, the youth may be unpopular in his school and has been referred to the counsellor for skipping school because he has been excluded by his peers. The counsellor tells him that she 'knows' about a (fictional) boy who 'prefers to stay home in his village because he is popular with the younger children there and enjoys being their leader, rather than go to school'. The counsellor talks about 'how good this (fictional) boy feels being looked up to by the younger children and how much he wishes he could experience this at school too'. The counsellor then asks the young person how this (fictional) boy might transfer his success in the village to the school setting. The youth benefits from this discussion because it mirrors his problem without tackling it head on, which could be too upsetting for him.

Discussion of the youth's interests and activities: Many young people communicate through actions or descriptions of actions or events rather than through a direct discussion of their feelings or problems. A youth may respond to questions about what he does rather than how he feels or what problems he has. For example, the counsellor might ask, 'What did you do with your family over the holidays?' rather than asking if any problems arose with the family members during the holidays.

Using metaphors to present difficult concepts: The counsellor can help young people understand their feelings and actions through the use of metaphors and visual images that interest them and that they can relate to. For example, a youth who takes impulsive aggressive actions may be better able to participate in a discussion about the buildup of his anger if the counsellor first talks to him about the way lava builds up in a volcano before finally bursting out. The youth may enjoy this discussion and benefit from it since it is more exciting and imaginative than a direct discussion about anger. The counsellor could use blackboards or flip charts with the youth.

Story-telling: Young people respond to stories which have themes and characters they can relate to. The stories and images should be tailored to the age of the young person and build upon his interests. For example, a 6-year-old boy who fears the dark may be interested in a fantasy hero, such as Superman, who overcomes dangers. The youth can be encouraged to make up his own fantasy hero whose power enables him to engage in all sorts of activities. The youth will find this exciting and interesting, and the counsellor can help him gradually understand that, like the superhero, he too can conquer his fears.

Cartoons, 'thought bubbles' and unfinished sentences: These can be an enjoyable and useful means of accessing a youth's thoughts and feelings. They can also be used to generate alternative ways of thinking or to highlight the fact that different people may have a range of thoughts about a particular event, e.g. if a youth is having arguments with a classmate, the counsellor could draw two figures and ask the youth to make a bubble above each figure and fill in what each one is thinking about and saying to the other.

Guessing aloud what the youth might be thinking: If the counsellor knows something about what the youth enjoys and/or is concerned about, she might tactfully and playfully make a remark on what the youth might be wishing, feeling or thinking. For example, she could venture, 'Let me guess what you like to do... eat ice cream with your friends?' or, 'Let me guess what you don't like to do... schoolwork which seems too hard?' This can be in the form of a game, e.g. asking the youth to wink or make a 'thumbs up' sign if the counsellor is right and wince or make a 'thumbs down' sign if she is wrong. Guessing aloud can become the basis for a discussion.

Application of core counselling skills

A session transcript to illustrate core counselling skills

Rita, a 10-year-old girl, has always been very lively and fun-loving. She is an average student. Recently, the teachers have noticed a change in her behaviour. She has become quiet, does not talk much to others and keeps to herself in the classroom. The quality of her homework has deteriorated and her grades have also fallen. Rita has started seeing the counsellor on the advice of her teacher. The counsellor has observed and interacted informally with Rita in the school setting on a number of occasions in the past. After the counsellor has welcomed her to the office and invited her to sit down, the interview begins.

Transcript of session	Technique
Counsellor: *'Good morning, Rita. You know me as the school counsellor. My name is Miss X. I want to thank you for taking time off from your school break to see me today.'*	Welcoming stance Affirmation
(Rita nods her head in agreement, but does not look at the counsellor.)	Observation
Counsellor: *'Rita, you are looking upset. You must be wondering why your class teacher suggested that you should meet with me.'*	Reflection (on observations) Open-ended question

Transcript of session	Technique
(Rita nods again, but says nothing.)	Observation
Counsellor: *'Rita, you have always been a lively person and all of us in the school have enjoyed your jokes and bright nature. You used to be very regular with your work and did well in your exams.'* *'But recently, it seems that things have changed. You have become very quiet, your homework is often incomplete and your grades have fallen.'* *'Looking at you now, I get a feeling that something is worrying you.'* *'Your teacher has suggested we speak today, but of course we will do so only if you are willing. Before I proceed, I want to assure you that whatever happens here will not go beyond these four walls.'* *'Would you like to talk about what has happened to bring about this change?'*	Positive asset Summarizing (the teacher's concerns) Observation Reflecting (an observation) Emphasizing personal choice Closed question
Rita: *'It's my mother. She has changed.'*	
Counsellor: *'Changed?'*	Encourager
Rita: *'Since my brother was born, she doesn't spend time with me. She doesn't love me anymore.'*	
Counsellor: *'You feel that your mother has stopped loving you since your brother was born.'*	Paraphrasing
(Rita starts crying. The counsellor pats her hand.)	Observation Reassuring body language
Counsellor: *'Could you tell me more about what makes you feel like this?'*	Open-ended question
Rita: *'She is just not interested in me anymore.'*	
Counsellor: *'Could you give me an example of something that has happened which makes you feel this way?'*	Open-ended question

Transcript of session	Technique
Rita: *'When I go back from school, she is feeding him. When I try to talk to her she just sends me off, saying I'll disturb him. All the time she is fussing over him.'*	
Counsellor: *'Sounds like she is very busy looking after your brother and you are lonely.'*	Paraphrasing
Rita: *'Yes, I get very angry with him* (her brother). *I hate him and feel like hitting him.'*	
Counsellor: *'You get so angry that you feel like hitting him, but you stop yourself, which uses a lot of self-control. I see a strong girl here.'*	Paraphrasing Positive asset search
(Rita smiles.)	
Counsellor: *'Rita, you've been talking about occasions when your mother doesn't spend time with you at all. Sounds like that little brother of yours keeps her very busy. Can you think of one instance in the last week when she spent time with you instead of your brother?'*	Summarizing
Rita: *'When he sleeps in the evening, she does sit with me and takes up lessons, but if he cries she goes to him. But daddy and I play in the evening.'*	
Counsellor: *'So daddy plays with you, which I imagine must be fun. But you still feel disappointed about mummy not having enough time for you.'*	Reflecting feelings and paraphrasing
Rita: *'Yes, but I guess she is very busy looking after him. Why do babies need so much of their mummy's time?'*	
Counsellor: *'Well Rita, babies really need their mothers for almost all their needs, even their need for food. You were once like that yourself! Every mother has to spend a lot of time looking after her baby.'*	Direct information-giving, but the counsellor gave this information only when Rita asked for it

Transcript of session	Technique
Counsellor: *'Rita, it seems that you have been upset since your brother was born because your mother spends less time with you. As a counsellor, I am trained to work with you to help you feel better about your situation.'*	Summarizing
(Rita looks down again, averting eye contact.) Rita: *'What good will it do talking to you? The problem is really my brother.'*	Observation (possibly indicating that Rita may not have faith in counselling)
Counsellor: *'So, your brother is the problem and if he disappeared from your life, everything would be okay again?'*	Amplified reflection
(Rita appears embarrassed by this reflection.) Rita: *'I know I need help, but just don't know what to do.'*	
Counsellor: *'You have been feeling sad since your brother was born, but at the same time, you know that he is a baby who needs your mother.'*	Summarizing
(Rita nods.)	
Counsellor: *'Perhaps we can work together through counselling to help you make sense of this situation and become the lively and happy person you used to be?'*	Affirmation Emphasizing personal choice

CHAPTER 6

COUNSELLING STRATEGIES, SETTINGS AND FORMATS

The first section of this chapter details the counselling strategies which the counsellor can choose to help the youth with his distress, disorder or disability. The counsellor skills, as well as the elements of the counselling relationship and the ethical standards described elsewhere in this casebook should always be kept in mind while implementing these strategies. The second section of this chapter describes supportive interventions which, in addition to counselling strategies, can help the youth recover. The final section of this chapter discusses the variety of settings and formats for delivering the strategies.

Counselling strategies: The strategies listed below are primarily aimed at improving the youth's mental health. Each strategy involves the use of specific techniques by the counsellor. In this casebook, we recommend the following nine strategies to address the mental health problems that young people may face:

- Youth psychoeducation
- Family psychoeducation
- Crisis counselling
- Problem-solving counselling
- Anger management counselling
- Social skills counselling
- Relaxation exercise
- Behavioural activation
- Cognitive restructuring.

Supportive interventions: These are interventions which support the youth in the school, home and community:

- Supportive interventions in the school
  ⇒ Consultation to benefit a specific youth

⇒ Consultation to improve the overall school atmosphere

- Supportive interventions in the home and the community.

Counselling settings and formats: This section describes the settings in which counselling can take place, e.g. at school or at home; and the formats in which it can occur, e.g. together with the family members or privately with the individual.

COUNSELLING STRATEGIES

Each strategy described in this chapter is organized as follows:

- Goals of the strategy
- The principles of the strategy
- Conditions for which the strategy is most useful
- Steps in delivering the strategy
- Challenges in the use of the strategy
- When the strategy should not be used.

YOUTH PSYCHOEDUCATION

Goals: The goals of youth psychoeducation are to engage the youth in the counselling process, help him gain a better understanding of his difficulty and emphasize the intended positive outcome of the counselling relationship and process. Youth psychoeducation also introduces the assessment process (explaining the purpose of the assessment phase to the youth) and concludes the assessment process (explaining the results of the assessment) (*see* Chapter 4). It continues throughout the counselling process, whenever the need arises.

Over the course of youth psychoeducation, the counsellor does the following:

- Explains the outcome of the assessment process to the youth in a clear and simple manner, building upon and respecting the youth's understanding of his problem. The counsellor avoids labelling the youth with a 'diagnosis', instead describing his difficulties to him in language that he can easily understand.

- Helps the youth recognize and understand how his problem affects his daily functioning.
- If necessary, explains why she requires additional information from his parents and/or teachers.
- Explains that the purpose of counselling is to support the youth's coping methods and help him improve upon them, and to work with him to develop new ways of coping with his problem.
- Explains the central features of the counselling relationship: confidentiality, predictability and working together.
- Explains the strategies and supportive interventions she has selected to address the youth's problem, as well as the counselling setting and format that will be the most effective.
- Makes an agreement with the youth on a counselling plan.

Principles: Youth psychoeducation is critical to engaging the youth in the counselling process and also has an important bearing on the outcome of the counselling. This is because it empowers the youth, making him an informed participant in the counselling process, creates a sense of purpose and optimism regarding the counselling and enhances his confidence in the counsellor as someone who is trained to help with problems. It is aimed at helping the youth gain a better understanding of his problem and the intended positive outcome that the counselling relationship and process hope to achieve.

When to use this strategy: Youth psychoeducation is the first step in all counselling. In addition, it is utilized to clarify any misunderstandings as the counselling proceeds. It must be tailored to the unique circumstances of the youth and the particular problem he presents with. While providing youth psychoeducation, the counsellor must take into account the youth's level of understanding, based on his developmental stage (*see* Chapter 1) and his unique difficulties (*see* Chapter 2).

Steps: This strategy consists of the following steps:

1. *Explaining the purpose of the assessment process.* During the first meeting with the youth, the counsellor explains the purpose of the assessment process.
2. *Obtaining consent.* If there is a need to gather additional information during the assessment process beyond that which has been obtained

during the individual interviews with the youth (*see* Chapter 4), the counsellor discusses the matter with the youth and obtains his consent for consulting other sources of information.

3. *Clarifying the assessment results.* Following the assessment, the counsellor communicates the results of the assessment tactfully, clearly and briefly. The goal at this stage is to clarify for the youth the problem he is experiencing. It is very important to avoid confusing or worrying the youth about his difficulty. The process of clarification includes the following:
   - The counsellor tries to understand from the youth's statements what he considers his problem to be. This shows respect for the youth's own opinion and is essential for ensuring that he is comfortable and engages with the counselling process. It will also help to involve him in the goal-setting task (*see* Chapter 4).
   - The counsellor incorporates the youth's language and definition of his problem into the explanation of what his problem is. She should avoid using a 'label', as far as possible, because this can give rise to discomfort or cause stigma. For example, the problem can be defined as 'getting cross all the time' instead of labelled as an 'oppositional defiant disorder'.
   - The counsellor focuses on the youth's strengths and coping capacities rather than his deficits.
   - The counsellor dispels any misunderstanding that the youth may have about the explanation.
4. *Instilling hope.* The counsellor instils hope that the counselling will help the youth with his daily life.
5. *Differentiating school lessons from counselling.* The counsellor distinguishes between school lessons and counselling, emphasizing that the counselling is intended to help the youth with the difficulties he is experiencing. However, if there are any academic difficulties, the counsellor explains that she will, with the youth's permission, work with his teachers and family to help him with these problems (*see* Supportive interventions).
6. *Explaining the unique features of counselling:*
   - Confidentiality (*see* Chapter 7)
   - Collaboration (*see* Chapter 3)

— Time-frame and the stages of counselling (*see* Chapters 3 and 4).

7. *Drawing up a counselling plan.* The counsellor and youth agree on a counselling plan (*see* Chapters 3 and 4), which includes the strategies and supportive interventions to be used, the counselling setting and format, the number of sessions and the expected duration of the counselling.
8. *Checking.* The counsellor checks with the youth to ascertain whether he has understood what has been explained to him thus far, answering questions and dispelling misconceptions.

Challenges in youth psychoeducation

- The youth may already be under stress due to the problem he is experiencing and giving him additional information about it may add to this stress. To avoid such a situation, the counsellor should carefully evaluate the youth's condition. In particular, she should try to ascertain how much the youth can understand comfortably and how much knowledge he can absorb in his current condition. Youth psychoeducation should be shaped to minimize the stress on the youth.
- The youth may have a tendency to feel criticized or guilty, i.e. he may blame himself for his problem. This challenge can be addressed by using normalizing statements, such as, 'Many young people have these difficulties,' and focusing on his strengths. It may be useful to emphasize that counselling is an aid, and not a punishment, and to praise him for participating in the counselling.
- In many instances, the level of motivation to change is low. The counsellor can deal with this by empathizing with the youth about his desire to have his life continue in the same way, while at the same time tapping his desire for a better life. For example, the counsellor might say, 'I can understand that avoiding your schoolmates may be the best solution you have found to avoid fights. But maybe there are some new ways we can think of together that might also work for you and even help to build friendships.'
- The youth may think that counselling is irrelevant to his life. In such cases, the counsellor can discuss an issue which the youth considers important and demonstrate how counselling can help in a practical and immediate way. For example, in the case of a person who is having

conflicts with a bossy older brother, the counsellor can introduce a role-play which includes ways of managing his brother that he has not thought of.

When not to use youth psychoeducation: Youth psychoeducation can be adapted to any circumstance. However, if a youth is suffering from a serious mental disorder and is unable to understand the information being given to him, youth psychoeducation should be deferred until he has stabilized (*see* Case Study 17).

FAMILY PSYCHOEDUCATION

Goals: The goals of family psychoeducation are to bring the family on board to assist their child in dealing with his problem and to facilitate his recovery. The counsellor can accomplish this in the following manner:

- Actively give the family practical knowledge regarding the nature of the child's mental health problem, with a description of the difficulties faced by their child and, where indicated, an appropriate diagnosis (if necessary, in collaboration with a specialist).
- Agree with the family on realistic goals for their child's recovery and a counselling plan.
- Instil hope and provide reassurance.
- Enhance the family's capability to help the child recover.
- Support the family's ability to make informed decisions on their child's care (*see* Chapter 4).
- Encourage the family to participate in helping their child adhere to counselling and any other interventions that have been recommended.
- Encourage the family to engage with specialized referral sources when needed, e.g. when the child may benefit from medication.
- Prepare the family members to continue to support their child to cope in a healthy manner following the closure of counselling.

Principles: Family-related factors which have a negative influence on a distressed child include the family having inadequate or incorrect information about their child's problems; the emotional/practical burdens that the child's problem imposes on the family; the family's inability to cope with their child's problems; negative attitudes/

behaviours among the family members towards their child; and negative family interactions. Family psychoeducation aims to address the influence of these factors.

When to use this strategy: Family psychoeducation is useful for most mental health problems because most children are embedded in a family structure which often contributes and responds to the child's problems. Educating families on their child's problems and on the resources and referrals available to address these problems increases their ability to help their child, and reduces the negative factors which may be contributing to the problems. It also reduces the families' sense of isolation or negative feelings associated with the problem. Family psychoeducation is particularly helpful for families which find their child's behaviour difficult to understand and are at a loss as to how to help. It can also serve a preventive function in the case of youth who are distressed, guiding the family members to follow specific steps to stabilize the family and the youth. For example, if there has been a recent loss or other change of circumstance in the family, the family can be advised on the need to comfort their child. Finally, in families in which the level of stress is severe and is affecting the child's functioning, e.g. if a parent is an alcoholic or abusive or the family is living in extreme poverty, family psychoeducation can help the family gain a clearer understanding of its own needs and facilitate its access to resources that could stabilize it.

Steps: This strategy has the following steps:

1. *Engaging the family.* All the elements of this first step are intended to establish a collaborative alliance between the counsellor and the family for the benefit of their child, and to alleviate any blame, guilt and anxiety that may be increasing the family's feelings of helplessness. These elements can be explored over a number of meetings, which may be attended by the child. The child may be excluded from the meetings if the counsellor feels that the discussion should take place without him. This could be the case, for example, if the discussion is going to focus on a serious family conflict, such as an impending divorce, or if the child's high-risk behaviours need to be discussed with his parents in private.

At these meetings, the counsellor should:

- — Ask the family members what they expect out of the counselling.
- — Identify the family's existing coping methods, especially those that work.
- — Elicit information on each family member's reaction to their child's problem and the behaviours that accompany it.
- — Explore each family member's understanding of their child's problem and its causes.
- — Make a brief evaluation of the strengths and difficulties of the family that have an impact on the child.
- — Describe clearly and simply to the family members how they could be involved in their child's recovery.
- — Describe clearly and simply to the family the role of the counsellor (and others involved in assisting the youth) in their child's recovery.

2. *Educating the family and creating a shared frame of reference within the child–family–counsellor alliance.* Education can be defined along a continuum, from simple suggestions and the provision of pamphlets to a comprehensive explanation of the child's problem and the various counselling strategies that can be implemented. This step includes:
   - — Giving a clear description of the behaviours that are symptoms of the child's problem and sharing the case formulation (*see* Chapter 4), adapting this suitably to the family's circumstances, i.e. not 'labelling' the child.
   - — Describing how the child feels with a view to increasing the family's understanding of and empathy for him, e.g. telling them that the child, who has academic difficulties, feels left out of his peer group in school and misguidedly acts like the class clown, thinking that this may make him popular.
   - — If the child's problem requires referral, explaining the rationale for this and suggesting the referral resource (*see* Chapter 4).
   - — Describing the expected outcomes of counselling and other interventions that have been recommended.
   - — Informing the family about the best techniques for the day-to-day management of their child and their interactions at home.
3. *Enhancing the family's positive coping skills.* The family's coping skills may be enhanced in the following ways:

— The counsellor should identify, together with the family, the destabilizing factors in the child's home life, and develop a plan to stabilize the home environment. For example, if a family employs authoritarian parenting practices, such as punishment and violence, the counsellor should explicitly address the matter and develop a plan with the family members to incorporate positive discipline practices.

— The counsellor must identify and assess difficulties in family communication, especially overly intense, distorted or negative communications and then use appropriate strategies (*see* Problem-solving counselling) to modify these patterns.

4. *Helping families address undesirable behaviours.* The following are some ways in which the counsellor can assist a family to address the undesirable behaviours of their child:

— The counsellor should guide the parents to make a list of the desirable behaviours that their child needs to learn. This can be a general list, which could include such behaviours as cooperation, honesty, kindness and responsibility.

— Similarly, the parents should be encouraged to make a list of the undesirable behaviours that their child exhibits. These behaviours need to be identified clearly. The parents may need help with this. The counsellor can help the parent identify when the behaviour occurs, how often, the settings which trigger it and how long the episodes last. Some common examples of undesirable behaviours include not listening to a parent's request, arguing, displaying aggression towards a sibling and throwing tantrums. This step may be skipped, e.g. when the counselling plan is focused on rewarding desirable behaviours rather than addressing undesirable behaviours, e.g. in the case of younger children.

— The counsellor should help the parents draw up a simple set of rules, which can be in the form of behaviour charts or contracts (*see* Appendix), for their child. These rules should focus on the immediate consequences of undesirable behaviours and the rewards for desirable behaviours.

— The parents should be advised to work with their child to make a list of rewards suitable to the child's age, as well as work out a plan for how these rewards will be earned. For example, the parent of a young child could decide, together with him, the privileges or rewards that he can 'earn' if he collects a predetermined number of stars, stickers or tokens. If the child collects a smaller number of stars, he may earn the reward of watching a television programme of his choice, while a larger number can be exchanged for a visit to the cinema. Older children can learn to save up for larger rewards (including money), e.g. through the collection of tokens such as buttons and counters.

— The counsellor should advise the parents to explain the rules clearly to their child. This can be done by role-playing with the parents, or the counsellor could facilitate a session between parents and their child. The parents should be advised to set positive goals and use an approach which is enjoyable for both themselves and their child. The counsellor could also discuss the possibility of using behaviour contracts (*see* Appendix) to give the child a clear picture of the behaviour that the parent wants him to display.

— The parents should be given guidance on how to help their child maintain desirable behaviours. The following are some simple tips the counsellor can give the child's parents:

  o Everyone involved, especially the child, must clearly understand the techniques being used to encourage desirable behaviours.
  o Keep the terms of a behaviour contract simple (*see* Appendix). The child may need to be given reminders of the rules (or the terms of the behaviour contract) from time to time.
  o To begin with, give small rewards quickly to help motivate the child to stick to the plan. For example, initially select behaviour which is easier to change.
  o Be patient. Be consistent for at least four weeks, however difficult this may be.
  o Take breaks to assess (with the counsellor, if necessary) whether the desirable behaviours are established and then revise the goals.
  o Praise behaviours which are desirable, however incidentally they occur.

5. *Expanding and strengthening the family's use of resources and social*

networks. The counsellor can work towards this in the following ways:

— Identify the resources that would be helpful to the youth, e.g. she could identify a social group for a youth with a learning disability to give him greater opportunities for socialization. She should then facilitate the utilization of such resources.

— Evaluate the family's social networks and their impact on the child's adjustment. For example, if the family is isolated because it has recently migrated, the counsellor can identify resources that will help the family integrate into their new community (*see* Supportive interventions in the home and the community).

Challenges in family psychoeducation

- Involving themselves in family psychoeducation may be a significant burden for the family members due to practical obstacles, such as transportation difficulties or competing demands, such as tending to other children in the family. This can be addressed by fixing meetings at times that suit the family members' schedules; offering to hold meetings with the family at a convenient location, such as the family home; meeting a family member individually; and emphasizing that meeting the counsellor can help ease the burden posed by their child's problem.
- Worries about the stigma associated with going to meet a counsellor can be eased by arranging meetings with the family after school hours or holding the meetings at the family's home. The counsellor may specifically discuss the stigma associated with counselling. It is also useful to instil the hope that the counselling can be helpful.
- Worries about the disclosure of private family matters to the counsellor can be addressed by emphasizing the principles of confidentiality underlying the counselling relationship (*see* Chapter 7).
- Family members may feel hopeless and convinced that nothing can change their child's problem. The counsellor should acknowledge that they have been trying hard to cope with their child's problems, and go on to add that she will work with them to consider alternative, new approaches that might have a positive impact on their child.
- If the youth does not want the counsellor to meet the family, the counsellor can explain to him how the principles of confidentiality

provide him with protection (*see* Chapter 7). The counsellor should also explain the specific reason for family psychoeducation, e.g. that she will work with the family members to help them and the youth communicate with one another in a more positive way.

- Explaining the youth's problems to him, his family and his teachers is a delicate task. During the assessment process, the counsellor may have gathered enough information to make a preliminary diagnosis of distress, disorder or a disability, e.g. attention deficit hyperactivity disorder or intellectual disability. In order to confirm the diagnosis, it is prudent for the counsellor to obtain feedback from a supervisor or mental health professional. In general, once a diagnosis has been made, it is important for the counsellor to describe the child's problems to him, his family and teachers so that they can understand his problems. Diagnostic terms must be used judiciously. At times, it is more beneficial to describe the problem than to use a diagnostic label. For example, the counsellor may feel that it will make the matter clearer and less stigmatizing for the family if she explains to the family that, 'Raj finds it difficult to concentrate on a given subject for a long period of time and tends to be distractible' rather than telling the family that their son is suffering from attention deficit hyperactivity disorder. On the other hand, providing the family with a diagnostic term can serve an important purpose when it underlines the fact that the child needs specialized care, such as in cases of serious mental disorders, or can help the family make use of certain benefits or services, such as specialized services for developmental disabilities.
- The family may take time to come to terms with their child's problem. This is especially common when the child has a disability that is not well known in the cultural setting. When there is a lack of familiarity with or discomfort regarding their child's problem, the counsellor will need to give family members time to understand the differences between their child and others and to accept these differences. Usually, when parents learn that their child has a disability, they experience a variety of emotions, such as shock, confusion, guilt, hopelessness, anger, unhappiness and disappointment. As they realize that the disability is permanent, they worry about their child's future. The counsellor should support the family members and encourage them

to seek continuing support as the child grows and develops. Some families may need to be referred to a mental health professional for further support.

When not to use family psychoeducation: Family psychoeducation is contraindicated if the youth does not give the counsellor permission to meet with his family despite all efforts to overcome his reluctance. It is also contraindicated when there is a possibility that family violence or physical/sexual abuse would increase if a family member were included in the counselling.

Crisis counselling

Goals: The goals of crisis counselling are as follows:

- To reduce the psychological distress caused to the youth by an emotionally stressful event. A youth is 'in crisis' when he experiences moderate to severe distress in response to such an event.
- To restore the youth's functioning to his pre-crisis level through brief supportive counselling aimed at minimizing the stress associated with the event and strengthening the youth's coping skills.

Principles: Stressful events, such as exposure to a natural disaster or an accident, and experiences that may trigger significant distress, such as the death of a loved one, may make a youth vulnerable to psychological difficulties and, in some cases, post-traumatic stress disorder (*see* Chapter 2). Crisis counselling is aimed at minimizing the adverse mental health consequences, such as feelings of depression and anxiety, following such events. The goals of crisis counselling are achieved by increasing the family's emotional support for the youth; enhancing the protective factors in his environment; fostering his adaptive coping mechanisms; and employing problem-solving counselling or other appropriate strategies and supportive interventions (*see* Supportive interventions). The duration of crisis counselling can vary, but it is generally intended to be a short-term supportive treatment, lasting up to two months after the event.

When to use this strategy: Crisis counselling should be used for youth experiencing moderate to extreme distress in response to a stressful event, e.g. a migration from home to a new location, an exposure to violence, a death of a loved one (Box 6.1).

Steps: This strategy consists of the following steps:

1. *Assessment.* The assessment ideally includes:
   — Understanding the nature of the event/experience and making a list of the stressors the youth was/is exposed to;
   — Getting an idea of the time frame (when the youth's distress began and how long it has continued);
   — Assessing the youth's level of functioning prior to the event/experience;
   — Assessing the youth's level of functioning immediately after and since the distressing event/experience;
   — Assessing the impact of the event/experience on the youth's developmental trajectory, such as a developmental regression (e.g. a previously toilet-trained child resumes bedwetting).

BOX 6.1: CRISIS COUNSELLING, APPLIED TO BEREAVEMENT

A 'bereaved youth' refers to a young person who has lost a loved one or a person he is close to. Crisis counselling specifically tailored to the bereaved youth is provided in the following manner:

Youth psychoeducation. This can help the youth understand the emotions he is experiencing and includes:

- Explaining to the youth that he may feel a wide range of emotions, including deep feelings of missing the person, sadness, anger, worry and guilt.
- Telling the youth that the death is not his fault.
- Telling the youth that it might help to talk about the loved one or close person who has died with a trusted person. For example, the youth may benefit from discussing with a friend the best times he has had with the departed person or the things he liked/misses most about the loved person. The counsellor may suggest that the youth might find it comforting to create

(*continued*)

BOX 6.1: CRISIS COUNSELLING, APPLIED TO BEREAVEMENT (*continued*)

a memory box of items that remind him of the loved one or making a diary or photo album.

- Explaining that it is not unusual to dream about the person or think he 'sees' the person.
- Emphasizing that while he will never forget this person, the pain of the loss will gradually diminish with time.

Family psychoeducation. The counsellor should guide the youth's family or caregivers, providing the following advice:

- To create a supportive and structured environment, which allows for open communication about the loss (e.g. by giving their child the opportunity to express feelings about his loss) and clearly dispels any feelings of guilt he may have.
- To increase their emotional support for their child through the use of physical (hug, smiles) and verbal (compliments) reassurance and through positive attention to their child's positive behaviours, qualities and ideas.
- To protect the child from being overwhelmed by their own distress. While they need not hide their distress from the child, they should reassure him that although they are sad now, they are strong and will overcome the adversity with time.
- To encourage them to provide their child with more opportunities to enhance his self-esteem. For example, they could support his emotional expression, enhance the quality of the family relationships and give him a chance to take part in activities he enjoys.
- To share memories, especially positive ones, of the departed person. The counsellor could also advise them to create memory boxes and albums; share feelings, including through symbolic communication, such as writing letters to the departed person; and participate in memorial activities together, such as visiting the grave.

2. *Family psychoeducation.* This focuses on enhancing the ability of the family to support their child after an extreme event or challenging life experience. It includes the following:
   - The family is encouraged to unite. Such unity helps to mobilize the family to support their child and protects him against the stress associated with an extreme event or distressing experience.
   - The family members are encouraged to set the child's mind at rest, and reassure him that they will provide safety and comfort and stay together.
   - The family is advised to listen to the child when he expresses his feelings. This includes giving him time to express himself and reassuring him, making sure not to minimize or ignore his feelings. The family members should be encouraged to allow the child to express emotions he may find difficult to handle, such as anger or grief. They should be advised to listen to their child's questions and answer them honestly, without volunteering more information than the child needs.
   - The counsellor should recommend normalization of the child's routine. If the family's routine has been disrupted, it should return to a routine as quickly as possible. This would include resuming his daily schedule, having the child attend school as usual and sending him to bed at the usual time. These routines signify a return to normal, provide the child with a sense of security and increase his confidence that the adults in the family are in control.
   - The family should be advised to control the child's exposure to 'reminders' of the extreme event. The reminders, for example, can be television news, conversations between adults and/or locations associated with the extreme event. They may also be highly specific, such as the colour of a dress worn by someone when the distressing event occurred.
3. *Youth psychoeducation.* The aim of this is to reduce the youth's psychological distress and includes the following:
   - The counsellor should listen to the youth's memory of the event or experience which is causing his distress, while not insisting that he tell his story if he is not comfortable doing so. Some young people generally speak about their feelings when they have a difficulty

and, for this type of youth, it might be helpful to ask him to recall the event because it is similar to what he would do naturally after a distressing event. Other youth, however, may tend not to talk about stressful events in their lives; in fact, they might try not to think about the event at all. There is nothing wrong with either style of coping. As a general rule, if a person shows signs of wanting to talk about the event, the counsellor should listen supportively, warmly, empathetically and genuinely; on the other hand, if it appears that talking about the event is uncomfortable or painful for the youth because it means re-experiencing unpleasant emotions, it is important not to force him to discuss it in detail, not to ask too many factual questions and not to express an opinion about what he should have or could have done.

— If the youth is comfortable discussing the event and his reactions to it, it is helpful to ascertain whether he has misinterpreted anything (e.g. he may believe that his actions caused his parent's death) and to give him the correct picture.

— If the youth is comfortable discussing the event and his reactions to it, it is useful to help him identify reminders which may cause him to re-experience the event, with the aim of reducing his exposure to these reminders. The counsellor should encourage him to communicate these thoughts and feelings to his parents and other trusted adults so that he can receive additional support when he is uncomfortable. The counsellor should listen for and address as needed themes of guilt, betrayal, revenge, helplessness, worry and sadness, since these emotions often accompany distressing events and experiences.

— The counsellor can help draw out the youth's natural resilience by providing reassurance, encouraging behaviours of positive coping and explaining that distress is normal under the circumstances. The counsellor can reassure him by emphasizing the hope that he will return to his normal way of functioning with time and support and by assisting the youth to seek social support, when necessary.

— The counsellor should recommend physical exercise, a healthy diet and regular sleep patterns.

— The counsellor should encourage social interactions and productive participation in tasks and in school.

— The use of alcohol and drugs, social isolation and excessive work should be discouraged.

Challenges in crisis counselling

- If the family situation exposes the youth to extreme events, such as family violence, and does not protect him, the counsellor should make an appropriate referral for his protection (*see* Chapter 7). Alternatively, the counsellor should creatively explore the possibility of finding other caregivers, such as a family member who lives nearby, is supportive and is able to take charge of the youth's care (*see* Supportive interventions in the home and the community).
- If the youth has developed post-traumatic stress disorder (*see* Chapter 2), he should be referred to a mental health professional for treatment for this disorder.
- If the youth suffered from a mental health disorder prior to experiencing a distressing event, some of his symptoms may arise from the pre-existing disorder. A thorough assessment should be made to find out how the youth functioned before the event/experience; and if the youth is suspected to have had a pre-existing disorder, it may be prudent to refer him to a mental health professional (*see* Chapter 4).

When to go beyond crisis counselling: If more than a reasonable period of time has passed since the loss, e.g. two months, and the youth continues to be distressed, the counsellor should maintain the supportive elements of crisis counselling while adding other useful strategies and supportive interventions suited to the particular problems of the youth. If at any point the youth has developed post-traumatic stress disorder in response to the extreme event, he should be referred to a mental health professional.

PROBLEM-SOLVING COUNSELLING

Goals: This strategy aims to increase the youth's capacity to solve problems by:

- Improving his ability to think through his problems and prioritize them.
- Increasing his ability to find solutions to his problems.

- Developing his capacity to evaluate potentially effective solutions, select the best options from among these and put them into practice.

Principles: Problem-solving counselling is intended to help the youth realize that there are links between how he feels and behaves and the difficulties he is encountering in his life. Problem-solving is a strategy that the youth can learn. This strategy includes breaking down difficulties into smaller, more manageable parts, and then learning how to generate and implement effective solutions. Problem-solving is based on the principle that difficulties in life can become overwhelming if one does not know how to reduce their impact on one's feelings and behaviours. In problem-solving counselling, the youth is taught skills to help him deal more effectively with the difficulties he encounters in life. These skills are empowering because they equip the youth to manage his difficulties himself and enable him to feel less helpless when faced with challenges. Youth are more likely to learn problem-solving skills if this learning experience is made enjoyable and the counsellor is supportive during the process; e.g. by brainstorming possible solutions in a playful way and using gentle humour in role-plays. The counsellor can praise the youth for the accomplishments he is making while going through the steps, empathize with him when he has any difficulty understanding the steps and be understanding about the problems the youth is facing.

When to use problem-solving counselling: This strategy is useful for most youth because it equips them with the practical skills necessary to manage real-life problems. It is especially useful for youth with emotional difficulties, such as depression, or behavioural problems, such as disruptive behaviours.

Steps: This strategy consists of the following steps:

1. *Explain the strategy.* The first step is to explain the strategy to the youth. The counsellor should tell him that there are links between life difficulties and mental health problems, and that mental health problems impair the ability to solve difficulties (Figure A). The counsellor should explain that problem-solving counselling will equip him to identify and prioritize difficulties, break them down into manageable parts and arrive at workable solutions. The counsellor may introduce the strategy in the following way: 'People with your

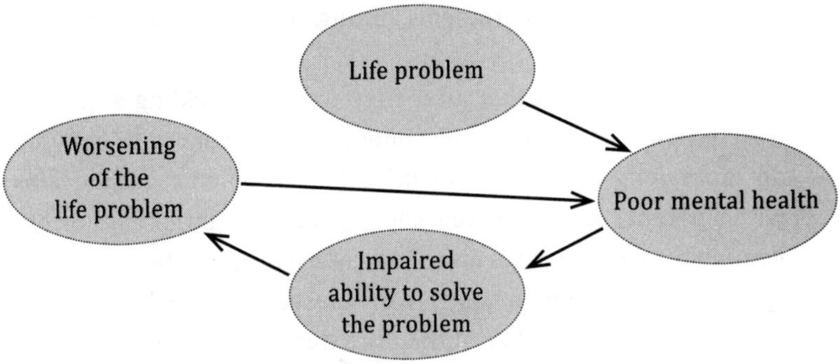

Figure A. The vicious cycle of life problems and poor mental health

type of problems can be helped by first looking at how they handle stress and deal with difficulties. With that in mind, I would like to discuss some of your difficulties with you and how you have tried to deal with them.'

2. *Define the problems.* To understand the nature of the youth's problems, the counsellor asks him about the difficulties he experiences in his daily life. The common difficulties faced by youth in their daily lives are of many different kinds; e.g. academic difficulties and difficulties with relationships.
3. *Summarize the problems.* Before moving on to the next step, summarizing the youth's key difficulties is very useful. For example, the counsellor could say, 'You have told me that since your baby brother's arrival a lot has changed in your life, especially the amount of time you get to spend with your parents. Also, your baby brother can be noisy, which interferes with your studies.'
4. *Select a problem and choose a goal.* The youth selects a specific difficulty and he and the counsellor work together to find solutions. Here are some suggestions of how the counsellor can help the youth select an appropriate difficulty:
   - Ask the youth to make a list of all of the difficulties he has and then identify those which concern him most.
   - Help the youth to target a difficulty which has a potential short-term solution, such as a recent difficulty coping with studies. The aim is to identify a difficulty for which the youth can potentially achieve success. It is not a good idea to try to tackle a long-standing

difficulty (e.g. such as problems getting along with a parent) in the first attempt.

- Explain to the youth that after they work on tackling a difficulty with a definitive solution, the counsellor will work with the youth on more long-standing difficulties (e.g. problems getting along with a parent) or a sensitive issue (e.g. in a romantic relationship).
- Remind the youth that the aim of the counselling is to teach problem-solving skills that he can apply to his present and future difficulties, rather than to solve all his difficulties during the counselling.
- Once a difficulty is selected, the counsellor confirms with the youth whether this is indeed a difficulty he wishes to tackle during counselling. For example, the counsellor identifies that the difficulty relates to the youth's getting into confrontations with a critical and aggressive peer, and the youth confirms whether or not this is a difficulty he wishes to tackle.

5. *Define solutions.* In this step, the youth learns to generate a variety of solutions ('brainstorming'), and to make sure that the solutions are realistic and attainable. The counsellor encourages the youth to think aloud about solutions, asking him to come up with any number of solutions, some of which may be silly and wishful, some which may be more practical. Brainstorming should be an enjoyable process for the youth. The counsellor writes down the solutions. Taking up each solution, the counsellor asks, 'Is this solution within your reach?' If it is not, the counsellor follows up with, 'Can you think of a solution which is more within your reach, which you can actually see yourself putting into action?' It is important to note that young people often come up with solutions that are not attainable, e.g. changing an aggressive classmate into a nicer person. The counsellor should show that she understands the youth's wish, while guiding him towards a solution within his reach. To take the earlier example, instead of aiming to change the aggressive classmate into a nicer person, the youth would do better to set the more achievable goal of avoiding confrontations with this classmate. The counsellor asks the youth to consider the pros and cons, i.e. the positive and negative consequences of the various solutions. The counsellor writes down the pros and cons that the youth mentions. She then guides the youth to select the most attainable solution (with the fewest cons and the maximum pros).

6. *Formulate a plan of action.* Next, the counsellor asks the youth to develop a plan for the implementation of the selected solution; e.g. that he will withdraw confidently when the aggressive classmate tries to intimidate him over the next school week. In addition, he should make a list of the obstacles or challenges he anticipates and also plan how he would address each of these. For example, one of the challenges the youth may identify is the possibility of the aggressive youth following him if he withdraws; he might plan to handle this by going to a safe place in the school, such as near the staff room. The counsellor should initiate a role-play with the youth to try out the plan, including the youth's ideas on how to manage the anticipated obstacles. The roles in the role-play should then be reversed. The role-play may lead to a reassessment of the selected solution and a return to an earlier step in order to select a more workable solution. Once a solution has been found to be workable, a plan can be agreed upon and made the basis for home practice; e.g. the youth implements the plan outside the counselling room and then reports how it went to the counsellor.
7. *Evaluate the impact.* At the next session, the counsellor specifically enquires about the youth's experience with the plan of action. Did he manage to go through with it? If not, why not? She asks the youth to enumerate the obstacles and how they can be addressed. If he did go through with his plan, what was the consequence? Did he get the result he had hoped for? If not, why not, and how can this be addressed next time? The counsellor asks the youth how this experience has affected the way he feels. On the basis of the discussion, the counsellor and youth may either continue to work on the same difficulty or move on to another difficulty the youth would like to tackle.

Challenges in problem-solving counselling

- In the case of young people living in extremely difficult situations which present many interlinked problems, the youth may find it very challenging to isolate specific target difficulties. An example is that of a home where alcoholism, family violence and child neglect are all present and intertwined. If a youth's situation is extremely complex, the counsellor should first aim to help the youth identify and solve more modest difficulties, e.g. difficulties that occur in the controlled setting of the classroom. Youth living in adverse circumstances (*see* Case Study 11) can also benefit from the supportive interventions of consultation with the school staff as well as supportive interventions in the home and the community. In addition, the counsellor should contact referral resources to assist with the youth's more complex social difficulties (*see* Chapter 4).

- Youth with certain mental health problems may have great difficulty mastering the problem-solving process. For example, a youth who is impulsive may feel that the problem-solving tasks require too much patience and as a result, may find the process of problem-solving counselling extremely frustrating.

When problem-solving counselling should not be used: Problem-solving counselling can be adapted to a wide range of intellectual abilities and mental health problems. However, for youth with moderate to severe intellectual disability, the problem-solving process might be too demanding and decrease the youth's self-confidence, especially if he is unable to recall the problem-solving process. For youth whose problems include difficulties with thought form and content, such as youth suffering from schizophrenia, the problem-solving process may be too difficult for them until their symptoms become less severe (*see* Case Study 17).

ANGER MANAGEMENT COUNSELLING

Goals: The goals of anger management counselling are to:

- Identify the youth's problems managing his anger;
- Increase the youth's understanding of the factors that trigger his anger;
- Increase the youth's ability to cope with situations which arouse his anger.

Principles: Anger management counselling is based on the premise that young people who are unable to control their anger and/or cannot express it constructively have a number of weaknesses. These include: misperceiving others' intentions, e.g. believing that someone intends to harm them when they do not; focusing narrowly on a perceived threat and disregarding other cues and thoughts; a limited ability to handle obstacles, e.g. difficulty with schoolwork; a distorted perception that others are responsible for conflict when they themselves may have caused it; mislabelling their feeling as anger rather than a more specific emotion, such as hurt; an inability to think of alternative responses to an aggressive action; poor verbal skills; weak problem-solving skills; and the belief that difficulties can be resolved only through the use of power. Many of these weaknesses are similar to the cognitive (or thinking) errors described later (*see* Cognitive restructuring).

When to use anger management counselling

- When a youth has specific problems (*see above* 'Principles') that lead to outbursts of anger;
- When a youth has a disruptive behaviour disorder (*see* Chapter 2);
- When a youth is exposed to family violence, bullying and/or punishment and humiliation.

Steps: This strategy consists of the following steps:

1. *Educating the youth about anger and techniques to manage anger.* The counsellor explains that anger is a normal emotion, and that there are socially acceptable and unacceptable ways of expressing it. The counsellor guides the youth to analyse his recent episodes of anger, reviewing their causes, the specific angry behaviours displayed and the consequences these episodes had for him. The counsellor also helps the youth identify his physical reactions caused by anger, e.g. tensing of the body, quickening of the heartbeat, clenching of the fists and his face flushing. She can ask the youth to give examples of occasions when someone used an angry tone with him and to compare his feelings at such times with how he felt when someone used a calm tone with him. The counsellor could also explain to the youth the 'vicious cycle of aggression' (Figure B). If anger is not checked appropriately when it is mounting, it results in an explosion which takes the form of either verbal or physical violence. The explosion is often followed by feelings of guilt and remorse, as well as fear of possible punishment.

   The counsellor describes the range of techniques the youth can use to control his anger. These entail consciously managing a reactive behaviour which could otherwise worsen the situation. Some

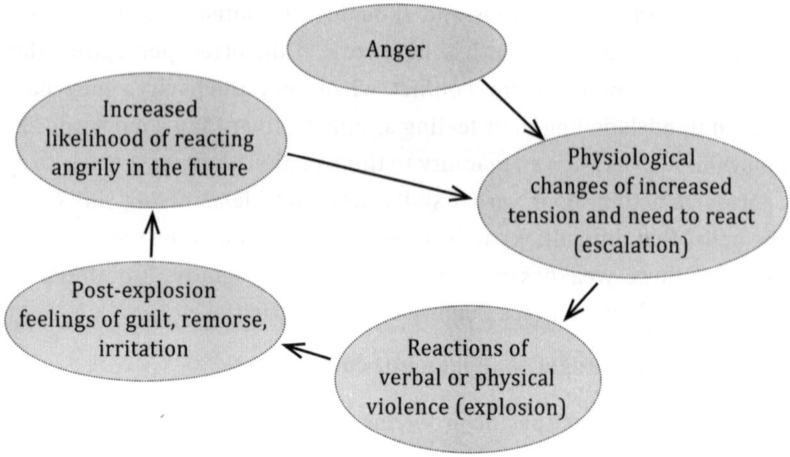

Figure B. The vicious cycle of anger

examples are:
- Ignoring the anger-provoking situation; e.g. by walking away.
- Attempting relaxation exercises to reduce angry arousal (*see* Relaxation exercise).
- Counting backwards until the mind is calm.
- Replacing aggressive responses, such as staring, making demands and threatening gestures and using harsh tones, with alternatives, such as using non-threatening eye contact, a calm tone of voice and gently requesting a change in the other person's behaviour.
- Using positive self-talk during a conflict situation, e.g. 'Keep cool,' and 'Don't get too angry—it isn't worth it!'

2. *Keeping and reviewing a record of angry episodes.* The counsellor sets the youth the specific task of noting down his angry episodes before the next session and recording the following in writing, soon after each angry episode: the cause of the episode, the angry behaviours he expressed and their consequences. At the follow-up session, these records are reviewed and alternative, more socially acceptable ways of reacting to the triggers are explored.
3. *Utilizing the problem-solving approach to anger management.* The counsellor can use a problem-solving approach to anger management, following the steps listed below:
   - Problem identification ('What is the problem I am experiencing?')
   - Defining the immediate goal ('What do I want to do?')

— Finding other solutions ('What are the various things I can do to solve the problem?')
— Taking stock of the possible consequences of each solution ('What might happen if I do X?')
— Selecting the best solution ('Which is the solution with the most positive aspects?')
— Implementing the selected solution ('I will now try it out.')
— Evaluating the outcome ('Did the solution I select solve the problem?')

The counsellor demonstrates the problem-solving approach to anger management through a role-play with the youth. In addition, the counsellor asks the youth to handle potential episodes of anger by following the steps described above and to apply these skills to different situations, e.g. episodes of anger with peers at school or with siblings at home. When reviewing the youth's approach in the role-plays and in various situations outside the counselling room, the counsellor should involve the youth in a discussion by asking him questions such as 'Did it work?', 'If so, why?' and 'If not, why not?' The counsellor should praise the youth for his participation in the role-plays and for his attempts to use anger management skills to handle various situations. If the youth's efforts to manage his anger have failed, the counsellor should reassure him by telling him that she is glad that he has tried, and that together they will come up with alternative solutions, practise them through role-play and then try again.

Challenges in anger management counselling: Some young people who have difficulty managing their anger are referred to the counsellor because others are distressed by their behaviour. The youth may have no insight into his unacceptable behaviours. He may be hostile towards the counsellor and believe that the real problem lies with others. With such youth, the counsellor may try to motivate the youth by pointing out that the adverse consequences of his angry responses can be very problematic for him; e.g. he might be suspended from school.

When not to use anger management counselling: Apart from the usual conditions which can affect the active participation of some young people in counselling (serious mental disorders and severe developmental disabilities), there are no specific situations in which anger management counselling may not be used.

SOCIAL SKILLS COUNSELLING

Goal: The goal of social skills counselling is to help young people improve key social skills to help reduce mental health problems. These skills include:

- Gaining acceptance of peers and adults;
- Establishing more satisfying relationships with peers;
- Being effectively assertive;
- Reducing isolation and loneliness.

Principles: Social skills counselling is based on the fact that youth with weak social skills cannot engage in social relationships effectively. This, in turn, leads to isolation and withdrawal, resulting in low self-esteem, impairing the individual's social skills further (Figure C). Deficits in social skills include the limited ability: to express feelings in a socially acceptable way; to recognize other people's emotions from either their verbal or non-verbal cues; to identify the demands or expectations of a social situation, such as a social interaction; and to be aware of when a social problem exists.

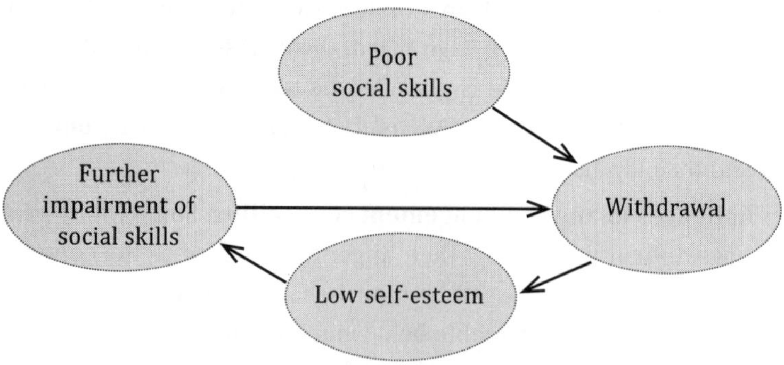

Figure C. The vicious cycle of poor social skills

When to use social skills counselling: Social skills counselling is useful when the youth is experiencing interpersonal difficulties, particularly with peers. It is beneficial for those displaying disruptive behaviours and those with depression, social anxiety and disabilities that affect communication skills, such as autism spectrum disorder and stammering. Social skills counselling can also help youth who are bullied or are bullies.

Social skills counselling focuses on improving the following core social skills:

- *Communication:* This refers to the ability to talk to others about interesting things, to listen to others, to communicate assertively, to use appropriate verbal and non-verbal responses and to maintain eye contact when listening and talking.
- *Cooperation:* This refers to the youth's ability to manage his anger (*see* Anger management counselling), follow directions and rules, take turns, share and be a good sport.
- *Validation:* This refers to the ability to be supportive, helpful and friendly towards others.
- *Participation:* This refers to the ability to engage in and show interest in group activities.

Steps: This strategy consists of the following steps:

1. *Giving information on the strategy.* Once the counsellor has built a rapport with the youth, she explains that that they will be working together to improve his social life and feelings about himself, an objective which the youth can accomplish by learning to engage more positively with his peers and others.
2. *Assessment of social skills problems.* Together with the youth, the counsellor makes a list of the interpersonal difficulties faced by the youth, ranking them from the least to the most difficult. Taking up each of these problematic situations separately, the counsellor asks the youth to explain why the situation is difficult for him, writing down the youth's explanation for each problematic situation.
3. *Selecting a specific social skill.* Choosing a difficulty which has been ranked among the least difficult, the counsellor and youth engage in role-plays to help him recognize how he contributes to these social difficulties. During the role-plays, the counsellor notes down the difficulties that are observed and then explains these to the youth. Referring to the list she made during the role-plays, the counsellor asks the youth to select the social behaviour he would like to work on first. For example, if the counsellor noticed that the youth made overly intense eye contact, spoke in a loud voice and stood too close, she asks the youth to prioritize which of these problems he would like to work

on first. If the youth selects the tone of voice as a starting point, the counsellor helps him understand the importance of the tone of voice in social interactions through explanations, and by modelling the use of an overly loud voice versus other tones of voice, such as a pleasant, moderate and calm voice. The counsellor asks the youth about his reactions to the various tones of voice and how each one makes him feel. The youth then engages in a role-play using the various tones of voice with the counsellor.

4. *Setting goals for the utilization of social skills.* The counsellor sets goals with the youth's agreement with respect to selected social skills. In the instance above, for example, the goal could be to use a moderate tone of voice when he talks to friends the following week (*see* Box 4.6). The youth could practise this tone of voice with a close friend, who could also become an ally ('buddy') in the youth's learning process (*see* Supportive interventions in the school).
5. *Reviewing the achievements of social skills.* In the follow-up sessions, the counsellor reviews how far the youth was able to meet the goals and discusses the challenges that arose while putting the skills into practice. Role-plays related to these challenges can help to increase the youth's confidence with the new skills. If, for example, his friends laughed at him when he tried to use a more modulated tone of voice, he can be encouraged to engage in a role-play with the counsellor to practise a casual response to his friends the next time they taunt him: 'This is my new voice. Pretty cool, huh?!'

Challenges in social skills counselling: Youth with disorders which result in impairment in understanding the rules of social engagement, such as autism spectrum disorder, often do not understand verbal cues, e.g. that a particular statement is meant to be sarcastic, or non-verbal cues, e.g. that a frown means someone is angry. Such individuals need more specialized social skills counselling by an appropriate professional.

When not to use social skills counselling: Social skills counselling can be adapted to any circumstance. If a youth is suffering from a serious mental disorder and cannot understand the information being given, social skills counselling can be deferred until the youth has been stabilized (*see* Case Study 17).

Relaxation exercise

Goals: This strategy aims to help the youth moderate or control heightened arousal, bodily tension or heightened reactivity associated with anxiety. There are a wide range of exercises that can be utilized to help the youth including progressive muscle relaxation, bio-feedback, guided imagery and breathing exercises. Breathing exercises, such as the one described below, can be easily taught in one session and do not interfere with the youth's routine.

Principles: Relaxation exercises aim to counter the physiological effects of stress (Figure D). These physiological effects trigger cognitive and physical experiences which further worsen anxiety. Breathing exercises break this vicious cycle by slowing down the person's breathing rhythm and reducing his mental focus on anxiety-provoking thoughts.

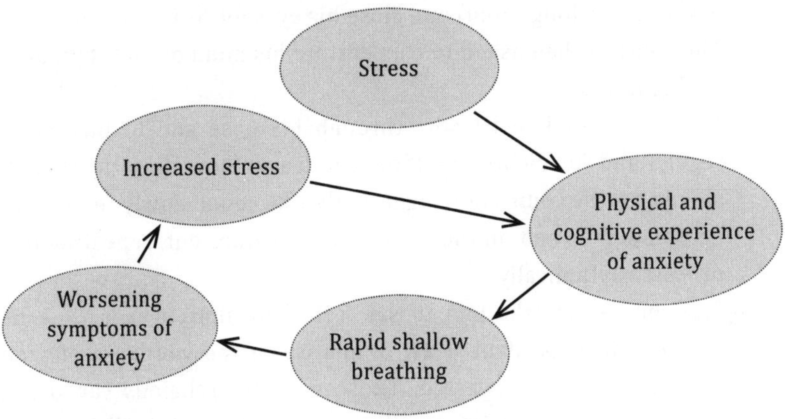

Figure D. The vicious cycle of stress and rapid breathing

When to use the relaxation exercise: This exercise can be used in any situation associated with anxiety, e.g. when a youth experiences stress or anxiety related to examinations, socializing or public speaking.

Steps: This strategy consists of the following steps:

1. *Educating the youth about the exercise.* The counsellor informs the youth that he will be taught a practical and useful breathing technique to relax his body and mind, and that this technique is also used in yoga and meditation; in fact, if courses on yoga or meditation are being offered at the school, the youth can also be encouraged to join

them. The exercise can be done in any position that the youth finds comfortable. Ideally, the youth should be sitting in a relaxed manner or lying down on his back in a quiet room. However, once the youth has learnt how to do this exercise, he can even try doing it while standing, e.g. as he waits his turn in a class debate. The youth can keep his eyes open or shut during the exercise, but it is usually more rewarding if they are closed.

2. *Demonstrating the exercise.* The counsellor should first demonstrate the exercise, and then ask the youth to do likewise. Next, she should ask the youth to do the exercise in silence for 3–5 minutes at a stretch. Finally, she should enquire how the youth felt during and after the exercise and encourage him to practise it regularly at home.

   The counsellor gives the youth the following instructions:

   — She tells the youth to choose a comfortable position (usually a chair in the counselling room) and close his eyes for 5–10 seconds.

   — The youth is then asked to concentrate his mind on the rhythm of his breathing.

   — Next, he is told to breathe through his nose and to take slow, regular and steady breaths. If the youth asks 'how slow' the rhythm should be, the counsellor suggests that he count slowly to three as he breathes in and do the same as he breathes out, repeating this process rhythmically.

   — The counsellor asks him to say 'relax' to himself each time he exhales. An equivalent word or phrase in the youth's preferred language can be suggested. Those who are religious can use a word or phrase associated with their faith. The counsellor should encourage the youth to practise the exercise for at least 10 minutes each day and, in addition, whenever he is faced with situations that arouse anxiety, until the anxiety subsides.

Challenges in the use of relaxation exercise

- Some people experience anxiety during the exercise. If the youth complains of palpitations (i.e. the sensation of the heart beating fast), tingling/numbness in his fingers or mouth, chest pain or any other physical discomfort during the exercise, it may mean that his breathing is too fast. The counsellor should suggest that he slow down the rhythm to one he finds more comfortable.

- In some young people, tension may be caused by a skill deficit, e.g. the youth becomes tense during social interactions. Should this occur, this relaxation exercise will be more effective if social skills counselling is used concurrently.

When not to use the relaxation exercise: This strategy should be avoided if the physical manifestations associated with anxiety persist, or get worse, despite the exercise.

BEHAVIOURAL ACTIVATION

Goals: The goals of behavioural activation (BA) are to address depression and depressive symptoms, e.g. low mood and low self-esteem, by helping the youth get active and engaged in specific ways that are pleasurable or productive ('activation').

Principles: Problems in a youth's life can lead to a combination of feelings, thoughts, physical experiences and actions that are typical of the disorder known as depression. Although a youth faced with challenges may find withdrawal from activities helpful in the short-term, in the longer term this withdrawal leads to dissatisfaction and unhappiness and increases distress (Figure E). The focus of BA is on what the youth does (rather than what the youth thinks). The counsellor's and youth's focus in BA are on identifying the links between what a youth does and how

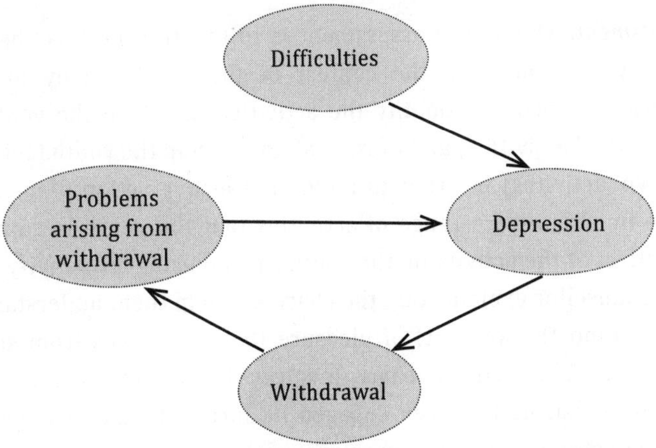

Figure E. The vicious cycle of depression

he feels, using this information to assign specific, structured between-session activities to improve mood. A central principle of BA is that if a youth is engaged in a manageable and structured programme which gradually reintroduces him to pleasurable activities, his involvement in these activities will increase over time because he will find that they reward and satisfy him and improve his mood.

When to use BA: BA has been most commonly used for young people presenting with depression and depressive symptoms.

Steps: This strategy consists of the following steps:

1. *Explain the strategy.* BA can be explained to the youth in the form of a simple diagram that illustrates the link between: the challenges in the youth's life, feeling depressed, subsequent withdrawal from activities resulting in worsening the depression. The counsellor explains this diagram to the youth and guides him to understand and remember it through questions that are simple and easy to recall. The diagram looks like this:

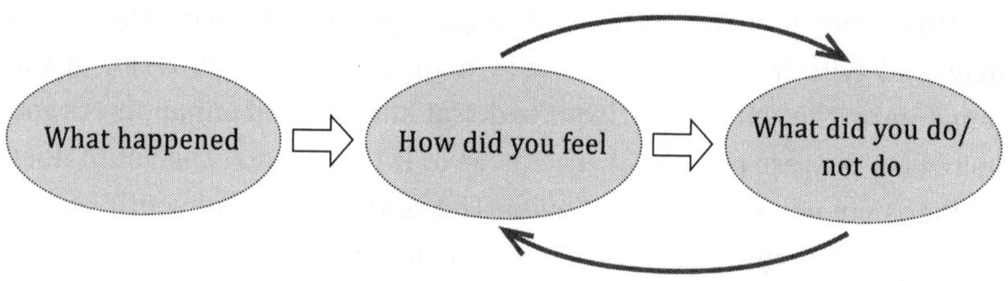

2. *Assessment.* The aim of assessment is to identify the links between activity and mood in the context of the youth's daily life. The counsellor needs to identify the activities that help the youth feel better ('up' activities) and those that do not help the youth feel better ('down' activites) in order to build an effective action plan. This is done by assessing a range of activities that the youth is doing and the effect of the activity on the youth's mood using an 'activity chart'. The counsellor explains that the chart will help them understand the extent (and the amount) of pleasure that he derives from specific activities. The activity chart involves having the youth record activities that he has been engaged in during the day. The youth is asked to monitor activities in chunks of time, i.e. activities done in the

BOX 6.2: ACTIVITY CHART

How to fill this form: For each part of the day, record your activities, including what you did, with whom, and where. Rate how you felt when you did each activity using a number between 1 and 10, with '*1 meaning the worst possible feeling*' and '*10 meaning the best possible feeling*'.

	Monday		Tuesday		Wednesday	
Time of day	What did you do?	How did you feel?	What did you do?	How did you feel?	What did you do?	How did you feel?
Morning	Having a bath Going to school	5 4				
Afternoon	Watching TV Listening to music	5 6				
Evening/ Night	Dinner with family	6				

Note: The actual form should include all the days of the week

morning, afternoon and night, over a specified number of days, e.g. over one or two weeks. Below each activity the youth is also asked to record his mood at the time of performing the activity. This is done on a 10-point scale, where 1 represents feeling very sad, 5 represents feeling all right and 10 represents feeling very happy. An example of such an assessment is given in Box 6.2.

3. *Selecting activities for the action plan.* Next, the counsellor explores the record of activities to find patterns in or links between the youth's activities and his moods. The record gives an indicator of the 'up' activities and the 'down' activities and guides the counsellor in the identification of the activities which should be used more frequently and those which should be used less frequently.

Common examples of 'down' activities	Common examples of 'up' activities
• Withdrawing from social activities or friends • Watching television alone for long hours at a time • Lying in bed for long periods • Not attending school • Neglecting personal appearance and hygiene	• Speaking with a friend • Playing with a sibling • Spending time with hobbies, such as reading or listening to music • Going for a walk • Helping a parent with a task, such as fetching groceries

The rule is to begin with activities that help the youth feel better and that he is most likely to do, even if it is a small activity. These activities will have a greater chance of success and will encourage the youth to try other activities.

4. *Structuring and scheduling activities.* It is important to break down more complex or challenging activities into smaller steps. The youth may find activities overwhelming and not know how to begin. Or, he may wish to achieve a lot in a short period of time. The rule of thumb therefore is to start small. For example, expecting the youth to go to a birthday party after he has failed an examination and has not seen his friends for nearly two months may be setting him up for failure; a better starting point might be to check with him whether he is willing to make a phone call to one of his closest friends.

Breaking down an activity into small steps: e.g. establishing contact with old friends

- Make a list of friends who the youth would like to contact.
- Get their contact details, e.g. telephone numbers.
- Identify who may be the easiest to contact.
- Choose a time/day for contacting them.
- Call the friend and have a conversation on the telephone.
- Arrange to meet for a short while.

The counsellor needs to then help the youth schedule the activity. This involves helping identify the duration (when and how long) as well as the intensity (how much) of the activity that he is going to perform. For example, if a youth is expected to spend more time with a friend, it may be helpful to plan when he is going to do the activity (in the morning/evening), for how long (e.g. for 20 minutes or 40 minutes) and how often (e.g. once/twice a week). Between the sessions, the youth is expected to attempt to keep to the schedule of activities agreed upon. He should then report back to the counsellor on how he fared, e.g. if he completed the activity, partially engaged in it or did not engage in it at all, as well as on the feelings he experienced. These records can be maintained in the same way as the chart used for assessment, or in any way that the counsellor and youth find useful.

5. *Addressing difficulties in doing an activity.* It is helpful to explain to the youth that he may not accomplish all the activities despite his best efforts because barriers may get in the way. Thinking ahead of the problems the youth may encounter and planning for how to overcome such difficulties is an important part of developing effective action plans. If a youth does not perform a planned activity, the counsellor should deal with it in a 'matter-of-fact' way. The dialogue below illustrates a 'matter-of-fact' approach.

Person	Conversation
Counsellor:	*'I see from your activity chart that you tried a lot of activities that we agreed on. I am curious about what happened to your grocery shopping.'*
Youth:	*'I didn't go.'*
Counsellor:	*'Could you tell me more about that?'*
Youth:	*'I was struggling with my maths homework and did not find the time to go in the morning. And when I start studying, I don't feel like leaving my room.'*
Counsellor:	*'So, I understand that you didn't have time in the evening either.'*
Youth:	*'The shop is closed in the evening.'*
Counsellor:	*'When does it open in the morning?'*
Youth:	*'Around nine.'*
Counsellor:	*'When do you start studying?'*
Youth:	*'Not before eleven.'*
Counsellor:	*'I was wondering if you could possibly go before you started studying.'*
Youth:	*'Hmmm . . . yeah, that's possible.'*
Counsellor:	*'Great! So can I put that in the plan we have worked out?'*

6. *Encouraging generalization.* In the closing sessions of counselling, the youth is encouraged to generalize the skills he has learned and to apply them to other circumstances in his life. The counsellor and youth jointly list situations which might trigger withdrawal, and then list the skills practised in BA that could help the youth engage in these activities. Take the case of a youth who tells the counsellor that worrying about preparing for examinations might lead him to withdraw from enjoyable activities, such as exercise. The counsellor should go over what they have discovered while working together, e.g. how withdrawing from enjoyable activities creates even more stress for the youth. It will be useful to again show the diagram that was used with the youth to explain BA at the beginning of counselling. She reminds the youth that scheduling exercise into his day even when he is feeling worried about studying for his examinations is necessary and will decrease his stress. The counsellor asks him to make a schedule to manage this problem.

Challenges in the use of behavioural activation

- *Trouble understanding the task:* The youth may have difficulty understanding the activity or task he has been assigned. To address this problem, the counsellor needs to describe the task in specific and clear terms. For example, instead of generally telling the youth to 'enjoy yourself more', the counsellor should take the time to identify specific activities that the youth enjoys and the specific steps that make up the activity.
- *Lack of skills:* A youth may have difficulty completing a task because he lacks a required skill. For example, the young person may not engage socially because he lacks communication skills. In such situations, consider other strategies that may be more appropriate, such as social skills counselling (*see* Social skills counselling), before assigning him the task of socializing.
- *The task is too difficult:* A common cause of failure is ignoring the rule of thumb of 'starting small'. The likelihood of success can be maximized if prior to scheduling a task, the counsellor makes a realistic assessment of the level of difficulty that the youth can handle with respect to the particular task.

When not to use behavioural activation: BA should be used primarily for individuals who are suffering from depression or depressive symptoms and who have withdrawn from pleasurable activities. It may be particularly difficult to use with youth who have moderate to severe intellectual disabilities or serious mental disorders, such as psychosis, since these difficulties may impair the youth's ability to engage in this collaborative strategy.

COGNITIVE RESTRUCTURING

Goals: The core aims of this strategy are to develop the youth's ability to:

- Identify and then modify negative thoughts and beliefs that lead to mental health problems.
- Replace negative thoughts and beliefs with more constructive thoughts and beliefs.

Cognitive restructuring is the most technically sophisticated strategy in this casebook. It is recommended that counsellors undertake specific training in cognitive behaviour therapy in order to implement this strategy successfully, although they can attempt to follow the simple instructions given in this casebook and improve upon their skills with regular practice.

Principles: The principle underlying cognitive restructuring is that a youth's mental health problems are caused by negative thoughts and beliefs, which impair his ability to adapt to difficult situations in a healthy, successful manner. For example, a young person displays a 'negative automatic thought' when, after failing an examination, he automatically thinks that his friends will not like him anymore; he displays a 'negative core belief' when he concludes that failing the exam means he is not as intelligent as his friends.

When to use cognitive restructuring: Cognitive restructuring is especially useful for individuals with depression, those who have low self-esteem and those prone to anxiety or anger. Cognitive restructuring requires the active collaboration of the young person, e.g. he regularly completes the home practice. Engaging the young person in the counselling process is often essential before attempting to use this strategy.

Steps: The counsellor helps the youth understand what a negative automatic thought is and how it affects him and then teaches the youth techniques to identify and to modify these thoughts. Then, the counsellor guides the youth to identify, understand and challenge his core beliefs.

1. *Understanding and identifying negative thoughts and their impact.* The counsellor explains what a negative thought is by using examples. She highlights specific thoughts that the youth has spoken about. For example, the youth may have told the counsellor that when he drops a catch during a cricket match he considers dropping out of the team because he thinks, 'I am a lousy player and my teammates want me off the team;' although he is, in fact, a valued and good player. The counsellor explains to him that most people have negative thoughts about themselves from time to time. The counsellor tells him that some of these thoughts occur extremely rapidly ('automatically') and that they do not reflect the real situation accurately. The counsellor then explains how these negative thoughts affect emotions which, in turn, fuel more negative thoughts (Figure F).

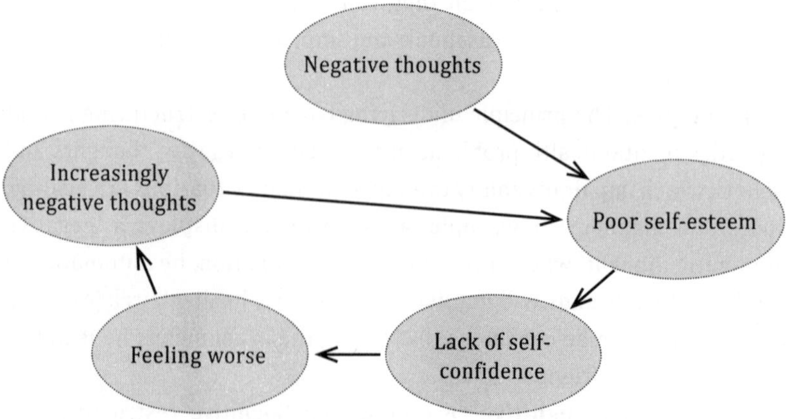

Figure F. The vicious cycle of negative thoughts and low self-esteem

2. *Acquainting the youth with various techniques which will help him become aware of negative automatic thoughts and notice how they*

influence his behaviours and emotions. These techniques include the following:

— *Guided discovery:* The counsellor listens attentively to what the youth says and how he expresses the problem; the counsellor asks open-ended questions about the youth's thoughts and beliefs; and communicates her understanding of the problem by summarizing what the youth has told her. Through this guided process, both the youth and counsellor discover the youth's negative automatic thoughts. The dialogue below is an example of guided discovery.

Person	Conversation
Counsellor:	*'Your mother suggested that you come to see me. Do you know why?'*
Youth:	*'No.'*
Counsellor:	*'Your mum told me that you have been fighting a lot with her.'*
Youth:	*'She and dad make me so mad!'*
Counsellor:	*'Why is that?'*
Youth:	*'I don't think my parents care too much about me.'* [Negative automatic thought]
Counsellor:	*'Has something happened recently that makes you feel like that?'*
Youth:	*'It was at my school annual function. All the parents had come; well, at least most of them. My parents decided not to turn up even though I had an important role in the school play.'* [Negative automatic thought]
Counsellor:	*'So what you are saying is that your parents did not make an effort to come for your school annual function, though it was important to you that they came.'* [Summarizing]
Youth:	*'Yes, I suppose so.'*
Counsellor:	*'When you say "decided not to turn up", do you mean that they promised to come and did not show up?'*
Youth:	*'No, they told me when they saw the invitation that they would not be able to come. My dad was travelling and mum was posted in the emergency unit of her hospital. Every nurse gets that duty twice a month and most of them hate*

it. So, nobody wanted to swap days with her because it was on a Friday.' [The counsellor notes that the youth might have perceived the situation in a negative way rather than realistically.]

Counsellor: ***'Have you been in a similar situation before?'***

Youth: ***'Meaning my parents not coming for school events?'***

Counsellor: ***'Well, what I was trying to understand is whether your parents often give work-related reasons to explain their absence from things that are important to you?'***

Youth: ***'Hmm . . . I don't think so.'*** [The counsellor has confirmed to herself that the youth has indeed come to a negative, inaccurate conclusion.]

Counsellor: ***'All right, so what do you know now that you didn't know earlier?'*** [The counsellor is indicating how the youth's perceptions may not have been accurate.]

Youth: ***'I'm thinking that my parents don't always do that and they tried . . . at least mum did. But, I feel horrible; I still feel that they don't care.'*** [The youth can glimpse that his perceptions are inaccurate, but still holds on to his negative conclusion.]

— *Noting mood shifts:* As a marked shift in mood may indicate the presence of an automatic thought, the counsellor should teach the youth to become aware of such shifts and then to recall his thoughts just before the shift. If a shift occurs during the counselling session, the counsellor can point it out to the youth and ask him to try to notice such shifts outside the sessions. A useful home practice is to ask the youth to take note of his mood shifts outside the session and then tell the counsellor what he has observed so that they can discuss it during the counselling session, in a manner similar to thought recording (*see below*).

— *Recording thoughts:* This is used to help the youth become aware of which situations trigger negative thoughts and how these are linked with negative emotions. The youth is asked to record his thoughts during the session and may also be asked to do so by way of home practice. Records of thoughts may be maintained in a diary in the following way:

Situation	Thought	Mood/Emotion
Rajesh and Sonia were talking about their favourite cartoon and did not listen to my poem.	*'I'm not cool enough.'*	Sad and angry

— *Identifying errors in the youth's way of thinking (cognitive errors):* Certain ways of thinking misrepresent reality, and this may lead to unhelpful ways of behaving and distressing emotions. The counsellor informs the youth about common cognitive errors and how they influence one's judgement and action. The common cognitive errors include the following:

- o The person forms an opinion on the basis of limited evidence. For example, he may think, 'Sonia and Ritu did not talk much to me during lunch. I think they don't like me at all.'
- o The person forms an opinion in the absence of any supporting evidence or even when they have contradictory evidence. Take the example of a child who is not included in the music classes because he does not meet the selection criteria. Even when this is explained to him, he assumes that he was left out because the music teacher does not like him for some reason.
- o The person thinks in extremes. A few examples are, 'I never borrow pens from my classmates. Anybody who borrows stuff is careless' and, 'If you are responsible you will never make a mistake.'
- o The person gives far more or much less importance to an event, behaviour or interaction than is logically merited. An example is that of a student who assumes that his dance group got the second prize because he missed a step, even though he was standing in the last row of the group.
- o The person takes excessive personal responsibility for events, behaviours and interactions. An example is a child holding himself responsible for his parents' divorce.
- o The person thinks of extremely negative outcomes even though there is little likelihood of the occurrence of such events. For example, a child who gets a C in the first semester examination may assume that he is going to get a poor result for the whole

year, since he thinks that his performance in the first semester indicates his performance for the entire year.

3. *Modifying negative automatic thoughts.* Once the youth has learned to identify negative automatic thoughts and understands how situations, thoughts and moods are linked, he can learn how to modify these thoughts. The counsellor asks the youth to evaluate his thought about himself with the help of the question, 'Is what I am thinking in fact true or is it false?' He then learns to ask himself if his thought matches the evidence and, if so, to what extent. This exercise is helpful because it enables the youth to evaluate the extent to which his thoughts about himself reflect reality. The counsellor and the youth practise this process through role-play during the counselling session, and then the counsellor asks the youth to practise it between sessions. She asks the youth to report examples of his experiences with the exercise in subsequent counselling sessions.

A number of techniques can be used to modify negative thoughts. These include the following:

- **Using thought change records:** This is an extension of recording thoughts (*described above*). The youth keeps a 'thought record diary', in which he identifies his negative automatic thoughts, evaluates how these thoughts influence his emotions and behaviours and identifies positive thoughts that can replace them. These records can be more detailed than the thought record discussed above and can include the following steps:
  - —Describing the event that led to an unpleasant emotion;
  - —Identifying, as clearly as possible, the thoughts that preceded these feelings;
  - —Specifying the emotion experienced;
  - —Identifying the negative automatic thought;
  - —Identifying a more accurate thought to replace the negative automatic thought;
  - —Describing any change in mental health when the rational, positive thought is applied.
- **Using 'positive self-talk':** 'Positive self-talk' helps a youth performing a task to talk himself through the task in a self-supporting way instead

of a self-defeating way. Teaching a person to apply this method includes the following steps: (i) as the youth watches and listens, the counsellor performs a task (e.g. pretending to write an exam paper), telling herself aloud that she is 'doing well and will succeed'; (ii) she then instructs the youth to perform the same task, using positive self-talk; (iii) she asks the youth to repeat the process, this time keeping the positive thoughts in his mind rather than speaking them aloud; and (iv) she suggests that the youth use this skill outside the sessions whenever necessary.

- **Understanding and identifying core beliefs.** The counsellor explains to the youth that core beliefs are the way an individual understands himself and the world around him. Core beliefs make up the youth's 'world-view' and are often based on the experiences he has had while growing up. An individual is likely to have both positive and negative core beliefs. The counsellor describes how, like negative automatic thoughts, negative core beliefs may lead to errors in thinking, which, in turn, give rise to irrational feelings and actions. The counsellor asks the youth to take up one of his negative automatic thoughts and then works with the youth to delve deeper to discover the negative core belief that underpins the thought. She poses a variety of questions to steer the youth towards his core belief. To minimize the chances of the youth getting irritated or bored during this somewhat difficult process, the counsellor explains her reasons for asking particular questions. The example below illustrates this technique.

Person	Conversation
Counsellor:	***'If I have understood this properly, your low scores in maths make you feel terrible.'*** [Identifying a negative thought]
Youth:	***'Yeah, I don't understand why I can't ever get things right.'*** [Cognitive error]
Counsellor:	***'What does it mean to you if you don't ever get things right?'***
Youth:	***'It means that . . . I haven't tried hard enough and also that I'm not smart.'*** [Cognitive error]
Counsellor:	***'Why is this such a big concern?'***
Youth:	***'I won't make it in the world.'*** [Negative core belief]

In addition to the particular questions mentioned in the example above, there are other questions that can help steer the youth towards his core belief. These include questions along the lines of: 'If that's true, so what?', 'What's so bad about . . . ?', 'What's the worst part about . . . ?', 'What does that show about you?'

- **Challenging negative core beliefs.** The following steps are useful for modifying negative core beliefs:
  - The youth and the counsellor make a list of the advantages and disadvantages of each core belief that has been identified.
  - The counsellor and the youth make a list of more adaptive core beliefs.
  - If the core belief is based on an actual limitation of the young person, e.g. academic weakness, the counsellor helps him overcome the limitation using problem-solving counselling.

When not to use cognitive restructuring: Cognitive restructuring is useful primarily for depression, low self-esteem, low mood, anxiety and anger. It is difficult to use with youth who have serious mental disorders or severe intellectual disabilities.

SUPPORTIVE INTERVENTIONS

In addition to employing the individual counselling strategies described above, the counsellor can build support for the youth in the school, home and community settings, if required. Such support is useful in many circumstances, including the following:

- The youth is not 'fitting in' with his peer group (*see* Case Studies 1, 9 and 14);
- The youth is disruptive (*see* Case Study 16);
- The youth is falling behind in his studies (*see* Case Studies 4, 5, 6 and 12);
- The youth has missed school for some time, e.g. due to illness (*see* Case Studies 2 and 18);
- The youth has made no educational or career plans (*see* Case Study 20);
- The youth lives in a vulnerable family and under extremely stressful conditions (*see* Case Study 11);

- The youth has experienced an extremely upsetting event (*see* Case Studies 3 and 7);
- The youth suffers from a serious mental disability and/or disorder (*see* Case Study 17);
- The youth is 'at risk' due to physical or sexual abuse (*see* Case Study 13);
- The youth is at risk of self-harm (*see* Case Study 19);
- The youth is at risk of harming others (*see* Case Study 10).

SUPPORTIVE INTERVENTIONS IN THE SCHOOL

The mental health and well-being of a youth influences, and is influenced by, how well he fits into school life, his academic success and how well he gets along with his peers and teachers. The counsellor can promote a supportive school environment in a variety of ways, including the following:

- **Consultations with the school staff to benefit a specific youth:** If the youth gives his permission (*see* Chapter 7), the counsellor can talk to his teachers about the difficulties affecting the youth. The purpose of these consultations is to promote the youth's recovery by providing the teachers useful information about his mental health problems, using a description of his problems rather than a diagnostic label, so that they can create a classroom and school environment that is more supportive for the youth. Some examples of the type of support that can be provided are: additional educational supports for a student who is having difficulty with schoolwork; specific actions for the student who is being excluded or bullied by peers (*see below*); alternative non-punitive methods of managing a youth who displays disruptive behaviours; decreasing academic pressure on a youth who has experienced a crisis; and encouraging the acceptance in class of a youth with a serious mental disorder or disability. The counsellor can refer to a special educator for scholastic interventions to address the particular learning style of the youth, e.g. hands-on activities for those who have difficulty understanding written descriptions. If the counsellor is faced with the exceptional circumstance of needing to refer to authorities outside the school, such as in the case of youth at risk due to physical or sexual abuse (*see* Case Study 13), she may discuss the matter with the head teacher, class teacher or school principal.

- **Consultations for improving the overall atmosphere of the school:** Ideally, the counsellor should be a respected person who is consulted by the teachers and school staff for advice on how to improve the overall atmosphere of the school for the benefit of both the specific student with a mental health problem, as well as for all students in the school. The counsellor might make recommendations such as the following:
  - Create an environment that does not discriminate between students along the lines of gender, caste and other personal characteristics.
  - Create an inclusive learning environment, taking into account individual differences in the ability to learn. For example, resource rooms should be established for those with learning problems.
  - Implement 'circle time' activities (Box 6.3). This classroom-based strategy, which consists of arranging a discussion in the classroom with the class as a group, can be used to address difficulties affecting the entire class. For example, the teacher can lead a discussion on bullying and encourage the students to participate by sharing their experiences and ideas on how to manage bullying in the class and on the campus. Circle time should ideally be used regularly to introduce values and ways of coping with difficult interpersonal issues that affect many young people rather than to address a particular youth's mental health problem.

BOX 6.3: CIRCLE TIME

Circle time (sometimes called 'group thinking time') is an active approach through which the facilitator (either the teacher or counsellor) encourages a group of students to explore issues that are of concern to them. The issues raised are usually those which are of relevance to the majority of the students. For example, the discussion can be devoted to discipline in the classroom or bullying in school. The students and counsellor sit together,

(*continued*)

BOX 6.3: CIRCLE TIME (*continued*)

ideally in a circle, to give the participants the feeling that they are in a safe and equal environment which is conducive to sharing their thoughts and feelings. In the case of young children, the counsellor may wish to sit on a smaller chair or on the ground to symbolize the equal nature of the engagement.

Circle time yields the best results if used with small groups, ideally consisting of not more than 25 students. If it is difficult to make all these arrangements, the counsellor can also use this strategy with the students sitting at their desks. The counsellor should set the rules of behaviour for this activity which include: respecting each person's opinion, giving each person an opportunity to speak, allowing individuals the freedom not to share (not forcing anyone to share something they do not want to) and respecting each other's right to confidentiality (not sharing with others outside the circle what has been communicated during the circle time).

The counsellor and students set the agenda for each session, with the focus of discussion spelled out clearly. Initially, the agendas may be set by the counsellor, but as the students become more familiar with the process, they may suggest issues that they want to discuss. The session usually consists of a beginning, which includes an introduction and a review of the rules; a middle, during which the key issue is discussed; and the closure, when the counsellor summarizes the discussion.

In the case of younger children, circle time can be devoted to issues such as managing emotions and building self-esteem, while in that of older students, it can be used to deal with topics such as substance misuse, bullying and decision-making (Box 6.5). The counsellor's role is to listen actively, in a non-judgemental way, and allow the members of the group to come up with their own solutions. Often, the circle time discussion does not lead to any conclusion and simply paves the way for further classroom discussions and debates.

— Implement a 'buddy' (peer pairing) system, especially for youth who are isolated. A buddy could, for example, help a peer with academic problems, help a student with a disability to manage physical obstacles on campus or help a youth who is being isolated by his peers (e.g. through bullying). Identifying buddies entails sensitizing the class or a group of peers (*see below*) and then requesting that volunteers serve as buddies.

— Implement strategies to manage challenging behaviours in the classroom (Box 6.4).

— Arrange poster competitions, assemblies, lectures or debates to build awareness of the factors that trigger mental health difficulties, e.g. bullying and substance abuse. Such events also help destigmatize mental health problems so that students in need seek help more readily. In addition, bringing taboo subjects, such as reproductive and sexual health, self-harm and drug/alcohol use out into the open, makes it easier for students to seek further information and help from the counsellor (Box 6.5).

— Celebrate internationally recognized days which promote gender equity and inclusion. These include International Women's Day (8 March), World Autism Awareness Day (2 April), World Mental Health Day (10 October) and the International Day for Persons with Disabilities (3 December).

- **Consultations with the school management:** The school management is the primary school-based body governing the approaches a school takes to create a nurturing, inclusive and health-promoting environment. The counsellor could encourage the school management to:

— Train the teachers in recognizing and handling behavioural and learning problems they might encounter in the classroom.

— Promote and train staff to deliver positive discipline practices.

— Conduct workshops on communication, team-building and conflict resolution to build a cohesive school team.

— Establish resource rooms, staffed by special educators, to help young people with special educational requirements, and promote an inclusive atmosphere in the school (*see* Case Studies 4 and 12).

—Encourage teachers to adapt and modify class curricula to make the school more inclusive (*see* Chapter 2).

BOX 6.4: MODIFYING BEHAVIOURS: ADVICE FOR TEACHERS

These guidelines are particularly useful for children who exhibit disruptive behaviours, such as impulsivity, defiance and aggression, in the classroom. The following are some general guidelines for the teacher to maintain discipline in the classroom:

- The teacher can make a list of the desirable behaviours she would like to see in the classroom. This can be a general list which includes behaviours such as cooperation, helpfulness and obedience.
- It is helpful to establish classroom rules which are short, simple and worded positively to encourage the behaviours that the teacher wants to see, for example, always let a classmate finish speaking before saying something yourself. The teacher should introduce the rules in the classroom and facilitate a discussion about the rules with the students.
- With the participation of the students, the teacher should decide upon the consequences a young person will have to face for exhibiting undesirable behaviour. The consequences should be developmentally appropriate, e.g. missing playtime in the case of a younger child. Care must be taken to use negative consequences sparingly.
- The teacher must deal with undesirable behaviours quickly and consistently.

The following guidelines can be used for modifying an individual student's disruptive behaviours in the classroom:

- The teacher should first identify the youth who is exhibiting disruptive behaviours.
- The teacher should agree upon a behaviour contract with the youth (*see* Appendix) to target specific behaviours and should choose an appropriate reward for desirable behaviours.
- Judicious use should be made of consequences which isolate the youth, e.g. exclusion from activities and those which require the youth's cooperation, e.g. assigning extra homework.
- The teacher should recognize and praise desirable behaviours.

BOX 6.5: ELEMENTS OF A LIFE SKILLS EDUCATION PROGRAMME

Life skills help a youth deal effectively with the demands and challenges of everyday life, and help him translate knowledge and values into positive actions. While acquiring life skills is a lifelong process, school-based life skills education programmes serve the important function of allowing young people to acquire knowledge and positive values in an age-appropriate manner, in a safe setting and through a participatory approach.

A comprehensive life skills education programme generally includes five pairs of related skills. These pairs of skills relate to the following areas:

- **Critical and creative thinking:** Critical thinking skills equip the person to objectively analyse information and experiences. Creative thinking skills, on the other hand, help the youth think 'outside the box' so that he can meet challenges in a flexible and creative way.
- **Decision-making and problem-solving:** Decision-making skills enable the youth to review all the information pertinent to a problem or challenge and to evaluate the various outcomes that would accompany alternative decisions. Problem-solving skills pertain to the execution of these decisions, as well as anticipating and managing the obstacles that may be encountered while executing them.
- **Interpersonal relationships and effective communication:** The skills of expressing opinions, desires and anxieties effectively and non-aggressively go hand in hand with building and consolidating important relationships in daily life.
- **Coping with emotions and stress:** The skills required for coping with emotions and stress are closely linked. These skills include recognizing the sources of stress, utilizing healthy ways of dealing with them and handling positive and negative emotions in a socially acceptable way.

(*continued*)

BOX 6.5: ELEMENTS OF A LIFE SKILLS EDUCATION PROGRAMME (*continued*)

- **Self-awareness and empathy:** Self-awareness involves the skill of recognizing one's temperament and character in order to anticipate and modify reactions in keeping with a situation. In the case of adolescents, self-awareness includes the ability to understand physiological changes and the emotional reactions accompanying puberty. Empathy is the ability to understand and accept others by 'putting oneself in the other person's shoes'. Empathy improves the youth's ability to form and maintain relationships.

— Make examination concessions for those with special needs.
— Invite the local health centre to carry out annual health check-ups.
— Implement a life skills education programme (Box 6.5) which includes building skills in social competencies, e.g. responsible decision-making and personal safety practices.
— Promote healthy school policies, including an anti-corporal punishment policy, an anti-bullying policy, a strong commitment to inclusion, promoting physical exercise and promoting healthy nutrition.
— Formulate a policy to address bereavement, both at the individual and collective levels. Thus, the policy should seek to help the individual youth who has lost a loved one and also the entire school when it has been affected by a death, such as that of a student or a staff member (*see* Case Study 7).

Supportive interventions in the home and the community

The counsellor should determine if the youth and/or his family might benefit from expanded ties with the community and/or greater involvement with members of the extended family. She can help the youth and family learn how to mobilize social support. If necessary, she can arrange for social support, provided the youth and/or family give their permission. The following are a few examples of social support resources:

- **Other family members:** There are occasions when relatives outside the nuclear family can be of help to the family and/or youth. For example, if a family is facing a crisis or loss, other family members can be approached to provide practical support and assist with caring for the youth (*see* Case Study 7). If the grades of a youth were not good enough for admission to college, or if a youth is not interested in a college education, the family members might be able to offer him employment or an apprenticeship (*see* Case Study 20). Enlisting extended family members can also be very important for youth who are in danger of abuse or who live in families where they witness or are subject to violence (*see* Chapter 4).
- **Religious organizations and leaders:** Many families have close connections with religious organizations. In such cases, the leaders and members of these organizations could be approached to support a family going through a crisis.
- **Community support groups:** In some settings, women's groups can be mobilized to support female members of families, e.g. women suffering from a mental illness (*see* Case Study 17).
- **Specific support groups:** Occasionally, families can use the help of support groups devoted to specific issues, such as Alcoholics Anonymous.
- **Sports and other activity clubs:** The youth can be encouraged to engage in recreational peer activities, such as sports activities. This can be useful, for example, if the youth is isolated, or if his family is too busy to engage with him constructively.

Counselling Settings and Formats

Counselling Settings

Counselling is usually carried out on the school premises, but other settings may be used occasionally. This section considers the variety of settings in which counselling may be delivered; and their strengths and limitations.

School setting: The school is the primary setting for school counselling. In order for the counsellor to provide effective counselling in this setting, the school administration and teaching staff require adequate information from the counsellor on the purpose that counselling is expected to serve for their students. There must also be a space in the school to conduct counselling (*see* Chapter 3). The primary advantage of the school setting is that it improves access to counselling. This is because the counsellor and youth are both at the school and the youth does not have to rely on a parent's willingness or ability to bring him to a counselling session after school hours. The school setting also offers a degree of privacy, assuming the counsellor has a private office. However, the school setting also has certain drawbacks. The youth may feel that there is not enough confidentiality since his peers might find out that he is seeing the counsellor and this, in turn, may lead him to fear that they and his teachers might stigmatize him. The youth may not feel assured about the confidentiality of the counselling if the school does not have a dedicated counselling room due to lack of resources. Finally, since educating the youth is the central purpose of a school, the teachers may not take to the idea of students missing their time in class and may limit the time spent on counselling as a result.

Community settings: Counselling can be offered in a setting outside the school, e.g. at a community centre, or as a part of other youth programmes, e.g. a scouts or guides programme. The choice of the setting must be acceptable to the counsellor, the youth, as well as the staff of the setting. The chief advantage of providing counselling services in a community setting is that it removes the need to compete with the academic work scheduled during school hours. However, it is difficult to find a space that is private enough for counselling and, of course, there is always a possibility of peers finding out. Further, there is a risk that the counselling relationship may be compromised due to the more informal nature of the setting. Thus, the counsellor needs to be particularly watchful about maintaining the professional relationship. Finally, counselling in a community setting may involve an additional burden on the time of the counsellor since it must take place after school hours.

Home setting: A home visit can be a useful part of the assessment because it gives the counsellor the opportunity to observe family interactions and gain a realistic understanding of the youth's family (*see* Chapter 4 and Case Study 11). Another strength of the home setting is that it offers a more private and convenient location for family psychoeducation and crisis counselling (for the family). The home setting can also be useful when the family members' work schedules and work locations make it difficult for them to gather at the school, or if the family is worried about lack of privacy in the school, or when the family is passing through extremely difficult circumstances (e.g. an ill parent, lack of availability of transport, a recent death in the family). The home setting has certain limitations as well. There may be various distractions in the home and also, it is difficult to assure confidentiality, e.g. relatives may wander in and out of the room where counselling is taking place. The home setting may also be personally unsafe for the counsellor, either because of the locality concerned or because of the possibility of the family members becoming aggressive. The family might also view the counsellor's presence in the home as an intrusion. Another possible disadvantage of the home setting is that it might be a burden on the counsellor to have to schedule an appointment outside school hours.

COUNSELLING FORMATS

Counselling can be delivered in a variety of formats: individual counselling with the youth, family counselling or group counselling. During the assessment phase (*see* Chapter 4), the counsellor gains an understanding of the interplay between the youth's problem and his school and family worlds. Depending on the formulation of the youth's problem (*see* Chapter 4), the counsellor selects a particular format for the delivery of counselling. Of course, family or group counselling involve different kinds of skills than those required for individual counselling and the counsellor may need some additional training for these formats since the focus of this casebook is individual counselling.

Individual counselling: Individual counselling is the format of choice for most of the strategies described in this casebook. The individual counselling format is often the ideal format in the school setting because counselling meetings can be arranged to take place regularly at the school. The counsellor and youth are at the school every day and a variety of individual schedules do not have to be juggled (as is the case for group or family counselling). The individual format is also ideal for building a rapport and trust, engaging the youth in the counselling process, facilitating a frank discussion with the youth about his concerns and tailoring the counselling to the youth's specific needs. The major limitation of individual counselling is that it could be less effective in dealing with family factors which have a bearing on the youth's problem; however, the counsellor can utilize family psychoeducation in addition to individual counselling in such instances.

Family counselling: Counsellors using the family counselling format meet selected or all members of the youth's family, often including the youth (either from the beginning or for selected sessions). The strategies employed in these meetings can include family psychoeducation, problem-solving counselling and crisis counselling (*described above*). This format is the most appropriate if the relationships within the family are the primary factors underlying the youth's problem, e.g. in cases of harsh parenting, marital discord and sibling rivalry. This format is also useful if the goal is to enlist the support of the family members to facilitate the youth's recovery, e.g. after an extreme event or the death of a family member. Before utilizing the family format, the counsellor needs to carefully evaluate the possible risks of engaging the family in counselling. For example, the family members might punish the child if they resent having to participate in counselling or if they feel blamed for their child's problem. They might lack empathy for the child or

firmly believe that harsh discipline is the only way of setting limits and, therefore, be resistant to family counselling.

Group counselling: In the group counselling format, the counsellor meets a group of young persons, typically in the school setting. The size of the group can vary from just two persons up to a dozen or more. This format is appropriate when problems with communication or relationships among a group of peers interfere significantly with their functioning and/or disrupt the learning or school environment. Some examples of such difficulties are teasing, rivalries and conflict. It may be appropriate to counsel in groups when a number of youth share a common developmental transition and can learn from each other, e.g. when students in Standard X or XII need to plan their future educational or vocational path, or children in Standard V are making a transition to the English medium from their primary school medium of their mother tongue. Groups may also help young people who share similar backgrounds and/or current life circumstances to build social networks and solidarity. An example is that of a group of boys who are coping with issues related to puberty. Ideally, group members should be of roughly the same age. The rules of working in groups are similar to those of circle time (*see* Box 6.3); e.g. the members should maintain confidentiality with respect to the group discussions, allow every member to participate fully and respect each other's views and comments.

CHAPTER 7

COUNSELLING ETHICS

The success of the counselling relationship depends on the counsellor respecting the youth's core human rights. These are the youth's dignity and her rights to privacy and autonomy. Respecting the youth's dignity entails displaying unconditional regard for her, irrespective of the nature of her problem and her reactions to the counsellor or counselling process. As for privacy, the counsellor should ensure that the counselling takes place in a private setting and that the information revealed during the process is kept confidential. The youth's right to autonomy is assured by ensuring that all decisions, including the decision to engage in the counselling process, are made collaboratively with her. However, it is important to note that under certain exceptional circumstances, it is necessary to curtail these rights in order to protect the youth or to protect others. The youth's basic rights and the exceptions to them, as well as the ethical standards that guide the counsellor, are discussed in this chapter.

The key ethical standards that guide counsellors working with the youth include:

- Ensuring autonomy
- Providing a competent and professional service
- Ensuring confidentiality
- Protecting the youth from self-harm
- Protecting the youth from harm
- Protecting others from harm by the youth.

ENSURING AUTONOMY

The nature and purpose of the counselling process should be discussed with the youth during the first meeting (*see* Chapter 4). Following the assessment, the counsellor should propose a counselling plan to the youth (*see* Chapter 4). She should then ask the youth for her views on the plan so that they can arrive at a mutually agreed consensus on how to proceed. Though the process of reaching an agreement on the counselling plan may require substantial modifications in the plan originally proposed by the counsellor, it is likely to facilitate the youth's engagement with the counselling (*see* Chapter 3).

A mutually agreed plan means that the youth has given her 'informed consent' to the plan, i.e. she is aware of and consents to the overall goals and details of the counselling plan. If family member(s) are participating in the counselling plan, e.g. through family psychoeducation (*see* Chapter 6), they too should be informed about the plan and provide their consent. It is always advisable to get parental consent for counselling in the case of young children in primary school. For adolescents, however, the need for parental consent should be evaluated on a case-by-case basis. In rare instances, a young person may not be willing to provide consent or may lack the capacity to do so. For example, she may be uncommunicative or appear not to understand what the counsellor is suggesting. In such cases, the counsellor should attempt to use other methods to communicate with the youth (*see* Chapter 5) in order to obtain her consent and seek the permission of her parent(s) or caregiver(s). As a general rule, if the young person remains uncommunicative or is unable to give consent despite the counsellor's best efforts, it may indicate that she is suffering from a serious mental disorder or disability and should be referred to a mental health professional (Box 7.1).

The counsellor should respect the youth's right to make her own decisions about the continuation or discontinuation of counselling. However, the counsellor should carefully assess the basis for the youth's desire to discontinue counselling. If the root cause is discomfort with counselling, the counsellor may be able to make the process a more satisfying experience for the young person. If the wish to discontinue arises from poor judgement on the youth's part, the counsellor may be able to help her understand the benefits of counselling. If the youth wishes to discontinue counselling even after the above possibilities have been addressed, the counsellor should respect her decision (Box 7.2). The counsellor should follow the guidelines for a planned closure of

BOX 7.1: WHEN THE YOUTH'S INFORMED CONSENT IS NOT POSSIBLE

A young person is referred to the counsellor by a teacher because he is unable to keep up with schoolwork. When the counsellor meets the youth, she finds that he is unable to follow what she is saying and she suspects that he may be suffering from serious intellectual delays. The counsellor decides to meet the youth's parents as the initial step in the assessment in order to understand the young person from the parents' perspectives. The parents are eager to come to the meeting, at which they describe how their son has shown delays in achieving key developmental milestones from childhood. Making sure she handles the issue with sensitivity, the counsellor brings up the possibility of a developmental disability and refers the parents to an educational psychologist for an evaluation of their son's intellectual level (*see* Chapter 4).

counselling in such a case (*see* Chapter 4). She should always keep in mind that the young person will be more inclined to consider the option of counselling in the future if she feels that she has been heard and respected at the close of the current experience of counselling.

However, if it is unadvisable to discontinue counselling because it could put the youth in danger, the counsellor will have to determine the level of risk and make alternative arrangements for the individual (*see* Protecting the youth from self-harm and protecting society from harm).

PROVIDING A COMPETENT AND PROFESSIONAL SERVICE

Counsellors must receive training both to provide competent counselling to young people and to recognize their own capacities and limitations in terms of skills. If the youth's problems are beyond the scope of the counsellor's abilities or roles, the counsellor is under an ethical obligation to refer her to an appropriate professional (*see* Chapter 4).

Providing a competent service to the youth also means conducting

BOX 7.2: PLANNED CLOSURE OF COUNSELLING INITIATED BY THE YOUTH

A 10-year-old boy has been attending counselling sessions for several months because he has difficulty making friends and is disruptive in class. He tells the counsellor that he is now able to better manage his relationships with his peers and does not need more counselling. The counsellor, however, is concerned that the youth's assessment of his ability to manage relationships in class may not be realistic. The teacher has told the counsellor that although the youth's behaviour has become less disruptive, he continues to get into fights with other students. The counsellor brings this up with the youth and suggests that they have a few more meetings to continue to work on his behaviour and feelings. However, the youth insists that he has 'improved', that he has learned how to handle peers and that he no longer wishes to meet the counsellor. The counsellor agrees to close counselling for the moment. She discusses the gains the youth has made, encourages him to practise the skills he has learnt and emphasizes that her door will always be open should he wish to return to counselling.

oneself professionally during and after the counselling relationship. While a counsellor must always maintain a caring attitude, it is of critical importance that as a professional, she must observe clear limits with respect to the level of informality or intimacy in her relationship with the youth. Of course, there is always a possibility that in certain circumstances, the counsellor's sympathies may be aroused to such an extent that she may be moved to behave more like a caregiver or friend, but she must always be alert to such feelings and manage them professionally. A common example of when a counsellor may lose her objectivity is if the circumstances in which the youth lives are very difficult, e.g. if the youth lives in an environment characterized by extreme poverty or family violence, or if her parent is mentally ill or has died. Faced with such a situation, the counsellor might develop a 'rescue fantasy'. In other words, a counsellor may imagine that she can save the youth from her circumstances, e.g. by befriending the youth rather than employing appropriate counselling strategies or informing the school or the authorities. Another example is when a youth is emotionally very upset, the counsellor may be tempted to touch her in a caring way, e.g. hug her. This can be misinterpreted by the youth, or frighten or embarrass her. The counsellor's role is to encourage the youth to talk about her concerns and the reasons why she is upset, and to gently guide her, through selected counselling strategies and supportive interventions, towards a solution (*see* Chapter 6). It is to be noted that a physical gesture, such as a reassuring touch, is permissible provided it is used judiciously (purely as a demonstration of an empathic counselling approach), is brief and involves a sexually 'neutral' part of the body, such as the shoulder or elbow.

The development of romantic feelings between the counsellor and youth clearly indicates that the professional relationship has been compromised. The counsellor must always be alert to the possibility of a romantic relationship, especially when working with adolescents. The counsellor should note any signals that show that she is harbouring romantic feelings for the youth. For example, the counsellor should notice whether she feels sexually attracted to the youth. The counsellor should also notice how the young person responds to her, e.g. whether the youth is flirting with her. If such feelings seem to be present, appropriate steps should be taken after discussing the matter with a supervisor or peer counsellor. Where feelings of attraction are involved, it may be prudent to consider closure of counselling (*see* Chapter 4) following a discussion of the reasons with the youth, who can be told, for example, that the counsellor is unable to offer competent services due to personal reasons. In certain circumstances, such as when no other counsellor is available to help the young person, it may be possible to continue counselling by setting firm limits and making use of supervision.

Another key element of a professional and competent service is 'non-discrimination'. When a counsellor's attitudes are affected by personal biases which give rise to negative views of the youth or negative actions towards her, they are said to be discriminatory. All counsellors bring a set of values and beliefs, based on their upbringing, training and other experiences, to the counselling relationship. They should be aware

BOX 7.3: PROTECTING A YOUNG PERSON EXPERIENCING DISCRIMINATION

The counsellor becomes aware that a young person in a hostel is being discriminated against by his peers because of his caste. After he has received the youth's consent, the counsellor raises the issue with the hostel warden. The counsellor and the warden discuss how to address discrimination along the lines of caste in the hostel. Together they come up with a plan to sensitize the boarders of the hostel to the injustice and impact of discrimination along the lines of caste. They initiate a discussion among the boarders about their understanding of what 'caste' means, how the caste system developed, how it has changed over time and ways to combat such discrimination.

of their discomfort with and personal biases regarding disability, caste, gender, religion, sexual orientation and different socioeconomic conditions so that their attitudes do not interfere with their counselling work. While counsellors need not eliminate their values and beliefs, they must strive to keep them at bay during the counselling to ensure that they understand and respect the youth's life experience and personal perspectives. In addition, if the counsellor becomes aware that the young person's school or schoolmates are discriminating against her, the counsellor should attempt to address the issue at the school level, e.g. by alerting the school management (Box 7.3; *see* Chapter 6).

Ensuring confidentiality

All information obtained during counselling must be kept strictly confidential, i.e. it should not be shared with any other person without the youth's explicit permission. The counsellor should take particular care to store the counselling records and other documents regarding the youth securely, e.g. in a locked cupboard. When a referral is to be made (*see* Chapter 4), the counsellor should obtain the youth's consent for disclosing the specific information that the counsellor has determined she would need to share. The counsellor should ask for the youth's consent only after she has informed her about the purpose of the referral and told her which information she thinks would be useful to share (Box 7.4). If the counsellor uses confidential case material in any other professional setting (e.g. supervision, case discussions), the case material must be disguised to protect the young person's identity. For example, the counsellor could use only the youth's first initial or change the youth's name for case discussion purposes.

In meetings with the youth's parents or teachers, the counsellor must maintain the youth's confidentiality by respecting her wishes regarding what can be shared. The parents or teachers may be informed of the course of the counselling in broader terms and relevant subjects can be approached in an indirect way. For example, if the youth has revealed that her father uses physical punishment at home, the counsellor can

BOX 7.4: OBTAINING CONSENT TO TALK TO A PARENT

An 8-year-old girl was referred to the counsellor by the school principal following a car accident. She was doing poorly in school, was 'jumpy' and had stopped participating in team sports. The counsellor met with the girl, who revealed that she worried that her parents might die in a car accident. The counsellor told her that she often met with the parents of a child to learn about the child's home life, at which point the girl said she did not want the counsellor to mention her fear to her parents. The counsellor sought her permission to talk to her parents about some of the things they had discussed in counselling, assuring her that she would not specifically mention her fear that they might die. The girl was relieved and agreed. The counsellor met with her parents, who were very worried because of the problems their daughter had developed since the accident. The counsellor discussed, in general terms, the time it takes a child to psychologically recover from having been involved in a car accident, the fears that follow such an event, including the fear of injury and death, and how they could comfort their daughter.

broach the topic with the parents by asking them what they do when they are angry with their daughter and whether they ever hit her. If the youth refuses to give her consent, the counsellor should gently explore the reasons for this and correct any misconceptions. If the counsellor determines that the youth is not in danger (*see* Protecting the youth from self-harm), she should honour the young person's refusal.

Protecting the youth from self-harm

When a counsellor determines that the youth is in danger of harming herself, she should take appropriate steps to protect her (*see* Chapter 4).

BOX 7.5: BREAKING CONFIDENTIALITY TO PROTECT A YOUNG PERSON FROM SELF-HARM

A 17-year-old youth, who has been receiving counselling for several months, stops attending the sessions. The counsellor often sees him in the school hallway, but the youth avoids eye contact. The counsellor, respecting his privacy, does not approach him. Under the mistaken impression that the youth is still attending counselling sessions, a teacher approaches the counsellor to tell her that the youth has been talking to his schoolmates about harming himself. The counsellor asks the teacher to suggest to the youth that he speak to the counsellor about these wishes. The student tells the teacher that he does not want to talk to anyone but his friends and that what is happening in his life is none of his or the counsellor's business. Because of what she knows about the young person's mental health, in addition to his statements in class and to the teacher, the counsellor speaks to the principal about the boy's risk of suicide. After some reflection, she decides to call the youth's parents and learns that he has been running away from home and not listening to them. The counsellor refers the parents to a mental health professional for an evaluation of their son's suicidal risk so that further plans can be made for his care (*see* Chapter 4).

In these situations, the young person's right to privacy may be waived, but only after reasonable efforts to obtain her permission have failed, if the risk of self-harm is judged to be moderate to severe and after the counsellor has explained clearly why she is breaking confidentiality. However, it must be kept in mind that even if the disclosure of confidential material is required, it should be restricted to the minimum to protect the youth (Box 7.5).

Protecting the Youth from Harm

Other circumstances in which concern for the safety of the youth may override her right to privacy include: when physical and/or sexual abuse is suspected; when the youth is being neglected or exploited, e.g. if she is overworked at home; and when a young person's health is jeopardized, e.g. if a youth is pregnant, poorly nourished or physically ill. In such situations, the counsellor must evaluate the seriousness of the matter and, if necessary, initiate a home visit, interview relevant people and make appropriate referrals (Box 7.6).

If the counsellor determines that any of these dangerous circumstances exists, she is obliged to take action to protect the youth. If it appears that the family or caregiver is the source of the harm, the counsellor must promptly report her concerns and the information on which her concerns are based to the school administration and, if appropriate, the legal authorities to avoid further harm. Her information may be based on reports from the youth or peers, observed physical evidence, collateral reports from the school nurse/teacher/doctor and other sources. In those instances where a family member is the perpetrator of violence or neglect, this needs to be handled with great sensitivity. If the source of danger is not a member of the immediate family or a caregiver, e.g. if he is a peer or teacher, the counsellor should first inform the immediate family or caregiver, either through a home visit or an appointment at the school. She should then work with the family to develop a plan to protect the youth, as well as a plan to inform the relevant authorities, such as the Special Juvenile Police Unit (SJPU) and the school principal (Box 7.7).

Ideally, in all cases in which there is a risk of harm, be it self-harm or

BOX 7.6: STEPS TO BE TAKEN WHEN THE YOUTH IS IN DANGER

- The counsellor should discuss the case with a supervisor, her colleagues, a member of the school team or the principal.
- It is essential to inform a responsible adult who is an important part of the youth's life so that he can take effective action to protect the youth. The person could be a parent. It would be best to do this in the young person's presence.
- The youth should be referred to a mental health professional (*see* Chapter 4) or to the appropriate authority, such as a social worker or the police, if the danger is acute or persistent (Box 7.7). Ideally, this should always be done after discussing the matter with the young person and/or his family, but it can be done without formal approval in instances of grave or persistent danger or sexual offences.
- The youth should be given the contact number of the local childline (Box 7.8).
- The counsellor should follow-up with the young person frequently until the dangerous situation has been resolved.

BOX 7.7: THE PROTECTION OF CHILDREN FROM SEXUAL OFFENCES ACT, 2012

The Protection of Children from Sexual Offences Act, 2012 is a new legislation which defines various types of sexual offences against children and provides penalties for such acts. A 'child' is defined as any individual below the age of 18 years. The law is 'gender-neutral' (both male and female children are covered) and clearly defines specific offences. It specifies child-friendly procedures for reporting and recording of evidence (e.g. recording the offence in the child's own words, providing children with disabilities with special educators to assist in communication) as

(*continued*)

BOX 7.7: THE PROTECTION OF CHILDREN FROM SEXUAL OFFENCES ACT, 2012 *(continued)*

well as for the investigation and trial. Sexual assault (including fondling, kissing and any act which is sexually gratifying for the perpetrator) and sexual harassment (e.g. voyeurism, showing a child pornographic material) constitute 'crimes against children'. To make the complaint and seek relief for and rehabilitation of the child, help should be sought from the local Special Juvenile Police Unit (SJPU) or local police, which have been given the responsibility of making immediate arrangements for the child's care and protection. These arrangements include measures such as admitting the child to a shelter home or to the nearest hospital within 24 hours of the report.

With respect to the reporting of sexual offences, the Act states that a person has an obligation to report such an offence if he has knowledge of it. When the counsellor is seriously concerned about the safety of the youth, her first steps should be to discuss the case with a supervisor; inform the youth that, as the counsellor, she must take action to protect her; provide the youth with the contact number of the local childline (Box 7.8); approach trusted persons in the school, family or community; and refer the youth and her family to a local child rights organization which can guide them on the practical steps that may be taken to protect the youth. The counsellor must seek the involvement of a social worker and/or a local child rights organization in those situations where she and the supervisor feel that the level of potential harm is significant and that other measures to ensure the youth's safety are insufficient. The social worker or child rights organization should be in a position to make a police report, if necessary. If this course of action is not feasible, the counsellor may take it upon herself to make a report to the SJPU. It is imperative for the counsellor to keep herself up to date on any new legislation which may have a bearing on her work with vulnerable young people.

BOX 7.8: CHILDLINE: CALL '1098'

Childline (www.childlineindia.org.in/) is a 24-hour toll-free emergency phone service for young people in need of assistance. This number is linked to local organization which responds to the needs of young people and links them to services for care or rehabilitation. The target group is any young person in need including those who are facing extremely stressful circumstances or violence and those who are in conflict with the law.

harm at another person's hands, the counsellor should make every effort to obtain the young person's consent to share pertinent confidential material with relevant others for her protection.

Protecting others from harm by the youth

Rarely, a counsellor might become aware that a young person intends to hurt somebody or damage property, but she cannot prevent this because the person is not willing to be counselled. In such cases, the counsellor should take reasonable and appropriate steps to protect these other parties from harm and may breach confidentiality for this purpose (Box 7.9).

BOX 7.9: A LOVE-STRUCK ADOLESCENT WHO IS ANGRY WITH HIS RIVAL

The school principal refers a 17-year-old young man to the counsellor because of his disruptive behaviour in school, targeted especially at one particular boy. He is reluctant to engage with the counsellor. Patiently, by focusing on the youth's feelings rather than his actions, the counsellor builds a rapport with him.

The counsellor learns that he has been very unhappy in recent months since his girlfriend broke up their relationship. The youth

(*continued*)

BOX 7.9: A LOVE-STRUCK ADOLESCENT WHO IS ANGRY WITH HIS RIVAL *(continued)*

says he has noticed that since the break-up, his ex-girlfriend has become very close to another boy in his class. He suspects that this boy engineered the break-up with his ex-girlfriend. The youth started several arguments with this boy, culminating in a fight, which led to the referral. Despite the counselling, however, the youth continues to be very angry and is convinced that he has to take 'revenge'.

The counsellor discusses her concerns with the young man. She explains that it is only natural for him to feel hurt and angry and goes on to say that the counselling sessions will help him cope better with his feelings, so that they will gradually become less intense. However, the counsellor is worried that before the young man learns to cope with his feelings, he might do something which would hurt the other boy and lead to a more serious problem. For this reason, the counsellor decides to meet the other boy and tell him that he should try to keep his distance from the young man for the time being. In addition, the counsellor continues to monitor the young man's level of anger so that, in case there is any escalation in his desire for revenge, she can take further action, such as notifying the principal.

CHAPTER 8

Becoming a more effective school counsellor

This chapter discusses how the counsellor can continuously improve her skills and take care of her own mental health so as to offer an even more effective service to youth. This chapter consists of two sections; the first focuses on building skills and the development and use of self-awareness; the second focuses on self-care.

- **Building professional skills**
  ⇒ Self-appraisal within the counselling context
  ⇒ Self-evaluation
  ⇒ Supervision
  ⇒ Continuing professional development
- **Looking after yourself**
  ⇒ The school counsellor's mental health
  ⇒ How a school counsellor can look after herself
  ⇒ When to seek professional help

Building professional skills

Reflecting upon and understanding one's strengths and weaknesses as a school counsellor is an ongoing process, which can be conducted in a variety of ways. All of the following methods are useful to the process of maturing as a counsellor. We recommend that the counsellor make use of a number of these methods, particularly self-evaluation and supervision.

Self-appraisal within the counselling context

The counsellor often comes up against the difficult situation of a youth failing to engage in counselling. The young person may, for example, refuse to talk about specific issues, repeatedly miss sessions or arrive late. This may not only disrupt the counselling plan, but also give rise to a number of unwelcome emotions in the counsellor. For example, the counsellor may feel angry about what she perceives as non-cooperation on the youth's part. She may feel frustrated at not being able to 'help' the youth. She may experience a feeling of inadequacy because she thinks her skills are not sufficient to help the youth, or she may worry that the youth is at risk for self-harm or some other kind of harm. A counsellor experiencing such feelings may find self-management strategies useful, for example:

- Calming down and thinking through the counselling problems without blaming either oneself or the youth;
- Applying some counselling strategies to oneself, in particular, managing negative thoughts with cognitive restructuring techniques such as 'positive self-talk' (*see* Chapter 6);
- Being patient with the youth and with oneself;
- Discussing the counselling challenges with a supervisor (*see* Supervision).

SELF-EVALUATION

Since self-evaluation requires some time, counsellors must factor it into their work plans. As a general rule, at least some of the counsellor's time should be set aside for self-evaluation. The self-evaluation techniques include:

- Keeping case records of good quality and regularly bringing them up to date (*see* Appendix);
- Reviewing the case records, evaluating the progress in each case, and analysing successes and failures by referring to the casebook and other resources (*see below,* Continuing professional development).

Keeping case records of good quality (*see* Chapter 4 and Appendix), reviewing them and thinking of ways of optimizing the youth's progress are not only good practices of case management, but also serve as means by which the counsellor can systematically and objectively assess the strengths and weaknesses of her counselling skills. Since it is not always easy to objectively evaluate one's own performance, inputs from colleagues and supervisors (*see below,* Supervision) often help to 'see' oneself accurately. With practice, self-evaluation becomes easier and one of the counsellor's many skills.

Supervision

This process is essential for the counsellor's growth and goes hand in hand with self-evaluation. Supervision entails regular meetings, during which the school counsellor presents her work to a more experienced mental health professional, such as a psychologist, psychiatrist, psychiatric social worker, or to a more experienced counsellor, for review and feedback. If this ideal situation does not exist, the school counsellor can present her work to a peer who is a school counsellor for 'peer supervision'. Peer supervision refers to receiving supervision from counsellors who share a similar level of education and experience, presenting cases to one another for review and feedback.

The supervisor's role is to ensure that the counsellor is providing effective counselling to the youth in her care. For this purpose, he must give the counsellor feedback which is both objective and supportive. The supervisor and counsellor must work towards building a positive, comfortable, mutually respectful and honest relationship with each other. The supervisor plays a number of roles in his relationship with the counsellor. These include:

- Supporting the counsellor so that she does not feel isolated;
- Providing consultation for challenging cases;
- Mentoring and encouraging independent decision-making;
- Monitoring and strengthening the quality of the counsellor's note-taking, case management and counselling skills.

The task of supervision is complex because the supervisor must be unbiased and analytical, while at the same time being nurturing in his approach to the counsellor and the supervision process. Supervision can be a challenging experience for the counsellor since a number of sensitive issues may emerge during the process. For example, the relationship with the supervisor may create anxiety in the counsellor because she may fear being judged, or the counsellor may become excessively dependent on the supervisor's inputs for individual case management (which could weaken the counsellor's skills). In a productive supervision relationship, the supervisor is able to help the counsellor become aware of the following issues:

- The supervisor helps the counsellor become aware of her strengths and weaknesses as a counsellor and helps her address the areas of weakness. In the process of supervision, the supervisor listens to the counsellor's presentation of the case and may provide feedback, brainstorm ideas with the counsellor and/or use role-play. For example, he can use role-play to demonstrate active listening skills.
- The supervisor makes the counsellor aware of how her personal values, beliefs and cultural background may affect her attitudes and behaviours in the counselling process. For example, the counsellor may have strong views against premarital sexual relationships and these might be affecting her ability to listen non-judgementally to a young person. The supervisor should challenge these views so that the counsellor can provide unbiased information to the adolescent, who will then be better equipped to make an informed decision.
- The supervisor advises the counsellor to refer a youth to another professional, if necessary (*see* Chapter 4). An example is when a youth's behaviour with the counsellor is becoming increasingly sexually provocative.

Continuing Professional Development

The counsellor should attend training workshops, particularly those on evidence-based counselling approaches for mental health problems of youth. Training that helps improve skills for case write-ups and the presentation of cases is also useful. Online courses, seminars, study groups and professional journals are all avenues for continuing professional development. Listed below are the resources that the school counsellor can make use of for continuing professional development.

Resource materials: These include manuals, practice guidelines and recommendations from local and international organizations. We list a few examples below and also strongly recommend that the school counsellor familiarize herself with useful sites on the Internet as well as search engines, such as 'Google Scholar'.

Local professional organizations/societies

- Indian Association of Clinical Psychologists (http://www.iacp.in/#)
- National Academy of Psychology (India) (http://www.naopindia.org/home)
- Indian School Psychology Association (http://inspa.info/index.html)
- CounselingIndia (http://www.counselingindia.com)

International organizations and guidelines

- British Association for Counselling and Psychotherapy (http://www.ccyp.co.uk/)
- School Counselling Services: Standards and Guidelines (http://www.gov.pe.ca/photos/original/ed_couns_svcs.pdf)

Journals

- *Indian Journal of Clinical Psychology* (http://www.iacp.in/2010/12/indian-journal-of-clinical-psychology.html)
- *British Journal of Guidance and Counselling* (http://www.tandf.co.uk/journals/carfax/03069885.html)
- *Journal of School Counselling* (http://jsc.montana.edu/)
- *VISTAS* (publications of the American Counselling Association) (http://counselingoutfitters.com/vistas/VISTAS_Home.htm)
- *Journal for Social Action in Counselling and Psychology* (http://jsacp.tumblr.com/post/3880811542/journal-for-social-action-in-counseling-and-psychology)
- *Journal of School Health* (http://onlinelibrary.wiley.com/journal/10.1111/(ISSN)1746-1561;issues)

Peer groups: School counsellor peer groups which meet regularly, i.e. at least once a month at a specific time and place, provide counsellors with a forum for sharing their mutual concerns and problems. Peer groups have distinct and varied missions. For example, the counsellors may use the meetings to discuss their emotional reactions to the different types of young persons they have encountered in the settings where they work and how they might approach the challenges they face as counselors with these youth. Some groups are organized as peer-supervisory groups, in which the counsellors take turns to present their cases for group discussion.

Workshops: Workshops are an excellent way to learn new skills and refine skills which have already been acquired. The following are some of the organizations that arrange workshops:

- The National Institute of Mental Health and Neuro Sciences (NIMHANS), Bengaluru organizes short training programmes on the management of mental disorders among children and adolescents (http://www.nimhans.kar.nic.in/conf/events.htm).
- The Indian School Psychology Association (InSPA) holds regular training workshops (http://www.inspa.info).
- Sangath organizes annual training programmes for school health counsellors (http://www.sangath.com).

Conferences: Conferences organized by professional bodies provide an excellent opportunity for understanding advances in the field and networking with peers. Further, conferences provide the opportunity to make presentations or present posters, and to receive feedback from peers and senior mental health professionals. The Indian Association of Clinical Psychologists (http://www.iacp.in/#) and the Indian School Psychology Association (http://inspa.info/index.html) organize conferences annually.

Membership in professional groups: Membership in a professional group allows the counsellor to network with peers, participate in the growth of the field of school counselling and become part of a larger community of professionals, e.g. Indian School Psychology Association.

LOOKING AFTER YOURSELF

THE SCHOOL COUNSELLOR'S MENTAL HEALTH

It is very important that the counsellor enjoys and derives satisfaction from her counselling work with youth. Helping a youth with a mental health problem and participating in her recovery can give rise to a deep sense of emotional satisfaction. At times, however, counselling youth with mental health problems can be a demanding experience for the counsellor, especially if she works in isolation. The following are some of the common problems a counsellor may experience:

Emotional exhaustion: Dealing with the problems and pain suffered by others can be difficult and stressful at times. The effort sometimes results in 'burn-out', with the counsellor feeling drained, fatigued, disinterested in and dissatisfied with her work.

Sense of inadequacy: Since the benefits of the counsellor's work are often difficult to measure, may become apparent only slowly or seem minor, or may not be valued by other staff members of the school or community centre, the school counsellor may at times feel frustrated or 'useless'.

Exaggerated sense of importance: Owing to her position in the school, the counsellor can fall into the trap of thinking that her work is more important than that of others within the school system. This may alienate her from the teachers and school staff and erode her effectiveness as an advocate for the youth.

Overlooking one's personal needs and family life: The counsellor's worries about and involvement in the problems of the young people she is working with may result in her putting aside personal and family responsibilities. This is more likely to happen if she carries home her day's work.

Continuing to be a counsellor outside the counselling room: Sometimes, counsellors carry over a counselling attitude into their personal lives. Though many of the counselling skills are useful in other settings, the counsellor should make sure that she does not allow her counselling attitudes to interfere with her other roles in life. She should always be a person first, and a professional second.

How a school counsellor can look after herself

To avoid the pitfalls described above, the counsellor can play an active role in looking after her own mental and physical health, and in creating a balance between her work and home lives. This can be done through a combination of the following:

Belonging to community groups: The counsellor may benefit from becoming a member of groups which are outside the school and counselling milieus. For example, she could participate in social, religious or sports clubs.

Distinguishing her professional self from her personal self: The counsellor needs to discipline herself so that she does not carry home her worries related to work. She should also remain objective about the youth she is helping even if the youth's problem touches upon some of her own personal concerns.

Relaxation exercise: When practised daily, relaxation exercises can be very helpful in dealing with stress. The counsellor might make use of the relaxation exercise described in this casebook (*see* Chapter 6), meditation techniques, yoga or prayer to cope better with the impact of stress.

Creative and enjoyable activities: It is important for the school counsellor to set aside some time each day for activities which she finds interesting or enjoyable, and which are unrelated to work. Spending 'fun' time with family or friends, reading a book, watching television, gardening, stitching or taking a walk in the neighbourhood are some examples of simple enjoyable daily activities. Creative activities may include writing a poem or story or making a drawing. These activities are especially helpful if the counsellor finds it difficult to share her feelings with others. Writing feelings down on paper can help to deal with them more objectively.

Improving the work surroundings: If the work surroundings are dirty or unpleasant, it is bound to have an effect on the school counsellor's mental health. Tidying up, fixing broken windows or chairs, putting up colourful drawings or posters on the walls, trying to cut down on noise and allowing natural light into the room can help improve the work environment and produce a feeling of well-being. The task of improving the surroundings is best achieved by working together with others who share the work setting.

Sharing and socializing: There is no real substitute for sharing and talking to others to improve one's mental health. Some examples are taking the time to talk to a spouse or friend about the workday, sharing special moments with others, listening to colleagues' experiences, supporting colleagues in their times of difficulty and learning coping methods from colleagues.

Participating in a peer group: This is a very useful and sustainable way of helping not only oneself, but colleagues as well (*see* Peer groups).

When to seek professional help

It is important to recognize that counsellors can develop mental health problems too. Being aware of one's emotions and behaviour is the main way of knowing when to seek help from a mental health professional (or supervisor who is senior to the school counsellor, and with whom the counsellor feels comfortable sharing personal problems).

There are two situations in which helping oneself may not be enough and it becomes essential to talk to someone else. These are as follows:

Suicidal feelings: Many people feel hopeless or wish to end their lives at some point. It is very helpful to talk about these feelings, however embarrassing it feels, to a trusted person. If the counsellor is experiencing such feelings and is considering taking her own life, professional help from a mental health professional should be arranged for urgently.

Problems with substance misuse: Like others, counsellors may also develop substance misuse problems. If the counsellor feels concerned or guilty about abusing drugs, alcohol or any other substances, or if her close relatives or friends express concern, the counsellor should seek professional help.

Part B

CASE STUDIES

CASE STUDIES

The case studies illustrate a range of mental health problems and the typical age of the problem's appearance in youth. The order of the case studies reflects the developmental continuum, from youngest to oldest.

CASE STUDY 1

THE CHILD WHO PLAYS ALONE

Tariq's story

THE PRESENTING PROBLEM

Tariq, a 6-year-old boy studying in Standard I, was referred to the counsellor by his teacher because of his unusual behaviours in the classroom. Since the beginning of the school year, Tariq had preferred to play by himself, barely engaged in classroom activities, and seemed to be in a 'world of his own'. The teacher had noted that even when he participated in activities with others, his behaviour was unusual; he rarely made eye contact with his peers, did not like to be touched by others and rarely shared what he was interested in with others. His mother agreed that his behaviour was unusual, especially when she compared it to his sister's, which had not been at all like Tariq's at the same age. Since the teachers in pre-school had never spoken about Tariq's behaviours to her, she thought that he would outgrow them. His mother said his favourite pastimes included lining up toy cars or animals and watching advertisements on television. She had noticed that he could be quite fussy. For example, he would wear T-shirts only if their labels had been snipped off and socks only if they were turned inside out since uneven textures bothered him. The mother mentioned that Tariq was very particular about routines. For example, he liked to follow the same schedule every day and got very upset if there was a change, such as during holidays. His way of managing his distress was to walk around in circles, sometimes flapping his hands, until he had calmed himself down.

Developmental history

According to his mother, the delivery was normal, as was Tariq's early childhood; though she had noticed that unlike her daughter, he was difficult to breastfeed. She had put him on bottle feeds very early on. Tariq started speaking late, though he managed well in other areas, such as motor development and self-help skills, including feeding himself and personal hygiene. When he started speaking, he was more comfortable repeating the jingles of television advertisements than conversing. As a young child, he used to often express his needs by taking his mother's hand and placing it on an object he wanted rather than by asking her for it. Tariq's mother had had some doubts regarding his development. However, her mother-in-law, who lived with the family, had reassured her that Tariq's father had also started speaking late, like some other boys in the family. The general practitioner had also reassured her during the boy's immunization visits.

Psychosocial history

Family history: Tariq was the only son, with a 12-year-old sister. His mother was a teacher's aide in a local pre-school and his father a businessman. His paternal grandmother lived with the family and helped look after the children. The family environment was stable.

Academic history: Tariq entered pre-school later than other children since he had not started talking yet and his mother was concerned that he would not be able to communicate his needs to the teacher. When he did enter pre-school at the age of 4, the teachers described him as a well-behaved boy who was very good at puzzles but reluctant to play with others in the class. Though he learned the nursery rhymes, he sang them to himself and rarely with the group.

Social history: Tariq's mother described him as a child who 'enjoys his own company'. Though he tolerated his sister, he never approached her to play. He had a fondness for his grandmother, but she had noticed that he did not like to be hugged or caressed. His mother did not understand this lack of affection, especially since her daughter was an affectionate child.

Mental status examination

Tariq entered the counsellor's room with his mother, immediately left her side and started working on some puzzles lying on the office table. When he completed the puzzles, he did not share his achievement with his mother or the counsellor and started tapping on the table. During the session, he solved many difficult puzzles with ease. When the counsellor called out his name, he did not respond and seemed to be staring at the pictures on the wall calendar. When the counsellor offered him a toy car, he took it, spun the wheels and seemed to examine it very closely; he did not roll it on the ground as one would with a toy car. The counsellor repeatedly tried to draw Tariq's attention by showing him interesting things in the room, but he responded only occasionally. When she asked him questions, he repeated the words that had been spoken rather than answering the question. For example, when the counsellor asked, 'Do you like puzzles?' he said, 'Puzzles...puzzles'. Tariq uttered only single words during the session. When it was time to leave, he walked out of the room without a backward glance. Throughout the session, Tariq had not once looked into the counsellor's eyes and had had a rather unusual fixed smile on his face.

CASE FORMULATION

Tariq, a 6-year-old boy studying in Standard I, is the second child in a stable and secure family. His older sister is 12 years old. Tariq was referred to the counsellor by his class teacher because she had noticed that he played only by himself. Tariq's language skills are delayed. He communicates infrequently and echoes speech which he has heard. He makes poor eye contact. His need to interact with others is minimal, and he does not show or share objects of interest with others, resists physical touch and does not play with his peers. His play activities consist of lining up toys and repeating television jingles, and he focuses on a part of the toy rather than the whole toy. He also uses unusual behaviours to calm himself (such as flapping his hands), has a need for fixed routines and restricted and rigid interests and mannerisms. His behaviours reflect core features of the developmental disability, autism spectrum disorder (*see* Chapter 2).

Strengths: Tariq is of average intelligence, as demonstrated by his ease in solving puzzles and good rote learning skills (learning through memorization, though this may not always imply comprehension of the material learnt). He belongs to a secure and stable family. He is good at following routines.

Difficulties: Tariq has limited eye contact. He has minimal language skills and rarely shares his interests or thoughts with others. He requires fixed routines. He has no relationships with his peers. A possible diagnosis of autism spectrum disorder has been made at a late age, so opportunities for early intervention have been missed.

Management plan

The primary strategy to help Tariq is family psychoeducation, which includes referring the parents to a specialist to complete a developmental assessment of their child and making them aware of autism-specific therapies once an assessment has been completed (*see below*, When to refer). In addition, supportive interventions in the school and supportive interventions in the home and the community are recommended.

Family psychoeducation: An example of an initial explanation that the counsellor can provide to help the parents understand Tariq's problem is: 'You may have noticed that Tariq finds it difficult to relate to others and that he has specific interests which are different from those of other children his age. These features are often characteristic of children who have certain developmental problems.' The counsellor can then go on to gently and clearly explain what a developmental disability is, why she suspects that Tariq might have one and why she recommends a developmental assessment with a specialist to determine the source of his difficulties (e.g. difficulty in communicating and interacting with others) at the earliest. The parents should be reassured that they are not to blame for their son's problems and that, with inputs from specialist doctors (who are developmental specialists), therapists and educators, their child could develop some communication and socialization skills (*see below*, When to refer). Only after the diagnosis is confirmed, should the counsellor help the parents understand the diagnosis, dispel any misconceptions they may have about it and help them understand that although there is no cure for autism, Tariq could make progress and develop his skills with the support of therapeutic inputs. The counsellor should maintain contact with the family, as well as the developmental experts involved in Tariq's care, to ensure that the family continues to adhere to any specific therapies that have been recommended. Since Tariq is still young, the importance of early and consistent intervention should be stressed.

Supportive interventions in the school: Due to his unique impairments in the area of communication, Tariq may not be able to learn the academic content of the curriculum unless the mainstream curriculum is adapted to his special needs. The curriculum needs to be modified for him on the basis of specialized evaluations of his learning style, as well as his strengths and difficulties. It is possible that he will need a functional curriculum that addresses the areas of self-help and communication and social skills. A special educator can assess Tariq's needs in this respect and implement the curriculum, either in a resource room or a mainstream classroom setting (*see* Chapter 2). The following can help Tariq anticipate and become comfortable with new upcoming events: visual timetables, i.e. pictorial representations of the daily schedule that clearly show transitions to new subjects or activities (*see* Appendix); social stories describing activities in a step-wise manner, e.g. a description of a school trip starting from the time of boarding the school bus to the time of returning to school, with details of all the events which will occur during the day.

When to refer: The counsellor should refer Tariq to a specialist with developmental expertise for a confirmation of the diagnosis and the commencement of appropriate treatments. Tariq should also have his hearing assessed to rule out any hearing impairment that might be contributing to his difficulty with speech and language. Appropriate treatments for autism include speech and language therapy; autism-specific behaviour therapies, which address challenging behaviours; social skills counselling, with an emphasis on interaction with peers; and occupational therapy, which aims to remedy any sensory sensitivity (in Tariq's case, this would be increased sensitivity to the texture of clothing labels). In addition, the family can be referred to a support group for families of children with special needs.

ASSESSMENT AND MANAGEMENT OF A CHILD WITH COMMUNICATION DIFFICULTIES OR DELAYS

THE PROBLEM

In the primary school years, children may present with a range of unusual behaviours which do not fit into the normal developmental pattern (*see* Chapter 2). The child's development may be delayed across all areas, e.g. a child who has intellectual disability and whose language, self-help and reasoning abilities are all delayed (*see* Case Study 4), or it may be delayed only in one specific area, e.g. a hearing impaired child whose speech is delayed but who has age-appropriate thinking skills.

Youth with autism spectrum disorder have an uneven developmental profile and always display varying degrees of impairment in social communication. Their level of development in certain areas, such as self-help and intellectual skills, may be appropriate, yet it may be significantly impaired in others, such as communication and socialization abilities. These individuals' abilities to engage socially and communicate vary (these abilities lie along a 'spectrum', ranging from mild to severe). Some young people diagnosed with autism spectrum disorder have no language skills at all, communicating neither through speech, nor non-verbal gestures. Some have a few language skills or are capable of some non-verbal gestures, but may have little or no interest in communicating with other people, seeming to be happier on their own. Others have some language skills and are capable of non-verbal gestures, but may find it difficult to understand social cues and the to-and-fro nature of a conversation (*see* Case Study 14). A significant number of young people with autism spectrum disorder have a coexisting intellectual disability; in these situations, the child's problems are noticed earlier and they often need an intensive special educational programme. Young people with autism spectrum disorder may also come to the counsellor's notice due to behavioural issues. These can include throwing significant 'temper tantrums', becoming unusually restless or even hurting themselves (e.g. head banging, biting themselves) and often result from an inability to communicate their need for sameness and routine, or because of their over-sensitivity to the world around them.

Assessment

Information from the youth

- Observing the youth with autism spectrum disorder in various settings in the school, such as in class and on the playground, often provides crucial information on the functioning of the youth. It is important for the counsellor to observe both his 'adaptive behaviours' (behaviours required for daily living) and his challenging behaviours (behaviours such as temper tantrums, excessive restlessness and aggression).
- During the assessment process, it is important for the counsellor to pinpoint and analyse the challenging behaviours of the youth. When do the difficult behaviours occur? How long do they last? What are the triggers? Are they related to specific issues in the environment, such as before snack time or prior to a toilet break? How frequently do they occur? How do the behaviours affect others in the environment?
- The counsellor can learn to interpret the youth's challenging behaviours with the help of a special educator. One reason for the youth's behaviour could be, for example, that he stands to gain something tangible, such as a toy he wants. It could also be that the behaviour is a result of his sensory needs and helps to soothe him. For example, jumping up and down may help to calm him down. The youth might behave in a particular way because it helps him avoid something he does not like (such as going to the sports ground), because it helps release tension or because it is a habit.

Information from the parent

- Have the parents noticed something unusual or different about their child's development?
- What steps have they taken to understand these differences?
- What do they think are the reasons for these differences?
- What are their concerns regarding the child?
- Are there any other children or adults in the family with a similar problem? If so, how are they doing?

Information from the teacher

- What problems has the teacher identified regarding the youth in the classroom?

- What has the teacher identified as the strengths of the youth that would make his inclusion in the mainstream classroom possible?
- What resources are available within the school to help the youth remain in a mainstream setting?

Management

With the family

- Family psychoeducation will encourage the family to follow up on a referral for a developmental assessment of the child (*see* Chapter 4) and, if a developmental disability is confirmed, will help them come to terms with a diagnosis which does not have a 'cure' (*see* Chapter 6). The diagnosis of autism spectrum disorder or other developmental disabilities often gives rise to a range of reactions in parents: denial, blame, guilt, sadness, and finally, acceptance. The parents sometimes move back and forth from one to the other of these emotions as they process the diagnosis. The counsellor should maintain regular contact with the family to provide emotional support. Helping the family maintain a sense of hope is an important part of family psychoeducation.

With teachers and school staff

- The counsellor should work with the youth's therapists and special educators to facilitate coordination of the management of the youth's disruptive and difficult behaviours within the school. Behaviour charts (*see* Chapter 6 and Appendix) can be useful tools for the management of behaviour. The youth's therapists and special educators can agree upon rewards and consequences that would accompany particular behaviours, e.g. a restless child could be allowed to walk around the class as a reward for completing an assigned activity.
- Educational inputs in a special education resource room enable young people to remain in the mainstream school setting while availing themselves of the benefits of a specialized curriculum (*see* Chapter 2). It is preferable for children with mild autism spectrum disorder to receive mainstream education because it most effectively supports healthy adjustment and social integration.
- Awareness and building of skills help teachers and staff understand

and address the special needs of young people with autism spectrum disorder and guide them to promote an inclusive school environment (*see* Chapter 6).

- Most young children who have autism spectrum disorder and a significant impairment in their ability to communicate cannot get their needs across effectively, possibly leading to social withdrawal or disruptive behaviour. In these situations, the counsellor could work with a special educator and a speech and language therapist to integrate specialized communication techniques, such as using gestures, sign language or pictures, into the classroom setting so that the child is better able to express his needs to the teacher and his fellow students.

When to refer: Youth who the counsellor suspects have a developmental disability must be referred as soon as possible to specialists with experience in the diagnosis and management of autism spectrum disorder. The earlier the interventions are introduced, the better the progress of the youth.

Key messages

- Autism spectrum disorders are lifelong developmental disabilities which affect the way the person communicates and relates to others, and which restrict his areas of interest.
- Youth with hearing impairment, a speech and language delay or an intellectual disability may display some of the features of autism spectrum disorder; however, their management and course are significantly different from those of the youth with autism spectrum disorder.
- Parents may need support to come to terms with the diagnosis of autism spectrum disorder and to attempt and adhere to the specific therapies that are recommended.
- When working with a youth with autism spectrum disorder, the counsellor's role includes: supporting the family; making appropriate referrals; and assisting the teachers in creating a parallel, specialized curriculum that makes it easier to include the youth in the mainstream classroom or helps the youth make good use of special classrooms or resource rooms.

CASE STUDY 2

THE CHILD WHO REFUSES TO GO TO SCHOOL

Gita's story

THE PRESENTING PROBLEM

Gita was a 7-year-old who studied in Standard II. She had been referred to the counsellor by her mother because she regularly missed school. On most mornings, she complained of headaches and refused to go to school. On a number of occasions, after dropping her tearful daughter to school, the mother would receive a call from the teacher saying that Gita was not well. The mother then picked her up from school. Once home, it hardly took any time for Gita to start feeling well.

The mother had consulted several doctors. All the medical reports had been normal and the doctors had reassured her that Gita did not

have any medical problem. Gita's mother had been very worried about her. Since she had missed school so often, Gita's notes were incomplete and her grades had fallen. At home, Gita constantly needed her mother for various reasons. This was particularly difficult for the mother because she also had a 3-month-old baby. Lately, when Gita had complained about going to school, her mother had been allowing her to stay at home.

Gita told the counsellor that she often had nausea and headaches in the morning. She said her mother did not believe that she was feeling sick and often shouted at her. Gita thought that the reason her mother wanted her to go to school was to be able to spend more time with her baby brother. She complained that since her brother had been born, her mother had not had the time to play with her or even help her with her studies.

Developmental history

Gita was born pre-term (at 8 months) and was described as a 'delicate' baby. Other than the fact that she frequently caught colds, she had generally been physically healthy throughout her childhood. However, Gita had always been shy and had a tendency to cling to her mother. It took her 3 months to adjust to pre-school, and she would cry and cling to her mother every morning during this period. Even after she adapted to the pre-school routine, there were many mornings when she would be in tears.

Psychosocial history

Family history: Gita was the eldest child and had a brother who was 3 months old. Her father worked in a company and was posted to another city, visiting the family twice monthly. Gita's grandparents lived with the family. Her mother was a housewife and looked after the children. Gita was very happy when her father came home. Her mother had been busy looking after her little brother and had had less time for Gita, who felt unhappy about this. Gita sometimes went out with her father alone, but did not enjoy this as much as when the whole family went out together.

Academic history: Gita's school performance had always been average. She was good at mathematics, but had difficulty with subjects that required memorization. Her mother had always assisted her with her lessons. She gave her tips and explained lessons that Gita had not understood. During her pregnancy, the mother began to encourage her daughter to study on her own because she knew that Gita's dependence on her could give rise to a problematic situation once the baby was born. However, Gita put up considerable resistance to this. Her mother gave up on trying to convince her, and continued supervising and assisting Gita with her studies. As she had anticipated, since the birth of her son, she had been unable to devote as much time to Gita's studies as she had provided earlier. Gita had been coming home with incomplete notes and the teachers had been complaining that she had been paying less attention to her studies. Gita said she found her class very noisy this year and claimed that her headaches were worse when she was in school. The teachers had no complaints about her behaviour, but were concerned about the fact that she did not pay attention in class and had been missing school frequently.

Social history: Gita said she was happy to have one best friend in her class. She talked to the girls in her class but rarely to the boys, whom she found too boisterous.

Mental status examination

Gita was not forthcoming with the counsellor. She spoke very softly and made poor eye contact. She was neatly dressed and had a careful manner. Whenever the counsellor enquired about her absenting herself from school, Gita became nervous and spoke in monosyllables. She was happier talking about her parents and the fun that she had when her father came home. She refused to talk about her little brother, though she said that her mother loved him more than she loved her. Since Gita did not speak much, it was difficult to know what she was thinking about. However, her behaviour and tone of voice indicated that she was upset about the attention that her brother received. She did not express any wish to harm her brother or herself. Her insight into her reactions was poor. The content of her thought appeared to be appropriate.

Case formulation

Gita, a 7-year-old girl studying in Standard II, is the eldest child and has a 3-month-old brother. She lives with her mother, grandparents and baby brother, and her father comes home twice monthly. She was referred to the counsellor by her mother. The primary problem is that Gita has been missing school and complaining of headaches and nausea, though the doctors have not found any medical cause. These complaints seem to have begun after the birth of her brother. Her mood and thoughts are otherwise normal. The most likely diagnosis is mental health distress with symptoms of anxiety (*see* Chapter 2), arising from feelings of insecurity and rejection following the birth of her brother and her mother's time spent caring for him. Gita's vulnerability during her pre-school years, when she showed symptoms of separation anxiety, may provide a background explanation for her current reactions.

Strengths: Among Gita's strengths are her average intelligence, a good relationship with her peers and teachers and a strong bond both with her parents and grandparents.

Difficulties: The difficulties include the relative lack of time and attention that Gita's mother can devote to her since her brother's birth; the additional pressures on the mother, whose husband is away much of the time and who now has to look after two children single-handedly; Gita's dependence on her mother for help with her homework; Gita frequently avoiding school in order to return or stay home; the difficulty Gita has expressing her emotions through words; and Gita's physical symptoms.

Management plan

The counselling strategies that can help Gita are youth psychoeducation, family psychoeducation and problem-solving counselling.

Youth psychoeducation: The counsellor can help Gita 'talk' about her thoughts and feelings through drawing and stories (*see* Chapter 5). He should try to help Gita understand that her mother's attentions to her brother may make her feel angry and left out, and that these feelings may cause headaches and result in a reluctance to leave home and go to school. The consequences of missing school should also be discussed. The counsellor should reassure Gita that her parents love her just as much as they did before the birth of her brother and that her mother is probably sad that she does not have the energy to give Gita the attention she needs. He should empathize with Gita, saying that it is natural for her to want her mother's attention, and explain that one of the aims of counselling is to help Gita and her mother find ways of spending time together. The counsellor needs to encourage Gita to come to school so that she can do well, spend time with her school friend as well as make new friends.

Family psychoeducation: It is important to tell Gita's mother about the emotional cause of her daughter's distress. It should be explained to her that since the doctors have not found a medical cause for Gita's headaches, the likeliest explanation for these, as well as her avoidance of school, is anxiety precipitated by the birth of her brother and the fact that she can no longer give Gita her full attention. The counsellor could describe Gita's distress to her mother as follows: 'Gita has been feeling insecure about losing your love and affection since her brother was born.' The fact that Gita experienced separation anxiety when she was younger could also be referred to as an indicator of a sensitive temperament and unease when she experiences less time with her mother. Further, if the parents also reassure Gita, as the counsellor has done, it will strengthen Gita's confidence in the process of counselling. For example, they could tell her that they love her just as much as they did before her brother was born. Her mother could say that she is sad about not having the energy to give Gita all the attention she needs, and that she will work with the counsellor to find more opportunities to spend time with Gita. To restore Gita's belief that she is important to and loved by her mother, the counsellor can help the mother think of ways of spending time with Gita and the baby together, as well as spending time with Gita individually. As an example of the first, the mother could enlist Gita's help in looking after the baby in ways that she is capable of and that she would enjoy. As for spending time with Gita individually, the mother might ask the grandmother to look after the baby at a particular time of the day so that she can spend some time exclusively with her daughter. Despite Gita's current problems, it is essential for the mother to be firm about expecting regular school attendance and following through on home routines.

Problem-solving counselling: The counsellor should help Gita identify and prioritize her problem areas, e.g. needing her mother's attention, needing to keep up with schoolwork, needing to come to school. The counsellor can then help her learn to find positive solutions to her problems. For example, instead of staying home with a headache, Gita might select a teacher, whom she particularly likes, to build a relationship with so that she may have a special reason to want to come to school. Gita can develop alternative ways of managing her feelings and behaviours. For example, she could find enjoyable ways of spending time when her mother is busy or could help her mother look after her brother.

The following intervention may also be useful:

Supportive interventions in the school: Gita may benefit from additional support from her teachers to help her learn to complete notes and manage some of the subjects that require memorization.

Assessment and Management of School Avoidance

The Problem

School avoidance (or refusal) refers to the situation when a young person repeatedly avoids attending school or is sent home from school due to physical symptoms which have an emotional basis. Young people who avoid school often have vague physical complaints, such as abdominal aches, headaches, nausea, palpitations, faintness or physical symptoms that accompany panic reactions, for which no medical cause can be found. Many also have low self-esteem. Typically, the youth experiences a physical symptom in the morning and this disappears by mid-morning if she is allowed to stay home. School avoidance usually has two causes: (i) anxiety associated with going to school, and (ii) the prospect of 'secondary gain(s)' associated with staying at home. Some reasons for the first are persisting separation anxiety disorder, worry about examinations or grades, anxiety about bullying at school, an upsetting change in family circumstances and distressing family dynamics. Among pre-school children, separation anxiety can be developmentally normal; however, if the symptoms are severe or if separation anxiety persists beyond the age of 6 years, it is possible that the youth is suffering from separation anxiety disorder (*see* Chapter 2). Secondary gains include the pleasure of receiving sympathy or special treatment at home, as well as the opportunity that staying home affords to avoid schoolwork.

Assessment

Information from the youth

- Is there anything at school or at home that is worrying the youth?

Information from the parent

- When did this problem begin? What is the parents' understanding of its causes?
- Does the child have symptoms only on school days or weekends as well?
- Has their child had difficulty separating from the parent in the past?
- Has there been any change in their child's life/family circumstances that may have caused her present insecurity, e.g. the birth of a sibling, marital conflict?
- Has anything changed in their child's school circumstances, e.g. does she have a new teacher or has her best friend moved away?
- What are the parents' attitudes to their child's distress and her missing school and staying at home?

Information from the teacher

- Has the teacher noticed anything unusual or a change in the youth's behaviour?
- Is there anything in the school environment (e.g. bullying, poor scholastic performance) which could be triggering the youth's anxiety?

- What helps the young person take an interest in school? What are her favourite school activities? What are her friendships like?

Management

With the youth

- Youth psychoeducation is useful in helping the youth understand how her body is reacting to emotional distress, and also, what is causing her distress.
- Problem-solving counselling helps the youth identify the problems that are stressful for her. It also aids the process of finding effective solutions to cope with the stress instead of resorting to school avoidance.
- Cognitive restructuring may be used to help the youth modify negative thoughts about herself.

With the family

- Family psychoeducation is used to help the family understand the reasons for their child's distress; to discourage them from blaming themselves or their child for her problem; to help them find practical solutions and use a system of positive rewards to encourage their child to take an interest in school again; and to explore the parenting attitudes and behaviours (e.g. overprotection, guilt, anxiety) which may interfere with their child's ability to attend school.

With teachers and school staff

- It is important to identify areas of stress for the youth in the school setting. The teacher and school staff should be assisted in encouraging her school attendance.
- It is useful to identify activities and peer relationships which can help engage the youth and sustain her interest in school.

When to refer: If the youth cannot attend counselling sessions because of school absence or if, despite a period of counselling, her anxiety symptoms continue to prevent her from attending school regularly, a referral to a mental health professional is necessary.

Key messages

- School avoidance is a common manifestation of anxiety in youth and, if it persists, can indicate a separation anxiety disorder.
- School avoidance can temporarily reduce anxiety and can also yield 'secondary gains', e.g. receiving extra attention at home.
- If the problem is not addressed, the youth may miss a significant amount of school and school avoidance can become an established maladaptive coping mechanism.
- Youth psychoeducation, problem-solving counselling for the youth and family psychoeducation for the parents can often effectively address school avoidance.

CASE STUDY 3

The child exposed to an overwhelming event

Bina's story

The presenting problem

Bina, a 7-year-old girl studying in Standard II, was referred to the counsellor by the principal about two weeks after she went through a serious car accident. Bina's parents spoke to the principal about her reluctance to go to school. She had not attended school for the week following the accident and, since then, had clung to her mother at the school gate, reluctant to leave her side. Her parents also said she found it difficult to sleep on her own and would come into their bedroom almost every night. In addition, she has been afraid to travel by car since the accident.

The counsellor first met with Bina's parents, who described what they knew about the accident. They recounted that two weeks ago, Bina's uncle had picked her up from school because both parents had been busy. She was in the back seat, where she was enjoying a snack. She and her uncle were chatting about her day in school when, at an intersection, a speeding car crashed into their car. Their car spun around and hit a compound wall. Over several seconds, Bina was hurled around in the back seat, her body banging against the front seat and the inside of the car. She suffered bruises on her arms and head, and slivers of glass from the shattered windscreen embedded in her hands. Fortunately, the airbags in the car inflated and protected her uncle from extensive injury; however, he had fainted. The police and an ambulance arrived and took Bina and her uncle to a hospital about 20 minutes away. The uncle needed to be put under observation and was hospitalized. Bina was examined in the emergency room, the slivers of glass removed and the wounded areas cleaned and bandaged. Bina's parents arrived at the hospital within an hour of receiving a call and took her home. Her uncle was discharged a few days later. Bina's parents told the counsellor that her problems began the day after the accident. They also expressed feelings of guilt, saying that if only they had picked Bina up from school that day, the accident may never have occurred.

Developmental history

According to her parents, Bina's development had been normal. Socially, she was a somewhat timid child, taking time to warm up to adults and children outside her family circle.

Psychosocial history

Family history: Bina was an only child. Her maternal grandparents lived nearby and visited the family often. Her father was a businessman and her mother a homemaker. The family was well regarded in the community and the father held a position of importance on the local temple committee.

Academic history: When Bina entered a local pre-school at the age of 3, she was initially very shy, but gradually adjusted to the routines. She entered primary school at the age of 6. She enjoyed learning to read, spell and write, though she found mathematics a little difficult. When Bina's parents met the counsellor, they expressed the apprehension that their daughter might lose ground academically, and that her fearfulness and reluctance to be away from her mother might affect her school attendance. She had already missed one week of school since the accident and it had been a struggle to get her to go to school every morning during the second week. She was reluctant to get up in the mornings, took a long time over breakfast and said she was 'scared' to go to school by car.

Social history: Since Bina was shy and reserved, her mother had always made efforts to help her develop and maintain friendships by arranging play dates. Her parents were now concerned that the fearfulness induced by the accident might affect Bina's friendships; she might become withdrawn or want to be with her mother at all times.

MENTAL STATUS EXAMINATION

Bina was happy to meet with the counsellor, after initially being hesitant. Although she was slow to warm up to the counsellor, she was friendly and cooperative, made good eye contact and spoke clearly. Bina was often quiet, and at times appeared sad and nervous, especially when talking about the car accident. Since Bina was reluctant to speak, the counsellor provided her with paper and coloured markers, which she told her she could use to draw whatever she liked (*see* Chapter 5). Bina drew a number of scenes, including a car accident, and talked about the accident. She admitted to feeling scared every time she was in a car and said she felt especially nervous if the car was being driven by people other than her parents. She also related that she had been waking up with nightmares about the accident and preferred to sleep in her parents' bedroom. Other than her preoccupation with these concerns, Bina's thought content was normal.

CASE FORMULATION

Bina is a 7-year-old girl who studies in Standard II and lives with her parents in a nuclear family. She was referred to the counsellor by the principal and her parents following a car accident. The primary concerns of Bina's parents include her reluctance to leave her mother in the mornings to go to school and also, at bedtime; her continuing fear of riding in a car; and the possibility that she may lose ground academically and become socially isolated. Bina has nightmares about the accident and finds it difficult to sleep in her own bed. She is experiencing mental health distress with symptoms of anxiety (*see* Chapter 2) as a consequence of having experienced a car accident.

Strengths: Bina is intellectually above average, and belongs to a secure and protective family. Her school environment is supportive.

Difficulties: Bina's difficulties include her fearfulness; increased dependence on her mother; her lost time from school; and aspects of her temperament, having always been shy and slow to warm up.

Management plan

The primary strategy to help Bina recover is crisis counselling (with Bina and with her family). In addition, supportive interventions in the school can be useful.

Crisis counselling (with the family): The counsellor should focus on helping the parents understand the connection between the car accident and Bina's current problems. She should also help them identify how they can facilitate Bina's recovery. To help the parents understand their daughter's problems, the counsellor might tell them, 'The car accident has shaken Bina's sense of security and it will be difficult for her to stop thinking about the accident for a while.' The parents can be advised to do the following to facilitate their daughter's recovery: listen to her description of what happened, if she wants to discuss it; allow her to express her emotions and respect these, e.g. expressions of fear that another accident could occur; empathize with her; reduce her fears by using realistic explanations; patiently correct any misconceptions she has about how and why the accident occurred; make sure that they are available to drive her to and from school until her fears subside; serve as role models for managing emotions; initially reduce her exposure to any reminders of the accident, such as avoiding driving down the road where the accident occurred, and gradually reintroduce her to the reminders as she is better able to manage her feelings; and maintain her routines. It is important for the counsellor to emphasize to the parents that Bina be encouraged to return to her school routines as quickly as possible (*see* Chapter 6). To help with this, they can make behaviour charts using a reward system for the days she attends school. For example, they could use a chart on which stars are marked every day she attends school, with a predetermined number of stars earning her a special reward, such as a favourite treat (*see* Chapter 6 and Appendix). In addition, the counsellor should address and try to decrease the parents' feelings of guilt about not having driven Bina home the day of the accident. An attempt should also be made to restore their confidence in their parenting skills.

Crisis counselling (with the youth): The counsellor should invite Bina to share her story to the extent that she wants to. Bina can be encouraged to talk and write about the accident and her feelings during and after it, or express herself through drawing (*see* Chapter 5). It is important to remember that Bina must not be forced to tell her story (*see* Chapter 6). The purpose of youth psychoeducation is to inform Bina how her experience during the accident is currently affecting her, e.g. causing her to cling to her mother, feeling afraid of riding in a car and having nightmares about the accident. Youth psychoeducation should also make her aware of how reminders of the accident might increase her anxiety and provide her with ways to deal with these reminders. For example, when she hears tyres screeching, in order to feel safe, she could tell herself that the sound may not be coming from the car she is in and then listen for where it is in fact coming. In addition, youth psychoeducation can be used to improve Bina's ability to communicate her feelings to her parents and other trusted adults (e.g. her grandparents). The counsellor should reassure Bina that although the accident was scary, with time, counselling and her parents' support, her feelings and life will return to normal. In addition, she should encourage Bina's positive coping behaviours and her return to the activities that she always enjoyed.

Supportive interventions in the school: The counsellor should inform the teachers and school staff (with permission from Bina and her parents) how the car accident has affected Bina, and should help them consider the school supports that could help her. Praising Bina when she comes to school and decreasing her workload may facilitate her transition to normalcy. It is common for young people who have experienced an overwhelming event to have difficulty concentrating on academic tasks because they are often thinking about the event. The counsellor can help the teachers understand this so that they do not misinterpret Bina's lack of concentration on academic tasks as intentional. They can support Bina by reducing her homework so that she can spend time with her parents after school, which in turn will restore her sense of security. In addition, the counsellor can advise the teachers to try to ensure that Bina engages with her peers if they see that she is withdrawing. For example, they could encourage her to participate in a group activity if she is sitting on the sidelines.

Assessment and management of youth who experience an overwhelming event

The problem

Exposure to an overwhelming event (e.g. experiencing or witnessing an accident or violence, being in a natural disaster) is destabilizing because it is unexpected and results in feelings of extreme helplessness. Such an event can affect a person in several ways. She may continue to experience the emotional and physical responses that occurred during the event, especially when faced with a reminder of the event. Among these feelings are terror, anxiety, anger, helplessness and physical symptoms (e.g. palpitations). The person may also fear or avoid cues that are reminders. Some young people regress to earlier phases of development which are associated with safety. For example, they may become very dependent on a parent or may need to sleep with their parents. Behavioural reactions, such as acting out behaviours marked by aggression or withdrawal from activities which the child previously enjoyed, may also occur. Most often, the youth's condition stabilizes with the passage of time and the consistent provision of support and a sense of safety. However, if the condition does not subside within a reasonable period of time following the overwhelming event, the youth might be suffering from post-traumatic stress syndrome (*see* Chapter 2) and require the assistance of a mental health professional.

Assessment

Information from the youth

- If the youth is comfortable describing what she recalls of the event, she can share this with the counsellor. However, it is important to note that she should not be pressed to describe the event (*see* Chapter 6).
- If the youth feels comfortable talking about the event, the counsellor can explore the reminders in her daily life that trigger feelings that she experienced during the event. If the youth describes reminders and the feelings associated with them, the counsellor should ask how

she handles these feelings.

- What other present or expected future events worry her?
- To what extent is the memory of the event affecting her friendships, family relationships and/or schoolwork? How is she coping with this?
- What other changes have taken place in her daily functioning? How is she coping with these changes?

Information from the parents

- What did their exposure to the event consist of? What do they recall?
- What is worrying them now about their child?
- Is their child talking about the event? If so, what has she told them?
- Does their child ever incorporate the event into her play, e.g. does she play out a car crash with toys? Have they discussed the event with her? If so, what has she told them?
- How are they supporting their child? What effect are their efforts having?
- How has this event and their child's condition influenced their parenting?

Information from the teacher

- How has the youth been functioning socially and academically since the event?
- What help have the teacher and school provided to support the youth's recovery?

Management

With the youth

- The crisis counselling with the youth restores the youth's ability to cope by helping her understand how the overwhelming event continues to affect her, by improving her ability to manage her reactions to reminders and by holding out the hope that she will recover.

With the parents

- The crisis counselling with the family educates the family members about the emotional and behavioural impacts of the overwhelming event, helps them find the best ways to support their child's recovery and makes it easier for them to cope with their reactions (e.g. reducing any self-blame they may experience).

With teachers and school staff

- Supportive interventions in the school help the teachers and school staff respond to the youth's distress in the school setting with appropriate emotional and academic support. They also equip the teachers to provide an explanation, if necessary, to the youth's peers regarding the effects of overwhelming events on young people in general and on the specific youth in particular (*see* Chapter 6).

When to refer: Immediately after an overwhelming event, a young person usually feels extremely worried, agitated, helpless and reactive to reminders. As mentioned earlier, these feelings usually subside with the passage of time and with support. However, if they do not subside

Key messages

- An individual exposed to an overwhelming event may have persistent recollections of the event, accompanied by symptoms of anxiety and arousal (e.g. feeling jumpy), especially when faced with reminders of the event.
- A youth who has experienced such an event may feel extremely vulnerable and may, without her awareness, regress to an earlier phase of development for a period of time, in search of care and comfort.
- It is useful to supplement crisis counselling with supportive interventions in the school.
- In most cases, the reactions to the overwhelming event subside with time and with the help of crisis counselling; if they do not, the youth may be suffering from post-traumatic stress disorder.

gradually after six weeks, or if they become more marked over the course of counselling, the youth may be suffering from post-traumatic stress disorder (*see* Chapter 2), which requires a referral to a mental health professional for evaluation and follow-up.

CASE STUDY 4

The child who is falling behind his peers

Somesh's story

The presenting problem

Somesh, an 8-year-old boy studying in Standard II, was referred to the counsellor by his class teacher because he was lagging behind his peers in his academic performance. Somesh's mother said that he had been struggling to keep up with his class since Standard I. His teachers had been complaining that he was very slow when it came to completing his assignments. His work was most often incomplete and his teachers had to supervise him very closely for him to submit completed work. He was quick to take out his books at the beginning of a class, but was then unable to follow the instructions being given. The teacher told the counsellor that though Somesh could recognize smaller numbers, say them by rote and recognize arithmetic signs, he was unable to carry out basic operations, such as addition, or to recognize bigger numbers. She sometimes felt his ability to understand concepts was not as developed as that of his classmates. He was good on the sports field and in arts/crafts, and enjoyed singing. Somesh was happy participating in extracurricular activities and was a helpful person. His mother related that he helped her with household chores such as sweeping. She was concerned about his schoolwork and complained that he forgot what he had learned. He had to be frequently reminded of his daily routines. She could not understand why Somesh could not do well in academics. Somesh said he liked going to school because he could play with his friends. He liked his art teacher because she allowed him to draw and because he did not have to read and write during her class. He also liked his environmental education class because the teacher sometimes took the class outdoors for lessons and to play games.

Developmental history

According to the history provided by his mother, Somesh was born at full term and the delivery was normal. He was shifted to a different hospital soon after his birth because he had some health complications. The doctors told his mother that he had to be kept in an incubator and under observation for a few days. His mother said that Somesh was 'not a very healthy baby', and that she had to often take him to the doctor. However, she did not report any major illnesses. He started walking when he was 2½ years old and speaking after he was 3. It took time to toilet train him. He achieved these milestones much later than his older sisters. His mother had thought he was a little 'slow' because he was a boy. He was a cheerful and affectionate child who did not cry much.

Psychosocial history

Family history: Somesh lived in a nuclear family with his two older sisters, mother and father. His father was a taxi driver and his mother a housewife. Somesh said he liked his father because he bought him toys and sweets and did not ask him to study. He did not like it when his mother shouted at him to get his schoolwork done.

Academic history: Somesh began attending a local pre-school at 5 years of age because he was not toilet trained until then. Since he did not begin talking until he was 3 years old, he had a little difficulty with rhymes, storytelling and other such verbal activities in pre-school. However, he seemed to understand the concepts conveyed in pre-school. He was physically very active, but not restless. His teachers in pre-school told his mother that Somesh would do well in school once his speech became fluent. The teacher who referred him to the counsellor described him as a child who was sociable in class and who was ready to help others with routine tasks, e.g. he liked to help distribute and collect books.

Social history: Somesh was very popular, both in his school and neighbourhood. He enjoyed outdoor sports. He said he had many friends and liked playing with them. His mother complained that he was out playing most of the time and she had to drag him back home to get him to complete his homework.

Mental status examination

Somesh made good eye contact with the counsellor. He wore clean clothes but seemed a little disorganized. For example, his shirt was not tucked in properly and his handkerchief was hanging out of a trouser pocket. Somesh was cooperative and it was easy to establish a rapport with him. He was interested in the puzzles and displayed a considerable ability to concentrate while trying to solve them, but he was not successful in putting all the pieces together. Sometimes his behaviour did not seem appropriate for his age. For example, he selected picture books which were meant for much younger children. He was of a very cheerful disposition and his mood was appropriate to the situation.

Case formulation

Somesh, an 8-year-old boy studying in Standard II, was referred to the counsellor by his class teacher because of his problems in coping with his studies. He is the youngest and the only male child among three siblings, and lives in a nuclear family with his parents and siblings. His father is a taxi driver and his mother a housewife. Somesh's history reflects a delay across all areas of development. Cognitively, his functioning is like that of a child younger than his age and he lags behind his peers academically. The most probable diagnosis is mild intellectual disability (*see* Chapter 2).

Strengths: Among the strengths in Somesh's environment are his caring home environment, his strong peer relationships and his helpful and cheerful nature.

Difficulties: His difficulties include his functioning at a level lower than his actual age in all areas except basic self-help skills and his parents' lack of awareness of his condition.

Management plan

The primary strategies and supportive interventions to help Somesh cope effectively are youth psychoeducation, family psychoeducation and supportive interventions in the school.

Youth psychoeducation: The counsellor should assess Somesh's understanding of the difference between his and others' learning abilities. On the basis of this assessment, she should explain, in a sensitive manner, the challenges he faces in acquiring new skills. She should avoid mentioning the diagnostic label since this might discourage him. While explaining the matter to him, the counsellor could tell him that he may require more time and practice than his friends to understand and complete his schoolwork, and that he will work with his teacher to find ways to help him with his schoolwork. The counsellor should also work with Somesh to identify his strengths, e.g. the fact that he is helpful and friendly, and tell him that he will also work with the teacher to identify opportunities within the class to build upon his strengths.

Family psychoeducation: The first step in family psychoeducation would be to make Somesh's parents aware of the need for an assessment of his intellectual abilities (*see below*, When to refer). The counsellor could explain this to the parents in the following way: 'Somesh finds it difficult to learn like other children of his age. It would help for you to have his learning abilities assessed so that we can understand what his learning potential is and tailor his academic work to suit his abilities.' If the assessment confirms that Somesh has an intellectual disability, the counsellor will need to give the parents emotional support so that they can understand and accept the diagnosis (*see* Chapter 6). This may take a number of meetings. Sharing the diagnostic term of 'mild intellectual disability' may help the parents support Somesh's ongoing development. However, they should be advised not to use the diagnostic term with Somesh as this could discourage him. Further, it is not necessary for him to know his diagnosis as long as he is aware that he has a learning difference and can benefit from additional inputs. The counsellor should emphasize how important it is for the key adults in Somesh's life to be patient and supportive. He can discuss Somesh's future needs and explain to his parents that Somesh is likely to continue to find it difficult to keep up with academic work, though hands-on activities (e.g. using counters to explain the idea of addition) and curriculum modification (*see* Chapter 2) can support his cognitive development. The counsellor can discuss and address the parents' long-term worries about Somesh's future. He could encourage them to continue to make use of counselling as Somesh develops, if necessary.

Supportive interventions in the school: It is of key importance for the school to understand Somesh's difficulties and support his development. Once his diagnosis has been confirmed, the counsellor should explain to the teachers and school staff why Somesh has academic difficulties and needs additional support to learn. It may be useful to mention the diagnostic term of mild intellectual disability. However, they should be strongly advised against using this term with Somesh or his schoolmates (about Somesh), since this could potentially stigmatize him. An empathetic student in Somesh's peer group could be designated as a 'buddy', who can prompt him to stay on course and complete his work. The teacher can be encouraged to make time to work individually with Somesh every day, e.g. during the break, to help him understand concepts. The school should be encouraged to adopt a curriculum tailored to his needs, as well as an individual educational plan (IEP) (*see* Chapter 2), which systematically breaks down the learning process into smaller units so that difficult concepts can be introduced in a step-wise manner. The family should be made aware of the content and focus of the IEP (*see* Chapter 4) so that further support can be provided at home, e.g. academic enrichment. The school management should be sensitized about the need for an inclusive atmosphere in the school. The school management should be persuaded to create such an atmosphere, e.g. by making resource rooms with special educators available and by encouraging children with various abilities to study together (*see* Chapters 2 and 6).

When to refer: It is important for Somesh to undergo developmental and psychoeducational assessments (*see* Chapter 4) to confirm the counsellor's suspicions, to help his parents and the school understand the level of his abilities and to facilitate modifications in the curriculum to suit his needs. Somesh should also be referred to a special educator who can implement the recommendations made in the assessment. The special educator would also support the mainstream teacher by providing information on Somesh's specific cognitive difficulties and suggest approaches to help him learn. For example, the special educator can help the mainstream teacher understand Somesh's difficulty with abstract concepts and can recommend teaching approaches which could help him understand these concepts. One such approach is the 'touch, feel, see, do' technique, which uses concrete examples and all the senses to help the youth understand abstract information. For example, if the concept that 'soft and hard' are different from one another is being taught, soft and hard objects can be given to the youth to compare and contrast. If the school cannot supply adequate academic support through a resource room, which would be the ideal solution, or if Somesh is not able to cope despite support, a referral to a special school (which is focused on teaching children functional skills rather than on academic skills) may be considered and discussed with his parents (*see* Chapter 2).

Assessment and Management of Intellectual Disability

The problem

Intellectual disability is manifested as delayed development across the major developmental areas, notably the cognitive (thinking, reasoning and recalling), motor, language and social domains. Individuals with intellectual disability typically show delays in achieving developmental milestones, such as sitting, walking and talking. As they grow older, they also lag behind their peers in the spheres of self-care, socialization, problem-solving, logical thinking and the ability to recall (*see* Chapter 2). A mild intellectual disability may not be noticed until the child starts formal schooling (Standard I). Given adequate support systems, including being allowed to learn at his own pace and given frequent opportunities to practise his skills, the child with mild to moderate intellectual disability can cope effectively in elementary (mainstream) school. However, as he grows, the curriculum focus may need to be shifted to 'functional academics', which addresses activities of daily living (such as telling what time it is and ensuring one's personal safety) and vocational options. It is also important for the counsellor to understand that a youth with intellectual disability may have coexisting mental health problems, such as anxiety disorder and attention deficit hyperactivity disorder (Panel 1).

Panel 1. Difference between mild intellectual disability and specific learning disability

Mild intellectual disability	Specific learning disability
The child will come to the teachers' notice during the early school years due to overall delay in many areas.	The child will come to the teachers' notice as academic pressures increase over the years.
The child will have difficulties across many areas of functioning, including self-help skills (e.g. becoming toilet trained later than his peers, needing reminders about daily routines), understanding concepts, retaining information and communicating.	The child will often have problems in a specific academic area, such as reading, writing or mathematics, and overall difficulty with processing information.
The child's achievements will match his intellectual level.	The child's achievements will be well below his intellectual level.
The child will score poorly on psychoeducational testing, indicating a problem with intellectual capacity.	The child will achieve an average or above average IQ score on psychoeducational testing, indicating that he has no problem with intellectual capacity.

Assessment

Information from the youth

- How does the youth get along with his peers? Does he feel included or left out?
- How does he fare in his studies? Which subjects does he enjoy and which are hard for him? What is his understanding of his academic difficulties?
- Which activities, at home or in school, does the youth enjoy? Which activities does he dislike? Why?
- How does he feel about himself (his self-image) relative to his peers?

Information from the parent

- What is their child's developmental history? Were there delays across

all areas or only in a specific area (such as language)?
- What is the parents' understanding of their child's learning difference?
- What are their child's current levels of thinking and functioning with respect to self-care?
- What are their child's strengths?
- Which of their child's difficulties concern the parents the most?

Information from the teacher

- What difficulties does the youth have with schoolwork?
- How does he function in specific areas, particularly socialization, self-care and academics?
- Have his difficulties increased as he has moved on from class to class?
- Are there any specific problems, e.g. social isolation or bullying, associated with the difference between him and his peers?

MANAGEMENT

With the youth

- Youth psychoeducation helps the youth understand in what ways the difficulties he is experiencing are related to differences in his ability relative to his peers. The counsellor makes the youth aware of and helps him build upon his strengths. The youth should be informed about his difficulties in as clear and sensitive a manner as possible.
- Social skills counselling helps the youth fit in with peer relationships.

With the family

- Family psychoeducation should encourage the youth's family to follow through with an educational assessment for the youth and, if he is diagnosed with an intellectual disability, help his parents come to terms with the diagnosis (*see* Chapter 6). An assessment by a special educator and a joint meeting with the special educator can enhance the parents' understanding of their child's abilities and difficulties and his likely academic future and provide the parents with approaches to his education and vocational future. 'Functional' education, e.g. teaching skills of daily living and vocational training,

are critically important for the youth's attainment of some degree of self-sufficiency.
- The parents must be prepared for transitions and changes which can affect the emotional and behavioural stability of their child. It is important that the counsellor provide the parents with 'anticipatory guidance' on developmental problems that they are likely to encounter as their child grows. For example, the parents should be advised in advance to teach their child about pubertal changes. They should also be advised on changes that may provoke a setback so that they can prepare their child in advance, e.g. a change in school or making a transition to English as the medium of instruction.

With teachers and school staff

- Supportive interventions in the school should emphasize the need for a special educational programme for the youth, with the goal of including him in the mainstream school programme as far as possible. This not only ensures that the youth keeps the company of children of his own age, but also promotes an inclusive atmosphere which is conducive to a greater awareness among everyone in the school of differences and diversity. An IEP sets out teaching and learning goals that will help the young person move towards functional independence (*see* Chapter 4).
- The counsellor should encourage the teachers to support a referral for a psychoeducational assessment (*see* Chapter 4) and the involvement of a special educator to advise them how to adapt the curriculum to the young person's needs.
- The counsellor should help the teachers understand that it is important to collaborate with the parents so that the parents can support their child's functional education in the home and view the teachers as allies in their child's development.
- The teachers should be sensitized to the possibility that the youth may be stigmatized when/if his peers notice his learning difference. The counsellor can guide the teachers to manage this in a sensitive manner.
- The counsellor should sensitize the school management to the needs

of children with different levels of ability and encourage it to establish resource rooms to address their needs (*see* Chapter 6).

When to refer: All children suspected to have an intellectual disability must undergo developmental and psychoeducational assessments (*see* Chapter 4) to confirm the diagnosis and to identify their strengths and limitations. This also helps determine if the youth has an intellectual disability or a specific learning disability (Panel 1). In the case of a child with intellectual disability, when the educational support required and the resources needed to tackle his behavioural problems exceed the capacity of the mainstream school setting, referral to and placement in a special school setting could be helpful to the child. Unusual behavioural changes, such as mood swings, unexplained aggressive behaviours and withdrawal, may also call for a referral to a mental health professional, in order to assess for coexisting mental health problems.

Key messages

- Intellectual disability is a condition characterized by delays in the acquisition of age-appropriate cognitive and functional skills.
- While moderate to severe intellectual disability is usually noticed in early childhood, mild intellectual disability may be noticed only when the child attends school and it becomes evident that the child has difficulty learning abstract concepts and generalizing from one situation to another.
- Young people with intellectual disability are at risk for coexisting mental health problems.
- Family psychoeducation helps the family understand and support their child, and supportive interventions in the school, such as appropriate educational support, can make it possible for the youth with mild to moderate intellectual disability to learn together with his peers in an inclusive atmosphere.

CASE STUDY 5

THE CHILD WHO IS INATTENTIVE AND RESTLESS

Pankaj's story

THE PRESENTING PROBLEM

Pankaj, an 8-year-old boy studying in Standard III, was referred to the counsellor by his class teacher because of his behavioural problems in the classroom. In the referral note, the teacher wrote that Pankaj got into trouble in class because of his restlessness, distractibility and tendency to leave his work incomplete. When the teacher was busy, Pankaj would often leave his seat and sometimes even leave the classroom to peep into an adjacent staff room. Although he was a bright child, had a good understanding of concepts and gave the correct answers orally, his overall academic performance was poor. He constantly disturbed the class, interrupting lessons or answering out of turn. When the teacher did not have her eyes on him, he would annoy the children sitting near him, for example, by snatching their books or grabbing their stationery. Quite often, the teacher had even punished him out of frustration. She had also tried to make him sit apart from the rest of the class, especially during instructions. However, contrary to what she had hoped for, this only worsened his behaviour and he would start to play the class 'clown'.

Pankaj's mother reported that he had always been much more restless than her two other sons and that he kept her 'on her feet' much more than even his younger brother. When he returned home from school, he scattered his things everywhere and it was hard to bring him to the table at meal times. He kept losing his belongings, especially his school stationery. She said that when Pankaj was supposed to be doing his homework, he would instead get up and wander around the house, complaining that he was thirsty or inventing other excuses. The mother said she felt exhausted by the time he finally went to bed.

Developmental history

According to the history provided by his mother, Pankaj was born at full term, by a normal delivery. He was difficult to nurse as a baby and it was hard to settle him into his sleep routines during his first year. His developmental milestones had all been within the normal range. When he was younger, he often did not understand the idea of something being 'dangerous'. For example, he would occasionally run across the main road chasing a football without looking. Pankaj's mother now makes sure that someone supervises his outdoor playtime.

Psychosocial history

Family history: Pankaj's father began working abroad when Pankaj was 3 years of age. He would return to visit his family every two years during the school holidays. His mother was a housewife and devoted most of her time to looking after the family. Pankaj was the middle child of three siblings. His older brother was 11 and his younger brother 3 years of age. His paternal grandparents lived with the family and helped his mother look after the children. Pankaj's grandfather had a particularly close relationship with him. While Pankaj's older brother got along well with him, his younger brother did not like playing with him because he grabbed his toys and broke them.

Academic history: During Pankaj's pre-school years, his teacher complained almost daily about his being 'excessively' active. His grades fell towards the end of his second year. Recently, his mother had noticed that his books were often incomplete and full of careless mistakes. She said she had to supervise him to have him complete them and had to correct his mistakes. She noticed that when she supervised his homework, he produced good work. Pankaj enjoyed oral work and dramatics.

Social history: Pankaj mentioned, with some regret, that he did not have many friends. The counsellor had noticed him on the playground, where he was always trying to redirect the games and make himself the focus of attention. His mother said he came home from the neighbourhood playground complaining that children did not include him in their games. In spite of his social difficulties, Pankaj loved outdoor play, especially physical games like football.

Mental status examination

Pankaj went to see the counsellor with his mother. He was cheerful and responded enthusiastically to the counsellor's greeting. Initially, he remained seated in a chair. While his mother was describing his problems to the counsellor, Pankaj's attention wandered. He started walking around, exploring the room. He briefly picked up a book and then opened puzzle boxes. He became increasingly restless as the session progressed. From time to time, he asked when he could go home. Pankaj's restlessness subsided when the counsellor attempted to involve him directly. He spent a short time drawing with the counsellor, after which he wanted to play with the puzzles again. He then flitted from one activity to another and wandered around the room. His speech was normal and his mood cheerful, except when he said with some sadness that he did not have many friends. He attributed this problem to the attitude of others: 'They don't listen to my rules. It's their fault.' He lacked insight into his social problems.

Case formulation

Pankaj, an 8-year-old boy studying in Standard III, was referred to the counsellor by his class teacher due to his behavioural problems and uneven academic performance. Pankaj has difficulty controlling his impulses, e.g. he blurts out answers, intrudes into other children's space and has a hard time waiting his turn. His restlessness is evident across various settings (home and school), and he has problems focusing his attention, makes careless mistakes and fails to finish tasks. Since his problems are in evidence across different settings and have been present since the age of 7 years, the probable diagnosis is attention deficit hyperactivity disorder (*see* Chapter 2).

Strengths: Pankaj's strengths include his above average intellectual abilities, his good memorization skills and his cheerful and outgoing personality. In addition, his family environment is supportive and stable, including a caring mother and good relationships with his older sibling and grandfather.

Difficulties: The difficulties for Pankaj include a behavioural disorder, his poor insight into his problems, his father's absence and a strained mother (due to her task of largely single parenting). Additional difficulties for Pankaj are his increasing isolation from his peers and the occasionally punitive school atmosphere.

Management plan

The primary strategies to help Pankaj include youth psychoeducation, family psychoeducation and social skills counselling. Supportive interventions in the school can help Pankaj improve further.

Youth psychoeducation: The counsellor should explain to Pankaj that his level of activity and restlessness prevent him from focusing and staying calm. He should emphasize that Pankaj's inability to control his impulses leads to conflict with his peers, resulting in social isolation. He should explain to Pankaj that with counselling, family psychoeducation and the counsellor's consultation to his teachers, his problems with restlessness, uneven academic performance and social isolation can be much improved. It is important for the counsellor to hold out the hope that things will get better as they work together. In addition, the counsellor can work with him to increase his knowledge and understanding of classroom and playground rules and the importance of abiding by them.

Family psychoeducation: The counsellor should meet with Pankaj's entire family, including his mother, his grandparents and his father (if present). He should explain Pankaj's behaviours to them and recommend further assessment. He could say, for example, 'Even though Pankaj may understand what is expected of him, it is difficult for him to comply because he has difficulty paying attention to detail and has a short attention span. Pankaj may need an assessment by a specialist for further advice.' The counsellor may choose to use the diagnostic term of attention deficit hyperactivity disorder with the family if the diagnosis has been confirmed by a mental health professional and also, if he thinks that using the term might help the family gain a better understanding of Pankaj's problem. He should inform the family that Pankaj's impulsive and restless behaviours will lessen or discontinue if they learn and employ three management strategies with Pankaj. The first is to reorganize his home schedules and help him learn to accomplish small, defined tasks. For example, he could be told to first have his breakfast and then put on his school uniform, instead of being given a more general directive such as 'get ready for school'. Second, all instructions to Pankaj would need to be clear and concise. The final strategy would be to establish a clear system of rewards (e.g. praise, an outing) for appropriate behaviours and consequences (e.g. denying him his favourite television show) for unacceptable behaviours. To motivate Pankaj to change his behaviours, the counsellor can teach the parents to use behaviour charts (*see* Chapter 6 and Appendix). The counsellor should integrate the techniques being used at home with those used in school so that Pankaj receives consistent messages in both settings. In addition to the three strategies, expanding the role of his father in his life, particularly when he returns from abroad, might have a beneficial effect on Pankaj's behaviour. For example, the father could be encouraged to take an interest in Pankaj's development and set clear rewards for acceptable behaviours.

Social skills counselling: The counsellor can help Pankaj understand the behaviours which lead to poor peer relationships, as well as aid in the process of identifying and practising social skills that will make it easier for him to fit in with classmates. For example, he can involve Pankaj in a role-play in which he plays out inviting a classmate to join him in a game.

Supportive interventions in the school: Since Pankaj's behaviours have a significant impact on his academic performance and disrupt the class, the counsellor must sensitize the school staff to the challenges faced by young people with attention deficit hyperactivity disorder. However, it is important for the counsellor to assess whether using this diagnostic term while speaking to the school staff will give rise to stigma against Pankaj. If it might, it is better for the counsellor to instead describe the set of behaviours without using a diagnostic term. The counsellor should advise the teachers to employ the following management strategies: ensure that Pankaj's seat is in a place where there are minimum distractions; allow him the freedom to use his high level of activity productively, e.g. let him distribute books or erase the blackboard; make sure that all instructions are repeated for him on a one-to-one basis, in short concise sentences; provide him with an easily observable written timetable of class activities; utilize behaviour charts (*see* Chapter 6 and Appendix); and set deadlines for the completion of smaller tasks which lead up to the larger work at hand. The teachers should also be informed about appropriate rewards and consequences in order to avoid unreasonable punishments. Examples of rewards include social praise, a special badge for the day and certificates of achievement, while an example of a consequence is to limit a favourite extracurricular activity.

When to refer: The counsellor may feel that even after all the approaches have been tried by the teachers and Pankaj's behaviour is still hard to manage, a referral should be considered to a mental health professional, for the possible use of medication.

ASSESSMENT AND MANAGEMENT OF INATTENTION AND RESTLESSNESS

THE PROBLEM

Pre-school children often have a degree of hyperactivity and impulsivity which is developmentally normal. However, when this behaviour is present across many settings (such as both home and school) and does not settle as the child grows, attention deficit hyperactivity disorder (*see* Chapter 2) may be considered a possible explanation. A young person with this disorder often has difficulty concentrating on schoolwork and homework, frequently interrupts conversations or activities and has difficulty remaining seated when required to do so. The restless behaviours characterizing attention deficit hyperactivity disorder often subside as the child passes through the primary school years; however, inattention and impulsivity often continue into middle childhood and adolescence, and even into adulthood. The symptoms of inattention, hyperactivity and impulsivity must be present across many situations and must have been present for over 6 months for the youth to qualify for this diagnosis. Some alternative explanations for symptoms of distractibility include anxiety arising from a crisis or a life change; depression; difficulty coping with increasing academic pressure due to learning disabilities; difficulties arising from a hearing impairment; inconsistent parenting; and living in adverse circumstances. Note that some children with attention deficit hyperactivity disorder also have a coexisting specific learning disability, which should be assessed and addressed while planning the treatment. Although attention deficit hyperactivity disorder is more common among boys, it may also be present among girls (*see* Chapter 2). In cases which do not respond adequately to behavioural interventions, supplementary medications (*see below,* When to refer) may be effective in combination with behavioural strategies at home and school.

Assessment

Information from the youth

- What is the youth's understanding of why he has been referred to the counsellor? What is his perception of why he gets into trouble?
- What difficulties does he face in managing his behaviour? What does he think makes him behave the way he does?
- What impact do his problems have on his daily life (at home, in class or in the schoolyard)?
- What helps him, if anything, to modify his behaviours or concentrate?

How much has this helped? What other ideas does he have about how to improve his behaviour and attention? What makes it more difficult for him concentrate or calm down?

Information from the parent

- What is his daily routine? How does his restless behaviour interfere with this routine?
- What is the family's perception of their child's problem?
- What parenting styles do they think might contribute to his problem?
- Have they tried to do anything, e.g. punishing him, to modify his behaviours? Has this helped?

Information from the teacher

- What is the most difficult aspect of his problem?
- What does the teacher view as his strengths?
- How do his problems affect the class and his academic performance?
- What strategies has the teacher tried to address his problem? What have been their effects?

MANAGEMENT

With the youth

- Youth psychoeducation gives the youth a better insight into his problem and improves his understanding of the links between his specific behaviours and his difficulties. The counsellor should hold out the hope that the youth's problem will become more manageable with counselling and with the guidance he will provide the youth's teachers and family.
- Social skills counselling and role-play help the youth forge and improve relationships with peers.

With the family

- Family psychoeducation helps the parents and family understand the underlying reasons for the youth's challenging behaviours. The counsellor should reassure them that their child's problems will be helped through counselling and classroom-based strategies. Family psychoeducation also helps the parents organize their routines and simplify their schedules, which, in turn, helps the youth to organize and follow through with tasks. Family psychoeducation includes teaching the parents positive methods to motivate and discipline their child, e.g. making use of rewards, including ways of interacting with him to avoid overreactions and harsh punishments (*see* Chapter 6). In general, when speaking to the family about their child's problems, the counsellor should avoid relying on the use of the diagnostic term attention deficit hyperactivity disorder and should, instead, help them understand their child by describing his behaviours in school, his strengths and how best to overcome his problem. Moreover, in considering using the diagnostic label with the family of attention deficit hyperactivity disorder, the counsellor should be guided by the level of confidence he has in the diagnosis, e.g. confirmation by a specialist would make for greater confidence; his assessment of whether using the diagnostic label would facilitate the family's acceptance of specialized treatments, e.g. the use of medication; and whether the diagnostic label might stigmatize rather than help the youth.

With teachers and school staff

- Supportive interventions in the school help teachers understand the causes of the youth's problems, and provide them with guidance to help him manage his school routines and meet expectations. The counsellor should encourage the staff to focus on the youth's strengths and guide them how to utilize the youth's strengths to overcome the challenges confronting him. In general, the school staff should receive training to help them appreciate the fact that young people who behave in an impulsive, restless and distracted manner do so because they have problems managing their behaviour and not because they are being wilfully 'naughty'. The school should create routines for children with attention deficit hyperactivity disorder (*see* Chapter 6). These routines can help the youth organize his belongings, e.g. how books are placed in his desk, and time management (e.g. by making a visual timetable for his school hours, *see* Appendix). Additional interventions that can help the child in school include simplifying instructions. For example, the teacher could tell the youth, 'Open your desk,' followed by, 'Take out your maths book,' and finally, 'Open it to the chapter on shapes,' instead of using one broad statement such as, 'Please open your maths book to the chapter on shapes.' The teacher can be advised that the child needs to be disciplined effectively, e.g. by using age-appropriate rewards for desired behaviours and consequences for unwanted actions. Another useful suggestion to the teachers is for them to create an environment that helps the youth remain focused, e.g. by decreasing distractions in the classroom. One way of achieving this is to seat him in front of the class and away from the windows. Similar practices can be used at home, creating consistency across different settings. It is important for the counsellor to suggest to the teacher (or special educator in the resource room) that she should review the youth's school books to determine if the youth has any coexisting specific learning disabilities (*see* Chapter 2). If a specific learning disability is suspected, the youth should be referred for a psychoeducational assessment (*see* Chapters 2 and 4), and if a specific learning disability is diagnosed, this should be taken into account when designing the youth's treatment plan.

When to refer: If, despite counselling, the youth's restlessness and inattention continue to significantly disrupt his learning and the school atmosphere, he should be referred to a mental health professional for an evaluation to consider medication. Parents may be reluctant to medicate their child for a number of reasons. For example, they may feel that putting their child on medication means that he would have to be on lifelong treatment, or they may think that his behaviour is not 'serious' enough to warrant medication. Even when a referral to a mental health professional is arranged and medication prescribed, it is important that the school continues to make significant efforts to create an atmosphere conducive to the youth's academic and behavioural improvements.

Key messages

- Attention deficit hyperactivity disorder is characterized by three core symptoms: hyperactivity, inattention and impulsivity (all present in varying degrees).
- Other mental health problems may give rise to impulsive and restless behaviours that 'look like' attention deficit hyperactivity disorder. These include mental health distress, hearing impairment, emotional disorders and/or specific learning disabilities.
- Attention deficit hyperactivity disorder often causes academic problems, as well as difficulties in relationships.
- The management of attention deficit hyperactivity disorder should focus on helping the youth and his family/teachers understand the nature of the problem and utilize behavioural techniques to manage the core symptoms.

CASE STUDY 6

THE CHILD WITH A DISABILITY

Shabana's story

THE PRESENTING PROBLEM

Shabana, an 8-year-old girl studying in Standard III, was referred to the counsellor by her teacher. The teacher had noticed that she missed school when she had to submit an oral assignment, she was reluctant to participate in class activities involving oral work and she was distracted and inattentive in class. Shabana went to the counsellor's office willingly; however, she was shy and reluctant to talk, and her speech was indistinct. When she did speak, her voice was very loud and unmodulated. Shabana said she found classwork difficult, primarily because it was hard for her to understand the teacher's instructions, especially when other children were talking. She said she was nervous about speaking in public. In this context, she described a poetry recitation eight months ago, when all the children laughed at her because she stumbled over a few words. She complained that the teachers were always telling her to speak clearly and stop mumbling. Of late, she had been telling her mother that she was unwell on days when there was oral work in school.

Developmental history

Her mother reported that Shabana was a pre-term baby and spent almost one month in hospital. During this time, she had jaundice, for which she was treated, as well as an infection that required antibiotics. When she was 1 month old, she seemed to be well enough to be discharged from hospital. Although Shabana had developed normally in most respects, there was a considerable delay in her speech and when she did begin to speak, her words were difficult to understand. However, she was able to communicate easily through gestures and expressions. Her family could now understand what she said, but others did not, especially when she was in a group setting. The family had noticed that when watching television, she turned up the volume very high. Her mother said one of the things which bothered her about Shabana was that she had to be called frequently before she responded. In the past few months, Shabana had often said she was unwell and missed school.

Psychosocial history

Family history: Shabana was the second daughter in a nuclear family. Her older sister studied in Standard VIII in the same school. Her father was an office assistant and her mother a housewife. There were close ties between the family members. The mother described Shabana and her sister as 'best friends'.

Academic history: Shabana's parents decided not to put Shabana in pre-school until she was 4 years old because she did not use single words until she was 18 months old, which was quite late compared to her sister. When she began pre-school, the teachers often complained that she did not pay attention to instructions and was absorbed in her own activities rather than playing with others. However, when they encouraged her to participate in activities with her peers, she would. Despite repeated comments from her teachers that she was inattentive in class and lacked confidence in her oral work, Shabana managed to proceed through school because she performed at the average level. She especially liked activities which did not involve others, such as reading and drawing.

Social history: Shabana described her classmates as kind and friendly, but she would not call any of them a 'close' friend. She said that even though her classmates seemed to welcome her into their group, it was hard for her to follow their conversations, especially when they all talked together, which prevented her from feeling like a part of any group. She also remarked that recent instances in which her peers had teased her for her oral work left her feeling hurt and isolated.

Mental status examination

Shabana seemed comfortable with the counsellor. The counsellor found it hard to understand Shabana's speech; her voice was poorly modulated and at times, she spoke very loudly. The counsellor also noticed that Shabana seemed to follow her lip movements when she spoke. With encouragement, Shabana described her difficulties, in particular that she felt fearful and anxious before and during any public speaking. She said that even the thought of speaking in front of the class made her heart beat very fast and her chest tighten. Her thought content was normal. She had some insight into her lack of confidence and avoidance of school, which she attributed to the fact that she had difficulty speaking 'like others'.

Case formulation

Shabana, an 8-year-old girl studying in Standard III, belongs to a secure nuclear family. She was referred to the counsellor because of her reluctance to participate in class activities involving oral work, erratic school attendance and inattentiveness in class. She has an average academic record. She suffers from symptoms of anxiety and low self-esteem, especially when public speaking is involved. Her delayed speech, habit of lip-reading, inattentiveness to instructions in class and at home, speech difficulties and tendency to listen to television with the volume turned up high indicate the presence of a hearing impairment. Together with this, Shabana suffers from symptoms of anxiety (*see* Chapter 2) related to public speaking.

Strengths: Shabana's strengths include her normal intelligence and insight into the reasons for her anxiety. Having a protective and secure family environment is also a positive factor.

Difficulties: A possible hearing impairment that has not been assessed and peers who tease her are factors that create difficulties for Shabana.

Management plan

The primary strategies to help Shabana manage her anxiety are youth psychoeducation, family psychoeducation, including referral to a specialist, problem-solving counselling, social skills counselling and relaxation exercise. Supportive interventions in the school are essential to help Shabana feel socially comfortable in school and achieve academic success.

Youth psychoeducation: The counsellor should explain to Shabana that she might have a hearing difficulty which is making it hard for her to form words properly and hear well. The counsellor should tell her that given her possible problems, it is natural for her to feel uncomfortable doing oral work, and also to feel very fearful and anxious when she is required to do so. The counsellor should praise Shabana for coping with school despite her difficulties. She can tell her that an assessment of her speech and hearing by a specialist will help her, her family and her teachers better understand her problems. An assessment would also help to formulate a plan to help her with oral work and other school activities. The counsellor should seek her permission to discuss her problems with her teachers and parents so that they can all work as a team to support her in all aspects of school.

Family psychoeducation: The counsellor should explain to Shabana's parents that her problems indicate that she likely has a hearing impairment, which will require a specialized speech/hearing assessment. Telling the parents that 'Shabana is having great difficulty enjoying herself and participating in school because she may have trouble hearing in class' may encourage the parents to take Shabana for an assessment. Once the referral has been made and a diagnosis established, it is important to help the parents understand and accept Shabana's special needs. Further, they should be guided to comply with any recommendations made, such as fitting a hearing aid and beginning speech and language therapy. The counsellor should advise the parents to tell Shabana how proud they are of her achievements and that she is equal to others in their eyes. To further bolster her self-esteem, the parents should encourage Shabana to do the things she enjoys and is good at, such as drawing. The parents should suggest that she practise oral presentations in front of them and her sister when she has oral work to prepare. For example, she could perform a mock recitation for them. If hearing aids are recommended, Shabana might feel uncomfortable about wearing them. For example, she might feel that they make her look less attractive, identify her as being different or may arouse her schoolmates' curiosity. These concerns need to be addressed through youth and family psychoeducation.

Problem-solving counselling: The counsellor should help Shabana identify the main challenges she faces, e.g. the anxiety she experiences during public speaking. With Shabana's participation, the counsellor can then identify practical ways of boosting her confidence. For example, Shabana could take up activities which do not rely on speaking, such as a sport. Activities that help manage the anxiety associated with public speaking would also be useful. An example is practising with her sister at home before an oral presentation in school.

Social skills counselling: The counsellor can brainstorm with Shabana how she can engage with her peers so that she may expand her circle of friends. If Shabana is diagnosed with a hearing impairment, the counsellor should encourage Shabana to share this information with classmates that she trusts and role-play with her how this can be done.

Relaxation exercise: The counsellor can demonstrate and teach Shabana relaxation exercises which she can use to help her calm down before public presentations.

Supportive interventions in the school: The counsellor can suggest to the teachers that they optimize Shabana's learning and participation in school through seating her near the front of the class so that she can hear the teacher and have a closer view of the blackboard; writing out instructions for her since she may find it difficult to follow oral instructions; speaking clearly and at a moderate speed; facing Shabana when they address the class so that she can read their lips, if necessary; writing the key words of an idea or lesson on the board so that Shabana is aware of the topic being covered; and appointing willing peers who can share notes with her.

Assessment and Management of a Youth with Disability

The Problem

Disabilities may be cognitive, scholastic, sensory or locomotor (due to physical impairments), or may affect social interaction and communication (*see* Chapter 2). Youth with disabilities are also referred to as having 'special needs'. Children with disabilities are often at a disadvantage in a social setting, being excluded by their peers and others and failing to gain their acceptance. Social and environmental barriers are sometimes more limiting than the disability itself. For example, a child who has a locomotor disability that makes it difficult for her to walk may not be able to attend school because the school does not have ramps, or because the school is a long distance away. The severity of a person's disability depends both on the severity of the biological impairment and how it affects her functioning. For example, a youth may be blind, yet well integrated into life, and may complete her education as well as hold a job. On the other hand, a youth who has mild mental retardation and no access to appropriate education may become completely isolated socially. Some disabilities are recognized early in infancy and childhood since they have obvious physical markers. Others, such as hearing impairment or poor vision, may not be detected until a later age, when a child is in school. The way a disabled youth feels about herself is also affected by certain subtle but powerful factors. These include the community's attitudes; the family's attitudes, e.g. siblings might be favoured; and the way the family feels about the time and costly services required by the child with a disability. These factors can have an impact on the child's adjustment and create serious social and mental health problems.

Assessment

Information from the youth

- Depending on the type and severity of disability and the intellectual capacity of the youth, her understanding of her condition and how much she has been told about her diagnosis should be explored.

- Which issues related to her disability does the youth find challenging?
- What are her expectations of herself? Are these realistic?
- How do her peers and family treat her? Does she get exceptional treatment due to her disability? Is she isolated from her peers due to her disability?
- Is she experiencing any associated mental health problems, such as depression? Is she anxious about any specific issues, e.g. difficulties with her studies, inability to participate in school activities, pubertal changes and concerns about her future?

Information from the parent

- Explore the parents' understanding of their child's disability. To what extent have they accepted it? What is their current emotional state regarding the disability?
- Have the parents approached their family doctor and others to try to understand their child's disability? If so, what have they learnt that has helped them facilitate their child's adaptation to school, community and home life?
- What have they told their child about her disability?
- Have any specific tests or assessments been done? Could copies of these be shared with the counsellor, after obtaining the necessary permission?
- How do they treat their child? Are they overprotective, indulgent or perhaps resentful?
- Are their expectations realistic? Do they understand the challenges their child faces now or may face in the future due to her disability?
- If the disabled child has siblings, how do they behave with her? How do the parents meet all of their children's needs?

Information from the teacher

- How has the school adapted its environment and/or curriculum to the youth's needs (Panel 2)?
- How is the youth's academic performance? Has there been a recent deterioration? If so, why?

Panel 2. Promoting an inclusive school environment

Disability	How to make a school inclusive
For all children with disabilities	Creating a school atmosphere which accepts differences among students; taking measures to ensure that all children can learn together; promoting among the teachers, staff and students a positive attitude to differences; employing a flexible curriculum that can be adapted to different ways of learning; providing teacher training in alternative teaching methods; peer pairing, i.e. encouraging another student to serve as a 'buddy'; praising the child to encourage him to achieve; challenging attitudes of discrimination through activities involving the whole school (e.g. assemblies, debates, competitions).
Hearing impairment	Helping the family learn sign language and encouraging the school staff and peers to also learn; seating the child close to the teacher and at the front of the class; placing the child in the quietest and best lit classroom in school; advocating the use of varied means of helping the youth understand, e.g. lip-reading and pictorial symbols or written instructions.
Visual impairment	Familiarizing the child to the campus; providing appropriate seating in class; using books with large print or Braille textbooks; replacing written assignments and examinations with oral assessments; reading everything on the blackboard aloud.
Locomotor impairments	Providing barrier-free access, such as ramps, hand rails and toilets accessible by wheelchair; making suitable arrangements for seating and transport to school.
Intellectual disability and autism spectrum disorder	Placing the child in an area where there is minimum distraction; getting a helper/volunteer to assist her in the classroom; arranging for special educators trained to design a parallel or overlapping curriculum; arranging for an IEP; breaking down a task into simpler steps. (For more tips, *see* Chapter 6 and Case Study 4.)

(continued)

Panel 2. Promoting an inclusive school environment (*continued*)

Disability	How to make a school inclusive
Specific learning disabilities and attention deficit hyperactivity disorder	Arranging for special educators trained in accommodating and adapting the class curriculum; allowing concessions in educational practices. (For more tips, *see* Case Studies 5 and 12.)

Management

With the youth

- Youth psychoeducation enhances the youth's understanding of her disability, besides helping her identify her strengths and set realistic expectations.
- The counsellor should be aware that the youth may develop a mental health problem in response to stresses in the environment, just like any other youth would. The mental health problem may, however, look different because of the disability. Any mental health problem should be addressed with the help of the same counselling approaches used with other youth, but special care should be taken to handle the youth's disability with sensitivity.
- The counsellor should look for opportunities that will help the youth

enhance her self-esteem. For example, she could be given a role in school that she could perform successfully.

- Social skills counselling can improve the youth's interactions with her peers.

With the family

- Family psychoeducation should explore the parents' attitudes to their child's disability, including their acceptance or denial of the disability, and help them articulate their disappointments and hopes (*see* Chapter 6) and follow through with a referral for an assessment. The counsellor should encourage the parents to recognize the child's likely potential in a realistic and compassionate manner. The parents should be advised to accept the disabled child and help her build on her strengths. For example, they could include her in family activities and encourage her to participate in whatever way she can. Simultaneously, the counsellor should refer the parents to local resources that provide support for children with special needs and the families of such children (Panels 3a and 3b).

Panel 3a. Disability resources—National

Programme/resource	Relevance
Sarva Shiksha Abhiyan	The Sarva Shiksha Abhiyan is responsible for overseeing the implementation of the Right to Education Act, 2010 for all children, including those with special needs.
Special needs training	The Rehabilitation Council of India runs courses to train special educators to address the educational needs of children with disabilities (http://rehabcouncil.nic.in/home.htm).
Disability-focused non-governmental organizations (local)	Certain NGOs provide assessment, training and intervention services at the local level.
Disability Rehabilitation Centre (district level)	At the district level, the DRC provides assessment, training and intervention services.

Panel 3b. Disability resources—International

Resource	Relevance
United Nations	The United Nations Convention on the Rights of Persons with Disabilities is a comprehensive document which has been ratified by India (http://www.un.org/disabilities/convention/conventionfull.shtml).

With teachers and school staff

- Supportive interventions in the school should be directed at making the school as inclusive as possible (Panel 2). Negative attitudes towards the child should be addressed by 'sensitizing' school youth and staff during class, assemblies and school events. 'Sensitizing', in this context, means encouraging people to recognize and appreciate the achievements of everyone in the school, irrespective of individual differences. In keeping with this goal, the counsellor can encourage the school management to introduce inclusive school practices, i.e. practices which ensure accommodation for children with disabilities.

When to refer: The family should be referred to medical and/or rehabilitation professionals for a professional assessment of the nature and severity of the youth's impairments, as well as for advice on the continuing care the youth may need. For example, a therapy programme might be recommended, glasses may be prescribed or hearing aids might be updated. It is important for the counsellor to learn as much as possible about the specific disability so that she can give advice on how to support the youth in school and at home. In order to be able to make key referrals, the counsellor should also familiarize herself with the programmes and resources which support the families of children with special needs (Panels 3a and 3b).

Key messages

- Disabilities affect about one out of every 20 children. Mild disabilities are often undetected and may be manifested as difficult classroom behaviours. In addition, the child may have poor peer relationships and low self-esteem.
- Disabilities can have a profound impact on the youth and her family. They can affect the youth's educational potential, her vocational opportunities in the future and her interpersonal relationships. Her family may experience stress due to the increase in the time and resources required to optimize the treatment of their child.
- A youth with a disability is vulnerable to mental health distress and disorders.
- Counselling should aim to enhance the youth's and her family's understanding of the disability, minimize the associated emotional and behavioural problems suffered by the youth, create an inclusive environment in the school and build on the youth's strengths.

CASE STUDY 7

THE CHILD WHOSE PARENT HAS DIED

Lakshmi's story

THE PRESENTING PROBLEM

Lakshmi, a 9-year-old girl studying in Standard IV, was referred to the counsellor by the school headmistress following her mother's death three weeks earlier after a brief stay in hospital. The teacher had noticed that since her mother's death, Lakshmi was mostly late for school and was less involved in school activities. It was with reluctance that she met the counsellor and during the session, preferred to draw rather than talk. Her drawings depicted a cheerful home, including a smiling mother, a father and two children, and a big sun and flowers. She gradually became more comfortable during the session and told the counsellor that she felt too tired to wake up in time for school. Her father came for a separate session and spoke about his wife's unexpected death following a severe infection of malaria. He informed the counsellor that Lakshmi had been an active and happy child, but since her mother's death, she had become quiet and less active at home. She spent little time with friends, had trouble waking up in the morning and had episodes of bedwetting. Her father was uncertain about whether he should force Lakshmi to get up in the morning and get ready for school. On a few occasions, Lakshmi had told her father that she missed her mother terribly.

Developmental history

According to her father, Lakshmi's birth and childhood had been normal. She had no health problems. He described Lakshmi as an active and outgoing child, but said that since her mother's death, she had become quiet and preferred being by herself.

Psychosocial history

Family history: Lakshmi was the younger of two daughters (her sister was 12 years old), and lived at home with her father and sister. Her mother had died three weeks earlier in the hospital due to an unexpected and severe infection of malaria. The sudden onset of the illness and the seriousness of the loss were very traumatic for the entire family. Lakshmi had been very close to her mother, and used to especially enjoy learning to cook from her. Her mother had been intimately involved in Lakshmi's upbringing. The father worked as a car mechanic. He kept regular hours, and was always home for dinner and on the weekends. Lakshmi and her sister had a fairly good relationship. The mother's sister lived nearby with her husband and children and had been helping the family out since the mother's death. She did the shopping, prepared meals and supervised the children after school until their father returned. However, the mother's sister had recently told the father that these additional responsibilities were beginning to put a strain on her.

Academic history: Lakshmi had mostly been a good student through the years, although she had always struggled to do well in mathematics. Her mother would help her with her mathematics homework, while Lakshmi was able to finish her other homework on her own. Her favourite subjects were English and history. Since her mother had died, Lakshmi had lost interest in doing her homework and had recently failed a mathematics review. She complained that her stomach aches interfered with her ability to complete her homework and sometimes interrupted her work during school.

Social history: Lakshmi had always found it easy to make friends and sustain her friendships. However, since her mother's death, the teachers had noticed that she would usually keep to herself on the school playground and in class. She would neither invite her friends to play, nor respond to their requests.

MENTAL STATUS EXAMINATION

Lakshmi was cooperative but quiet during her meetings with the counsellor. She was well dressed and polite. She told the counsellor that she did not have much to say. She preferred to draw and mostly avoided discussions about her mother. When she answered direct questions by the counsellor, the pace and volume of her speech were normal. Her mood was subdued and appropriate to the feelings she was experiencing due to the recent loss of her mother. She and her father reported that she was eating well, but had frequent stomach aches. Her sleep was disturbed at night and she had difficulty waking up in the morning. She had insight into her sad mood and spoke about how 'unhappy my life is now'. However, she did not openly discuss her mother's passing away, her reluctance to come to school or mention her episodes of bedwetting.

Case formulation

Lakshmi, a 9-year-old girl studying in Standard IV, lives at home with her father and older sister. She was referred to the counsellor by the school headmistress following the sudden death of her mother, to whom she was very close. Since her mother's death, she has been finding it difficult to reach school on time and has become less involved in school and social activities. She has had episodes of bedwetting, often has stomach aches, her sleep is disturbed and her mood is subdued. Lakshmi appears to be experiencing mental health distress in response to the loss of her mother.

Strengths: The strengths in Lakshmi's environment include her supportive father, an aunt who is able to help out, a good relationship with her older sister and concerned school staff. Further strengths include that she is intelligent and has a history of strong academic commitment and performance.

Difficulties: The foremost problems for Lakshmi are the recent loss of her mother and the significant distress associated with this. The fact that the aunt is beginning to feel burdened by the additional responsibilities she has taken on since the death poses another challenge.

Management plan

The primary strategy to help Lakshmi come to terms with the loss of her mother is crisis counselling specifically focused on bereavement (*see* Chapter 6). Supportive interventions in the school can be used to support her during the period of adjustment to the loss of her mother.

Crisis counselling (with the youth): The purpose of crisis counselling is to help Lakshmi understand her reactions to her mother's death, to work with her to find ways to soothe herself, to strengthen her relationships with her family members and to help her become involved in her school and social activities again. The counsellor should explore her understanding of death and help her understand that it is natural for her to want to turn the clock back to a time when she was younger and her mother was home with her, e.g. wanting to stay home rather than going to school in the morning. The counsellor should introduce methods to Lakshmi that can help her soothe her distress. These include verbalizing her feelings about missing her mother more often and asking her father and aunt to hug her when she is particularly sad. It is important to help Lakshmi strengthen her ties to her father, sister and aunt. She could do this, for example, by sharing fond memories of her mother with them and sharing enjoyable activities with them. The counsellor should help her practise how to tell her friends why she is feeling sad right now. Further, as far as activities with her peers are concerned, the counsellor should guide her to participate with them in a way that feels appropriate to her at this time. Lakshmi should also be encouraged to reach out to teachers whom she likes for help with schoolwork, especially mathematics. She might enjoy sharing memories of her mother with the counsellor through various means, such as making a journal or 'memory box' of items that remind her of her mother and their relationship. These could include photographs, notes or letters and other objects. The counsellor should reassure Lakshmi that though she is very sad about the loss of her mother at present, these feelings are normal and will become less painful with time. It should be explained to Lakshmi that her stomach aches and difficulty getting up in the morning are connected with her sadness. The counsellor should describe how the counselling will help her with her feelings, her physical and social reactions and her recent problems related to school. The counsellor should tell Lakshmi that with her permission, she would like to talk to her father, aunt and teachers so that they can help ease her emotional burden.

Crisis counselling (with the family): The purpose of crisis counselling is to help Lakshmi's family members understand how to support her after the death, as well as how to comfort themselves. Her father will be mourning the death himself, and if he needs someone to speak to about his feelings and reactions, he could be referred to a mental health professional. In order to help him understand how Lakshmi's problems are linked to her mother's death, he could be given a simple explanation such as, 'Lakshmi really misses her mother and it is possible that she does not completely understand what has happened to her. Her sadness is interfering with her involvement in school, and resulting in bedwetting and stomach aches.' The counsellor should seek to learn about the parenting challenges the father is facing and offer guidance. For example, if he does not know how to reach out to Lakshmi when she retreats in sadness, the counsellor could suggest that he hug her and offer to draw with her. Ways of sustaining the aunt's involvement should be explored. For example, the counsellor can advise the father to see whether there is another family member who might not mind sharing the additional responsibilities being taken on by the aunt. The counsellor can advise the father that it would help him with his and his daughters' grief to engage in shared activities with his daughters. These could include recounting or sharing memories of the mother through such activities as sitting together and making a journal of their memories of her or with photographs of her. It is also important for the counsellor to encourage the father to maintain Lakshmi's daily routines, e.g. she should not be allowed to miss school. In addition, a family meeting, at which the aunt and sister are present together with Lakshmi and her father, could facilitate a discussion among them about how they can all support one another. The counsellor should also explain to the father that Lakshmi's regression to an earlier developmental stage (from being toilet-trained to again wetting her bed) is a common symptom of bereavement among children, that it will pass and that he needs to handle it with patience.

Supportive interventions in the school: The counsellor should help the teachers understand that it is very important to reach out to and support Lakshmi to demonstrate to her that they care about her feelings and recognize that this period of grieving is very difficult for her. In addition, the counsellor can talk to the teachers about how they could temporarily reduce the academic pressure on Lakshmi to accommodate her emotional distress. To increase Lakshmi's ability to handle tasks in mathematics independently in the long run, it would be helpful to arrange for remediation in school. Since it can be disturbing for young people to see one of their friends affected by death, especially if they have no personal experience of such a loss, the counsellor can give the teachers advice on how to help Lakshmi's friends reach out to her. For example, they could advise Lakshmi's peers to make small statements of support from time to time; these could include telling her that they understand she must be feeling very sad. In addition, the teachers should be advised to reassure Lakshmi's schoolmates that the death of a parent is a rare event. The counsellor can also suggest supportive interventions, such as assigning a buddy (the peer pairing system) and arranging circle time activities for her class that address issues related to bereavement (*see* Chapter 6). There are child-friendly books which can help children think about their experiences without having to face the pressure of talking about them, and/or which enhance their ability to talk about their feelings if they are inclined to do so (*see* Appendix).

ASSESSMENT AND MANAGEMENT OF CHILDHOOD BEREAVEMENT

THE PROBLEM

The nature of a young person's grief following the death of a loved one varies according to the child's age and type of relationship to the person who has died, e.g. whether the departed one was a parent, sibling, member of extended family, classmate; the nature of the relationship between the youth and the person, e.g. whether it was a loving relationship or one marked by conflict; the nature of the death, e.g. whether it was due to an accident or other traumatic event versus a long-term illness; the characteristics of the particular family; and the child's degree of innate resilience. Children in pre-school do not understand the permanence of death and think that the person will return. Between the pre-school years and approximately 10 years of age, the child may waver between understanding that death is final and believing that their loved one will return. Older children and adolescents often understand the irreversible nature of death. Depending on their understanding of death, younger children may harbour feelings of guilt, e.g. thinking that their 'naughtiness' caused the death, go through changes in their sleep routine, display regressive behaviour (including bedwetting at times) or insist that the person will return. The reactions seen among older children and adolescents include outbursts of anger, 'acting out' behaviours, unexpected tears, changes in the sleep routine and difficulty concentrating. Sadness, social withdrawal and physical symptoms, such as stomach aches, headaches and fatigue, are common emotional responses among all age groups. For most youth, these reactions are temporary and pass with time and emotional support. In some youth, however, they are more persistent and cause severe impairment in functioning. If the grief reactions do not start subsiding naturally over a reasonable period of time, e.g. 6 months, the counsellor should consider the possibility that the youth is suffering from depression. It is also important to recognize that adults are often uncomfortable talking about death, especially with a child. This is often compounded by the fact that the adult is preoccupied with his own struggle to come to terms with the death.

ASSESSMENT

Information from the youth

- How is the youth related to the person who has died and what was the quality of the relationship? How is she coping with the loss? What is her understanding of what death is?
- What was the nature of the death, e.g. did it result from a traumatic event or was it an expected death following a long illness?
- How does the youth get along with the other family members? How are the family members coping with the death?
- Are there reminders of the death in the home or school environment that increase the youth's distress?
- What does she think would help her come to terms with the loss?
- To what degree has grieving been possible?

Information from the parent

- **What is the parent's relationship with the person who has died?**
- **How is the parent coping with the loss?**
- **What is the parent's understanding of the difficulties faced by their child in adjusting to the death?**
- **What is the nature of the communication between the parent and child?**
- **What kind of help are the extended family and community providing to the family and the children who have suffered the loss, and will this continue?**
- **Are there any anticipated difficulties that may add to the parenting burden?**

Information from the teacher

- Are there other specific issues, e.g. academic problems, affecting the youth's adjustment in school?
- How can the teachers help the youth's peers understand what has happened? How can the teachers support the bereaved youth?
- How can the teachers make good use of the youth's academic and other strengths (i.e. protective factors) to facilitate her healthy adjustment?

MANAGEMENT

With the youth

- Crisis counselling (with the youth) enhances the youth's understanding of her reactions to her loss, helps to stabilize her and facilitates her return to her previous level of functioning and coping. While exploring the youth's understanding of the loss, the counsellor must not force her to accept the finality of death if she is not ready to do so. The counsellor should provide her with opportunities to express her feelings and grieve at her own pace, e.g. through conversations, drawings, play-acting, going through photo albums and creating a 'memory box'.

With the family

- Crisis counselling (with the family) helps the parent and members of the extended family understand the reasons for the youth's problems, manage their worries about the youth, effectively care for the youth as she copes with the loss and manage their own grief. The counsellor should advise the family to maintain the normal routines, e.g. encouraging the child to attend school and keeping to the usual daily schedule. She should advise them how to address the topic of death with the child, e.g. by sharing memories, going through photo albums and making a 'memory box'. Ways of including the child in the rituals associated with the loss should also be discussed. For example, with preparation, the child could attend the funeral and other ceremonies marking the death.

With teachers and school staff

- The counsellor can help the teachers and staff understand the source of the youth's present problems in school and make suggestions about how to assist her in coping with academic stress. For example, they could place fewer academic demands on her and set smaller tasks. The teachers and staff should also be advised on ways of providing emotional support. For example, when they see that the youth has withdrawn, they could comfort her with a gentle pat on the shoulder and say something reassuring.
- The counsellor can help the teachers address the concerns of the youth's peers. This would include advising the teachers how to help the students understand their feelings and fears about the death of a fellow student (Panel 4).
- The counsellor could arrange with the teachers that she provide circle time for the students to discuss general issues related to loss and grieving (*see* Chapter 6); or help the bereaved youth by sensitizing peers and encouraging them to support her as buddies (peer pairing, *see* Chapter 6).

When to refer: If, despite counselling, the youth's grief reactions

Panel 4. When a student dies

The death of a school friend can have an impact on the entire student body. The following are some ways of addressing this impact:

Sharing the information
A carefully drafted note containing the key facts about the loss should be read out in all the classes. The terms used should be age-appropriate. The note should mention the youth's name and include a simple statement of empathy for the family in their time of loss. An example is, 'I am so very sorry to announce that we lost one of our Standard X students (insert the name) through a terrible road accident yesterday.' If the death was a suicide, the fact that it was a suicide should not be made public. Hence, though the name of the student should be mentioned, the way the death occurred should not. An example is, 'I am very saddened to announce that one of our Standard XI students (insert the name) passed away unexpectedly yesterday.' A similar note should be sent to the parents of the students in the school to inform them about the death and encourage them to talk to their children. This note should include simple tips on how to help their children through the grieving process. Also, it should inform them that the counsellor is available to help out any child who seems to be severely affected by the loss.

Acknowledging the loss
The school should arrange a simple event in remembrance of the student. For example, a moment of silence could be observed during the school assembly.

Working with the students
The counsellor can work with the teachers to organize class-based activities that allow students to share their grief and express their emotions as well as coordinate a counsellor led circle time. These are especially useful for the class of the student who has died.

Working with individuals
The counsellor should offer drop-in sessions to any student who needs further support, e.g. a close friend of the deceased youth.

Working with the staff
The counsellor should also try to support staff members who may be shocked themselves. Follow-up sessions should be conducted with staff members as well as students to address issues that may arise subsequently. If the youth died through suicide, the counsellor must make the staff aware of the possibility of other students being vulnerable and encourage them to refer those at risk for counselling, e.g. a student who, as a close friend of that youth, could feel responsible for not having saved her friend.

increase or do not abate, she should be referred to a mental health professional for evaluation and follow-up counselling.

Key messages

- Grief reactions can be expected to last for up to 6 months following the death of a parent (or other loved one). Bereaved young people exhibit features of depression or, less commonly, disruptive behaviours. Grief is a normal and adaptive reaction to the loss of a significant person in the youth's life.
- If the grief reactions are prolonged and the symptoms severely hamper the young person's daily functioning, if she regresses to previous developmental levels, or if her mood is marked by extreme sadness and/or her behaviour becomes disruptive, she may have developed a mental health disorder.
- Grief reactions can impair the youth's daily functioning, academic performance and social engagement.
- Crisis counselling with the youth and the family are the most useful strategies to assist the bereaved youth. In addition, supportive interventions in the school can be very helpful for the bereaved youth as well as for her peers.

CASE STUDY 8

The Anxious Child

Manish's story

The presenting problem

Manish, a 10-year-old boy studying in Standard V, was referred to the counsellor by his mother because he had recently failed in four subjects. Manish complained that for almost 6 months, he had been having difficulty writing because of a 'pain' in his wrist, though he did not feel this 'pain' when using a computer. His mother had taken him to the family doctor a year before to get his wrist examined. After the examination and an X-ray, the doctor had reassured them that there was nothing wrong medically. However, Manish was not able to write the answers to most of the questions during his terminal examination because the pain in his wrist had increased. His mother was extremely upset and approached the counsellor for 'help with his studies'.

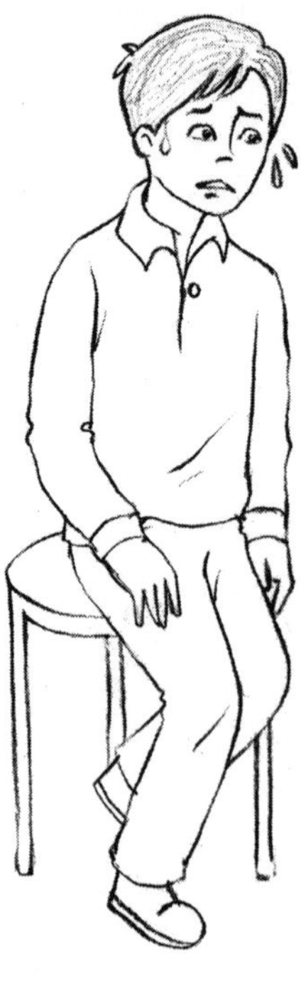

When he met with the counsellor, Manish said he felt nervous and tense in a number of situations. He could easily identify some of these situations, including when he was asked to talk to people he did not know well and when his mother asked to review his homework. He described that at these times, his heart started beating fast, he began perspiring and he felt an urgent need to go to the toilet. He believed that his mother did not think he was a 'good boy' because of his poor school performance. As a result he had stopped showing her his test results when he fared badly. Manish said that during the examinations, he found it hard to write, his hands had become sweaty, he was trembling and his mind had 'gone blank'. Just before an examination, his thoughts revolved around how little he knew and how he would disappoint his mother again; he felt breathless and became tearful and had trouble concentrating on the task at hand. He was really keen to pass his examinations to make his mother 'happy' and also, because she had promised to buy him a new cycle if he passed.

Developmental history

According to his mother, there was nothing extraordinary about Manish's developmental history. He had had no major health problem, other than the 'pain' in his wrist. His mother described him as always having been a 'worrier' and said he tended to avoid situations that made him uncomfortable, e.g. meeting unfamiliar people. He used to cling to her as a young child and did not want to part from her when she dropped him at school. She recalled having to wait outside his pre-school on many occasions, until he settled down.

Psychosocial history

Family history: Manish was an only child and lived in a nuclear family. His father was a goldsmith and his mother a housewife. His father worked long hours and pampered his son by buying him potato chips and aerated drinks. Manish said he was a little afraid of his mother because she got very angry if he did not get good marks in school. He felt more comfortable with his father and especially enjoyed the time they spent together during the weekends.

Academic history: Manish did well in primary school. However, his results in the first term of middle school were poor, leading to his mother supervising his homework. In the second term, his results deteriorated further. The teachers described Manish as a well-behaved student, who was good at recalling academic subject matter when it had been orally presented and when he had managed to write down what he had been taught in class (although he made many spelling mistakes). He could not understand some English words because he had studied in the local language up to Standard IV and English was not spoken at home. Manish could not understand why he 'blanked out' during examinations. He had recently taken to praying before examinations, hoping this would help him. Manish's mother thought he was just not working hard enough.

Social history: Manish had two close friends in class with whom he played cricket after school. He was well-liked by his classmates and teachers. He said he was happy with the number of friends he had. He was not interested in making new friends because he thought he would not have anything interesting to say to them.

Mental status examination

Manish was cooperative during his meetings with the counsellor, although he made minimal eye contact. He was well-dressed and his behaviour was socially appropriate. However, he looked uncomfortable and spoke softly when talking about situations that make him 'nervous', e.g. examinations and having to speak to unfamiliar people. Manish's speech was otherwise normal. His mood shifted between anxiety and sadness. He did not report harbouring any suicidal thoughts. His mood was appropriate to his thought content and the situations he described. Even though Manish was worried about passing his examinations, the matter did not constantly preoccupy him. He had moderate insight and his descriptions of the situations that caused him distress were clear.

Case formulation

Manish, a 10-year-old boy studying in Standard V, is an only child who lives with his parents. He was referred to the counsellor by his mother after he failed in four subjects. His primary complaint is that he experiences tension in a variety of situations, including examinations and meeting new people, and suffers a 'pain' in his wrist when writing during examinations. He has moderate insight into his problems and tries to cope with them by praying. Manish has symptoms of persistent and excessive anxiety and worrying, which he finds difficult to control. The most probable diagnosis is an anxiety disorder (*see* Chapter 2). In addition, he has depressive symptoms. His symptoms of anxiety and depression stem from a tendency to be fearful that began in early childhood, difficulty in coping with the English language in middle school, difficulties with writing, a fear of disappointing his mother and the worry that he would not be accepted by his peers because he is 'not an interesting person'.

Strengths: Among Manish's strengths are his above average intelligence and his insight into his predicament. In addition, he is liked and supported by his friends and teachers. His strong bond with his father is another advantage.

Difficulties: The challenges for Manish are his severe anxiety, which affect his academic performance, as well as his poor self-esteem. His mother's constant pressure on Manish to improve his academic performance and her tendency to show displeasure with his results pose additional challenges. The different parenting attitudes and styles of Manish's mother and father also pose difficulties.

Management plan

The primary strategies to help Manish include youth psychoeducation, family psychoeducation, relaxation exercise and cognitive restructuring.

Youth psychoeducation: The counsellor should reassure Manish that though he is suffering from a number of distressing problems due to anxiety, these problems are likely to decrease with the help of counselling. She should describe the counselling approaches that will help him feel better, cope more successfully and reduce his worries and difficulties. In addition, the counsellor should seek Manish's permission to meet with his parents so that she can provide them with advice on how best to support him.

Family psychoeducation: The counsellor should help Manish's parents understand that he needs their support. She should describe how the great difference in their approaches to him adds to his anxiety. The reasons for Manish's poor performance could be explained by a statement such as, 'Manish feels very unsure of himself in a number of circumstances which are stressful for him. At times, this makes his body tense and makes his mind go blank.' The counsellor can apply the problem-solving strategy to help the parents think through a more coordinated approach to parenting, to help Manish improve his school performance and to help him feel more comfortable in social situations. The counsellor can suggest that the father play a larger role in Manish's upbringing. The mother needs to be encouraged to acknowledge Manish's strengths, e.g. that he is an obedient and affectionate child. Both parents should be advised to provide Manish with the kind of support that will help improve his functioning. For example, they could praise and hug him rather than punish or give him junk food.

Relaxation exercise: The counsellor should explain to Manish that some of his symptoms get aggravated when he breathes very fast because he is nervous. She should suggest that he slow down his breathing when he is under pressure as this will alleviate many of his symptoms. Manish should be advised to spend five minutes practising the relaxation exercise before an examination, in addition to practising it on a daily basis.

Cognitive restructuring: The counsellor should explain to Manish that with her assistance, he can learn to identify, and then tackle, the negative thoughts which cause his feelings and symptoms of anxiety. For example, with relation to his anxiety about examinations, the counsellor can suggest that he ask himself the following questions, as these might help him get to the root of the problem: 'What thoughts do I have when I enter the examination hall?'; 'Do I feel I haven't studied enough?'; 'Will my hand begin to hurt again during the exam?'; and, 'Will my mother be upset if I do badly in the exam?' Once he has identified his negative thoughts, the counsellor can advise him to challenge these thoughts, e.g. through positive self-talk: 'There is nothing wrong with my hand. In fact, I am going to write very well for the exam,' or 'I have studied really well,' or 'I am going to be able to write everything.'

The following are some other interventions which may be useful:

- **Social skills counselling:** The counsellor could suggest to Manish, as well as to school staff who work with him, that he meet new people in non-threatening situations to increase his social confidence. For example, the school coach can help to integrate him into a football team with children from other classes. The counsellor can use role-play to demonstrate how to deal with new social situations, and Manish can practise these social skills with the counsellor.

- **Problem-solving counselling:** The counsellor could work with Manish to identify specific situations which generate anxiety, e.g. telling his mother about his test results. She could then involve him in a discussion of the practical solutions, such as first giving his mother the positive news from school so that she is possibly more receptive to any poor results. He could also make sure that his father is in the house when the results are discussed.
- **Supportive interventions in the school:** The counsellor can help the teachers understand the possible educational factors that may account for Manish's difficulties with examinations. She can also help them ascertain his level of comprehension in English, as well as his writing skills, in order to arrange for appropriate educational support.

ASSESSMENT AND MANAGEMENT OF HIGH LEVELS OF ANXIETY

THE PROBLEM

Anxiety is a common, and normal, emotional response to anticipated difficulties, dangers or stress. However, the degree of anxiety experienced in particular situations and its impact on the youth's life can vary considerably. While a moderate level of anxiety can optimize performance, a high level can be incapacitating. The factors which can lead to higher levels of anxiety or an anxiety disorder include: having parents who respond to situations with anxiety; being in a punitive or harsh school or family environment; having experienced an overwhelming event in the past; and having an anxious temperament.

ASSESSMENT

Information from the youth

- What happens when he feels anxious?
- What triggers the anxiety? Are there any particular precipitating events?
- What impact does the anxiety have on his everyday functioning and how often does he feel anxious?

- How does he cope with his anxiety and what are the effects of these coping strategies on his anxiety? What helps him to feel calm?
- Which factors at home or in school increase the anxiety?
- Are there any associated problems which are aggravated by his anxiety (Panel 5)?

Information from the parent

- What are their parenting styles, particularly those which may enhance anxiety (e.g. punitive parenting, differences in parenting styles)?
- What are their expectations, particularly those which may enhance anxiety (e.g. unrealistic academic expectations)?
- What is their understanding of and what are their approaches to their child's problem?

Information from the teacher

- What is the teachers' assessment of the youth's academic abilities?
- What is the impact of the youth's anxiety on his academic performance and classroom behaviour?
- Have they observed any factors, such as bullying, which might be increasing the youth's anxiety?

MANAGEMENT

With the youth

- Youth psychoeducation enhances the youth's understanding of his problem and the links between his difficulties and his anxiety.
- Relaxation exercise helps the youth manage physical and emotional reactions to stress.
- Cognitive restructuring aids the youth through replacement of negative thoughts with more positive ones, helping to decrease anxiety.
- Problem-solving counselling teaches the youth to identify his difficulties and generate solutions to help manage his anxiety.
- Social skills counselling can help the youth participate in social situations, instead of avoiding them due to anxiety.

Panel 5. Stammering: A communication disorder worsened by anxiety

Stammering is a communication disorder in which the normal flow of speech is affected ('dysfluency'). It affects boys more frequently than girls and occurs more often when there is a family history of stammering or other speech and language disorders. Many children below the age of 5 lisp and hesitate when pronouncing new words; however, as they develop confidence and acquire language skills, they grow out of this dysfluency. When dysfluency does not stop by the age of 6, it may develop into stammering.

Common presentations
The speech of a child with this disorder is more difficult to understand than that of their peers. The child lacks fluency in speech because he hesitates, tends to repeat certain sounds or prolongs sounds. He may also have a lisp. A 'blockage' often occurs in cases of severe stammering, i.e. when the child is speaking or tries to speak, he becomes blocked at a certain point and cannot say the word at all. This is often accompanied by facial grimacing.

Consequences
Stammering can severely affect the young person's confidence and self-esteem. Younger children get frustrated when they are not understood or become shy about speaking to others. As a child with this disorder grows, he may be teased and mocked not only by peers, but also by adults. This tends to make him more nervous and increases the likelihood of stammering. The child may also feel ashamed and, because of this, refuse to make eye contact while speaking.

Counselling strategies and supportive interventions
Youth psychoeducation, family psychoeducation, including referral to a speech and language therapist (*see* Chapter 4) and supportive interventions in the school are recommended for youth who stammer. The youth can be advised to speak at a slower speed and take a deep breath before starting to speak. He should be taught how to manage anxiety and how to interact effectively with peers. The family members can be advised to regularly hold one-on-one conversations with their child, proceeding at a slow pace and making sure not to pressure him. It is important that the counsellor stress that they should empathize with and encourage their child, and avoid drawing attention to his dysfluency. The family and school can be advised to bolster the child's self-esteem by encouraging him to participate in activities that he can excel in. The counsellor should inform the teachers and family that young people with this disorder can be bullied, and that they should prevent any attempts at bullying (*see* Case Study 9).

With the family

- Family psychoeducation helps the parents manage their worries about their child and equips them with effective parenting approaches. These include providing their child with opportunities to succeed, making sure that their expectations of him are realistic and showing him how to deal with stress adaptively.

With teachers and school staff

- Supportive interventions in the school enhance the teachers' understanding of the sources of the youth's anxiety and equip them to help the youth manage academic stress. For example, the counsellor can advise the teachers to reduce the academic demands on the youth and set smaller tasks to help him succeed. This, in turn, would build his self-esteem.

When to refer: If, despite counselling, the youth's anxiety continues to impair his functioning significantly, or if the youth has developed depression as well, he should be referred for further evaluation to a mental health professional.

Key messages

- Anxiety is a common emotional experience, characterized by fearful thoughts and feelings about everyday situations, and often accompanied by physical complaints such as headaches, stomach aches and palpitations ('the heart beating fast').
- Anxiety is often transient and situational. However, it can become a persistent disorder in some cases.
- An anxiety disorder can seriously impair a young person's well-being and academic performance.
- Youth and family psychoeducation, relaxation exercise, problem-solving counselling, cognitive restructuring and social skills counselling are the most useful strategies for addressing anxiety disorder.

CASE STUDY 9

THE CHILD WHO IS BULLIED

Salim's story

THE PRESENTING PROBLEM

Salim, an 11-year-old boy in Standard VI, was referred to the school counsellor because of his erratic school attendance in the current academic term. According to Salim, his problems began soon after a new boy arrived in his class at the beginning of the year. In contrast to Salim, the new boy was a talented sportsperson. Salim had been on the new boy's team when they had lost a football game. Since then, the new boy and two others had been taunting him, calling him 'fatty'. They pushed him around in the corridors during the break and snatched his tiffin. Salim described these episodes as humiliating and wished he did not have to go to school. When he had tried to tell the sports teacher

about the problem, the teacher had been dismissive and told him to 'toughen up'. The result was that Salim had become increasingly nervous and begun to have lunch in the classroom to avoid the boys who were troubling him. Salim had not told anyone at home about his problem with his peers since he felt his sports teacher was right. On days when he was teased in school, he found that going home to a sweet, hot snack helped him feel better, but he then regretted having the snack because he knew it could cause him to gain weight. On some days, he felt so badly about himself that he wished he could discontinue school and help his father in the shop. His mother had noticed that of late, Salim had often been complaining of stomach aches and staying at home due to the pain. She consulted a doctor, who said there was nothing physically wrong with Salim. She told the counsellor that Salim had a good appetite and 'loves to eat'. Though he did not talk about his day in school, she could often sense that he was troubled.

Developmental history

Salim's early and middle childhood had been normal.

Psychosocial history

Family history: Salim lived at home with his parents and one of his three siblings. He was the youngest child and the only boy in the family. Two of his three sisters were married, while the third was in school. Salim had been a much awaited male child and, as a result, had often been given preferential treatment at home, with domestic chores being assigned to his sisters. His father ran a small grocery store close to their home and his mother was a housewife.

Academic history: Salim had been a good student and performed well in class tests until the end of the previous academic year. Doing well academically was very important to him. He was now worried because he had missed quite a lot of school and feared his grades would fall.

Social history: Salim had a few friends in class. However, they never came forward to help him when he was being bullied since they were scared of the possibility of being bullied themselves. He had a few friends in the neighbourhood and felt safe with them because they had known him since childhood and treated him well.

Mental status examination

Salim appeared to be a reserved, likeable young man. He was overweight. He readily participated in the counselling session. He spoke with confidence and expressed his anger appropriately while describing the bully. Though he seemed sad when describing the bullying episodes, he did not express ideas of self-harm or excessive anger. He admitted he craved food, especially when upset, and said he got stomach aches when he was nervous about going to school.

Case formulation

Salim is an 11-year-old boy who studies in Standard VI and comes from a stable nuclear family. He was referred to the counsellor by his class teacher because of a recent drop in his school attendance. Salim is being bullied, in part because he is overweight. The bullying has caused mental health distress, manifested as anxiety (nervousness during the breaktimes in school and experiencing stomach aches) and low self-esteem. He manages these feelings by eating, which he finds comforting, and by avoiding school. Intellectually, his abilities are above average. He has insight into his problems.

Strengths: Salim generally has an easy-going temperament as well as normal intelligence and good insight. In addition, he has a supportive and loving family and good friends.

Difficulties: Salim is overweight and overeats as a way to feel better. Being the object of bullying presents a major challenge and the overindulgent family atmosphere interferes with his ability to increase his resilience.

Management plan

The primary strategies to help Salim recover from his anxiety and raise his self-esteem include youth psychoeducation and problem-solving counselling. Supportive interventions in the school may also prove useful.

Youth psychoeducation: The counsellor should inform Salim that what he is being subjected to by the schoolboys is called 'bullying' and that bullying should not be tolerated on or off the school grounds. She should explain that she will suggest methods, both to him and the school, to counter bullying. For example, she will ask the school management to introduce a strict policy against bullying (Panel 6). The counsellor should inform Salim that his stomach aches, his desire to avoid school and his habit of eating to comfort himself on his return from school result from the anxiety he is experiencing due to the bullying. She should describe how counselling will help him learn ways to manage the bullying, as well as his anxiety. In addition, it would be helpful for Salim if the counsellor addressed his overeating and the need for him to lose weight, making sure she handles these subjects in a sensitive manner. She could provide him with appropriate information on diet and exercise to help him reduce his weight and maintain it at a healthy level.

Problem-solving counselling: The counsellor should help Salim develop the ability to anticipate when and where the episodes of bullying might take place and guide Salim to think of ways to avoid them. For example, Salim could move around in a group during the break and approach trusted teachers for help when he is bullied. The counsellor should also help Salim think of methods to deflect the bullying, such as using humour against verbal bullying. For example, when taunted about his size, he could try to disarm the bully by saying in an easy tone, 'Hey, yes I am fat, but still friendly.' In addition, he could request his friends to come to his aid if he is bullied. The counsellor could also offer to speak to his friends about this, if Salim would like additional support. If he feels his weight is a problem, the counsellor can help him identify activities that may help him lose weight, such as taking brisk walks or cycling. This will make him feel more positive about himself. The counsellor should also work with Salim to find alternatives to overeating, e.g. replacing eating with a walk.

Supportive interventions in the school: The counsellor should inform the teachers and management about bullying in the school and its effects on the students. She should work with the teachers and school administration to establish an anti-bullying school policy (Panel 6) and monitor its effectiveness. Circle time activities, the school assembly and art/poster competitions (*see* Chapter 6) should be used to empower the students to actively discourage bullying. In addition, with Salim's permission, supportive and empathetic friends can be identified and

Panel 6. A zero-tolerance anti-bullying policy

• All incidents of bullying should be reported without fear of reprisal.
• All complaints must be investigated impartially by the school.
• The views both of the victim and the bully need to be heard.
• Concerned teachers and the counsellor should arrange for both the bully and the victim to receive counselling by separate counsellors, if available.
• All incidents of bullying should be dealt with firmly, with a clearly defined system of sanctions. For example, it might be a good idea to have graded measures, beginning with verbal warnings, followed by written warnings, then suspension from enjoyable activities, then detention from break time and finally, asking the bully to perform community service in or outside school. Expulsion could be considered as a last resort for those involved in episodes of severe and unrelenting bullying.

encouraged to support him when he is in a vulnerable situation. The friends can, for example, be encouraged to ask the school staff for help if Salim is bullied or they can continue to include him in a group even if some peers want to exclude him.

The following are other interventions which may be useful:

Cognitive restructuring: The counsellor could help Salim identify thoughts which can build his self-esteem and learn to recall these thoughts when he is feeling despondent about himself. Some examples are that he is a much loved child and a good student, and that he has many friends.

Social skills counselling: The counsellor could encourage Salim to expand his circle of friends. She should also demonstrate through role-play how he could approach children he is not familiar with and engage them in conversation. It is important to help Salim develop 'assertiveness skills' (the ability to honestly express your opinions, feelings, attitudes and rights, without undue anxiety, in a way that does not hurt others) so that he can effectively stand up for himself when targeted by the bully.

Family psychoeducation: With Salim's consent, the counsellor could meet his parents and explain to them that 'Some boys in school are picking on and bullying Salim. This has been very hard on him. He has been trying to avoid situations in which he is bullied and tries to comfort himself by overeating.' Once the parents have gained an understanding of their son's problems, they can work with the counsellor to find ways to assist him that would be more effective than overindulging him. These would include helping him develop healthy eating habits and enrolling him in after-school activities to build his skills and self-confidence.

ASSESSMENT AND MANAGEMENT OF BULLYING

THE PROBLEM

Bullying is defined as deliberately hurtful behaviour. Common forms of bullying include physical bullying (pushing, tripping or hitting), emotional bullying (the use of peer pressure and manipulation to isolate and hurt a person's feelings) and verbal bullying (teasing, mocking, threatening, taunting, and spreading rumours and lies). A new kind of bullying is 'cyber bullying', which makes use of technology (e.g. cell phones, the Internet) to harass individuals. Young people who are bullied may experience a number of distressing reactions, including anxiety, depression, low self-esteem and unexplained physical complaints. Often, when a youth is bullied, other students avoid getting involved in the situation or disassociate themselves from him; as a result, the victim's circle of friends shrinks. Occasionally, bullying results in a vicious cycle: the bullying gives rise to emotional distress, which takes a toll on the victim's school performance and this, in turn, leads to more bullying. Out of frustration, the victim may retaliate. The violence may be directed towards himself (self-harm), the school in general or towards the bully. If the bullying is continuous, and if the victim feels overwhelmed and helpless and has no support system, he may take to substance abuse.

ASSESSMENT

Information from the youth

- What are the bullying episodes like and how frequently do they occur (including where they occur, who is involved, the nature of the bullying and the level of danger the youth is feeling)?

- What steps has the youth taken to counter the bullying and how effective are they?
- What are the youth's social networks? How can these be used to combat the bullying?
- What are his coping strategies? How effective are these strategies?

Information from the parent

- Is the family aware of the bullying occurring in school? Does it occur in any other setting?
- What steps have they taken to support their child?
- Have they noticed any changes in the child's behaviours and performance across the academic and social settings?

Information from the teacher

- Have the teachers noticed any problems with the youth?
- Are the teachers aware of bullying being an issue within the school setting and are they concerned about it?
- What is the school's policy on bullying and how can this be strengthened?
- What actions are the teachers and school officials taking to address bullying within the school?

MANAGEMENT

With the youth

- The counsellor's primary goal should be to ensure the safety of the victim, protecting him from bullying as well as from any risk of self-harm.
- Youth psychoeducation enhances the youth's understanding of the fact that bullying in any form is unacceptable, that he is not responsible for the bullying and that there are things that both he and the school can do to reduce bullying.
- Problem-solving counselling helps the youth identify the different sorts of bullying that occur and develop varied tactics to avoid the

bullying (e.g. identifying and avoiding places where bullying occurs, identifying and making use of support networks, walking away from a threatening situation, using humour to disarm the bully and reporting the incident to a trusted adult).

- Cognitive restructuring helps the young person recover his self-esteem by replacing self-criticism with 'positive self-talk'. This breaks the cycle of victimhood.
- Social skills counselling should include assertiveness training so that the youth can stand up for himself.
- Anger management counselling could be useful for those who respond aggressively to the bully.

With the family

- Family psychoeducation helps the parents develop skills to see their child through a difficult time. For example, they can learn to offer their child protection, model ways for him to manage bullying and work with the school to safeguard their child.

With teachers and school staff

- The counsellor should find out from the school staff who the bully is. Arrangements can then be made for a counsellor to see him so as to uncover the factors that make him a bully and to discuss with him the ways in which he can control his bullying behaviours (*see* Case Study 16).
- The counsellor should encourage the school to implement and monitor a zero-tolerance anti-bullying policy covering the entire school to create a safe school environment for all students (Panel 6). The policy should be adopted by the school management and the parent–teacher association, and then shared with the entire school community. All policies should be prominently displayed on the school notice board.

When to refer: Should the bullying escalate and the victim's symptoms increase despite the counselling and supportive interventions in the school, the youth should be referred to a mental health professional and the school management should seek further consultation.

Key messages

- Bullying is common in schools and greatly affects the mental health of the person who is bullied.
- Bullies often have low self-esteem and many have experienced violence and humiliation themselves.
- Youth psychoeducation and problem-solving counselling are the key strategies for helping the victim address the bullying and its emotional consequences. Supportive interventions in the school are essential to protect the bullied youth.
- A strong zero-tolerance anti-bullying policy is the foundation for a secure school environment to benefit the entire student body.

CASE STUDY 10

THE YOUTH WITH PROBLEMS CONTROLLING ANGER

Navin's story

THE PRESENTING PROBLEM

Navin, an 11-year-old boy studying in Standard VI in a boarding school, was referred to the counsellor by the headmaster and his class teacher for using abusive language with others and hitting classmates, as well as due to his poor academic performance.

Navin was sent to the boarding school when he was 10 years old, after he had thrown a glass bottle at a classmate on the playground of his former school. He described this incident as a retaliation for what he had perceived to be a negative remark (the classmate had said that Navin should run faster on the football field). Navin's father reported that his son had been hot-tempered since early childhood, but had not been physically aggressive until the age of 10. While observing Navin on the playground, the counsellor noted that he was a good football player. However, when he did not manage to get the ball, or if someone said something even slightly critical to him, he immediately became aggressive. As for the classroom, the teacher reported that he tended to interpret harmless conversation as criticism and was overly sensitive to remarks made by his classmates. Navin said that when he struck out physically and verbally in response to such remarks, the harrassment stopped. He added that, although his actions stopped the remarks against him, his temper created many problems for him, including losing friends. He said he did not know how to deal with his temper or with schoolmates when they made hurtful remarks. Once, when he hit a classmate in the face and the boy began to bleed, Navin was frightened. He had meant to warn, not hurt, his classmate.

Developmental history

According to the history provided by the father, Navin's developmental history was normal.

Psychosocial history

Family history: Navin's father worked intermittently as a manual labourer and was a heavy drinker. His mother had begun working abroad as domestic help when Navin was 9 and had rarely been in touch with her son since her move. Navin had three older siblings. None of his family members visited him at the boarding school. Navin reported that he had been beaten with a stick and verbally 'put down' by his father since his early childhood. His father confirmed that this was his method of 'controlling' Navin. Navin did not provide any information about his relationship with his mother, but said that he missed her. He was fond of his elder sister, whom he said was the only one who cared for him when he went home during the holidays. He did not feel that his relationships with his older brothers were close. One of them was taking a technical course; the other had dropped out of school and was working in a restaurant.

Academic history: When the medium of instruction in Navin's primary school was in his mother tongue, he had fared well. He started failing class tests in Standard V, when the medium of instruction switched to English. In the last examination, he had failed in three subjects. He said he had trouble reading English. However, he felt comfortable speaking both in his mother tongue and English, and enjoyed school debates in English. He found his studies 'boring', though he was convinced that he could pass, given some help and if he put in more effort. He said he wanted to pass in all subjects so that he could complete his schooling and find a good job.

Social history: Navin had befriended two boys upon his arrival at the boarding school, but said they were not such great friends. He did not like to go home over the weekends or during the holidays because his father beat him, his mother was not home and nobody cared for him except his sister.

Mental status examination

Navin was distrustful when he first met the counsellor, but warmed up as the counselling progressed. He was dressed sloppily. His speech was normal. Navin's mood varied during the session. At times, he appeared sad, e.g. when talking about his home life; at other times, he was irritable, e.g. when talking about being slighted by his peers. Often he seemed disinterested. He had a poor self-image. For example, he expressed the perception that his parents favoured his siblings when there was no evidence for this. He said he found it difficult to control his anger because he often felt intensely hurt by the comments and actions of others. He instantly felt 'really mad' when others 'put me down'. He said his body turned 'hot' and his breathing became 'fast'. He agreed that he often overreacted and sometimes misread others' intentions, and said he became aware of this only after he 'cools down'.

Case formulation

Navin is an 11-year-old boy who studies in Standard VI of a boarding school. He is the youngest of four siblings. His mother works abroad and his father is a manual labourer who drinks heavily. Navin was referred to the counsellor by the headmaster and his class teacher for using abusive language with others and hitting classmates, and due to his poor academic performance. Navin's primary problems are his difficulty in managing his anger and his extreme sensitivity to perceived criticism from his peers. His mood is low and irritable at times. He expresses remorse for his angry outbursts and is aware that his outbursts are often overreactions. He is experiencing mental health distress. This distress is probably the result of the separation from and lack of contact with his mother and the chronic physical violence and humiliation by his alcoholic father.

Strengths: Navin's strengths include good motor skills, normal intelligence and insight into his behaviour. Living in a boarding school, where he is protected from his father's violence and supported by his teachers, is helpful for him. The presence of a caring sister at home is also beneficial.

Difficulties: Navin's challenges include extreme sensitivity to criticism and his difficulty in managing his anger. The violence he faces at his father's hands during the holidays, the fact that his mother works abroad and does not keep in touch with him, and his brothers' lack of interest in him are significant challenges in addition. In the academic arena, Navin's poor reading skill in English is a significant difficulty.

Management plan

The primary counselling strategies to help Navin are youth psycho-education, anger management counselling, problem-solving counselling, family psychoeducation, relaxation exercise and supportive interventions in the school.

Youth psychoeducation: The counsellor should help Navin understand his problems, that he responds to hurt feelings by getting angry and that he anticipates criticism even when there is unlikely to be any. The counsellor should explain that anger is a 'normal' emotion, but it is how a person behaves when he is angry that may cause problems. He and Navin should agree on a counselling plan.

Anger management counselling: The counsellor should help Navin identify the triggers which lead to his aggressive behaviour towards his peers and work with him to replace angry outbursts with socially acceptable responses. With the counsellor's help, Navin can identify situations which provoke him to respond angrily. For example, he might feel provoked if a schoolmate laughs at his clothes. The counsellor should then help Navin find alternative ways to manage his hurt feelings and angry responses. For example, he should try to recognize any tense feelings he has in response to a peer's remark, take a moment to assess the situation and attempt to calm himself down, refuse to counter the remark and walk away. The counsellor might make use of role-play, simulating situations which arouse his anger and practising new ways of thinking about these situations and responding to them. Later, the counsellor should review with Navin how he is managing his anger and praise him when he has managed it successfully.

Relaxation exercise: The counsellor can teach Navin the relaxation exercise and discuss how to use this technique when he is beginning to feel angry in order to calm himself.

Problem-solving counselling: The counsellor should work with Navin to identify the other problem areas in his life, such as the lack of contact with his mother and his father's aggression towards him, and help him find solutions. For example, he could write to his mother and go out of the house until his father's anger subsides.

Family psychoeducation: With Navin's permission, the counsellor can meet the father to gain an understanding of his difficulties with parenting and work with him to improve his parenting skills. A statement such as, 'Navin is unable to handle his anger, especially when he feels hurt' may help the father understand the causes of his son's behaviours and motivate him to modify his style of parenting. While explaining Navin's tendency to lose his temper, the counsellor can gently tell the father that his son's behaviour is modelled after what he sees and experiences at home. If the father is receptive he should advise him on how to manage his own anger. He could, for example, seek individual counselling and reduce his intake of alcohol, both in general and especially when Navin is home for the holidays. The counsellor should consider enlisting the sister's help so that she can support Navin when he goes home.

Supportive interventions in the school: The counsellor can request that Navin's teachers create opportunities for him to build positive peer relationships, e.g. by encouraging him to participate in cooperative projects which utilize his talents. He should advise the school administration to provide Navin with academic remediation, particularly in English. The teachers can also use behaviour charts (*see* Chapter 6 and Appendix) to help motivate Navin to behave acceptably in the school setting.

When to refer: If the youth's outbursts of anger are part of a larger group of disruptive behaviours (*see* Case Study 16), the counsellor may consider referring the youth to a mental health professional.

Assessment and Management of 'Problem' Anger

The Problem

Anger is one of the many 'normal' emotions. It is not a 'bad' emotion in itself, but can be damaging when it is too intense, is triggered too easily, does not match the situation or leads to socially unacceptable reactions. Individuals feel angry when they perceive that they have been wronged or threatened, when they are or perceive that they have been hurt emotionally or physically, when they feel frustrated or when they think that people they care about are being mistreated. When managed properly, the youth tries to understand why he has become angry, controls his anger and addresses the situation that has produced the anger effectively and appropriately. Angry overreactions may temporarily relieve feelings of hurt and anger, but often lead to subsequent feelings of shame, social marginalization and further destructive acts. The most common causes of poor management of anger are low self-esteem and living in an environment in which the youth witnesses and/or experiences violence. Anger may also be associated with mental health distress or disorders such as depression, conduct disorders and drug/ alcohol abuse. The anger management skills of young people with coexisting problems such as specific learning disabilities or attention deficit hyperactivity disorder may be poorly developed.

Assessment

From the youth

- What makes him angry and how does he feel when he is angry?
- Has he ever hurt/felt like hurting others when he is angry?
- What does he do to try to control his anger? Does this help?
- Does he have other sorts of behaviours that he considers problematic?
- How has his mood been recently? Has he been feeling depressed or low?
- Does he face stressors, especially violence, at home? Does he face stressors in school, for example being bullied (*see* Case Study 9)?

From the parents

- What do they think has contributed to their child's problem with anger?
- What are their reactions to their child's behaviours?
- What can they do to help their child manage his difficulties?
- Which skills would they like to model for their child in order to teach him how to manage his anger?

From the teacher

- How does the student interact with his peers and with the teacher?
- How often does he have an angry outburst?
- How does his anger interfere with his academic performance and social relationships?
- Does he have academic problems?

MANAGEMENT

With the youth

- Youth psychoeducation enhances the youth's understanding of his problem, as well as of its causes and consequences.
- Anger management counselling can help the youth identify the 'triggers' for his anger, recognize the signs which indicate that he is losing his temper and develop skills to manage his emotional reactions.
- Relaxation exercise can help the youth calm himself down when he anticipates trouble and when his anger has been triggered.
- Problem-solving counselling enhances the youth's ability to think of and then implement more adaptive responses to challenging situations.

With the family

- Family psychoeducation helps the parents understand how their behaviours and approaches to their child affect his feelings and actions. It aims to replace problematic styles of parenting with effective and caring approaches to their child.

With teachers and school staff

- Using supportive interventions in the school, the counsellor can guide the teachers and school staff to develop non-punitive techniques to manage the youth's disruptive behaviours in the classroom. The counsellor can provide the teachers with skills to determine whether academic difficulties are contributing to a youth's distress and help them to identify supportive educational remedies that might benefit the youth. If bullying is an issue, *see* Case Study 9.

When to refer: The counsellor should refer the youth to a mental health professional for further evaluation if the instances of aggression due to anger are serious, e.g. if they have led to a serious injury; if there is evidence suggesting a mental health disorder, e.g. depression or a conduct disorder; or if the counsellor's interventions have had little impact. If academic difficulties are present, assessments for specific learning disabilities should be conducted (*see* Chapter 4).

Key messages

- Anger is a normal emotion. However, when it is frequent and intense or has a negative impact on the youth as well as others, the youth would benefit from an assessment.
- Intense anger may lead to social marginalization and academic decline. It may also increase the risk of harming oneself or others.
- The presence of intense, sustained anger may indicate a mood disorder, e.g. depression, or a conduct disorder.
- Youth psychoeducation, anger management counselling, problem-solving counselling and relaxation exercise are useful strategies to help the youth manage his anger; family psychoeducation is helpful to the youth's family.

CASE STUDY 11

THE YOUTH LIVING IN EXTREMELY STRESSFUL CIRCUMSTANCES

Varuna's story

THE PRESENTING PROBLEM

Varuna, a 12-year-old girl studying in Standard VI, came to the school counsellor on her own (self-referred). She had heard a class presentation by the counsellor on how counselling can 'help with worries' and had then put a note in the 'Speak Out' Box (*see* Chapter 3). The note briefly described her problem and expressed her wish to meet with the counsellor.

During her first meeting with the counsellor, Varuna said she had occasional headaches, was worried about her family and her studies, and felt angry with her father. She said she had been having difficulty coping with her studies since the summer break. Varuna was especially worried about being unable to focus on her studies and about the fall in her marks over the course of the school year. She told the counsellor that she 'needed' to do well in school because if she did not, her future would be bleak. She said she understood her schoolwork, but could not concentrate on her assignments or complete them. As she warmed up to the counsellor over the course of several meetings, Varuna revealed that her home environment was extremely distressing for her and that she often felt angry because of the problems at home. She lived in a joint family with her parents, younger brother and paternal uncle's family. They shared a kitchen, though both families cooked separately. She said her father drank every day, and would return home drunk and often beat her mother. Her mother had become 'very sick' over the past few months. When asked about the nature of her mother's illness, Varuna said she did not know what her mother was suffering from, but she was always weak, stayed in bed for days at a stretch and sometimes vomited or cried out in pain. She said she was worried that her mother might die soon. When her mother was feeling particularly weak, she was unable to look after Varuna and her younger brother, cook or clean. As a result, on many days, Varuna had to take over the household chores, cook breakfast and dinner, and help her 6-year-old brother prepare for school. An additional problem was that her father's income was declining and the adults in the joint family had frequent quarrels about money. Varuna said that her family had become isolated and the children in the neighbourhood avoided making eye contact with her when she passed by. She thought this was because of her father's alcohol abuse, her mother's illness and the loud arguments that the neighbours could probably hear.

In response to the counsellor's questions, Varuna expressed hopelessness about her home situation. She said that quite often she got into arguments with her father because she could not control her annoyance and anger with him. The arguments regularly spun out of control. She later felt guilty about her outbursts. The situation usually proceeded in the following way: the father would shout at the mother, Varuna would angrily defend her mother, the father would hit Varuna and tell her to 'mind your own business', the mother, feeling upset by this, would then argue with the father, and the father would beat the mother. Varuna told the counsellor that she wanted this vicious cycle to stop. She also said she wanted her father to stop drinking and her mother to get well.

Developmental history

With Varuna's permission, the counsellor made a home visit (*see* Chapter 6) so that she could learn more about Varuna's family life and collect a developmental history. Since the visit was during the day, the only adult at home was the mother. The counsellor noticed that Varuna's home was subdivided into two living quarters. The section occupied by her uncle's family was relatively well kept, but the living quarters of Varuna's family were badly maintained. Throughout the home visit, the mother remained in bed and appeared unwell, though she was neatly dressed. While talking to the counsellor, she shared her fear that she had a chronic illness, though she did not know the diagnosis. She said she was concerned that Varuna had to see to the household chores since she could not manage them. She described the members of her brother-in-law's family as helpful, but added that they were getting increasingly fed up with her husband's behaviours, with the result that there were frequent arguments between the brothers. The mother did not say much about her husband, but admitted that she was finding it difficult to make ends meet. In response to the counsellor's questions about Varuna's history, the mother reported that her developmental history had been normal. She said she had recently noticed that Varuna seemed impatient and got angry easily. She was proud of Varuna because she had always been motivated to 'have a future'.

Psychosocial history

Family history: Varuna was the older of two children. Her younger brother was 6 years old. Her father used to work as a driver, but because of his drinking problem, he did not have a steady job. Due to financial difficulties, Varuna's mother, although physically weak, made snacks at home which were sold at a stall by a local vendor. Varuna lived in an extended family with her paternal uncle and his family. The relationship between the two brothers was strained primarily due to the father's abuse of alcohol. Varuna's aunt used to be quite close to Varuna's mother before the relationship between the brothers started deteriorating the previous summer.

Academic history: Varuna had done very well in primary school and most of middle school. Until Standard VI, when her mother had been well enough to supervise her studies, Varuna had had no academic problems. However, since her mother had become unwell recently, Varuna's performance had deteriorated. When she tried to study, she became distracted and gave up. Throughout Standard VI, she had been faring poorly in all her subjects.

Social history: Varuna used to have friends in her class, but had recently stopped interacting with her peers because they 'gossiped' about her and even teased her when she shared her difficulties with them. She used to enjoy participating in races with them during the school breaks. She now kept to herself because she felt embarrassed about her family life and her declining marks. She had one friend, but was worried that this friendship, too, might not last. She had no friends in the neighbourhood and she was lonely.

Mental status examination

Varuna was forthcoming and cooperative during the counselling sessions and made good eye contact. Her appearance was neat. Her behaviour and mood were appropriate to the situations she described. She seemed slightly embarrassed when she became tearful while talking about her home situation. Generally, the tone and pace of her speech were normal, but the pitch rose and the pace increased when she spoke about her anger with her father. She told the counsellor that she sometimes felt hopeless about her home situation, saying, 'It will never improve.' She disclosed that she often got into arguments with her parents, particularly her father, because she 'cannot control her angry feelings'. Following these episodes, she would feel guilty. Varuna was noticeably sad and anxious, in an appropriate manner, when she discussed her mother's health and her worry about her academic performance. She did not report any thoughts of self-harm. She had insight into her problems, and expressed a strong desire to see an improvement in her home life, to succeed in school so that she could have a bright future and to make friends.

Case formulation

Varuna, a 12-year-old girl studying in Standard VI, visited the counsellor on her own. She lives with her parents and 6-year-old brother in an extended family. Her primary complaints are that she has been having difficulty in coping with her studies over the past several months and that she worries about her mother and family all the time. She is facing a number of significant problems in her home. Notable among these are that her father is a chronic alcoholic who abuses her mother and her, and that her mother appears to be suffering from an undiagnosed medical condition. Varuna has to shoulder many of the household responsibilities since her mother is unwell. In addition, the family is experiencing financial difficulties. Varuna says she feels worried, angry and hopeless, and complains that she often gets headaches. She is aware that her feelings and functioning are being affected by her family's problems. Her symptoms reflect mental health distress in response to a chronically stressful home situation, compounded by the more recent emotional and practical stresses arising from her mother's illness.

Strengths: Varuna's strengths include her strong motivation to do well in school, as well as her insight into her difficulties and her intelligence. The fact that she has sought the counsellor's help on her own is a positive factor. The other advantages are the presence of a supportive mother and the possibility of enlisting the support of other adults in the joint family.

Difficulties: These include the mother's chronic ill health, the absence of information about the cause of or appropriate treatment for her mother's illness and the mother's inability to perform the household chores or help Varuna with her studies. The father's alcohol abuse and tendency to physical violence, together with the marital conflict between Varuna's parents, present major difficulties. In addition, the father has no steady employment and the family is facing financial problems; there are frequent arguments between Varuna's father and uncle; and the family is becoming socially isolated. Finally, Varuna is being bullied in school and her grades are falling.

Management plan

The primary strategies that can help Varuna recover are youth psychoeducation, family psychoeducation, problem-solving counselling, anger management counselling and relaxation exercise. Supportive interventions in the school can also play an important role.

Youth psychoeducation: The counsellor should praise Varuna for seeking help. She should then explain that her problems arise from the increased pressure that her mother's illness has put on her and from her continuing worries about her family, particularly her mother's health. The counsellor can reassure her that her situation can be improved if she and her family receive counselling, and if supportive measures are implemented in school and at home.

Family psychoeducation: With Varuna's permission, the counsellor should attempt to provide family psychoeducation to the parents to address the multiple challenges at home and explore whatever support might be available to stabilize the family. In order for the family psychoeducation to have a chance of succeeding, the counsellor would need to build a non-judgemental and supportive relationship with Varuna's parents, over time. This could help the counsellor tackle the numerous issues facing the family and Varuna. The counsellor should request that the parents meet her in the school; if this is not possible, she should meet them in their home. The major concern being the mother's physical condition, the counsellor should encourage the parents to ensure that she goes for a medical check-up and receives appropriate care. It may be advisable to make a referral to social services, which can arrange for an intervention on the mother's behalf, given her deteriorating health and also, if the home situation does not improve (*see* Chapter 4). The father's alcoholism should be addressed by first obtaining the history of his problem from him, then assessing his motivation to change and finally, encouraging him to seek help from the family doctor or a counselling facility (*see* Chapter 4). The counsellor can also highlight how tackling his alcoholism might help him secure a steady job and overcome his financial difficulties. She should then discuss how the parents can work together to provide a more nurturing environment for their children. Informing them about the impact of family problems on child development and mental health can help to improve their parenting. So that the parents can understand Varuna's distress better and increase their hope that their home life can improve, the counsellor can empathize with them and tell them, 'Varuna is feeling very worried about all of the stresses the family is experiencing and this is affecting how she feels and copes, including with her schoolwork. Also, perhaps you have some worries at this time about Varuna and about your family.' In order to reduce the mother's and the family's isolation, the counsellor, together with the family, could think of how they can engage with the community. For example, if the mother has had good relationships with some of the women in the community, she and the counsellor could think of ways to cultivate these relationships. The mother could also re-build her relationship with her sister-in-law.

Problem-solving counselling: The counsellor should first take up problems which are relatively easy to tackle so that Varuna can experience a sense of mastery. For example, she could take up the issue of Varuna isolating herself from her classmates because they tease her. The counsellor can help her find ways of interacting with her peers again, e.g. Varuna could lend a hand in class events or help a classmate with her studies. She should then use role-plays which would help Varuna practise how to handle these situations. Further, the counsellor and she can discuss the activities which she would like to participate in (such as sports), which would give her pleasure as well as involve her peers. Varuna will need assistance in identifying people with whom she can share private information and determining when it might be best to talk to these people about her family problems. The counsellor can assist Varuna to find ways to ensure her safety, as well as to identify the resources she can access when her home environment is feeling unsafe (*see* Chapter 4).

Anger management counselling: The counsellor should explore with Varuna what thoughts and physical responses she experiences when she gets angry. She can be taught how to recognize her anger when it first arises and to identify and implement acceptable alternative responses. For example, when her father's behaviour is making her angry, she can remove herself from the situation, use a calm voice with her father or calm herself with self-talk. Role-playing the possible situations and solutions will help Varuna gain confidence that she can manage her anger successfully.

Relaxation exercise: The counsellor can teach Varuna this exercise and explain how it can be useful when her worry about her problems interferes with her ability to concentrate.

Supportive interventions in the school: It is important that the counsellor, with Varuna's permission, help the teachers understand that Varuna is experiencing extreme stress and that, although motivated and bright, she is having great difficulty concentrating because of her problems at home. The counsellor should suggest that they reduce or modify her homework until she is better able to concentrate. In addition, the teachers should be advised to protect Varuna from teasing and to help her participate in enjoyable activities with her peers so that she can rebuild her friendships.

When to refer: If the situation in Varuna's home remains unchanged despite the counsellor's efforts and her consultations with her supervisor, the counsellor should contact a social worker, child rights organization and/or the local authorities.

Assessment and Management of Youth Living in Extremely Stressful Circumstances

The Problem

Extremely stressful home situations include: abnormal intra-familial relationships, e.g. lack of warmth in parent–child relationships, familial discord, hostility towards the child and family violence; illness in the youth's primary support group; isolation of the family; unsafe circumstances, e.g. extreme poverty resulting in compromises to hygiene and nutritional needs and/or physical danger; being discriminated against by the community; and migration into a new community. Young people living with high degrees of stress often suffer from mental health distress and the symptoms accompanying it (impulsivity, regressive reactions such as bedwetting, anxiety and depressive symptoms). In addition, chronically stressful circumstances can lead to the development of emotional disorders, particularly depression and anxiety disorders; behavioural disorders, particularly oppositional defiant disorder and conduct disorder; and substance abuse.

Assessment

Information from the youth

- What are the youth's symptoms? How do they affect her everyday functioning?
- What problems is the youth facing at home, in the school and in her community?

- When did these problems begin? How do they affect her overall health?
- How does she cope with these problems?
- What makes her feel better? What makes her feel worse?
- Who does she count on the most for support?

Information from the parent

- What problems is the family facing?
- How do they manage these problems, e.g. do they take the help of other family members or of community agencies? What has proved to be effective? What makes matters worse?
- How are these problems affecting their child? What have they done to protect her?
- What are the family's social support networks?

Information from the teacher

- What have the teachers and school staff noticed with respect to the youth's problems?
- Has the family approached the school for help with their child or their difficulties? What kind of help have they sought? What help has the school been able to offer?
- How has the youth's academic performance been? Has it been declining recently? If so, how have the teachers addressed this?
- Have the teachers noticed anything unusual about the youth's peer relationships? If she is having problems with her peers, what are they and how have the teachers tried to help?

MANAGEMENT

With the youth

- Youth psychoeducation enhances the young person's understanding of the problems she is facing and the potential remedies that counselling can offer.
- Relaxation exercise aids in the management of physical and emotional reactions associated with anxiety.

- Problem-solving counselling helps the youth to first identify problems that are relatively easy to tackle so that she can experience a sense of mastery and feel less powerless, and then equips her with skills to help her address more difficult situations.

With the family

- Family psychoeducation aims to enhance the family's understanding of the impact of the stressful home environment on the child's mental health, and to help them decrease the family's stress and manage the problems at home.
- Supportive interventions in the home and the community help families without sufficient emotional and practical resources to locate support outside the home, e.g. from local social service agencies, local religious leaders and groups, support groups and community leaders.

With teachers and other school staff

- Supportive interventions in the school enhance the teachers' understanding of the link between the youth's academic problems and the stress she is going through. The counsellor helps the youth by encouraging the teachers to be more empathetic towards her, as well as by suggesting modifications in the curriculum and homework (decreasing the academic pressure on the youth) until her situation improves. If the youth has become socially withdrawn, the teachers can be advised how to help her rebuild her relationships.

When to refer: If the youth does not respond to the counselling strategies or is suicidal (*see* Chapter 4), she must be referred to a mental health professional for further evaluation and follow-up. When a youth living in extremely stressful circumstances is in physical and/ or emotional danger or is a risk to others, the counsellor must assess the situation with her supervisor and report it to a social worker, a child rights organization or, if necessary, the local authorities (*see* Chapter 7).

Key messages

- Examples of stressful experiences include illness and/or loss in the youth's primary support group, inadequate or distorted intra-familial communication, family conflict (especially parental conflict), social isolation, dangerous living conditions, impoverishment and exposure to physical or sexual abuse.
- The reactions to such stressful experiences include mental health distress and emotional and behavioural disorders.
- Accessing resources in the youth's environment as well as reducing the stress in the home environment are vital to address the youth's mental health problems.
- Youth psychoeducation, family psychoeducation, problem-solving counselling and relaxation exercise are the most useful counselling strategies for promoting the mental health of young people living with severe stress. Additionally, supportive interventions in the school and supportive interventions in the home and the community are important supportive interventions.

CASE STUDY 12

The Youth Who Has Difficulty with His Studies

Ravi's story

The Presenting Problem

Ravi, a 12-year-old boy studying in Standard VII, was referred to the counsellor by his teacher because he had been experiencing difficulty with his academic work.

Ravi's parents and teachers were worried about his performance in the last examination. His scores had been very low in almost all subjects, except mathematics. His teachers had been complaining about his declining academic performance since Standard V and were puzzled because he seemed to be bright. His mother found it frustrating to supervise his studies because whatever she taught him seemed to 'slip out of his head'. Not knowing what to do, she had enrolled him for private tuitions. The teacher who gave Ravi tuitions had also begun complaining

that he lacked motivation and did not focus on his work. He said that Ravi made 'careless' spelling mistakes and errors while reading, often seemed to be in a dream world and did not complete his assignments on time. Ravi's mother remarked that even though he revised and seemed to understand all his work, he did badly in the examinations. Ravi explained that he got confused while doing assignments at home. He said the questions in the tests and assignments were often 'hard to understand'. When he realized that he could not make sense of his work, he 'switched off' and instead, started to think about things which interested him, such as a football match he had watched on television.

Developmental history

According to his mother, Ravi was born at full term by a Caesarean section. Though she had not given much thought to his development during his early years, she now recognized that compared to his younger brother, Ravi probably spoke much less at the same age.

Psychosocial history

Family history: Ravi had an 8-year-old brother. His paternal grandparents lived with his family. His mother was a teacher and his father a manager in a corporate house. Ravi's mother complained that his academic performance had been very embarrassing for the family. Since both parents were well educated, they had high academic expectations for their children. The younger son was faring very well in school. The father, constantly busy with work commitments, spent very little time with the family. The mother was also very busy, dividing her time between work and looking after the house and the children.

Academic history: Ravi's mother said that looking back, she realized Ravi had been 'behind other children in pre-school' as far as his ability to speak was concerned. He could not utter single words until 2 years of age and started putting words together only at the age of 3. However, his speech improved rapidly by the end of pre-school and he subsequently caught up with his peers. While in pre-school, Ravi initially had trouble learning the names of letters, colours and shapes. His mother had also noted that he had difficulty buttoning his clothes and tying his shoelaces. She reported that Ravi's teachers in pre-school had observed that he could not colour well between the lines. In primary school, though he had problems with spelling and writing, he managed to get average grades with his mother's assistance. This trend had lasted until Standard IV. His performance had begun deteriorating from Standard V. Recently, his teachers had remarked that he was bright but lost marks because his written work in tests 'does not make sense'. They said he was 'careless' in his work and lacked the motivation to study, especially when it came to written work. In class, his oral responses were praiseworthy and he sometimes provided answers to questions that many children found confusing and difficult. His mother said he was 'lazy' when it came to studies and completed his home assignments only after numerous reminders and shouting (which she found stressful). Ravi named mathematics, science, music and physical education as his favourite subjects. He disliked history because he could not remember the dates and the sequence of historical events properly. He found map-reading difficult in geography. Further, studying grammar, whether of English or another language, confused him. He enjoyed learning about plants and animals in the science classes, but did not like the written assignments. He said he liked mathematics because the teacher gave him grades for the answers and not for his tidiness.

Social history: Ravi was popular with his friends in school and in his neighbourhood and enjoyed outdoor games. His teachers liked him because he was a bright, well-mannered boy, who was always ready to help others. His mother said he was the favourite grandchild of his grandparents and that they 'spoiled' him.

MENTAL STATUS EXAMINATION

Ravi was well groomed. Although he was a little nervous at first, he made good eye contact and was cooperative. As the session progressed, he relaxed and began talking about his problems. He said that he did not like going to school and felt happy on holidays. Ravi's speech was normal and his behaviour socially appropriate. His mood was appropriate to his thought content and to the situations he described. The form and content of his thinking were normal. Though he disliked school and described it as 'frustrating', he understood that it was important for him to complete his studies and was concerned about his performance. Ravi had good insight into his problems and wanted to overcome them.

Case formulation

Ravi, a 12-year-old boy studying in Standard VII, is the elder child in a family of two children. He lives with his parents and paternal grandparents. He was referred to the counsellor by his teacher due to his poor academic performance. The primary complaint is that he scores low marks in most subjects and seems to lack the motivation to study. Ravi knows that he is having difficulty with his studies, but he does not know how to remedy this. He has problems with reading, writing and spelling. The most probable diagnosis for Ravi is a specific learning disability.

Strengths: Among Ravi's strengths are his above average intelligence, his ability to perform well in mathematics and his awareness of his academic problem. The other factors in his favour are that the teachers are keenly interested in helping him improve academically, and that he has good peer relationships, a caring home environment and good self-esteem.

Difficulties: Ravi is having trouble with academic work and dislikes written work. His parents' high expectations, as well as the fact that they have little time to help him with his studies, are additional obstacles for Ravi.

Management plan

The counselling strategies of youth psychoeducation, family psychoeducation and supportive interventions in the school can help Ravi cope with his academic problems.

Youth psychoeducation: The counsellor should praise Ravi for his determination to persevere with his studies and for his intelligence. After explaining that learning is a complex process, she should introduce the subject of the difficulties he seems to be facing with respect to learning. The counsellor should explain that due to these difficulties, he may need some additional educational support to help him develop his learning skills. She should emphasize that a psychoeducational assessment would help everyone concerned gain an understanding of his learning strengths and weaknesses. It would also be useful to determine the kind of learning support he should be given in school and at home to help him do well academically.

Family psychoeducation: Ideally, the counsellor should try and meet with Ravi's parents as soon as possible after meeting with Ravi. The goal of the meeting should be to help them understand that his problems may result from a specific learning disability and are not due to 'laziness'. The counsellor should clarify that Ravi's intellect, which is above average, allowed him to cope with the curriculum through primary school, but with the increase in academic pressure, he is finding it difficult to keep pace with his peers. The counsellor should refer him to a clinical psychologist for psychoeducational testing, helping the parents understand the reason for the referral by explaining: 'It seems that Ravi is finding it very difficult to make sense of the information that is given to him in class. An assessment with a specialist will allow us to pinpoint the problem' (*see* Chapter 4). If Ravi is found to have a specific learning disability, the counsellor should explain to his parents that remedial education, modifications to the curriculum and concessions by the examination board will help improve their son's academic performance. The counsellor should also emphasize that recognizing their son's strengths and praising him for his efforts will boost his self-esteem and improve his engagement with the learning process. The parents should be advised to strike a balance between their expectations for Ravi and his abilities, reduce their pressure on him, encourage him in the areas of his strengths and devote some extra time helping him with his studies.

Supportive interventions in the school: If the psychoeducational assessment confirms that Ravi has a specific learning disability, the counsellor can ask the clinical psychologist to coordinate with his teachers to determine the best techniques to help him learn effectively.

The classroom adaptations which could be useful include: placing Ravi in the front of the classroom, so that he can clearly see the teacher and blackboard; making sure that he has understood the instructions given to him; giving preference to oral assessments over written assessments; and giving him a choice of subjects which bring out his strengths. The counsellor should encourage the teachers to help this bright boy do well in the classroom despite the fact that his learning needs are different from those of others.

When to refer: Ravi should be referred for psychoeducational assessment to clearly identify the source of his academic difficulties and confirm the specific learning disability he may have. A clinical psychologist or a special educator can recommend remedial techniques, as well as suggest modifications to the curriculum to give Ravi the best chance to overcome his problems.

ASSESSMENT AND MANAGEMENT OF SPECIFIC LEARNING DISABILITIES

THE PROBLEM

Specific learning disabilities comprise a broad category of learning problems. The difficulty for young people with specific learning disabilities is an impairment in how they receive, organize and understand information, i.e. 'process' information. This affects their performance in mathematics, reading, writing and reasoning skills, and listening or speaking skills, even though their level of intelligence is normal. Individuals with specific learning disabilities usually have strengths in certain areas and problems in others, e.g. problems with reading and writing but not mathematics. The early signs of specific learning disabilities are: problems pronouncing words; trouble finding the right word; trouble learning the alphabet, numbers, and names of colours, shapes or days of the week; difficulty following directions or learning routines; difficulty using pencils and scissors; and difficulty colouring within the lines. As the child passes through primary school, he may have difficulty understanding the connection between letters and sounds; have trouble blending sounds to form words; confuse basic words when reading, e.g. 'when' for 'then' or 'where' for 'there'; consistently misspell words; make frequent errors while reading; or have trouble learning basic concepts in mathematics. As academic pressures increase in middle school, the youth with a specific learning disability has difficulty coping with the curriculum and often comes to the teacher's notice because of his problems with writing, reading, comprehension or mathematical reasoning. Because of the problems he is experiencing, the youth may dislike reading and writing, become disorganized at home and in school, and 'daydream' in class (*see* Chapter 2). The learning challenges may lower the youth's self-esteem and/ or result in behavioural and emotional disorders. Underlying sensory impairments, such as poor hearing and vision, should always be ruled out in young people suspected to have specific learning disabilities (*see* Chapter 2).

Assessment

Information from the youth

- Which subjects does he enjoy learning?
- Which subjects does he have difficulty with? What are the problems he experiences, e.g. understanding what the teachers say or recalling what he has heard/read?
- How does he feel about his academic performance? Does he feel sad or hopeless about his situation?
- What has he done to cope with his difficulties? How much has this helped?

Information from the parent

- How did their child perform in pre-school and primary school?
- When and how were his academic problems first noticed?
- What kinds of difficulties has he been experiencing?
- What are his strengths?

- What has the family done so far to help their child? What effect have these measures had?

Information from the teacher

- What are the academic areas of concern (e.g. reading, writing, comprehension, mathematical reasoning)?
- What have the teachers done to help the youth learn? What effect have their efforts had? What are their suggestions regarding curriculum adaptations?

Management

With the youth

- The first step is to understand the nature of the youth's learning problem through a psychoeducational assessment. This would require a referral.
- Youth psychoeducation helps the youth understand the nature of his learning difficulty.
- If the youth exhibits signs of low self-esteem, problem-solving counselling can help him identify its causes and help him to develop and implement coping strategies.

With the family

- Family psychoeducation helps the parents understand their child's problems so that they can provide him with the necessary support. The counsellor gives them tips on how to establish study routines that fit the child's learning style. The family is encouraged to support the child's strengths in non-academic areas, such as art and sport.

With teachers and school staff

- Supportive interventions in the school include informing the teachers about the results of the psychoeducational assessment and then facilitating the formulation of a remedial education plan. Adapting the curriculum and modifying the assessment and evaluation procedures

Panel 7. Addressing different learning styles: Advice for teachers

- Students should be allowed to do their academic work in a quiet place, without distractions.
- New information should be presented in small units and the instructions accompanying each step should be brief.
- The teacher should frequently confirm whether the youth has understood each step.
- A phonetics approach, in which letters are linked to sounds, is useful for those with a reading difficulty.
- The youth should be permitted to work at his own pace.
- The study space, and even the writing tools and other materials, can be adjusted to accommodate the child's specific difficulty. For example, provision could be made for pencils with grips for a child who has trouble holding pencils of the normal size.
- Various techniques should be used to assess the child, e.g. oral assessment is preferable if he has problems with writing. The assessments should evaluate his knowledge, and not his performance.
- Negative comments should be avoided and, instead, all efforts made by the youth should be praised.
- It is useful to try alternative methods of teaching that are geared to the youth's strengths to enhance his learning. An example is the 'touch–feel–see–do' technique, which employs all the senses of the child to convey abstract concepts. In this method, the child may learn through means such as constructing models, listening to audiovisual presentations and conducting experiments.

for the youth can be of considerable help (Panel 7). The counsellor should also advise the school management to set up resource rooms (for academic support and remediation) and to approach examination boards to arrange concessions for older children.

When to refer: Whenever there is a possibility of a child having a specific learning disability, he must be referred for a psychoeducational assessment. If the youth is suffering from an emotional and behavioural disorder which has not been relieved by counselling, he should be referred to a mental health professional.

Key messages

- Specific learning disability is an umbrella term which includes disorders in which the normal pattern of learning (reading, writing, language abilities, mathematical reasoning, memory and/or attention) is disturbed due to problems with processing information.
- Because of his learning difficulties, the young person experiences problems in many areas of functioning, predominantly academics.
- Specific learning disability can also compromise emotional health, leading to low self-esteem, and emotional and behavioural disorders.
- The most useful strategies for specific learning disability are youth psychoeducation and family psychoeducation. Supportive interventions in the school are of critical importance as the youth can benefit greatly from specialized academic interventions, educational support through a resource room or special educator and the creation of an inclusive atmosphere in the school.

CASE STUDY 13

THE YOUTH WHO IS SEXUALLY ABUSED

Kareena's story

THE PRESENTING PROBLEM

Kareena, a 12-year-old girl in Standard VII, was referred to the counsellor by a teacher because she had become less interested in schoolwork and had recently failed in two subjects. She refused to reply when the teacher asked her questions in class and argued with the teacher when she pressed Kareena to answer.

Kareena came for the counselling session readily and revealed that she was very worried about the actions towards her by her 17-year-old cousin, Suraj, who lived with her in a joint family. The joint family consisted of Kareena's family and her father's two brothers and their respective families, among others. She described how Suraj approached her a number of times when she was watching television or studying and had tried to touch her on her breasts and thighs. He had teased her, telling her not to be so stuck-up, and implored her to enjoy his attentions. On such occasions, Kareena had quickly left the room. She had been confused and unsure about what her next steps should be. She had told her mother that Suraj 'does not let me study', but had not discussed the issue further. Kareena's mother had mentioned her daughter's complaint to Suraj's mother and the two had had a terrible argument, in which Suraj's mother had accused Kareena of 'blaming' her son for her poor marks. In addition, Kareena's remark had led to a huge fight between her father and his brothers. Kareena had not told her elder sister because she felt she would not be of much help since her sister was quite timid.

Developmental history

According to her mother, Kareena's birth and growth had been normal and she had not had any health problems. She described Kareena as a child who had always been intelligent and very friendly. She had always been assertive, and her frankness had sometimes been 'misinterpreted' as rudeness and lack of respect, especially in the joint family setting.

Psychosocial history

Family history: Kareena lived with her father, mother and elder sister in a joint family consisting of 15 members. Each of her father's two brothers' families had their own small living space and kitchen within a jointly owned property. The brothers constantly fought among themselves over the property. The eldest brother was a domineering person, who was always arguing with Kareena's parents. Kareena's parents owned a sweetmeat business, which required them to work late on weekdays. While they were away, either of Kareena's two aunts looked after her and her sister, or the girls stayed with a great aunt who lived nearby. Kareena worried that her eldest uncle might take over her family's part of the jointly held property while her parents were out. Kareena was very protective of her elder sister (in Standard IX), describing her as 'very shy and scared'. At school, Kareena had once thrown her sandal at some boys when they were bothering her sister and the school authorities had spoken to her parents regarding disciplinary issues raised by this incident.

Academic history: Kareena passed with average grades in Standard VI, but was lagging behind in Standard VII. Since entering Standard VII, she described having difficulty with mathematics and science, in part because she was preoccupied with the tensions at home. She also said that it was hard for her to sustain her attention on schoolwork while studying at home since she was always worried that Suraj would suddenly appear. She reported that her father beat her when she got poor marks. In her opinion, her father's bad temper could be attributed to the constant arguments over property. Kareena also reported that her mother got angry with her and ignored her when she did not do well academically; although she knew her mother cared for her. Her teachers described her behaviour over the past few months as distracted and combative.

Social history: Kareena generally got along with her peers, who admired her for her assertiveness, as well as for her protectiveness towards her elder sister. However, when she felt that someone was treating another person unfairly, she was quick to lose her temper and this could disrupt her friendships. She named both boys and girls in her circle of friends.

Mental status examination

Kareena was communicative and cooperative during her meetings with the counsellor. When she described her cousin's behaviour towards her, she appeared slightly nervous and fixed her gaze on her handkerchief, which she kept knotting and unknotting. She was well groomed and appeared to take pride in her appearance. Her mood varied between sadness and anger, and she seemed to think that the counsellor may not believe her story. The pace and tone of her speech were normal. She did not report any thoughts of self-harm. She was having trouble concentrating on her studies, but this seemed to be linked to her worries rather than any intellectual or learning difficulty. She had adequate insight into her problems and could clearly describe the situations that were causing her distress (the arguments in the joint family and her cousin's inappropriate advances). Her judgement was good, although she was often overly assertive even if the situation did not require it, e.g. when she argued with the teacher.

Case formulation

Kareena, a 12-year-old girl in Standard VII, lives with her mother, father and elder sister in a joint family consisting of 15 members. She was referred to the counsellor by the teacher because her academic performance had deteriorated recently and she was misbehaving in class. Kareena is preoccupied by her older male cousin's attempts to touch her inappropriately whenever he gets a chance. She is unable to tell her parents or sister about this because she does not want to burden them. In addition, she is very worried about her father's brothers' constant arguments over property and worried that her elder uncle would take over her family's property. The most probable diagnosis is mental health distress (*see* Chapter 2) consequent to sexual abuse and family stressors.

Strengths: Kareena's strengths include her normal intelligence, her insight into her family problems and her confidence and ability to speak out. Her protectiveness towards her sister is another positive factor, as well as the fact that she feels remorseful about not doing well academically.

Difficulties: The difficulties Kareena faces include her stressful home environment, her parents' frequent absence from home due to the demands of their work and the sexual abuse by her cousin and corporal punishment by her father. Kareena's acting out behaviours, e.g. arguing with her teachers, are also difficulties for her.

Management plan

The primary strategies to address Kareena's distress are youth psychoeducation, problem-solving counselling, anger management counselling, family psychoeducation and supportive interventions in the school. The counsellor should consider discussing Kareena's case with a supervisor, as well as a child rights organization. She may also consider reporting the matter of sexual harassment by the cousin to the Special Juvenile Police Unit or its equivalent (*see* Chapter 7).

Youth psychoeducation: Kareena should be praised for her decision to be frank about her problems with the counsellor. The counsellor should emphasize that the cousin's behaviour is completely unacceptable and amounts to sexual abuse, since he is making sexual advances towards her and attempting to engage her in inappropriate sexual activity against her will. Kareena should be informed about the objectives of the counselling: to enable her to deal more effectively with her cousin's sexual advances; to develop her communication skills so that she can effectively express her concerns about the sexual abuse she is facing and her distress about the conflicts in the family; to build on her ability to be assertive while enabling her to control her temper; and to help her perform well in school despite the challenges at home.

Problem-solving counselling: The counsellor should encourage Kareena to identify her problems; break them down into manageable components; and explore, select and implement solutions. The counsellor can work with her to devise a safety plan to avoid abuse by the cousin, and together they can think of ways to implement this plan. The plan could include: identifying a family member who can provide her with support when her parents are absent, e.g. by being nearby when she is studying; identifying strategies aimed at deterring her cousin from making advances, e.g. telling him loudly that she disapproves of his behaviour and going into another room so that she is not alone with him and calling the helpline (Childline) when her cousin is abusing her (*see* Chapter 7).

Anger management counselling: The counsellor should help Kareena identify what triggers her anger and help her, through utilizing role-play, to respond to these triggers more effectively.

Family psychoeducation: With Kareena's permission, the counsellor should meet her parents. Before this meeting, it is important that the counsellor and Kareena agree on how to inform her parents about her cousin's inappropriate behaviour. An example of how to inform the parents about the gravity of the situation is: 'Kareena is being sexually harassed by her older cousin. This is a very serious situation, which is causing her great distress. We must put our heads together to find ways to ensure her safety.' Once the parents have been informed and are willing to work on the issue with the counsellor, the three of them should collaboratively devise a safety plan for both daughters. For example, the mother could be at home more frequently; the girls could go to the aunt's home after school and return to their own home when their parents return; and/or the parents could report the matter to the Special Juvenile Police Unit (*see* Chapter 7). In addition, with Kareena's permission, the counsellor should speak to the parents about who should approach the cousin and his parents to discuss the issue and how this should be done. The counsellor should also explain to the parents how the sexual abuse and conflict in the home are affecting Kareena's ability to concentrate on studies. It is important for the father to understand that Kareena is not performing poorly on purpose, and that her poor performance is caused by her inability to concentrate due to the problems at home. The counsellor can encourage the parents to approach either a social worker, or an elder in the family or community for advice on how to create a safe environment for Kareena. They will also need to decide whether or not to pursue legal options.

Supportive interventions in the school: With Kareena's permission, the counsellor can inform the teachers about the level of stress Kareena is facing, without breaching confidentiality regarding the details of the matter. This may help them view Kareena with more compassion and also understand that she is not just being wilfully disruptive. The teachers and counsellor can consult each other on how to modify the amount of homework in order to reduce the pressure on Kareena to study at home and to help her accomplish as much as possible during school hours.

When to refer: If, even after the above steps have been taken, the counsellor finds that Kareena remains vulnerable to sexual abuse, e.g. in case her parents have not taken the issue seriously or the cousin continues to make advances towards her, the counsellor should discuss the case with her supervisor and consider contacting a social worker, a child rights organization and/or the local authorities.

Assessment and Management of Child Sexual Abuse

The Problem

Child sexual abuse covers any type of sexual behaviour, ranging from touching sexual parts to sexual acts, towards a child below the age of consent, i.e. 18 years of age (*see* Chapter 7). Often the victim is forced into these activities because of the superior power, whether physical, social or intellectual, of the perpetrator (the abuser). The abuser may use various methods to wield his power, such as threatening or emotionally manipulating the victim. For example, the abuser often blames the victim, telling her that she is 'asking for it' and thus making her believe that the sexual encounters are her fault. Other abusers 'groom' the victim by building a relationship with her with the intent of abusing her in the future. For example, they may compliment the young person in communications on the Internet or buy her gifts. In the majority of cases, the perpetrator is a person known to the victim and is often from her family. Boys as well as girls can be the victims of sexual abuse. The anguish of the victims is reflected in changes in their mood and behaviours. They may develop mental health distress, emotional disorders (including post-traumatic stress disorder) and behavioural disorders. If sexual intercourse occurs, the victim may suffer physical injury to the sexual organs, become pregnant or contract a sexually transmitted disease. The experience of sexual abuse frequently has an impact on the youth's school attendance, scholastic performance and interactions with her peers.

Assessment

Information from the youth

- What is the nature of the sexual abuse? When did it start? Who is the perpetrator?
- Who has the youth approached for help? What was their response?
- How is the youth coping with the situation? Is she safe at present?
- How much has the youth told trustworthy members of her family? The counsellor should obtain the youth's permission to approach protective members of the youth's immediate family.
- Has the incident been reported to the appropriate authorities?

Information from the family

- What do they know about the sexual abuse that their child is experiencing?
- What is their response? What have they done to protect their child?
- What are their suggestions on how they can reduce the risk of harm to their child?
- What does the family plan with respect to taking legal action?

Information from the teacher

- What changes have they noted in the youth's behaviour and academic performance?
- If any changes have been noted, what are the perceived causes? It is important not to breach the youth's confidentiality by letting the school staff know that her specific problem is being the victim of sexual abuse unless, for example, a member of the school staff is the

perpetrator or if situations arise in which the youth's safety is at risk and the school is in a position to protect her.

Management

With the youth

- Through youth psychoeducation, the young person learns that what she is experiencing is sexual abuse and that sexual abuse is totally unacceptable. She is reassured that what is happening is not her fault. She is also informed that sexual abuse is illegal and that she, her family or the counsellor must report the matter to the authorities (*see* Chapter 7).
- Crisis counselling is helpful if the sexual abuse is recent and the young person is under acute stress.
- Problem-solving counselling helps the young person identify how to ensure her safety in the future. It also facilitates the task of identifying people whom she can trust and who can support her. These could be members of the family, school staff or community members.

With the family

- The first step the counsellor should take is to convince the family members to take urgent steps to ensure that the young person is safe. For example, they could see to it that the child has no further contact with the perpetrator. The family should also be told that it is important to make sure that the sexual abuse stops immediately.
- The counsellor should help the family contact child rights organizations and the Special Juvenile Police Unit. However, if the family is uncooperative, as may happen, for example, if the perpetrator is a family member, the counsellor may need to report the case to the authorities directly after discussing the matter with her supervisor and the victim (*see* Chapter 7).

With teachers and school staff

- School life skills programmes which give students information on reproductive and sexual health, besides including components related to child rights and personal safety, empower youth by helping them understand how to keep their bodies safe and identify persons they can trust in case of an emergency. The life skills programme can include school-wide campaigns to increase the students' awareness of the Protection of Children from Sexual Offences Act, 2012 (*see* Chapters 6 and 7), as well as the services provided by local child rights organizations.

When to refer: The counsellor should immediately consult her supervisor and take steps to secure the safety of the child who has been sexually abused if the child continues to be at risk, e.g. if the family is unable to ensure the child's safety or if the perpetrator is a close family member.

Key messages

- Child sexual abuse is often a hidden issue. The perpetrator is most often known to the victim.
- Sexual abuse includes a wide range of sexually inappropriate behaviours and can affect both boys and girls.
- The victim is often made to feel responsible for the abuse. This can lower their self-esteem and cause mental health problems. The victim may also develop sexual health problems.
- The primary goal of counselling is to ensure the young person's safety by seeing to it that the sexual abuse ceases, and enlisting the support of trustworthy adults in the youth's environment. Youth and family psychoeducation and crisis counselling are the most useful counselling strategies to help the victim recover.
- Child sexual abuse needs to be reported to the relevant authorities in line with the Protection of Children from Sexual Offences Act, 2012.

CASE STUDY 14

THE YOUTH WHO HAS DIFFICULTY MAKING FRIENDS

Amar's story

THE PRESENTING PROBLEM

Amar, a 13-year-old boy, studied in Standard VII. His class teacher referred him to the counsellor because she had noticed that he was often left out of group activities. Further, when he was asked a question in class, he gave long, irrelevant answers, causing his classmates to mock him. Amar was initially reluctant to go to the counsellor's office and grumbled that he did not need anyone's help. He told the counsellor that he was not unhappy, but felt he was different from his classmates. He described himself as being the 'odd one out'. Amar said he often thought of leaving school, but did not do so because he liked learning about new things. He named a few people in his class, but did not qualify them as friends. He said his peers constantly annoyed him by interrupting him whenever he talked. Amar did not enjoy sports, but had taken to the new computer classes and was a voracious reader. The counsellor noticed that Amar was usually alone during the breaks.

Developmental history

Amar's early developmental history was normal. His mother reported that he had always had a narrow range of interests. His recent passion was cars and he could recite the names of all the latest models. He had been an independent child and very rarely asked others for help. He often tried to dominate conversations at home, expressing his opinions vociferously. His mother felt that Amar was like his father, who did not have many friends and was happiest reading a book.

Psychosocial history

Family history: Amar lived with his parents and two older siblings. His father was a laboratory technician in a local college and his mother worked as an office assistant. His elder sister was a teacher and his elder brother was completing his bachelor's degree. The family, a nuclear one, was stable and Amar's grandmother, who was very caring, lived close by. Amar had a good relationship with both his siblings, especially his brother, who helped him with his homework.

Academic history: Amar had always struggled in school, especially with writing. However, with the hard work he put in, he had always managed to maintain his academic performance at an average level.

Social history: Amar did not have any friends in school or in the neighbourhood, but had good relationships with his family members.

Drug/alcohol use: Amar did not report the use of any drugs or alcohol.

Mental status examination

Amar was well-mannered, though nervous, during the first session. He gradually relaxed and seemed to enjoy his time with the counsellor. He often strayed from the point when the counsellor asked him questions, drifting into talk about the car industry. For example, he would name the various car manufacturers and describe the details of their logos. The counsellor tried hard to get Amar to focus on answering her questions, but he kept returning to his favourite topic. His speech was monotonous and odd, and he occasionally recited a television car advertisement. His mood was stable, though he tended to become irritable when the topic of conversation veered away from the car industry. Amar said he felt different from his classmates, but could not explain exactly how. He had a poor self-image, e.g. he felt he was the worst student in class and 'hopeless' on the sports field. He did not harbour any thoughts of self-harm. He reported no problems with his sleep or eating habits. Other than the fact that he was preoccupied with the car industry, his thought content was normal. He lacked insight into how his behaviour may affect his relationships.

Case formulation

Amar, a 13-year-old boy from a stable and supportive family, has become very isolated from his peers over the years. His teacher referred him to the counsellor because of this isolation, and also because his answers to questions in class were long and irrelevant, causing his peers to mock him. His problems appear to be related to his unusual way of dominating his peers with his ideas. His narrow interests and poor self-image compound his social isolation. He has very little insight into how his social behaviours could lead to social isolation. He has fine motor difficulties which affect his ability to write clearly. His long-standing problems with social interaction, his narrow range of interests and normal intelligence point to a diagnosis of Asperger syndrome, a type of autism spectrum disorder, a developmental disability (*see* Chapter 2).

Strengths: Amar's normal intelligence, his caring home environment and his class teacher's awareness of and concern about his social isolation are Amar's strengths.

Difficulties: In addition to the fact that Amar has a developmental disability, his difficulties include his poor insight into his problems and his low self-esteem. Further, he is mocked by and isolated from his peers.

Management plan

The primary strategies to address Amar's social isolation are youth psychoeducation, social skills counselling, supportive interventions in the school setting and family psychoeducation.

Youth psychoeducation: The counsellor should explain to Amar how his problems with social interactions and with forming and maintaining relationships isolate him. She should inform him that social skills counselling can help him with these problems. There is no need to tell him the diagnosis since this might compound his feeling of being the 'odd one out' and affect his self-esteem negatively. The counsellor and youth should come to an agreement on a counselling plan.

Social skills counselling: The counsellor should help Amar develop social relationship skills that he can utilize while interacting with his peers and the school staff. She can model for him how people greet each other, as well as the basics of to-and-fro conversation. Further, she should show him how to 'read' social cues so that he can avoid alienating someone before it is too late. For example, the counsellor can play the role of a person who is losing interest in a conversation. She should role-play these behaviours with Amar until he is able to comfortably generalize them to social settings in the real world. She can then encourage him to join a specific school club or activity which would provide him with more opportunities to socialize with his peers. Later, the two of them can regularly review his interactions in the club or during the activity.

Supportive interventions in the school: The counsellor can sensitize the teachers and school staff to Amar's needs with respect to socialization and give them tips on how to actively include him in the school setting. For example, the teachers could be encouraged to provide Amar with an opportunity to make a presentation on the car industry. This would help him gain social recognition through use of his interests. The counsellor need not share Amar's diagnosis with the teachers and could, instead, describe his social awkwardness as his primary difficulty, and discuss how they might help him build peer relationships. However, the counsellor should consider whether sharing the diagnosis with the school (with the family's permission) would be of any advantage to him or his family. For example, providing a diagnosis may be necessary for him to be eligible for concessions during examinations. The teachers could encourage Amar to practise fine motor strengthening exercises, such as clay modelling and craft work, to help improve his writing abilities. Teachers can identify classmates for peer pairing, with Amar's permission, and the teacher can explain to potential 'buddies' that Amar needs their support to make and keep friends (*see* Chapter 6).

Family psychoeducation: When talking to the family, the counsellor should emphasize the need for an assessment by a specialist to diagnose whether their child has a developmental disability. The counsellor can begin by informing the family about Amar's problems, saying, for example, that 'Amar has difficulty understanding the rules of social interactions. Because of this, his peers avoid him and he lacks friends.' If the family agrees, an assessment by a specialist should be arranged (*see* Chapter 4). If the assessment confirms a developmental disability, the counsellor must make sure she approaches the parents with sensitivity while explaining the diagnosis. This is important because many families do not understand the diagnosis of autism spectrum disorder, especially that of Asperger syndrome, because the youth seems to be functioning relatively well in most areas (*see* Chapter 6). In addition to helping the family understand the diagnosis, the counsellor should make specific suggestions on how to enhance Amar's socialization skills (*see below*, Management: With the family).

When to refer: Besides the developmental assessment to confirm the counsellor's suspicions of a developmental disability, Amar may benefit from a referral to an occupational therapist (*see* Chapter 4) who can assess his fine motor skills and suggest strengthening exercises to address his handwriting difficulty.

ASSESSMENT AND MANAGEMENT OF YOUTH WHO ARE SOCIALLY ISOLATED

THE PROBLEM

A young person who is socially isolated spends time by himself rather than participating in the activities of social groups. Social isolation is characterized by being friendless, ignored and excluded from group activities. This is quite different from the situation of a young person who enjoys his private time more than socializing, but is able to socialize. There are two main pathways to social isolation, though there may be various underlying causes. The first pathway is social rejection by the person's peers, e.g. because he is aggressive or of a different social status, or has a disability. The second pathway is rejection of and withdrawal from others by the person himself. This situation could occur, for example, because he is shy or has low self-esteem. The effects of social isolation reflect the pathways which have led to it. For example, a young person who has been rejected by his peers may exhibit hostile or antisocial behaviours or drop out of school, while one with poor self-esteem may withdraw. Significant isolation may cause a person to misuse substances or attempt self-harm. The young person who is socially isolated is rarely referred to the counsellor, unless he is playing truant or his behaviour is disrupting the class. He generally does not self-refer to a counsellor because he is disengaged or lacks confidence.

Assessment

Information from the youth

- What does the youth feel about his social relationships? What does he think are the reasons for his social isolation?
- What efforts has he made to overcome his isolation? What have been the results of these efforts?
- What impact has his social isolation had on his daily life and, in particular, his mental health?
- What changes would he like to see in his life?

Information from the parent

- What is the family's opinion about their child's social functioning at home?
- What does the family do to help their child interact with others?

Information from the teacher

- Which aspects of the youth's behaviour cause his peers to avoid him?

Management

With the youth

- Youth psychoeducation enhances the youth's understanding of his problem and of the links between his social difficulties and his behaviours. It thus increases his insight into the reasons for his social isolation.

- Social skills counselling helps develop the youth's ability to engage positively with his peer group.
- Problem-solving counselling helps the youth identify his problems and then generate, select and implement solutions to manage these challenges.

With the family

- Family psychoeducation helps parents understand their child's problems, and also helps them develop ways to support his integration into his peer group and minimize the impact of social isolation on his functioning. The parents' efforts should focus on helping their child understand the informal 'rules' of social engagement. This could include: how to start, maintain and end a social interaction; how to be flexible, cooperative and share with others. The family can make use of explanations and role-playing, and also model acceptable behaviours for their child. Simple stories, as well as episodes on television and in the films, can be used to point out the usual behaviours that people display in various situations. These might help the child learn, for example, the gestures and body language that young people use upon greeting each other.
- The youth should be referred to a developmental specialist for further assessment (*see* Chapter 4) and confirmation of the diagnosis of autism spectrum disorder, as well as the provision of specific interventions for autism spectrum disorder.

With teachers and school staff

- Supportive interventions in the school sensitize the teachers and school staff to the risks faced by young people who are socially isolated (e.g. poor school attendance, low self-esteem, increasing isolation, high-risk behaviours). The teachers and staff should also be made aware of the mental health difficulties which can arise as a result of social isolation (e.g. anxiety and depression). To reduce the youth's isolation, the teachers and staff can be advised to encourage others to include him in group activities.

When to refer: If, despite counselling, the youth continues to be so socially isolated that it has an impact on his emotional health, or if he has other mental health problems, he should be referred to a mental health professional for further evaluation.

Key messages

- Social isolation refers to a situation in which a youth is isolated from his peer group. It can be due to either rejection of the youth by his peers or the youth's withdrawal from his peers.
- Youth with autism spectrum disorder and other developmental disorders are often socially isolated. The confirmation of a disorder requires an assessment by a specialist.
- Social isolation places the young person at risk of mental health problems, particularly anxiety and depression. It can also lead to other difficulties, such as the inability to function as part of a team, poor school attendance and high-risk behaviours.
- Social skills counselling may help integrate the youth into his peer group. The treatment of autism spectrum disorder may also require specialist interventions.

CASE STUDY 15

THE YOUTH WHO IS WORRIED ABOUT A ROMANTIC RELATIONSHIP

Pooja's story

THE PRESENTING PROBLEM

Pooja, a 15-year-old girl studying in Standard IX, was referred to the counsellor by her teacher because she had lost interest in her studies, did not pay attention in class and seemed generally distracted. Her teachers told the counsellor that they suspected something might be going on in her life these days since she had been a consistent student until a few months ago. When Pooja met the counsellor, she was initially reluctant to talk. When asked why she thought she had been referred for counselling, she mentioned that she had done poorly in her examinations. When further encouraged by the counsellor, Pooja said she found studies very boring and confusing. She was more forthcoming in a subsequent session, when she revealed that she felt burdened taking care of her two younger siblings and complained that her mother asked her to perform too many household chores. She felt her mother mostly gave her orders and very little positive attention. Gradually, however, Pooja admitted that the relationship which mattered most to her was the one she had with a boy named Rajesh, whom she shyly referred to as her 'boyfriend'. Over a number of sessions, as Pooja's trust in the counsellor grew, she talked more about Rajesh and their relationship. Rajesh was 17 years old, lived in the neighbourhood, had dropped out of secondary school and was taking a vocational course. Pooja often met him after school or in the evening, when she went for a walk in the neighbourhood with her best friend. She always felt excited at the prospect of these meetings, during which they talked and held hands. Of late, however, she had started to feel a bit nervous since Rajesh had told her he wanted to meet her alone and threatened to leave her if she refused. Pooja told the counsellor that this troubled and confused her. She said that on the one hand, she wanted to have a good reputation with her friends and follow her parents' advice that one should not get into a sexual relationship until marriage. On the other hand, she loved Rajesh's attentions, and was taken by his expressions of true love and his promise to marry her one day. Pooja also asked the counsellor whether she thought it was safe to use a much-advertised 'fairness' cream. She was concerned about her skin being rather dark and was of the opinion that the cream would make her look more attractive.

Developmental history

Pooja's parents were not asked about her developmental history since Pooja was uneasy about the counsellor talking to them. She did not report any problems during her growing up, apart from abdominal cramps during her menstrual periods.

Psychosocial history

Family history: Pooja was the eldest of three siblings and lived in a nuclear family. Her father was an accountant and her mother a housewife. The father spent long days out of the home at work. Pooja said that her mother's interaction with her consisted mainly of trying to ensure that she and her siblings did well in their studies, as well as asking her to help out with the domestic chores. Pooja described her mother as a perfectionist and said she even felt somewhat afraid of her mother's occasional anger when things were not how she expected them to be. She felt more comfortable with her father and especially enjoyed the time they spent together during the weekends.

Academic history: Pooja had done well in primary school. However, her grades started falling when she reached Standard VIII. She had always struggled with mathematics and had been regularly receiving tuitions in the subject. The teachers described Pooja as a well-behaved, soft-spoken, shy girl. They said she was an average student who had recently become distracted, leading to a deterioration in her academic performance.

Social history: Pooja said she had a very close friend, Seema, with whom she walked to and from school. She also had two other good friends whose company she kept in school. Her classmates and teachers liked her. She stated that her boyfriend was very caring, loving and generous, i.e. he gave her many gifts, and that her favourite part of the day was when she was with him.

Drug/alcohol use: Pooja denied any use of alcohol, drugs or tobacco.

Mental status examination

Pooja was cooperative during the meetings with the counsellor, although she made little eye contact. She was well-groomed. Her behaviour was socially appropriate, but she seemed shy. She said she felt 'angry and sad' when her mother scolded her. She also mentioned that she was 'worried' that her boyfriend would become interested in someone else. Pooja's speech was normal and her mood was appropriate to the situations she described. She did not report any suicidal ideas. She said her worry about losing Rajesh distracted her from her schoolwork. Pooja had good insight and she clearly described the situations that made her happy or caused distress.

Case formulation

Pooja, a 15-year-old girl studying in Standard IX, lives in a nuclear family with her two younger siblings and parents. Her teacher referred her to the counsellor because of a fall in her grades and her distracted behaviour. Pooja's primary complaints are that she is having difficulty concentrating on her studies and can think only about her boyfriend. She is torn between her boyfriend's demand for intimacy and her fear that it is not yet time for her to get sexually involved with him. Pooja is experiencing mental health distress, characterized by excessive worry, confusion and distractibility, due to her conflict over her romantic involvement with a young man.

Strengths: Pooja's strengths include her average intelligence and her insight into her predicament and how her choices can affect her school success and family relationships. Further, her friends and teachers like and support her. She enjoys a good relationship with her father and the family has strong values.

Difficulties: The difficulties that Pooja has to contend with are the boyfriend's insistence on sexual intimacy and the possibility that Pooja can be at risk of child sexual abuse if she engages in sexual intimacy (since she is below 18 years of age). An additional hardship for Pooja is her mother's pressure that Pooja perform household chores.

Management plan

The primary strategies to help Pooja recover from her problems are youth psychoeducation, problem-solving counselling, social skills counselling and family psychoeducation.

Youth psychoeducation: The counsellor should help Pooja understand that the way she feels and behaves is due to the worries she has. The counselling strategies that will be the most helpful should be described to her. The counsellor should praise Pooja for the positive manner in which she is handling the situation at present, i.e. her refusal to give in to her boyfriend's pressure. She should also praise Pooja for her efforts to cope with the conflicting feelings she has about becoming physically intimate at this stage. In addition, Pooja needs to be reassured that she is an attractive young person, and that what makes her so is not only her appearance but also her personality. As for using 'fairness' creams, the counsellor should inform Pooja about the risks (e.g. allergic reactions) and should give her simple tips on how to maintain skin hygiene. The counsellor should seek to learn about Pooja's understanding of physical intimacy and its outcomes and increase Pooja's awareness of reproductive and sexual health (Panel 8). The counsellor should inform her in a non-judgemental, supportive and caring way about the possible risks and consequences of sexual experimentation at her age. It is essential to inform Pooja about the laws with respect to child sexual abuse (*see* Chapter 7). The counsellor should involve Pooja in a discussion of the potential risks of physical intimacy with Rajesh since simply telling her that sexual intimacy at her age is 'against the law' is less likely to stimulate the thinking process essential to take a healthy decision on her own (*see* Chapter 3). The counsellor should tell Pooja that

Panel 8. Common physical problems which concern youth

Problems	Psychoeducation
Skin problems: These include an increase in skin secretions, pimples and at times, severe acne.	Taking a balanced diet and drinking enough water help regulate the hormonal changes which give rise to acne. Skin hygiene should be maintained through the use of a mild soap, and creams should not be applied, unless prescribed.
There may be strong body odour due to hormonal changes and increased perspiration.	Personal hygiene should be maintained by bathing daily. The person can use talcum powder or a deodorant.
Breast development occurs at varying ages. Whether girls develop breast tissue earlier or later, they can feel embarrassed.	It should be explained that each individual has her own rate of growth. The use of bras or supporting vests should be encouraged.
Young people are often preoccupied by their physical appearance, whether it concerns their hair, height, weight or the colour of their skin.	Life skills programmes and circle time activities should include components aimed at helping students appreciate the diversity of 'good looks' and the importance of personality as against physical appearance.

it is natural for her to have difficulty concentrating on her studies due to her present dilemmas, and should empathize with her. She should also provide Pooja with guidance on effective study skills, making timetables and time management.

Problem-solving counselling: The counsellor should guide Pooja to identify the situations which cause her worry at home and help her develop practical solutions to these situations. For example, regarding her mother's expectation that she should perform many of the household chores, Pooja could begin to solve this problem by communicating effectively with her mother about how burdensome these demands feel to her.

Social skills counselling: The counsellor should work with Pooja to enhance her self-esteem by building her social skills, as well as improving her assertive communication skills with her peers, family members, teachers and Rajesh. It would be helpful for the counsellor to role-play assertive communication and encourage Pooja to try this out with her boyfriend.

Family psychoeducation: With Pooja's permission, the counsellor can meet her parents and explain that Pooja needs their steady support to help her improve her academic performance. The counsellor can help the parents understand that Pooja is experiencing distressing emotions which are common during adolescence with the help of a statement such as, 'Pooja is undergoing the normal physical and emotional changes of adolescence. There are many thoughts distracting her from her studies due to this.' The mother should be encouraged to see Pooja's strengths, e.g. that she is obedient and helpful, and to support her with praise, smiles and hugs rather than use verbal punishments. Effective family psychoeducation may result in the development of trust and understanding which, in turn, may lead Pooja to share some of her personal problems with her parents and reduce her insecurity. It may also make it possible for her to count on her parents' support in the event of a break-up with her boyfriend. The counsellor should not reveal confidential details regarding Pooja's feelings and activities to her family unless Pooja gives her explicit permission to do so (*see* Chapter 7). If, however, the counsellor feels that the relationship with Rajesh is threatening Pooja's well-being, she should discuss these concerns with Pooja and emphasize the need to inform her parents. If the situation is extreme, e.g. if Pooja is at risk of harming herself or being sexually abused, the counsellor may break the rule of confidentiality (*see* Chapter 7) and talk to her parents without Pooja's permission about the problems she is facing in her relationship with Rajesh.

ASSESSMENT AND MANAGEMENT OF DIFFICULTIES IN ROMANTIC RELATIONSHIPS

THE PROBLEM

Sexuality is a natural part of everyone's life. Sexuality influences an individual's physical and emotional needs, wishes and self-image. Sexuality evolves as a child grows. During adolescence there is a rapid development of the secondary sexual characteristics, accompanied by emotional and physical feelings that are new to the individual (*see* Chapter 1). Young people are often preoccupied by the changes in their physical appearance (Panel 8). The feelings of young people going through these changes should be anticipated and addressed through a life skills programme and circle time activities (*see* Chapter 6). Throughout adolescence, young people are curious about sex and begin to explore the various aspects of physical intimacy in romantic relationships (hugging, kissing, fondling and sexually intimate bodily contact). Falling in love and being sexually attracted to another person is a normal part of growing up. However, children and adolescents below the age of 18 may not be cognitively, physically or emotionally mature enough to engage in intimate sexual acts. They are vulnerable to negative physical consequences, e.g. teenage pregnancy and sexually transmitted infections, as well as emotional consequences, e.g. low self-esteem and guilt. However, the reality is that though the laws are clear about the definitions of child sexual abuse, people under the age of 18 generally engage in sexual experimentation. The factors which may lead to problems in romantic relationships include premature sexual activity (especially when it is coercive), negative reactions on the part of the youth's parents and the break-up of the relationship.

Assessment

Information from the youth

- What is the nature and history of the relationship?
- What is the nature and history of any physical intimacy that there may have been between the young pair? To what extent is it consensual? Is the youth using protection? If so, what kind?
- What does the youth know about the Protection of Children from Sexual Offences Act, 2012? Does she understand what the law means with respect to consensual and non-consensual sexual acts involving young people under the age of 18?
- What does the youth know about the risks of pregnancy and sexually

transmitted infections?
- How does the youth feel about the sexual intimacy she is permitting or contemplating?
- Has the youth ever been pregnant? If so, how was the pregnancy handled?
- What do the youth's family members know about her relationship? What is their attitude to the relationship?
- What does the youth feel about her standing in the relationship? Does she feel nurtured and equal?

Information from the family

- Consent from the youth is essential for the counsellor to speak to the family. Great care must be taken while assessing the family's knowledge of, and attitude towards, their child's relationship so as to maintain confidentiality.
- The counsellor can explore the role the family can play to assist their child if there is any suspicion that the relationship is coercive.

MANAGEMENT

With the youth

- Youth psychoeducation aims to enable the youth to make a fully informed decision about the degree of sexual intimacy she wants to have with her partner. The counsellor should make a thorough effort to determine how well the youth understands reproductive and sexual health issues, and then provide her with adequate information to allow her to make appropriate decisions. As a general rule, for health and emotional reasons, the counsellor should actively discourage anyone below the age of 18 years from engaging in sexual acts. If the young person has already become involved in sexual activities, the emphasis should be on ensuring her safety and health, e.g. by encouraging the use of contraception. Simultaneously, without alienating the youth, the counsellor must provide her with information on the sexual abuse laws in India (*see* Chapter 7).
- Problem-solving counselling helps the youth learn how to think about

the practical problems she is experiencing as a result of her romantic relationship, as well as select an appropriate approach to address them. For example, she could explore ways to prevent the relationship from interfering with her studies.
- Social skills counselling helps the youth assert herself in a more effective manner when she is with her partner. For example, it will equip her to explain to her partner why she is not ready for a sexual relationship. Social skills counselling can also help the youth broach the topic of her romantic relationship with her parents.

With the family

- Family psychoeducation may be required for families in conflict with their child due to her involvement in a romantic and/or intimate physical relationship. The counsellor should make the parents aware of the normal developmental experiences that young people go through, mentioning that adolescents feel curious about sex. Demystifying issues related to sexuality and encouraging the parents to talk about these issues may help them communicate with their child without alienating her and put them in a better position to persuade her to make healthy decisions. Family psychoeducation can also include reassuring parents who are worried about their child's relationship, providing them with guidance on the acceptable levels of freedom within adolescent relationships and supporting their efforts to set limits that are appropriate to the child's age and the culture.
- If the counsellor feels that the youth is in harm's way because of her romantic relationship, the family will possibly need to be informed of this (*see* Chapter 7).

When to refer: The counsellor should consider a referral of the youth to a physician for appropriate advice on contraception and sexual health if she is already involved in a full physical relationship. If there is any element of threat, blackmail, coercion or violence in the relationship, the youth should be encouraged to disclose this to her parents or other trusted adults and, if necessary, to the police. If she does not, the counsellor may have to breach confidentiality to protect her from harm (*see* Chapter 7). If the youth is experiencing symptoms of anxiety or depression, or if she has suicidal ideas, she should be referred to a mental health professional for further evaluation (*see* Chapter 4).

Key messages

- Adolescence is characterized by rapid sexual maturation, the development of romantic attractions and the exploration of physical intimacy.
- Sexual development, sexual feelings and romantic involvements may be accompanied by anxiety and mood changes, related particularly to worries about rejection, parental reactions and physical relationships.
- An intimate physical relationship may affect the youth's well-being and academic performance. Further, it could result in pregnancy or a sexually transmitted infection.
- Youth psychoeducation should focus on providing 'anticipatory guidance', i.e. helping the youth anticipate and prepare for upcoming changes and challenges. It is equally important to provide emotional support and empower the youth by giving her accurate information on reproductive and sexual health. This will help her focus on age-appropriate activities and delay her forays into the most intimate aspects of sexual behaviour until she reaches adulthood.

CASE STUDY 16

THE YOUTH WHO IS ANTISOCIAL

Dev's story

THE PRESENTING PROBLEM

Dev, a 15-year-old boy studying in Standard X, was referred to the counsellor by his teacher because he had been absent from class for a number of days. When the teacher contacted his mother, the mother informed her that Dev had been leaving for school regularly every morning. According to his teachers, Dev's school attendance had been poor since the beginning of Standard X. When he returned to school following an absence, he claimed that he had been unwell and submitted leave notes bearing the forged signature of his mother. During this academic year, his classmates had accused him of stealing money from them. When questioned about his absence from school, Dev acted vague, saying that he got 'bored' in class. He finally admitted that he spent time playing cricket with older boys in his neighbourhood. He emphatically denied stealing any money. The counsellor observed that Dev did not have friends in school and was always alone during the breaks. Dev's mother said she occasionally felt a little afraid of him, particularly because she had seen him kicking and hitting their dog in anger. When she would try to stop him, he would shout and threaten her. After a few sessions, Dev admitted to the counsellor that twice he had taken money from his classmates' bags to buy alcohol, which he drank with his friends in his neighbourhood. He confessed that he had started smoking and chewing tobacco regularly.

Developmental history

According to his mother, Dev's childhood and development had been normal. She said his academic performance had begun to deteriorate in Standard V. However, it was in Standard X that his school attendance began to suffer and his other problematic behaviours came to the fore. She said he had never been a particularly affectionate child and had always had problems 'sticking to a task'.

Psychosocial history

Family history: Dev's father was an alcoholic and had died 5 years ago. He had been violent towards Dev and his mother. He had worked in a factory and Dev's mother supplemented the family's income by tailoring clothes at home (this was now the only source of family income). Dev's older sister lived with his maternal uncle's family because his mother thought that the high school in that neighbourhood was better. His sister, who was studying in Standard XII, came home for holidays. Dev said that he cared for his mother but that she annoyed him because she 'complains about her life'. He did not mention his sister and did not seem to have a close relationship with her. When asked about his father, he shrugged and refused to talk about him.

Academic history: Dev was an average student. However, in Standard X, Dev's school attendance had become erratic. He described studying as 'very boring' and said that none of the subjects interested him. He shrugged when asked about his future plans. He said he found it difficult to concentrate when he tried to study and preferred to go out and play cricket.

Social history: Dev could not name a single 'good' friend in school. He especially liked to tease the studious boys and did not care if this made him unpopular. Over this past year, he had befriended a group of older boys from his neighbourhood. These boys were school drop-outs, worked odd jobs and spent their time playing cricket and drinking beer.

Drug/alcohol use: Dev admitted to chewing tobacco, smoking cigarettes and drinking beer.

Mental status examination

During the first session with the counsellor, Dev was defensive and uncooperative. He was restless and fidgeted in his chair, and his eye contact was poor. His appearance was neat, though his shoes, socks and trousers were dirty. It took quite a few sessions to build a rapport, after which he became somewhat amenable to talk more openly. His mood varied from one of disinterest to mild anxiety. For example, he seemed mildly anxious when he admitted to stealing and forging his mother's signature. The pace and tone of his speech were normal, as were the form and content of his thoughts. His ambitions for the future ('I want to be an engineer') seemed unrealistic, given his poor academic performance. He recognized that his actions were unacceptable, but seemed unconcerned about his antisocial behaviours and poor academic performance.

CASE FORMULATION

Dev, a 15-year-old boy studying in Standard X, was referred to the counsellor by his teacher for playing truant from school. Dev lives with his widowed mother. His alcoholic father died 5 years ago. Dev and his mother had been victims of his father's violence. When he skips school, he lies to his teacher, telling her he has been sick. He smokes and chews tobacco, drinks beer and has forged his mother's signature on leave notes. He does not have any relationships with his school peers, socializing instead with older unemployed boys in the neighbourhood. He admits that he has stolen money and abused the family pet. Academically, he has average abilities. Dev shows little remorse for any of his actions. He has some awareness of the fact that he is unpopular in school. His truancy, antisocial behaviour and lack of remorse for this behaviour indicate that he has a conduct disorder (*see* Chapter 2).

Strengths: Among Dev's strengths are his average academic abilities and intellectual skills. The school environment is good, and he has a concerned and loving mother. Because his disruptive behaviours started at a later stage, there is more likelihood that his problems will decrease with counselling and supportive interventions. In addition, he is able to build some rapport with the counsellor and is able to admit to some of his wrongdoings.

Difficulties: Dev's lack of interest in academic work is problematic. The absence of a male role model at home; his exposure to his father's alcoholism; his father's violence towards him and his mother; and his father's death are all difficulties for Dev. The family's economic difficulties pose another problem, as do Dev's substance abuse and the fact that his chosen peer group engages in high-risk behaviours.

Management plan

The main strategies that can be of assistance to Dev are youth psychoeducation, problem-solving counselling, social skills counselling and family psychoeducation. Supportive interventions in the home and the community and supportive interventions in the school will also help Dev.

Youth psychoeducation: The counsellor needs to continue to make efforts to win Dev's trust. For example, talking to him about how to increase his vocational options for the future, rather than focusing on his wrongdoings, may convince him that the counsellor is interested in helping him find a direction. Once some trust has been established, the counsellor should attempt to enhance Dev's understanding of why his actions are self-destructive and destructive towards others. He should explain how, with the help of counselling, Dev can develop more positive relationships with his peers and mother. Dev should also be informed about the risks associated with substance abuse and encouraged to stop the tobacco and alcohol use.

Problem-solving counselling: The counsellor should help Dev identify the specific difficulties he has and how these hinder him from participating positively in daily life. He can be given the example of how keeping the company of drop-outs isolates him from his school peer group and results in his missing school. The counsellor should then help Dev select the difficulties he thinks are the most important to address and to work with him to explore and implement solutions. For example, to establish positive interactions with his school peers, he could join the school cricket team. Simultaneously, the counsellor should work with Dev to enhance his study skills so that he can achieve academic success. The counsellor and Dev could, for example, set study routines and fix a regular time for Dev to complete homework.

Social skills counselling: The counsellor should encourage Dev to participate in school and after-school activities with his school peers so that he can learn how to interact with a healthy peer group. The counsellor can role-play how Dev can interact positively with his peers so that he can develop friendships.

Family psychoeducation: With Dev's permission, the counsellor can describe to his mother the issues that are adversely affecting Dev. The counsellor can tell his mother, 'Dev's behaviour has been causing considerable problems in school. He needs clear guidelines on what are acceptable behaviours and the consequences of unacceptable behaviours.' The counsellor should suggest strategies to Dev's mother so that she can better manage his behaviour. For example, he should inform the mother how to set limits and how to implement a reward system to motivate Dev to attend school (*see* Chapter 6). The counsellor can also encourage the mother to work towards strengthening the bond between the siblings so that Dev begins to value the family and participate in its activities. For example, the mother could create 'family time', during which she, the sister and Dev do something enjoyable (e.g. going to a film) as a family unit during the sister's visits home. The counsellor might also help the mother work out a system for monitoring Dev's whereabouts. In addition, Dev's mother can be encouraged to create opportunities for him to interact with school friends and the family, as an alternative to the neighbourhood drop-outs.

Supportive interventions in the home and the community: If Dev's uncle can serve as a positive male role model for him, the counsellor should advise the mother to encourage this relationship. In addition, the void created by the death of Dev's father can be partially filled if he is enrolled in a community or sports club which has male adult members, e.g. a sports coach, who can serve as a positive male role model.

Supportive interventions in the school: The counsellor should speak to the teachers about motivating him to attend school using behaviour contracts and appropriate rewards. He should advise the school to access vocational guidance to identify Dev's strengths, interests and skills and match these with potential training options for future vocations.

Assessment and Management of Conduct Disorder

The Problem

Conduct disorder (*see* Chapter 2) is a pattern of disruptive behaviour which can include aggression towards people and animals, lying, stealing, truancy from school and deliberate destruction of property. Handling young people with this disorder can be an extremely challenging task for the parent, teacher and counsellor because they often do not experience remorse for their disruptive behaviours. When a younger child exhibits hostile and defiant behaviours, it may be referred to as oppositional defiant disorder. If such a child's feelings and behaviours are not addressed effectively, his problematic behaviours may intensify during adolescence and evolve into conduct disorder. Children with oppositional defiant disorder or adolescents with conduct disorder may also suffer from attention deficit hyperactivity disorder and/or perform poorly in academics. These children's problems may be related to the presence of a learning disability. Male gender, poverty, violence in the family, the absence of a parent of the same sex who could have served as a role model and exposure to peer groups which are involved in high-risk activities may contribute to the development of antisocial behaviours. The long-term outlook for young people who develop a conduct disorder during adolescence is better than the outlook for those who have had a childhood history of oppositional defiant disorder which develops into conduct disorder during adolescence.

Assessment

Information from the youth

- Regarding the specific antisocial behaviours the youth exhibits, explore the history, frequency, reasons for and consequences of each behaviour. For example, when did the youth begin missing school? What does he do during the hours he is away from school? Whose company does he keep when he is not in school?
- What is the youth's attitude to the situations he creates or is involved in? Does he feel any remorse for his antisocial behaviours?

- What methods has the youth tried to counter his antisocial behaviours? To what effect?
- What positive role models or friends does he connect with?
- What are his plans for the future? How will he implement these?
- How do his parents respond to and handle his behaviours?

Information from the parent

- Since when has their child been exhibiting these undesirable behaviours?
- What parenting methods are being used (e.g. severely punitive or extremely lax)?
- What difficulties is the family facing (e.g. violence)?
- What do they see as their child's strengths and weaknesses?
- Who in their child's environment serves/may serve as a positive role model?

Information from the teacher

- What problems have they noticed in the school setting? What impact have these problems had on the youth's academic and social functioning (e.g. bullying or being bullied)?
- What are the youth's strengths and weaknesses?

Management

With the youth

- Youth psychoeducation helps the young person understand why he conducts himself as he does, how his behaviours are linked to certain consequences and how the proposed counselling strategies and supportive interventions may help him improve his behaviour. Since individuals with moderate to severe conduct disorder are usually not sufficiently motivated to change, frequent counselling sessions are required to build a rapport and elicit their cooperation.
- Problem-solving counselling helps the young person identify his problem areas and develop socially acceptable solutions.
- Social skills counselling enhances the young person's social skills

so that he may engage in healthy activities with his peer group. The counsellor should identify healthy, age-appropriate activities that the youth enjoys and guide him to engage in these activities.

With the family

- Family psychoeducation helps the parent(s) decide upon limits that can effectively regulate their child's activities and behaviours, as well as design consequences. For example, family psychoeducation can help them develop clear guidelines on their child's school attendance, with a follow-up plan to monitor his attendance which includes positive feedback for attending school. This strategy also helps them learn how to communicate productively with each other and their child, e.g. without hostility or blaming each other. Single parents may face great difficulty handling the youth who exhibits antisocial behaviours because they lack the support of another adult. The single parent can be informed about the usefulness of positive role models and be encouraged to identify such persons in the youth's environment. A positive role model could be, for example, a member of the extended family. If the youth's family is contributing to his antisocial behaviours, family psychoeducation should focus on the link between the youth's behaviours and the family's difficulties and help the family better manage their difficulties. For example, developing conflict management skills would be useful for families that resort to violence. Family sessions, including the youth and his parent(s), can be used to help them develop a behavioural contract. This contract would specify the rewards the youth may expect for good conduct and the consequences for bad conduct, as well as rules for effective communication (*see* Chapter 6 and Appendix).

With teachers and school staff

- Supportive interventions in the school setting help the teachers develop and implement effective techniques for behaviour management. These techniques should be aimed at curbing the youth's disruptive behaviour in the classroom and on the campus. For example, the teachers can establish effective limits for the youth, closely monitor his school attendance and create opportunities for him to engage in school activities (*see* Chapter 6). In addition, young people with conduct disorder may need help with any coexisting specific learning disability, e.g. introducing methods to increase concentration.

When to refer: If the youth's antisocial behaviours persist despite counselling, or if the behaviours are very serious, e.g. if he harms others, he should be referred to a mental health professional for further evaluation. He may also need referral for psychoeducational testing if there is a possibility of a specific learning disability, or to a mental health professional for an assessment if any coexisting disorder, such as attention deficit hyperactivity disorder, is suspected. The youth can be referred for vocational guidance if he is disengaged from academics in secondary school.

Key messages

- Conduct disorder is characterized by antisocial behaviours, such as repeated lying, stealing and aggression towards human beings and animals; high-risk behaviours; and lack of remorse for these behaviours.
- Conduct disorder results in poor academic performance, marginalization from the appropriate peer group and school failure or expulsion from school.
- Youth with conduct disorder may have underlying attention deficit hyperactivity disorder or a specific learning disability.
- Establishing a counselling relationship with a young person with a conduct disorder can be challenging. The counsellor should try to build a rapport through a variety of counselling skills which increase the youth's confidence that the counsellor has an interest in and values him.

CASE STUDY 17

The youth with a serious mental disorder

Uday's story

The presenting problem

Uday, a 17-year-old boy in Standard XI, was referred to the counsellor by his class teacher because his school attendance had decreased, his academic performance was uneven, he had become increasingly isolated from his peers and he displayed some unusual behaviours. His father and aunt said he had always been an outgoing and pleasant boy, but seemed to have lost interest in most things over the past 6 months. He had stopped meeting his friends after school, was listless at home and preferred to lock himself in his room. Over the past few weeks, the family members had become increasingly worried because they had noticed that he talked to himself and became extremely irritable and moody when they interacted with him.

Developmental history

Uday's early childhood and subsequent development had been normal.

Psychosocial history

Family history: Uday was the eldest son and lived in an extended family with his two younger brothers (11 and 9 years old). His father's brother's family lived with them and the families shared a kitchen. His father and uncle were agricultural labourers. His aunt described Uday's mother as 'unusual', although she had been well adjusted before the birth of her third son. When Uday was 10 years old the family noticed that his mother had become increasingly unreasonable. For example, she would shout at the children for no particular reason, say that the family was trying to poison her and retreat to a separate room in the house. The aunt had willingly taken over the care of the three boys.

Academic history: Uday had been an average student until the last academic year. However, his performance had deteriorated in Standard X and he barely scraped through the board examinations.

Social history: The teacher had noticed a gradual change in Uday's behaviour over the past three months. The main changes were that he had become irritable when asked questions and had withdrawn from his classmates. She had also noticed that during the breaks, he either spent his time alone in the classroom or wandered around by himself along the boundaries of the school grounds.

Drug/alcohol use: Uday was not reported to use drugs or alcohol.

Mental status examination

Uday missed two of his appointments with the counsellor. Eventually, the counsellor had to locate him personally and guide him to her office. Uday's appearance was untidy. His eye contact with the counsellor was consistently poor and it was very difficult to build a rapport with him. His behaviour was unusual, e.g. he repeatedly tapped his head, and he seemed to be listening to conversations not audible to the counsellor. He was very distracted throughout the session. On at least two occasions, he started mumbling to himself and it seemed like he was telling someone to go away. However, he denied that he was 'hearing voices'. He told the counsellor that he did not enjoy school, stating that many of the students were against him. He named a few students who he felt were out to harm him, but could not explain why they would wish to do so. He said that he had received clear warnings about the dangers posed by these classmates while watching television news. He did not think he was ill and was convinced that his unusual beliefs were real.

Case formulation

Uday, a 17-year-old studying in Standard XI, was referred to the counsellor by the class teacher due to a deterioration in his school performance and his increasingly unusual behaviours. He lives in a joint family with his two younger brothers, his father, who is a farmer, and his mother, who probably has an undiagnosed mental disorder. He has abnormal persecutory thoughts and possibly auditory hallucinations, and he is increasingly withdrawing from social interaction. These symptoms suggest the possibility of psychosis, a serious mental disorder (*see* Chapter 2).

Strengths: Uday's strengths include an average intelligence and a normal developmental profile up until his current illness. Other strengths include a caring home environment and an aunt who is willing to participate in the plan for his recovery.

Difficulties: Uday's difficulties include his serious symptoms, lack of insight and the possibility that his mother has a mental illness.

MANAGEMENT PLAN

The primary counselling strategies that can help Uday are youth psychoeducation, family psychoeducation and supportive interventions in the school setting.

Youth psychoeducation: The counsellor should explain to Uday that his very unusual symptoms are probably signs of a serious mental disorder. He should be reassured that an assessment with a psychiatrist will help him and his family understand why this is happening and allow him to get appropriate treatment in the form of medication. Uday may have apprehensions upon hearing this information; for example, he may have concerns that people will call him 'mad'. The counsellor should address these concerns by reassuring him that she will support him if such incidents occur. After a diagnostic assessment, if Uday is prescribed medication, the counsellor should help him adhere to the medication, for example by reassuring him that the medication will help him recover, improve and maintain his mental health. Once Uday has improved and is able to interact with the counsellor more comfortably, she can utilize strategies with him that may be useful for his overall functioning, such as social skills counselling.

Family psychoeducation: As soon as possible after meeting with the youth, the counsellor should meet with his family. An urgent referral to a psychiatrist is the immediate priority. The counsellor can first convey her concerns to the family with a clear statement such as, 'Uday has very serious symptoms. I suggest that he immediately see a psychiatrist who can help us understand how to help him.' The family members' understanding of Uday's problem and its causes should be explored and corrected if necessary, e.g. they might think that Uday is the victim of a curse. The counsellor should also find out whether they have already taken any steps in response to Uday's behaviours. After hearing them out, she must emphasize that the problem may be due to a mental health disorder and explain that a psychiatric assessment, which may recommend treatment with medication, is critical to Uday's recovery. If Uday's family members take him for a psychiatric evaluation and specific treatments are recommended, e.g. medication, they should be informed that it is essential for them to help him adhere to the treatment plan advised by the psychiatrist. With the family's permission, the counsellor may discuss the care of the youth with the psychiatrist. The counsellor should help the family deal with the issue of shame or fear. For example, she can help the family members plan for how to include Uday in social events, since they may be worried about what others might say or do to him. In addition, the family should be encouraged to use the opportunity to seek help for Uday's mother, who also seems to be suffering from a mental health problem and would benefit from a psychiatric evaluation.

Supportive interventions in the school setting: The counsellor should inform the teachers that Uday is suffering from a serious mental disorder and that she is working with his family to address his problems. The teachers may be worried about Uday's behaviour in the classroom. If it is disruptive, the counsellor should meet the school principal and his family to discuss how to manage him in school until he recovers, or whether he should remain at home until he is better. To reduce academic stress, which could worsen Uday's symptoms, the counsellor should ask the teachers if they can make academic concessions for Uday. They could, for example, not put pressure on him to meet homework deadlines until he has stabilized. Once he is better, the teachers can be advised on how to gradually steer him back to his previous level of academic functioning and to provide remediation for the work he has missed.

The following intervention may also be useful:

Social skills counselling: Once Uday's symptoms start coming under control with medication, the counsellor can use social skills counselling to facilitate his re-integration with his peers. He can also be encouraged to join school clubs which provide opportunities for socialization.

ASSESSMENT AND MANAGEMENT OF A YOUTH WITH A PSYCHOSIS

THE PROBLEM

The psychoses are among the most serious of all mental disorders. The most common type of psychosis affecting young people is schizophrenia. The cardinal features of these conditions are abnormal thoughts, disconnection from reality and disordered behaviour. Psychoses should be diagnosed only by a mental health professional after a thorough assessment. Although these disorders are relatively rare, they are associated with tremendous suffering and disability, and the person can benefit greatly from appropriate medication. An additional problem faced by a person with a severe mental disorder is society's reaction to him and his family, i.e. stigma. 'Stigma' is a term that refers to the negative and biased views people harbour about individuals who are different. Individuals with mental disorders and disabilities are easily identified as different and often bear the brunt of discriminatory behaviours. These behaviours include social exclusion, name-calling, ridicule and bullying. The counsellor should attempt to reduce stigma by informing the whole school (e.g. in an assembly organized by the school administration) about the causes of and proper attitudes towards mental health problems, without identifying any specific students suffering with this disorder (*see* Chapter 6).

ASSESSMENT

Young people with psychoses are usually referred to counsellors by their teachers or family because of a deterioration in their school performance and poor school attendance, or due to their unusual behaviours. Occasionally, the individual visits the counsellor himself in the early stages of the disorder, when he might worry about his persecutory thoughts and has the feeling that his thoughts are going out of control. Building a rapport with the youth with a serious mental disorder may prove challenging when he is acutely unwell. Occasionally, the counsellor unwittingly becomes a target of suspicion, as part of the general feeling of suspicion that the young person is experiencing. She may need to step back until the youth's suspiciousness decreases following the initiation of medication.

Information from the youth

- How is he feeling, particularly with respect to his distressing mental experiences?
- How are things at home, in school and with his friends?
- Is he drinking alcohol or using drugs? Certain drugs, such as cannabis, can aggravate the illness. How do these make him feel?
- Is he taking his medicines? Have they been of any benefit? Are there any side-effects?

Information from the parent

- How is their child doing at home?
- Have any aspects of his life changed recently? What are these and what is the extent of the changes? What impact have these changes had on their child?
- How are the family members coping with the illness? Have they come up against the problem of stigma or exclusion?
- Are there other family members with similar problems? How have these problems been addressed?
- What kind of help have they sought for his problems? How do they treat the youth at home?

Information from the teacher

- How is the youth performing in school?
- Has his academic performance changed recently?
- Has his behaviour towards his peers and school staff changed? If so, how?

Information from the psychiatrist

- What is her assessment of the youth's mental health? What are her recommendations?

- Has she prescribed medication? What is the medication? What is the medication schedule? What are the side-effects of the medication?
- What has the psychiatrist told the youth and his family members about the illness?

Management

Although the primary goal should be to successfully refer the young person to a psychiatrist for an assessment and, if necessary, appropriate medical treatment, the counsellor can also play an important role in the continuing care of the youth.

With the youth

- The most urgent priority is to refer the young person to a psychiatrist for a psychiatric evaluation. The counsellor and family should collaborate with the psychiatrist and follow her recommendations.
- The counsellor can help the youth understand the nature of his problem through youth psychoeducation only after a diagnosis has been made and she has clear information regarding the type of illness the youth is suffering from. It is important that the counsellor encourage the youth to take the medication prescribed by the psychiatrist and visit his psychiatrist for regular reviews.
- Social skills counselling can help the youth re-enter social spaces that he has withdrawn from once he is better. Helping him identify school and social activities that he can engage in and supporting his participation in these activities will help the youth build self-esteem and rejoin his peer group.

With the family

- Family psychoeducation helps family members understand the nature of the youth's problem, enabling them to be more empathetic towards him and thereby possibly reduce the occurrence/intensity of behaviours which isolate him further or worsen his symptoms. The counsellor should emphasize that it is essential for the family to help the young person adhere to his medication to facilitate his recovery.

With teachers and school staff

- Supportive interventions in the school give the teachers and school staff a better understanding of the nature of the youth's problems and help them empathize with him. Supportive interventions help the youth academically during and after the illness, as well as integrate him into school and peer activities. Further, they guide the teachers and school staff on how to minimize discriminatory behaviour, such as name-calling, teasing, bullying and social exclusion, against the youth. If the youth is in a very disturbed state, the school should be encouraged to permit him to stay at home until his medication produces enough of an improvement to allow him to engage in school activities.

When to refer: All youth suspected of having a serious mental disorder must be referred to a mental health professional for assessment and, if need be, for continuing care.

Key messages

- Psychoses are serious and rare mental health disorders, characterized by abnormal thoughts (such as 'delusions'), unusual behaviours (such as agitation) and sensory experiences (such as 'hallucinations').
- Psychoses can seriously impair the youth's well-being and academic performance, and are often associated with discrimination and stigma.
- An immediate psychiatric assessment is needed to establish the diagnosis and initiate appropriate medical treatment.
- Youth psychoeducation and family psychoeducation should aim to help the youth and his family understand the disorder, adhere to the prescribed schedule of medication and continue to work with the psychiatrist. Once the youth's symptoms have been managed through medication, social skills counselling may help reduce his isolation and support his re-integration into his social world.

CASE STUDY 18

The youth with unexplained physical symptoms

Alisha's story

The presenting problem

Alisha, a 17-year-old girl studying in Standard XI, had been suffering from headaches that became worse before school examinations. Her parents spoke to her class teacher, who suggested that Alisha see the school counsellor. Alisha told the counsellor that over the past year, she had been getting headaches, which had become a daily occurrence recently. Her night's sleep was disturbed and she felt fatigued. Her headaches were worse in the morning and she had been missing school. She said she found it hard to get to sleep at night because she was usually worried about the next day at school. She had noticed that although she studied, her ability to concentrate was poor and she was distracted by negative thoughts about how she would fare in her examinations. On enquiry, Alisha had denied having any thoughts of harming herself. The counsellor also spoke to Alisha's parents, who told her that their child had always been shy and quiet. She seemed to have a difficult relationship with her older sister, with whom she fought frequently. In the past year, she had become withdrawn and quieter. The doctors had not found any medical explanation for her headaches and her eye test did not indicate the need for spectacles.

Developmental history

The parents reported that Alisha's birth had been a normal one. Although she had suffered from asthma as a child, she had outgrown the wheezing episodes and had had a normal developmental history.

Psychosocial history

Family history: Alisha's father was a college teacher and her mother a teacher at her school. Alisha told the counsellor that her father was very strict and had very high academic expectations for her. She said that most of their conversations revolved around academics. Her father did much of the parenting since her mother was usually quite busy preparing for her classroom lessons. Alisha said she liked her sister, but got annoyed with her father's constant comparisons between their academic performances. Her sister, who was two years older than Alisha, had done very well in her board examinations, had performed exceptionally well in a national entrance examination and was about to leave home to study in a top technology institute. Alisha said her parents never talked about her with the kind of pride that was apparent when they talked about her sister. She said she felt sad 'that I will never be as accomplished as my sister'.

Academic history: Alisha remembered enjoying primary and middle school, when she used to find studying easy and did well. She had also done well in her Standard X board examinations. She had opted for the science stream since her father thought she should be a doctor. However, she had begun to find the sciences difficult, though she was doing well in mathematics. With sadness, Alisha mentioned that she had had to ignore her love of singing and creative writing since she had to now concentrate on getting good marks in her Standard XII board examinations. Most of her time after school was devoted to studying and she felt very frustrated when she did not get the marks she expected.

Social history: Alisha mentioned having one close friend in her class. Though she talked to her classmates, she rarely got involved in any group activities. Since she had been missing school recently due to her headaches, she needed to complete class work after school hours and could not see her close friend as often as before.

Drug/alcohol use: Alisha was not reported to be abusing any drug or alcohol.

MENTAL STATUS EXAMINATION

Alisha was an anxious and fidgety girl, who was shy and neatly dressed.

Her speech, perceptions and memory were normal. In the second session, she became tearful while describing how helpless she felt when she was unable to understand what she was studying even though she spent a lot of time with her books. She described being unable to sleep at night, getting up exhausted and lacking energy throughout the day. By evening she described having severe headaches which disturbed her sleep. She felt she would never be able to fulfil her father's dream that she become a doctor and worried about disappointing him. Alisha had thought of running away from home; however, she had never thought of harming herself. She was relieved that she could discuss her problems with the counsellor and was keen to see her again.

Case formulation

Alisha is a 17-year-old girl studying in Standard XI. She was referred to the counsellor by her teacher because her parents expressed concern about the fact that she suffered from headaches which had no obvious cause. Alisha belongs to a nuclear family, the members of which are high achievers, and her parents have tremendous academic expectations for her. Alisha has been missing school over the past 6 months, complaining of constant headaches and fatigue. She is very hard-working and her performance, which is average, does not match her parents' expectations. She has one close friend and her contact with this friend has decreased since she has been missing school due to ill health. Alisha shows symptoms of anxiety and depression, including worrying, low self-esteem and feelings of helplessness about her ability to change her situation. She has no thoughts of self-harm. The most probable diagnosis is depression.

Strengths: Factors that can work to Alisha's advantage are that she is a sensitive person who has insight into the stresses she is experiencing in her environment. In addition, she is hard-working, of normal intelligence and has a close friend.

Difficulties: Low self-esteem, the mismatch between her academic abilities and her aspirations, and the parental pressure for her to achieve academic excellence may be obstacles to Alisha's recovery.

MANAGEMENT PLAN

The following strategies are recommended to address Alisha's problems: youth psychoeducation, cognitive restructuring, behavioural activation and family psychoeducation. Supportive interventions in the school will help Alisha adjust in school.

Youth psychoeducation: The counsellor should explain to Alisha that her physical problems are likely related to her worries and low self-esteem; and that these problems result from her attempts to meet her own and her parents' academic aspirations. In addition, the counsellor should explain that her negative thoughts about herself are creating feelings of helplessness, as well as interfering with her ability to concentrate and perform well academically. The counsellor should give Alisha an idea of how counselling will help her; e.g. the counsellor could tell Alisha, 'We will work together to understand what triggers your negative thoughts about yourself and develop your ability to focus on your strengths at those times.' The counsellor should also seek Alisha's permission to speak to her parents, explaining that family psychoeducation may help her parents develop realistic expectations for her academic performance and, as a result, reduce their pressure.

Cognitive restructuring: The counsellor should work with Alisha to identify the thoughts which affect her self-esteem, e.g. that she is not as talented as her sister and that she is disappointing her father. The counsellor can then help her learn to replace these thoughts through positive self-talk that focuses on her personal strengths, e.g. reminding herself that she has her own talents and interests, which have as much merit as her sister's.

Behavioural activation: The counsellor can encourage Alisha to increase her participation in activities that have a positive effect on her mood. For example, she could pursue her interests in creative writing and singing by joining extracurricular classes. The counsellor can help her structure her schedule to achieve a balance between studies and pleasurable activities.

Family psychoeducation: With Alisha's permission, the counsellor should meet her parents and explain that their daughter is suffering from depression and very poor self-esteem. The parents may gain a better understanding of the link between Alisha's physical symptoms and her emotions if they are given an explanation such as, 'Alisha is feeling overwhelmed with sad thoughts, which are affecting every aspect of her life. She may be suffering from depression, which is causing her physical complaints.' It is important to help the parents understand that their high expectations for Alisha, the pressure they put on her for academic achievement and the unfavourable comparisons they make with her sister are causing Alisha's depression. They must be made aware of the possibility that there is a mismatch between Alisha's aptitude and interests and their choice of career for her.

Supportive interventions in the school: With Alisha's permission, the counsellor can help the teachers understand that Alisha is not intentionally missing school, but instead, is feeling a great deal of pressure to do well. It is important for the teachers to involve her not only in academic activities, but also other school activities that will allow her to use her talents in creative writing and singing.

Additional interventions which may be useful include the following:

Problem-solving counselling: The counsellor can help Alisha identify what is troubling her and seek realistic alternatives for herself. For example, she could reassess her current career goals and develop alternative achievable career plans, or she could find ways of using her creative talents, such as participating in extracurricular activities.

Social skills training: The counsellor can assist Alisha in developing social skills that will engage her peers, expanding her social circle and communicating assertively with her parents. Role-playing a variety of social situations with the counsellor would help Alisha acquire skills to improve her relationships.

Relaxation exercise: The counsellor can teach Alisha deep breathing, which she can utilize when she feels anxious.

When to refer: If after using the above counselling strategies, Alisha still continues to have symptoms of depression, or has thoughts of self-harm, the counsellor must set up a referral with a mental health professional. The counsellor should first try and get Alisha's consent to speak to her parents; however, if she feels that Alisha is at a risk of self-harm the counsellor can directly contact her parents (*see* Chapter 5).

Assessment and Management of Medically Unexplained Physical Complaints

The problem

Mental health distress, depression and/or anxiety (*see* Chapter 2) are common among adolescents and often manifest themselves in medically unexplained physical complaints, such as headaches, stomach aches, fatigue and disturbances in sleep and appetite. Depressed adolescents may also abandon their normal routines and withdraw from their usual activities. Less often, they exhibit disruptive behaviours, e.g. they may participate in high-risk activities such as substance abuse. If undetected or not taken seriously, the symptoms may worsen and the youth may plan to commit suicide or make deliberate attempts to harm herself. The stressors of daily life, such as academic pressure, problems with relationships (family/friends), the break-up of a romantic relationship, bullying and rejection by peers, are common causes of depression. It is to be noted that physical complaints must not be interpreted as mental health problems until any medical conditions which might be causing them have been ruled out. To take the example of headaches, short-sightedness and migraines should be ruled out.

Assessment

Information from the youth

- How does she describe her physical symptoms, particularly how they began and what makes them worse or better?
- What are the stressors in the youth's life? Do the physical symptoms coincide with a particular stressor?
- What is the youth doing to manage the stress she is undergoing?
- Has she had any thoughts of hopelessness and helplessness which have led her to think of harming herself?

Information from the parent

- Have the pains their child is experiencing been investigated medically?

If so, what are the results?

- Have the parents noticed any link between their child's physical complaints and stressors in the home or other environments?
- What are the parents' attitudes towards their child's complaints?

Information from the teacher

- Has the teacher noticed a change in the youth's behaviour or her academic performance?
- Are there any school-related stressors, e.g. examinations or being the victim of bullying, which may be affecting the youth?

MANAGEMENT

With the youth

- Youth psychoeducation helps the youth become aware that her physical symptoms are related to the stress she is feeling and helps her understand the various strategies the counsellor selects to help her manage stress more effectively.
- Cognitive restructuring helps the youth learn how to replace negative thoughts about herself and her abilities with more positive ones.
- Behavioural activation aims to involve the youth in pleasurable activities, in order to enhance her self-esteem and improve her mood.
- Problem-solving counselling can help the youth identify the problems that are causing stress and find effective solutions to these problems. Both these processes can enhance her sense of mastery over her situation.

With the family

- Family psychoeducation enhances the parents' understanding of their child's problems and helps them modify the factors contributing to her discomfort.

With teachers and school staff

- Supportive interventions in the school guide the teachers and school staff to be sympathetic about the youth's stress and take steps to decrease the stress associated with the youth's school experience.

When to refer: If the counsellor feels that the youth's mood continues to be a cause for concern even after a period of counselling, if the depression is causing significant changes in the youth's sleep and appetite or if she expresses the wish to harm herself, the counsellor should make a referral to a mental health professional for an evaluation and follow-up.

Key messages

- Young people who have physical complaints may be suffering from mental health distress or a disorder, such as depression or anxiety.
- Physical complaints should be medically investigated to rule out any organic cause before being identified as symptoms of mental health distress or a disorder.
- Underlying distress or a disorder will have an impact on the youth's social and academic functioning.
- Youth psychoeducation, cognitive restructuring, behavioural activation and problem-solving counselling are useful for helping youth with physical symptoms related to mental health distress or disorders.

CASE STUDY 19

THE YOUTH WHO ATTEMPTS SELF-HARM

Kevin's story

THE PRESENTING PROBLEM

Kevin, a 17-year-old boy studying in Standard XII, was referred to the counsellor by the headmaster and his parents. He had swallowed a strip of pills and had to be admitted to the hospital. He had recovered from the overdose. Kevin was not willing to tell his parents the reason for what he had done. The principal asked him if he would talk to the counsellor and he agreed. His parents spoke to the counsellor privately to express their distress and worry over Kevin. They were also concerned about how this incident would affect his academic performance, with the pressure to do well in the final year of higher secondary school. Kevin's mother told the counsellor that she thought the incident had to do with a disappointment in a relationship with a girl. The mother's niece had informed her that she had seen some of Kevin's posts on Facebook about feeling heartbroken. When Kevin met the counsellor, he said he had met a really attractive new girl named Gita in the last academic year. She lived in his neighbourhood and they used to walk to school together. Gradually, they came to like each other very much and began dating. However, Kevin was very careful about where they met and did not tell his parents about the relationship because he thought they would disapprove. Recently, he had noticed a change in Gita. She seemed to avoid meeting him and had stopped calling him or replying to his text messages. Two weeks earlier, she had told him that she wanted to end their relationship because she was interested in another boy. Kevin said he had felt extremely shocked and heartbroken. He had begged Gita to give him another chance and explain to him what had gone wrong, but she had just not been interested. Following this, he started having difficulty concentrating on his studies and began drinking and smoking 'to forget about her'. Last week, he felt especially upset when he saw Gita laughing and enjoying herself with her friends in the shops in the locality. He had rushed home, picked up his grandmother's sleeping pills and swallowed one strip. His mother had found him asleep on his bed and, upon finding the empty strip, rushed him to the hospital. Kevin realized that his parents were very upset and felt a bit silly about what he had done. He was now determined to forget about Gita and instead, concentrate on his examinations, but said he was finding this difficult. When questioned about his attempt to harm himself, Kevin said he had not planned it beforehand. It was when he had come home upset and seen his grandmother's pills on the table that he had thought it would teach everyone, especially Gita, a lesson if he died. He said he had thought that Gita would feel awful, regret breaking up with him and miss him. In retrospect, after seeing how badly he had upset his family and friends, he realized that he had behaved in an immature way. He still thought about Gita and now planned to work hard and succeed in school in order to impress her and win her back.

Developmental history

Kevin's parents reported that he had a normal childhood. He had always been a shy child, with only a few good friends. At home, he was a quiet and obedient young man.

Psychosocial history

Family history: Kevin lived with his mother, father and younger sister, who was 14 years old. His paternal grandmother had been staying with the family for the past three months. His father was unemployed and his mother was a teacher. His father used to be the captain of a merchant vessel, but was forced to retire due to ill health. Kevin described his father as a strict disciplinarian, who often got into fights with him over trivial issues, such as his returning late from school. Kevin's mother seemed to be finding it difficult to balance her work and family obligations. She and his father had different parenting styles; the mother felt that her husband was too strict with their children while the father felt that she indulged the children. The step that Kevin had taken recently had made his mother wonder if she should be more strict, like the husband.

Academic history: Kevin had done well throughout his school years. He wanted to become an electrical engineer and join a professional course after completing Standard XII. Because of this, he was very concerned about his falling grades and the fact that he could not concentrate.

Social history: Kevin had two close friends with whom he played music after school. He had a fairly good relationship with his mother and sister, but did not get along with his father. He helped his sister with her homework and they often went to the cinema together. He had never discussed his romantic relationship with anyone in the family, but had told his friends about it.

Drug/alcohol use: Kevin disclosed that he began drinking beer and smoking in the company of his friends following the break-up with Gita.

Mental status examination

Kevin was dressed neatly and, though slightly ill at ease, made good eye contact. His mood was variable. He appeared sad while speaking about the break-up, but seemed happy when talking about playing music with his friends. He expressed irritation with his father. When he spoke about his academic deterioration or his having swallowed pills, he seemed ashamed. His mood matched the content of his thinking. The form and content of his thinking were normal. He complained of poor concentration but his sleep and appetite were normal. He did not mention feeling hopeless or harbouring suicidal ideas. He had good insight and was clear about why he was distressed. He was also aware of the need to 'move on'.

Case formulation

Kevin is a 17-year-old boy studying in Standard XII. He was referred to the counsellor by the headmaster and his parents after he attempted suicide by swallowing pills. This act was an impulsive one, without prior planning, and was precipitated by the break-up of a romantic relationship. Since the break-up, Kevin has difficulty concentrating, his mood has become low and he has been smoking and consuming alcohol to manage his hurt feelings. Since the attempted overdose, he has not expressed suicidal ideas and does not appear to have the symptoms of a mental health disorder. He wishes to refocus on his studies and future career plan. The diagnosis is mental health distress (*see* Chapter 2) due to the break-up of a romantic relationship. His attempt to harm himself was impulsive and was followed by feelings of remorse and regret.

Strengths: Kevin's strengths include above average intelligence; motivation to do well academically; musical abilities; a clear future career plan; a high level of insight and motivation to get on with his life; good social skills; and good relationships with his friends, his mother and sister.

Difficulties: The problem areas include Kevin's difficult relationship with his father; the break-up of a romantic relationship, which still preoccupies him; and his parents' divergent parenting styles.

Management plan

The core strategies to help Kevin include youth psychoeducation, cognitive restructuring, problem-solving counselling, social skills counselling and family psychoeducation.

Youth psychoeducation: The counsellor should carry out a suicide risk assessment (*see* Chapter 4) to determine if Kevin is still at a risk of harming himself. She should explain the counselling process to him. This should include a discussion of the selected strategies that will help him develop effective coping mechanisms he can use when faced with disappointments. These coping mechanisms could help him manage his emotions so that he would not resort to impulsive and risky behaviours. The counsellor should also make Kevin aware of the negative consequences of substance abuse. She should motivate him to discontinue smoking and drinking alcohol, explaining that with continued use, his health and career plans would suffer.

Cognitive restructuring: The counsellor should help Kevin identify any negative thoughts he has about himself. She should then teach him to replace these thoughts with positive ones, using positive self-talk. This skill is very important for Kevin, given his tendency to harbour negative thoughts about himself when faced with interpersonal disappointment.

An example of positive self-talk would be to remind himself about all of his attractive qualities, e.g. his musical abilities when he is feeling unattractive.

Problem-solving counselling: The counsellor should help Kevin identify and prioritize his problems. He may feel that the loss of his friendship with Gita has left a void in his life. The counsellor should find out if he would like to identify other avenues for making new friends. Another important problem area for Kevin is his communication with his parents. Kevin can problem solve how he can share his concerns with his parents about his future. Role-plays can equip Kevin with methods to build a more positive relationship with his father and to decrease conflict in their interactions

Social skills counselling: The counsellor should help Kevin identify and prioritize his problems. Kevin's key problem is his extremely self-deprecating reaction to disappointments in relationships. Kevin can learn to identify those interactions with peers and romantic interests which make him feel badly. Role-plays, with a focus on these social situations, will point out to Kevin what elements of these interactions distress him. The counsellor should then work with him to develop socially effective solutions to these problematic interactions. Implementing these solutions will develop his self-pride and provide him with a sense of mastery.

Family psychoeducation: With Kevin's permission, the counsellor should meet with his parents. To help them understand why Kevin attempted to harm himself and the objectives of counselling, the counsellor could say, 'Kevin seems to have had his heart broken by someone he liked very much and this has caused him to harm himself impulsively. He seems to realize his mistake now, but needs counselling so that he can manage disappointments without resorting to self-harm.' Since the parents will no doubt be worried about the possibility of Kevin making another such attempt, the counsellor should work with them to draw up a safety contract with Kevin. This contract should include an assurance by Kevin that if he ever has thoughts of harming himself again, he will reach out to his parents (or another identified individual) to ensure his safety. The counsellor should also address the difference in parenting styles and involve the parents in a discussion of positive parenting techniques which they would both be willing to employ. In addition, she should encourage them to assist Kevin with his academic work so that he can gradually return to his previous level of academic performance.

When to refer: If the counsellor finds that Kevin's thoughts of self-harm persist, and/or if he begins to show signs of depression, she should refer him to a mental health professional.

Assessment and Management of Self-Harm

The Problem

Thoughts of suicide and self-harm are very common during adolescence. 'I want to die' or 'I feel like killing myself' are thoughts commonly experienced by young people. Most often, these are transitory and do not result in attempts at self-harm. However, suicide is one of the most common causes of death among youth, in part due to the impulsivity which is characteristic of this age group. Because of this, any threat of self-harm must be taken seriously. Suicidal behaviours can occur when a youth experiences mental health distress, depression or schizophrenia. The precipitating causes include interpersonal problems, e.g. the break-up of a romantic relationship, difficulty making friends, loneliness and being a victim of bullying; educational problems, e.g. inability to cope with studies and school failure; familial reasons, e.g. discord in the family, divorce, violence in the family and punitive parenting; physical concerns, e.g. feeling that one is unattractive and/or self-conscious about a disability; and sexual concerns, e.g. sexual abuse and alternative sexual orientation. Management of a youth who is experiencing suicidal thoughts or has attempted suicide requires a detailed suicide risk assessment (*see* Chapter 4). It is very important that the counsellor maintains the youth's confidentiality when communicating with his family and teachers; however, when communication about the youth is necessary to protect the youth from self-harm or other exceptional circumstances (*see* Chapter 7), the counsellor may have to breach confidentiality.

Assessment

Information from the youth

- A suicide risk assessment is essential (*see* Chapter 4).
- Ascertain the details of the episode of self-harm. For example, what was the method used and the motivation/reason for the attempt, and was it planned? Did the youth share his thoughts about harming himself with anybody and, if so, with whom?
- What is his reaction following the attempt? For example, does he regret that he survived (which would indicate a continuing risk of self-harm)? Does he feel he lacks support? If so, in relation to what in particular? What support does he need?
- What are his plans for the future?

Information from the parent

- What do the parents know about the stressors in their child's life?
- What is the family's attitude towards their child's suicide attempt?
- What parenting styles do the mother and father employ?
- Are there any risk factors, such as violence in the family, drug and alcohol abuse or a family history of depression or suicide?
- What steps can the family take to ensure their child's safety?

Information from the teacher

- What did the teachers notice about the youth's behaviour or academic performance in the period immediately before the suicide attempt?
- What might have precipitated these changes?

Management

With the youth

- Youth psychoeducation can help the youth understand why he harmed himself. It can make him aware of how counselling will help him handle disappointments in daily life in a way that does not place him at risk.
- Problem-solving counselling can help the youth identify the specific

problems in his daily life that are linked to his low self-esteem. Further, it can guide him to find and select adaptive solutions to these problems. Two common problems associated with suicidal behaviours are disappointment with academic performance and problems in peer relationships.

- Social skills counselling is beneficial for youth who have difficulty in making and keeping friends or who are facing problems with romantic relationships. This counselling strategy equips the youth with methods to manage interpersonal disappointment and develops the youth's ability to make and maintain friendships.
- Behavioural activation is useful for the person who has withdrawn from daily activities, is going through depression and is suffering from low self-esteem. This strategy aims to help him re-engage in activities he previously enjoyed.
- Cognitive restructuring is useful for young people who exhibit symptoms of depression and are troubled by negative thoughts and beliefs about themselves. This counselling strategy helps the youth identify his negative thoughts, and then develop and utilize positive thoughts to counter them.

With the family

- Family psychoeducation helps parents understand their child's feelings and behaviours, identify when he is coping poorly and communicate with him more effectively. Family psychoeducation helps parents strengthen their parenting skills so that they can be of greater assistance to their child, particularly when he is distressed and uncommunicative. It is always important for the counsellor to maintain the youth's confidentiality, except in exceptional circumstances (*see* Chapter 7).

With teachers and school staff

- Supportive interventions in the school sensitize teachers to the stresses that young people can experience in their daily lives. It is important for the school staff to become familiar with signs indicating that a youth is stressed, e.g. changes in behaviour or academic performance, and to make a referral to the counsellor. When a youth has attempted self-harm, it is important that the counsellor maintain the youth's confidentiality while sensitizing the teachers to his need for their support. The counsellor can guide the school staff and management to raise the general awareness among the students and teachers of the risk factors associated with suicide through a life skills programme (*see* Chapter 6). She can also advise them to enlist peer support, through peer pairing, for a youth at risk (*see* Chapter 6).

When to refer: If the youth's symptoms persist despite counselling or if the counsellor feels at any time that he is at risk of self-harm (*see* Chapter 4), the youth should be referred to a mental health professional.

Key messages

- Thoughts of self-harm are not unusual among adolescents. Usually, such thoughts are transient and do not lead to a suicide attempt.
- Suicide attempts are one of the most common causes of hospitalization among young people and suicide is among the most common causes of death in this age group.
- Mental health distress and depression are the most common mental health problems associated with suicide. These are usually triggered by disappointments, e.g. deterioration in academic performance or break-up of a romantic relationship.
- Youth psychoeducation, problem-solving counselling, cognitive restructuring, behavioural activation and family psycho-education are important strategies to help a young person who has attempted self-harm.

CASE STUDY 20

THE YOUTH WITHOUT REALISTIC FUTURE PLANS

Yash's story

THE PRESENTING PROBLEM

Yash, an 18-year-old boy studying in Standard XII, was referred to the counsellor because he was becoming increasingly apathetic as his final school term was coming to a close. The teacher who had referred him was concerned that he lacked the motivation to study throughout secondary school and that the problem had worsened in the current school term.

Yash described studies as 'boring' and said he found football 'exciting'. He had always been keenly interested in playing football. He said he had no plans for what he would do after graduating from secondary school and added that he felt 'down' because he did not think it likely that he could play professional football. His coach had told him that he was a 'fairly good player but not excellent'. In addition, since he had fractured his leg in a motorcycle accident the summer before entering Standard XII, he had been unable to play football throughout the current school year. As a result, he had been unable to improve his football skills. He told the counsellor that football was the only thing he had ever cared about.

Developmental history

According to his mother, Yash's developmental history was normal. His health history had been uneventful until he fractured his leg in a motorcycle accident the summer before entering Standard XII. His mother described him as a happy person who especially enjoyed playing outdoor sports.

Psychosocial history

Family history: Yash lived with his mother. His father had died in a car accident when he was 3 years old. He had an older sister who was married and lived nearby. However, she rarely visited her brother and mother because she had young children of her own to look after. He had several paternal uncles, who sometimes gave him part-time work at a restaurant they owned near his home. His mother had started working as a housekeeper after her husband's death. She worked the entire week and arrived home very late in the evenings. Yash usually prepared his own dinner and had begun to go out with friends in the evenings, sometimes returning home later than his mother. He was close to his mother and felt protective of her. She also cared about Yash, but had no time or energy to guide him after a full day's work.

Academic history: Yash said he had never been interested in schoolwork, and even less so in secondary school, when football had become the centre of his life. His academic performance had consistently been average and he had just managed to pass each year. In primary school, he had undergone educational testing, which had revealed that he was of above average intelligence and had no learning disability. His teacher reported that during the last school year, Yash had been even less inclined to do schoolwork and often put his head down on his desk or looked out the classroom window during class.

Social history: Yash was well liked by his classmates. He had an interest in girls his age and enjoyed flirting in the schoolyard. The girls seemed to enjoy his attention. He had close friends in the football team, but had lost touch with them over the past year since he had stopped playing football due to his fracture. He felt the members of the football team did not respect him anymore and believed this was because he had stopped playing football.

Drug/alcohol use: Yash smoked five cigarettes a day. He denied drinking alcohol.

MENTAL STATUS EXAMINATION

Yash was cooperative, polite and fairly quiet during his meetings with the counsellor. His appearance was casual. He had a faint odour of cigarette smoke. The pace and tone of his speech were normal. He was subdued and tended to appear sad. He did not report having any suicidal ideas. The form and content of his thinking were generally normal. He spoke of a passionate dream of pursuing a career in football, but seemed to have no back-up plan in case this did not materialize. He showed a degree of insight into his predicament when he expressed his worry that though he had always counted on professional football as his future career, he now knew that this was 'not going to happen'. He admitted that he was feeling 'down' and 'pissed off' with himself for not being up to the mark in football.

CASE FORMULATION

Yash, an 18-year-old boy studying in Standard XII, lives with his widowed mother. He was referred to the counsellor by his teacher because he had become increasingly apathetic about school. Yash has no plans for his future career, and has no guidance to help him develop a future career plan. His academic performance has consistently been average. He has dreamed of a career in professional football; however, since fracturing his leg the previous summer, he has been struggling to come to terms with the fact that this was not a realistic option. He is suffering from mental health distress with features of low self-esteem and loss of interest in his studies. He is also smoking tobacco regularly.

Strengths: Yash's strengths include an average intelligence; some insight into his predicament; a close relationship with his mother; and being generally liked by his schoolmates and teachers.

Difficulties: The absence of adult guidance or a male role model at home poses a problem. Other challenges are Yash's inability to play football since he has fractured his leg, the fact that his former football teammates seem to have lost respect for him and his habit of smoking. Yash's history of lack of interest in academics and his failure to make plans for the future are other problem areas.

MANAGEMENT PLAN

The primary strategies to promote Yash's recovery include youth psychoeducation and problem-solving counselling. Useful supportive interventions include supportive interventions in the school and supportive interventions in the home and the community

Youth psychoeducation: The counsellor should reassure Yash that though this is an emotionally difficult period of transition for him, the two of them will work together to make a plan for his future. He should praise him for recognizing that the plan he has treasured for so long is not realistic for him. The counsellor should explain that the transition into young adulthood is a complex process for most young people and that Yash will ultimately find a career which is both realistic and matches his interests. He should also provide Yash with information about the risks of smoking tobacco, mentioning its impact on his health and how it will further compromise his participation in outdoor sports. The counsellor should suggest various smoking cessation methods, such as stopping completely or following a plan for a gradual decrease.

Problem-solving counselling: The counsellor should involve Yash in a discussion of the obstacles to establishing a future direction and help him find solutions that will provide a realistic way forward. He could ask Yash what he enjoys about football, and discuss how he might find other activities and future options that will provide similar opportunities for pleasure. For example, if he likes the teamwork aspect of football, the counsellor can encourage him to think of team-oriented activities that might give him the same kind of satisfaction. As for his recent inability to play football, the counsellor should engage Yash in a discussion about the obstacles that have been limiting his participation and encourage him to find solutions to these problems. For example, Yash could consult the doctor who had treated him for his fracture and ask him about exercises that could help him return to the football field or engage in other outdoor sports.

Supportive interventions in the home and the community: The counsellor can help Yash identify adults whom he can consult about his future career options. He could, for example, consult his uncles or other relatives, his former coach, or his mother or elder sister.

Supportive interventions in the school: The counsellor should work with the teachers to arrange a referral for aptitude testing and career guidance (*see* Chapter 4). This would help determine Yash's interests and abilities, as well as identify possible career options suitable to his strengths and interests. If the school does not have access to such a referral resource, the counsellor, together with the school management, should explore and arrange for such resources for Yash and other young people in secondary school.

Family psychoeducation: With Yash's permission, the counsellor should help his mother understand the problems he is facing while making the transition into adulthood. The counsellor could explain that 'Yash is feeling very directionless and having difficulty shaping his future plans.' He should encourage the mother to increase her involvement in Yash's life at this critical juncture. The counsellor should also ask her for suggestions on how to assist him. For example, the mother could share her ideas about the people Yash can talk to about career options. With Yash's permission, the counsellor can also meet his uncles to find out if they have any opportunities and advice to offer Yash.

Assessment and Management of a Youth without Realistic Future Plans

The Problem

Worry about the future is common among young people preparing to leave secondary school. However, the degree of the young person's worry about, as well as his preparation for, his future varies considerably depending on whether there is a match between his skills and his interests; the opportunities available for him in his environment; his social networks; the support he receives from adult mentors; and the availability of vocational guidance in the school setting. A different type of problem that can occur in this context is when there is a conflict between the youth and his parents about his choice of career, e.g. if the parent refuses to allow him to pursue a career that he selects. A young person who is worried about his future for any of these reasons may experience anxiety, a fall in self-esteem or feelings of depression. Other possible fallouts are social withdrawal, self-destructive behaviours and indulging in high-risk behaviours.

Assessment

Information from the youth

- What are his plans for what he will do upon leaving secondary school?
- Which are his skills and interests? Are they aligned?
- What are his thoughts and feelings about the steps he will take next?
- Which factors at home or in school are hindering or helping him to take these steps?

Information from the parent

- What are their concerns about their child's future once he completes secondary school?
- How are they addressing these concerns?
- What kind of career guidance do they provide? Do they have any particular career in mind for their child and how does he react to this choice?
- Who can they count on to help support their child's transition into adulthood?

Information from the teacher

- What are the youth's strengths and interests? Are they aligned?
- Which careers do they feel might suit the youth?
- Which teachers or school staff might be recruited as mentors for the youth?

Management

With the youth

- Youth psychoeducation enhances the youth's understanding of the concerns he may have regarding his future and how these are affecting his mental health. The counsellor should reassure him that counselling will help him gain more clarity on his future choices and select an appropriate direction. Psychoeducation also provides information about healthy ways to manage stress, e.g. participating in outdoor sports rather than substance misuse. An important aspect of psychoeducation is that the counsellor and youth agree on the counselling strategies and supportive interventions necessary to achieve a realistic plan for the youth's future.
- Problem-solving counselling helps the youth to identify the problems he is facing finding a future direction and to generate solutions to these problems.
- Supportive interventions in the home and the community provide a network which the youth can use for guidance and to find future work opportunities.

With the family

- Family psychoeducation helps parents provide guidance to their child as he makes the transition into adulthood. The parents are advised to network with the extended family and other key adults in their social network with the aim of enlarging their child's future options. If there is a conflict between the family's choice of career for the youth and the youth's choice, family psychoeducation should explore the conflict and encourage the family to respect the youth's choice.

With the teachers and school staff

- Supportive interventions in the school include arranging for aptitude testing and career guidance to help the youth make realistic career choices, as well as to promote the development of skills that are aligned with his interests and abilities (*see* Chapter 4). Ideally, such guidance should be routinely available to all students in the school.

If this is not the case, the youth could be referred to a professional career counsellor outside the school.

When to refer: If the youth is unable to give up self-destructive ways of managing stress (e.g. continuing to abuse substances) or has developed an accompanying mental health disorder, he should be referred to a mental health professional for further evaluation.

Key messages

- Making the transition from secondary school into young adulthood is stressful for many students since they have to decide on a future that suits them and they are leaving a structured school environment.
- If a young person does not have a clear sense of direction or is in conflict with his parents about his future career, he can become discouraged and depressed and might engage in unhealthy behaviours.
- Career/vocational guidance is useful for those students in secondary school who are having difficulty planning for their future.
- Youth psychoeducation, problem-solving counselling and family psychoeducation are beneficial for young people who experience mental health distress associated with making the transition into adulthood. Supportive interventions in the school and supportive interventions in the home and the community can also help the youth.

Appendix

A. Sample counselling forms

Individual Information Sheet

Date:	Name:				
Date of birth:			Class:		
Mother's/Father's/Guardian's name:					
Occupation:			Contact information:		
Informants	Youth	Teachers	Principal	Parents	Other
Presenting complaints					
Developmental history					
Family history					
Academic history					
Social history					
Experience of bullying or other types of violence					
Medical history					
Substance use and frequency	Tobacco		Alcohol		Other
Mental Status Examination Appearance Speech Mood Thoughts Cognitive function Insight					
Suicide risk	Low		Moderate		High

Summary of Strengths and Difficulties

Date:	Name:	
Date of birth:	Class:	
	Strengths	Difficulties
Physical health		
Mental health		
Academic performance		
Social relationships in school (peers/teachers)		
Social relationships at home (family)		
Any other (specify)		

Case Formulation

Date:	Name:
Date of birth:	Class:
Case formulation	
Counselling plans	
Plan for next session	
Follow-up session	

Follow-up Counselling Form
(For each session)

<table>
<tr><td colspan="2">Date:</td><td colspan="4">Name:</td></tr>
<tr><td colspan="3">Date of birth:</td><td colspan="3">Class:</td></tr>
<tr><td colspan="6">Duration of counselling meeting:</td></tr>
<tr><td colspan="6">Location of counselling: School/Home/Other</td></tr>
<tr><td>Informants</td><td>Youth</td><td>Teachers</td><td>Principal</td><td>Parents</td><td>Other</td></tr>
<tr><td>Change in presenting problem</td><td colspan="5"></td></tr>
<tr><td>New problems/ concerns</td><td colspan="5"></td></tr>
<tr><td>Overall status</td><td>Worsening</td><td>Same/Minimal improvement</td><td>Moderate/Good improvement</td><td colspan="2">Recovered</td></tr>
<tr><td>Summary of session</td><td colspan="5"></td></tr>
<tr><td>Counselling plans</td><td colspan="5"></td></tr>
<tr><td>Plan for next session</td><td colspan="5"></td></tr>
<tr><td>Follow-up appointment</td><td colspan="5"></td></tr>
</table>

B. Behaviour contract and chart

We are all motivated to work towards gaining a reward or pleasure. Rewards are of two kinds: token rewards and main rewards. Token rewards are those which can be collected (e.g. stars or points) with a view to receiving a main reward (e.g. ten stars will give a child a special treat or will allow the child to do something they like). A behaviour 'contract' is an agreement by an adult (e.g. a counsellor, teacher or parent) with the youth on specific behavioural goals and their associated rewards once the goals are achieved. This helps motivate and engage the youth and clarifies the system of rewards. A behaviour chart is a visual reminder which can be used to support a contract, especially in the case of younger children.

A contract, with its associated chart, should follow the guidelines discussed below:

- Keep the goals specific. For example, 'completing homework' instead of 'behaving well'.
- Keep the initial goals attainable. For example, 'completing homework three times every week' instead of 'everyday'. This enhances the probability of success, and thus, creates a sense of achievement.
- As far as possible, the goals should be stated in a positive way (e.g. 'Hari will wait for his turn'; rather than 'Hari will not push others when in the queue').
- Create a reward which will motivate the child (e.g. a reward which appeals to the child because it links to a hobby or activity he enjoys; or a simple treat such as a new set of crayons).
- Keep the reward collection within a reasonable time span (e.g. within a week of achieving the goals; though teenagers may be able to wait a bit longer).
- The adult must be consistent and not be pressured to give rewards if goals are not achieved.
- The behaviour chart should be attractive, interactive and age-

appropriate (e.g. the younger child can colour in a star or apply a sticker to indicate achievement).

- Remember that contracts do not always work. If the youth has difficulty achieving the goals, take a break and start again.

An example of a behaviour contract (with its associated chart) is given below:

Examples of activity to be achieved	Monday	Tuesday	Wednesday	Thursday	Friday	Saturday	Sunday
Cleaning my room							
Completing my homework							

I will get one point/sticker/star for every time I complete the activity. When I collect ______ points/stickers/stars, I will get to ____________ .

Child's/Student's signature

Parent's/Teacher's signature

C. Visual timetable

Time	Activity
9:00–9:20 a.m. Assembly	
9:20–9:30 a.m. Attendance	
9:30–10:30 a.m. Mathematics	
10:30–11:00 a.m. English	
11:00–11:15 a.m. Break (snack time)	
11:15–12:00 noon Hindi	

D. Resources

Resources can generally be located through Flipkart, Amazon or Scholastic India unless otherwise noted.

Child and Adolescent Development

- Hutchison E. (2011). ***Dimensions of Human Behaviour: The changing life course***. Thousand Oaks, USA: SAGE Publications.
  This book reviews, in an engaging and readable format, theories of child development, developmental stages and treatment approaches to youth.
- Talking About Reproductive and Sexual Health Issues (TARSHI).
  The Orange Book: A teachers' workbook on sexuality education (2010). *This workbook serves as a guide to teachers so that they can provide comprehensive sexuality education to youth with confidence and ease.*
  The Red Book *(1999) contains information about growing up, bodily changes and other issues that young people between the ages of 10 and 14 are curious about.*
  The Blue Book *(1999) contains information about growing up, bodily changes, sexuality and how to stay smart and safe for youth over 15 years of age.*
  The Orange Book *can be purchased from the TARSHI website: http://www.tarshi.net. Hindi versions of* The Red Book *and* The Blue Book *can be downloaded directly from the TARSHI website at no cost.*

Counselling Youth with Mental Health Problems

- Augustyn M, Zuckerman B, Caronna EB. (2010). ***The Zuckerman Parker Handbook of Developmental and Behavioral Pediatrics for Primary Care.*** Philadelphia, PA: Lippincott, Williams & Wilkins.
  Although primarily directed at paediatricians, this book's practical approach to child development and mental health issues can also be useful for counsellors interested in more information about child development and youth mental health.

- Weisz JR. (2004). ***Psychotherapy for Children and Adolescents: Evidence-based treatments and case examples.*** Cambridge: Cambridge University Press.
  This book describes evidence-based treatment approaches, utilizing case examples, for a broad range of social, emotional and behavioural problems that children and youth can experience.
- The National Child Traumatic Stress Network (NCTSN) and the National Center for Post-traumatic Stress Disorder (PTSD). ***Psychological First Aid—Field operations manual.*** 2nd ed. (2006).
  This manual, which is accessible on the web, http://www.nctsn.org/content/psychological-first-aid, provides guidance to mental health workers working with youth who have been subjected to traumatic events.
- Patel V. (2003). ***Where There is No Psychiatrist: A mental healthcare manual***; Eapen V, Graham P, Srinath S. (2012). ***Where There is No Child Psychiatrist: A mental healthcare manual.*** London, UK: RC Psych Publications.
  Both these books are intended for the non-specialist working with people with mental health problems. 'Where There is No Psychiatrist' is available through http://www.talcuk.org and covers mental health problems and interventions for both children and adults. 'Where There is No Child Psychiatrist' is available through http://www.rcpsych.ac.uk/publications/books/rcpp/9781908020482.aspx and is focused on the mental health problems of infants, children and adolescents and interventions to address these problems.
- Central Board of Secondary Education (2010). ***Teachers Manual on Life Skills.*** New Delhi: CBSE; Bharath S, Kumar K. (2005). ***Activity Manual for Teachers on Health Promotion Using Life Skills Approach.*** Bengaluru: National Institute of Mental Health and Neuro Sciences (NIMHANS).
  These are among a number of life skills manuals providing guidance to teachers which can also be useful for counsellors. The CBSE manuals can be downloaded from http://www.cbse.nic.in and are available in Hindi. The NIMHANS manual can be obtained from the author at srikala@nimhans.kar.nic.in.

- McMullen Carol S. (2005). ***Creating a Bully-Free Classroom.*** New York: Scholastic, Inc.
This book prepares primary school teachers to help students discuss, plan and practice social skills so that they can react strategically to any bullying situation.

Resources for Youth (and their families)

- Grollman EA. (1993). ***Straight Talk About Death for Teenagers: How to cope with losing someone you love.*** Boston: Beacon Press.
This book offers advice to grieving adolescents and answers the kinds of questions that they are likely to ask when someone they have been close to has died.
- Heegaard M. (1996). ***When Someone Very Special Dies: Children can learn to cope with grief.*** Minnesota, MN: Woodland Press.
This book helps the younger child understand the concept of death and develop skills to cope with feelings following a death.
- ***The Let's Talk Library.*** New York: Powerkids Press (2000). Examples of books in this series: *'Let's Talk About Smoking', 'Let's Talk About Being Afraid', 'Let's Talk About Feeling Lonely'.*
This series of picture books is aimed at the younger age groups and tackles a range of emotional and health concerns.
- ***Brainworks Creative Learning.*** Brainworks Live and Learn Series. Mumbai: Popular Prakashan. Examples of books in this series: *'It's Called Dyslexia', 'It's OK to Be Me', 'Winning Isn't Everything', 'It's Hard Being a Kid'.*
This series, for the younger child and his parents, covers specific learning disabilities, developmental disabilities and low self-esteem. These books include a short story for the young child and an information sheet and activities for parents to help their child.
- ***Joy Berry Enterprise Series*** (2010). New York: Joy Berry Enterprise.
This series includes easy to read books which can be read by children independently or can be used with a counsellor's guidance:
Help Me Be Good Series. Examples of books in this series: *'Being Forgetful', 'Being Careless', 'Being Messy', 'Being a Bad Sport', 'Being Selfish', 'Being Greedy', 'Breaking Promises', 'Disobeying', 'Lying',*

'Throwing Tantrums', 'Complaining', 'Being Rude', 'Snooping', 'Cheating', 'Stealing', 'Being Bossy'.

Good Answers to Tough Questions Series. Examples of books in this series: *'Good Answers to Tough Questions: Divorce'.*

Let's Talk About Series. Examples of books in this series: *'Let's Talk About Feeling Worried', 'Let's Talk About New Situations', 'Let's Talk About Feeling Rejected', 'Let's Talk About Playing With Others'.*

- ***Janine Amos's Good and Bad Series*** (2006). London: Evans Publishing Group. These books include six titles: *'Moody', 'Cheat', 'Thief', 'Liar', 'Selfish'* and *'Bully'.*

  These books, aimed at the older child, show examples of good and bad behaviour in a variety of situations. They include questions linked to short stories which allow the child to think through options of how to behave.

Films

The following are the mainstream films that a counsellor could use to introduce discussions within a school setting or as a part of school-wide awareness campaign:

- **Dahaavi Pha** (Marathi, 2002)

  About students in the 'F' division in a school who object to and struggle with the stigma of being the worst performing class in their academic year.
- **Taare Zameen Par** (Hindi, 2007)

  About a young child's struggle with specific learning disabilities.
- **3 Idiots** (Hindi, 2009)

  About the exam pressures on youth and parental academic expectations for youth to succeed academically. The film also includes issues of bullying and suicide.
- **Shala** (Marathi, 2011)

  About youth on the threshold of leaving school; their dreams, aspirations and emotions during the growing up process.
- **Barfi!** (Hindi, 2012)

  About young adults with autism and hearing impairment.

My Personal Resource List

You may wish to list the resources that you have found helpful: